RAB BUTLER

RAB BUTLER

The Best Prime Minister We Never Had?

MICHAEL JAGO

Biteback Publishing

First published in Great Britain in 2015 by
Biteback Publishing Ltd
Westminster Tower
3 Albert Embankment
London SE1 7SP
Copyright © Michael Jago 2015

ISBN 978-1-84954-920-2

10 9 8 7 6 5 4 3 2 1

A CIP catalogue record for this book is available from the British Library.

Set in Adobe Caslon Pro

Printed and bound in Great Britain by
CPI Group (UK) Ltd, Croydon CR0 4YY

MIX
Paper from
responsible sources
FSC
www.fsc.org
FSC® C020471

For Carol

CONTENTS

ACKNOWLEDGEMENTS

The number of people to whom I owe gratitude is large, for Rab Butler was a complex man who has caused me to put to many friends a question that was an apparent *non sequitur*. The several forms of this question boiled down to 'Would Rab really have done that?' or 'How could he have allowed that to happen?' To all those people, I owe thanks for their tolerance.

Most specifically, I thank my wife Carol for being the person behind me, wielding the hammer, as largely through her sensitive editorial antennae and her frequent identifications of one adverb too far has this book achieved whatever semblance of style it now possesses. To those friends and relatives who have been pressured to read all or part of the book in different stages of evolution I offer unreserved thanks, in particular to Dr Raymond Davis (Belfast and University College, Oxford) and Dr Patricia Owens (Oriel College, Oxford and Sussex).

Many people have contributed their knowledge of the several areas addressed by Richard Austen Butler. For a grasp of educational issues, I am indebted to Patrick Cootes and Rachel Fisher; for an insight into Rab's psychological make-up, to Dr Elizabeth Jago; for the view from Washington, to Major Dr Seth Johnston; for help with the arcane science of economics, to Mark Vandevelde; for Rab as Master of Trinity College, to Max King and Charles Moore and other graduates of Trinity College, Cambridge. As ever, I am grateful to my son James Jago for his insights, his trans-Atlantic perspective and encouragement. For assistance with photographs I am indebted to Trinity College, Cambridge Archives, to Sitesh Patel and Laura Wagg of Press

Association Images; and to Pressdram Ltd for permission to include images from *Private Eye*.

The trawling of Rab's papers in Trinity College was facilitated by Jonathan Smith and the staff of the Wren Library; that of Harold Macmillan's and Conservative Party papers by the staff of the Weston Library of Oxford University. Their unfailing help to a stumbling researcher made the journey seem navigable after all. For invaluable legwork in the National Archives and the British Library I am indebted, once again, to Simon Fowler, research assistant *par excellence*.

I am most grateful to my agent, Andrew Lownie; to Mick Smith, Olivia Beattie and Victoria Godden at Biteback Publishing. Their experience of their professions and of what constitutes a book has been invaluable. Sustenance in various forms was provided by Juliet Jamieson and Iain Harris, by Chris and Frances Pye, by Jonathan and Sarah Dancy, by Robin and Amanda Shield, by Jerry and Jane Scott, by Bill and Jean Whaley, by la famille Pégué of L'Hôtel La Mère Hamard in Semblançay, and by all those friends who, perhaps unwittingly, have contributed to the completion of this book. I thank you all unstintingly.

INTRODUCTION

On the morning of 10 January 1957, the Lord Privy Seal sat alone at the table in the Privy Council Chamber, a splendid room with high windows looking onto Horse Guards Parade. Unusually – for he was a notoriously prodigious worker – he had no papers in front of him. No ministerial red boxes; no files demanded his attention. He had no Great Office of State whose business occupied him. He was waiting.

On the previous day, the Prime Minister, Sir Anthony Eden, had resigned, and that morning almost every daily newspaper in Britain had predicted that the Lord Privy Seal, Richard Austen ('Rab') Butler, would be summoned to Buckingham Palace and asked to form a government.[1] That was the summons he awaited. It would come to him, he was confident, by right. Since 1953 he had chaired Cabinet meetings when first Winston Churchill and later Eden had been indisposed. If he looked at the recent past, he could point to four years as an inspired and creative Chancellor of the Exchequer. If his thoughts ranged further back, he would recall with pride his rebuilding of the Conservative Party in the years after its crushing defeat in the 1945 election.

It was Butler who had refashioned the image of the Tories, Butler who had fathered the 1944 Education Act, a truly revolutionary Bill whose far-reaching, radical proposals earned the admiration and gratitude of post-war Britain. A Member of Parliament since 1929 and a junior minister in Neville Chamberlain's government at the age

---

1   In his autobiography, Ted Heath recalled, 'As I entered, his face lit up with its familiar, charming smile. Every newspaper that morning, save one, had announced that he would be the next Prime Minister.' Heath, *The Course of My Life* (London: Hodder & Stoughton, 1998), p. 179.

of twenty-nine, he had worked at the India Office, the Ministry of Labour, the Foreign Office and the Board of Education before going to the Treasury in 1951. Most recently, he had picked up the pieces after Eden's disastrous attempt to reclaim the Suez Canal. No one, he could reasonably have argued, had done more for the Conservative Party in the twentieth century. No one had more clearly identified the Tories as the natural party of governance in Britain.

That was the view of the press and would certainly have been the view of the general electorate. Rab Butler's claim to the Conservative leadership and, therefore, to 10 Downing Street, was self-evident. A progressive Tory, possessed of a first-class mind, he was the embodiment of the 'modern' Conservative whose centrist instincts would restate the government's mission after the fractious fifteen months of Eden's administration. Butler would administer 'the smack of firm government' that the *Daily Telegraph* demanded.[2]

It was thus that Edward Heath, the Government Chief Whip, found him when he came to tell Butler the party's choice of Eden's successor. It was thus, recalling his service to the party and rehearsing his first speech as Prime Minister, that Rab sat alone. To this imposing and iconic figure Heath, fourteen years his junior, elected to parliament six years after the 1944 Butler Education Act, gave the unadorned news that his party had chosen Harold Macmillan as its new leader.[3] At the age of fifty-four, Rab Butler staked his claim to the sobriquet that has remained with him ever since – the Best Prime Minister That Britain Never Had.

This book is not a balance sheet of the virtues and shortcomings of a puzzling politician; rather, it is written as a triptych – a tableau in which, reading from left to right, we see to the left Rab, the young Cambridge don and aspiring Foreign Service officer; to the right, Rab returning to Cambridge, Lord Butler of Saffron Walden, Master of Trinity College. In the centre is Rab's 35-year political career, a long and arduous campaign, whose *point d'appui* is the twenty-month span that destroyed his political aspirations.

---

2   *Daily Telegraph*, 3 January 1956.
3   Heath wrote, 'I had a sad mission to carry out, but there was nothing I could do to soften the blow. "I am sorry, Rab," I said, "it's Harold." He looked utterly dumbfounded.' Heath, loc. cit.

Between April 1955 and January 1957, Rab Butler, the intellectual giant who held three of the four Great Offices of State, the architect of the 1944 Education Act that bears his name, the rebuilder of the post-war Conservative Party, destroyed his reputation and cast away his almost certain right of succession to the highest office. It was the ultimate 'Rabism', a series of misjudgements and indiscretions that seem almost wantonly self-destructive. From an apparently impregnable position of prominence, the only candidate qualified to succeed Churchill if Eden's health had failed him (as seemed probable), Rab had become within two years the discredited associate of a disgraced Prime Minister, vilified for his part in a Middle Eastern adventure of which he had disapproved from the outset. As Chancellor of the Exchequer in 1955 and Lord Privy Seal in 1956, he squandered the political capital laboriously built up since 1941. Seven years later, after one final disappointment, one final hurdle that he failed (or disdained) to jump, he returned to Cambridge, to the pastures that many friends and associates felt he should never have left.

The practice of politics for Rab Butler was not the adventure that it was for Franklin Roosevelt or Harold Macmillan, for Winston Churchill or Bill Clinton. It was a mixture of duty and ambition – a calling, as it had been for Adlai Stevenson or, bizarrely, as it was for the 14th Earl of Home, the man who in 1963 acquired the crown that had eluded Rab for a decade.

When Lord Home succeeded Macmillan, a cry went up from Iain Macleod, Reginald Maudling and Enoch Powell that Rab had been stabbed in the back. None of those three younger ministers led a pro-Rab party; they proposed him as a 'Stop Home' candidate. Rab's brilliance and ability, his massive stature in the Conservative Party, ensured that he would be a candidate for as long as he drew political breath. Yet he was a repeatedly unsuccessful one. At the last fence, his supporters – and, arguably, his own resolve – deserted him.

On three occasions he might have entered 10 Downing Street: in June 1953, when Churchill and Eden were incapacitated; in January 1957, when Eden resigned after Suez; and in October 1963, when Macmillan stepped down. On each occasion he started strongly and finished badly. On each occasion it is easy to see how he faltered.

At the heart of the story and of this book is the Suez Crisis of the summer and autumn of 1956. Shrewd observers such as Reggie Maudling and Harold Nicolson have stated with conviction that Rab's actions during Suez dispatched forever his chances of the premiership. They are not inaccurate. Yet their analysis falls short of addressing the more fundamental truth that Rab, for all his ability, never stood tall at the head of the Tory Party. Not in 1953; no more so in 1957; and not in 1963. After Suez, that truth became apparent. The *coup de grâce* administered seven years later by Macmillan was posthumous.

To refer to Rab Butler as 'the best Prime Minister that Britain never had' is flattering but inaccurate. Certainly he was one of the most able Cabinet ministers never to be rewarded with the top job, the general of the cohort of 'modern' Conservatives in the post-war period who revolutionised the party. His patience, drive and pertinacity in piloting the 1944 Education Act were gargantuan. Yet, when Lord Butler of Saffron Walden returned to Cambridge, the waters closed over his political career. His great achievements were on the periphery, not in the mainstream – not in *détente*, a Test-Ban Treaty, in achieving world peace or Britain's membership of the Common Market. He was probably the best Chancellor of the Exchequer since the war but his achievements at the Treasury between 1951 and 1954 are barely remembered. Grotesquely, it is for the 'Pots and Pans' Budget of 1955 that his tenure is most commonly recalled. By 1970, after five years of Ted Heath's leadership, the *Evening Standard* wrote of the mood at the Conservative conference:

> It was aggressive Toryism at last. A far cry from the defensive Toryism of Rab Butler which had shared room and board with Socialism for the last twenty-two years. Heath was pulling down the Butler boarding house … Instead he plans to build a skyscraper with self-operating lifts.[4]

With so much in the credit column, it might seem a trifling entry on the debit side to assert that Rab lacked the qualities required of a

---

4   *Evening Standard*, 12 October 1970. Cited by Campbell, *Edward Heath* (London: Jonathan Cape, 1993), p. 312.

prime minister. He was so close to power for so long that the accession was popularly seen as his right. He himself certainly saw it in that light. The abiding tragedy is that he failed to distinguish between the roles of competent chairman and chief executive, between Philosopher and Philosopher-King.

CHAPTER 1

FAMILY AND CHILDHOOD, 1902–21

Richard Austen Butler was born on 9 December 1902 at Attock, where North-West Frontier Province and the Punjab met, about sixty miles west of Islamabad. His family largely comprised academics and divines, strongly rooted in Harrow and Cambridge, and civil servants who served their Queen-Empress in India. The infant Richard, whom his father dubbed 'Rab' so that he would have a distinctive handle,[1] was the first child born to Montagu Sherard Dawes Butler and his wife Ann (*née* Smith). Their immediate family, later to include two sons and two daughters, was known to family and friends as the 'Monty Butlers'.

Since 1742, Butler had followed Butler in the Church of England and since the late eighteenth century in the headship of public schools and as Fellows of Cambridge colleges. Rab's great-grandfather, Dr George Butler, was Senior Wrangler at Sidney Sussex College, Cambridge, a Fellow of his college, and later a devoted headmaster of Harrow School. His children included a Dean of Winchester, a Head of Haileybury and Vice Provost of Oriel College, Oxford, and Henry Montagu, the youngest son, who, aged twenty-six, followed his father as headmaster of Harrow. In 1886, Henry Montagu returned to Cambridge as Master of Trinity, his old college.

---

1   Rab records that by the time he went to prep school he was known by that nickname, which his father 'had deliberately designed as a useful sobriquet for life'. Rab Butler, *The Art of the Possible* (London: Hamish Hamilton, 1971), p. 9.

The least distinguished of George Butler's sons was Spencer Perceval Butler, named after the assassinated Prime Minister. A modestly successful solicitor, he compensated for his lack of glittering prizes by fathering four knights among his nine sons. Sir Cyril Butler, a financier, acquired a large estate in Berkshire that served Rab as a base in England during his youth; Sir Harcourt Butler, an administrator in India, introduced dyarchy in the United Provinces and in Burma. Sir Geoffrey Gilbert Butler, the youngest, was both a Cambridge don and politician, Member of Parliament for Cambridge University from 1923 and author of *The Tory Tradition*. The third son of Spencer Perceval Butler was Sir Montagu Sherard Dawes Butler, *paterfamilias* of the Monty Butlers.

Montagu Butler, twenty-nine when Rab was born, had attended Haileybury and Pembroke College, Cambridge, where he won a double first in the classical Tripos, coxed his college boat and was president of the Union. Top of the list in the Indian Civil Service exam, he embarked on a distinguished career in the Punjab in 1896. In 1901 he married Ann Gertrude Smith, whose father George was principal of Doveton College, a boys' school in Calcutta.

The Smiths and the Butlers had long-established ties to India and both Monty and Rab's Uncle Dunlop decided soon after Rab's birth that his future lay on the subcontinent. Uncle Dunlop dedicated *Attock-on-the-Indus: A Rhyming Geography* to him in 1904.[2] From earliest years, Rab was marked out by his family as a special child; Dunlop and Monty, two old India hands, imagined him a future Viceroy. Late in life, Rab confessed that becoming Viceroy of India was his one unrealised ambition. That was Rab the romantic speaking, for his most patent unfulfilled ambition was to be Prime Minister; but the notion of ruling India had perhaps been hinted at, spoken of, accepted as his destiny when he was young. In Monty's world – and, less immediately, in Dunlop's – this was the height of achievement.

Rab was absent from India from his departure to prep school until his honeymoon in 1926. Of his birthplace he wrote unromantically in

---

2   Trinity: Butler Papers, RAB, F1.3.

1929 that 'Attock has one foot in the grave, and now the other one is nearly in as well.'[3] By then, married to a wealthy woman with a reasonably safe Tory seat at his disposal, he had grander ambitions than to govern the disintegrating Raj.

Rab's relations with his parents were typical of a late Victorian family. With his father, whom he loved and respected, relations were warm but formal. Towards his mother, Rab recalled with understatement, he was 'the devoted son of a loving mother'. Her love, Rab describes as 'permanent and all-surrounding. She supported me in all my ventures with grace and shrewdness.'[4]

Ann was the epitome of the Victorian *memsahib*. Chief of the Girl Guide movement in India, she had a high sense of public duty, inherited from her father. She had a genuine and infectious friendliness and an 'astonishing facility for putting a shy stranger at ease in the first few minutes'.[5] Combining a quiet Christian faith with a radiant cheerfulness, she was a fiercely loyal wife to Rab's father.

She was devoted to all her children, but it was for Rab, her firstborn, that she had the greatest ambition. It was to Monty, however, that she owed primary loyalty, and Monty's decisions settled all family decisions. The smooth, symbiotic working of their household was exemplary:

> Subtle, charitable, feminine and game, she relied on [Monty's] wisdom, his tenacity and his cheerful, ordered mind. It is easy to picture his broad Butler head and her tall distinction as at some family gathering he made the jokes and she provided the light-hearted, leisurely atmosphere.[6]

Her letters to Rab, addressed to 'Dearest of Rabs' or 'Rabin', are chatty, occasionally formal, more often recording the moment – a mixture of Presbyterian earnestness with very feminine impressions, interspersed with local government gossip. During Rab's teens she signed

---

3   Trinity: Butler Papers, RAB, F1.6; from Rab's essay on Attock.
4   Butler, *The Art of the Possible*, p. 4.
5   *The Times*, Obituary of Lady Butler, 24 July 1953; Trinity: Butler Papers, RAB, B21.299.
6   *The Times*, 4 August 1953; Trinity: Butler Papers, RAB, B21.300.

her letters 'Mother'. Later she became more informal, signing them simply 'M'. She used every square inch of every page to write. She never ended a letter halfway down the page but often finished it by carrying on from the last page to the unused space on the first page for one final thought. The letters are spontaneous and full of local news in florid handwriting, crossings out and additions. Quite the opposite of Monty's and Rab's logically structured epistles.

Her letters breathe India, largely incomprehensible to someone unfamiliar with the subcontinent. When Rab was away in England she missed him badly and might insert an expression of love – 'You're a nice boy, Rabin. I love you very much' – into the middle of a paragraph, and then resume her narrative.[7] She would discuss a problem with Rab but, when Monty expressed his opinion, his word was law. On one occasion, Ann and Rab had been weighing his sister Dorothy's immediate future until Monty made a unilateral pronouncement. That ended the dialogue; Ann tore up the letter she was writing to Rab and wrote again. Monty had spoken.[8]

Her zest for life was inexhaustible. She wrote to Rab of 'this pretty strenuous and extremely interesting game of living'.[9] She was scatty and forgetful, but ever proud of Rab, as she demonstrated after his election to Parliament:

> Darling, there's some people called Kingsford Letheridge in the Fusiliers. She said to me, 'Is it your nephew who is member for Saffron Walden?' I said 'Yes' for I wasn't listening, and when I did I got most excited and explained of course you were my son.[10]

She followed Rab's career closely, never without an opinion on his fortunes or his colleagues. These might be interspersed with gossip, talk of articles in *Vogue*, the Cuthbertson [*sic*] Forcing Convention and the

---

7   Trinity: Butler Papers, RAB, A67.4, Ann to Rab, 29 December 1928.
8   Trinity: Butler Papers, RAB, A67.229, Ann to Rab, 12 January 1926.
9   Trinity: Butler Papers, RAB, A67.40, Ann to Rab, 23 May 1931.
10 Trinity: Butler Papers, RAB, A67.29, Ann to Rab, 5 March 1931.

English weather, so that one suddenly stumbles on the sentence 'Duff Cooper sounds an ass'.[11]

Rab's memoir, a concise volume of 262 pages and a masterpiece of succinctness, opens with a wistfully descriptive chapter describing his early years. In vivid contrast to the brisk and businesslike descriptions of his later life stand the few pages devoted to his childhood. More than sixty years later, he infused his writing with an almost tactile quality when he spoke of India, blending his account with the practical understanding of administration that he acquired by observation:

> We all went to camp, with a train of camels carrying tents, furniture and crockery. My sister Iris and I travelled in a cart pulled by two ponies … our parents rode everywhere and sometimes changed to elephant transport for crossing rivers. The tents were pitched by a grove of trees and we were let loose to wander in and out of tent-ropes and to climb the tent sides and slide down them. We went quite near the table placed by the office where father sat to receive petitions and give judgement and settle quarrels. Thus we witnessed the grassroots of government.

Rab grew up entranced by India, by 'the rich smells of wet marigolds round the neck … the burning dung fires in the evening, the stone bathroom, the tent and rope smells, the horses and ponies, the deluge of the monsoons, the brilliant-coloured shrubs coming out after the rains'.[12] From the hot plains the family, accompanied by a stern Aberdonian nanny, went up every spring to Simla, 'like a garden city plastered on the edge of huge mountains'. Here, in July 1909, aged six, Rab was thrown from his pony Prince, breaking his right arm in three places.

A doctor at the Walker Military Hospital set the arm and assured Rab's mother that there would be no permanent damage. His optimism was unjustified; Ann wrote to her husband that the arm was

---

11 Trinity: Butler Papers, RAB, A67.43, Ann to Rab, 23 June 1931. By the 'Cuthbertson' convention Ann, of course, meant the Culbertson system of bridge bidding.

12 Butler, *The Art of the Possible*, pp. 5–6. The reader cannot help noticing that Rab's descriptions of India contain very few Indian people.

not straight, a problem that was to be rectified by tying a one-pound weight to his hand.[13] Unsurprisingly, this failed to achieve the desired result and the injury remained with Rab throughout his life.

Rab's father, harbouring grand ambitions for his son and recognising that competitive sports at public school were an essential ingredient of success, was devastated. 'My father's sorrow was terrible,' Rab recalled. 'He was brought up in the public school tradition and felt that my whole future as an athlete would be prejudiced.' Somewhat laconically, Rab added, 'Indeed this proved to be so.'[14]

Boys who attended private preparatory schools, even in the last days of Empire, remember those of their fellows with parents in far-flung places still pink on the map – in Malaya, in Borneo, in exotically named African nations. They spent their school holidays with relatives, with schoolfriends, legatees of British imperial greatness, while their parents and sisters kept the flag flying abroad. In the early twentieth century, before air travel, this was the natural life of the male offspring of imperial administrators.

Uncomplaining, they sailed 'home', to a country they knew not at all. From the age of seven or eight they became orphaned nomads, spending Easter, Christmas and often summers with relations, through prep school and public school, until they, in their turn, entered the ranks of the Civil Service, in one of the professions, or in the City of London. Rab joined this band of cultural nomads in 1911, the shock of transplantation at first mitigated by his mother who scooped up his sisters Iris and Dorothy, along with Nanny, and sailed with him.

To his two sisters, Rab was always the imposing elder brother. Dorothy remained in awe of him, while Iris would tease him gently for his magisterial, somewhat pompous manner. When she met and fell in love with their father's aide de camp 'Buzz' Portal, she wrote to Rab that 'You will probably think Buzz terribly old as he's 36, but a younger person never lived. He is much younger than you, darling

---

13 Letter from Ann Butler to Montagu Butler, 14 August 1909. Butler family papers, cited by
     Howard, *RAB* (London: Jonathan Cape, 1987), p. 7.
14 Butler, *The Art of the Possible*, p. 7.

Rab, for instance.'[15] Well into adulthood Rab treated 'Irey' as a naughty younger sister, sending her a note on her thirtieth birthday: 'I write to wish you many happy returns of the day, and the enclosed wherewith you can purchase some confection for yourself.'[16]

When Rab, his mother and sisters sailed to England in 1911, it was the end of his Indian childhood. He was now to attend The Wick, a preparatory school in Hove run by Laurence and Mary Thring. Brother and sister, they were great-nephew and great-niece of Edward Thring, the innovative headmaster of Uppingham from 1853 to 1887. Of the two, Rab has the more vivid memory of Mary, whom he describes as 'very stern'.

He was granted a temporary reprieve from imperial orphanage by his father's appointment as Secretary of the Islington Commission, a royal commission on public services in India. In 1912, when the Commission's work began, he sailed to join his family in Britain. Ann was loaned a house in the village of Bourton in the Vale of the White Horse, where Monty's brother Cyril had a grand estate, and this became the family's English home until November 1916, when Ann, the girls and Nanny followed Monty back to India.

Ann used her sabbatical in Britain well. Rab, Iris and Dorothy were taken to meet Ann's family as well as the Cyril Butlers. Ann's father, George Smith, returned from Calcutta, was living in Edinburgh; his son, George Adam, was Principal of Aberdeen University. The Smith family also had close connections with India, and Rab grew up in awe of the family's unconventional approach to life. 'Uncle Will kept a tame bear in his tea garden in Assam,' Rab records, while 'Aunt Kate was baptised by a missionary called Mr Jagadisha Battarcharjia.'[17] Uncle Charles and Uncle Dunlop were also old India hands, the former as Resident in Gilgit and the latter as Private Secretary to Lord Minto. Rab and Iris, avid readers of *Stories of Indian Gods and Heroes*, thought the Smiths exotic creatures and substituted them for characters in the stories.

---

15 Trinity: Butler Papers, RAB, A3.33.
16 Trinity: Butler Papers, RAB, A.60, Rab to Iris, 30 May 1935.
17 Butler, *The Art of the Possible*, p. 4.

By the time his parents returned to India, the First World War had
raged for two years and Rab had moved on from his prep school. It
had been assumed that he would go on to Harrow and his place was
reserved there. Two members of his family had been headmasters; a
Butler was a housemaster; there were cousins already at the school.
It caused a stir, therefore, when Rab declared that he wanted to go to
Eton instead. With his mother's support and encouragement, he went
to sit the scholarship exam. Such was his confidence that, when his
name was not read out as required for further examination, he boldly
but vainly challenged the master reading the list.

With both Eton and Harrow excluded, the family chose Marlborough, principally for its proximity to Bourton and because Rab's
cousin Charles Sorley, the war poet, was an Old Marlburian. In the
autumn of 1916, Rab started at his public school and his mother and
sisters departed. Severance from his birthplace had been softened by
their presence; now it was absolute. By the time he returned in 1926,
his future assuredly lay in London and not in Delhi.

His arrival at Marlborough coincided with that of Cyril Norwood,
an outstanding classical scholar who had been appointed headmaster
of Bristol Grammar School at the age of thirty. In ten years, between
1906 and 1916, Norwood gave the school a new identity, trebling enrolment, expanding the physical facilities and establishing his own
reputation as an effective reformer. In 1916, he was eager to take on
the refashioning of a famous public school and in his application for
the headship in April he cannily balanced his ambition to advance
Marlborough's academic reputation with respect for 'the building of
character and the training for citizenship which at Marlborough must
be the first considerations'.[18]

In retrospect, Rab recognised Norwood's achievement in revolu-
tionising the curriculum and urging the school's governors to move
with the times and use the new developments such as the school certificate and higher school certificate examinations. Over a decade he

---

18 Dr Norwood's application for headship at Marlborough College, April 1916, cited by *Oxford
Dictionary of National Biography* (article by Gary McCulloch).

succeeded in dramatically altering the character of the school. Rab was impressed by the way that the school soon 'came right to the front in obtaining scholarships at the universities'.[19]

That was the judgement of a mature Rab; the teenage Butler had a less enthusiastic view of school life. The environment he found constricting as, he judged, 'the great need of a public school is to look outward and not into its monastic self'. He was disappointed by the lack of debating and literary activities and, in later life, when he and John Betjeman discussed Marlborough, they concluded that they had 'not contributed enough'.[20] All in all, Rab gives the impression that it was a period of his life to be tolerated rather than enjoyed. It was a necessary rite of passage that would, in due course, lead him to Cambridge, at which point his intellectual training would begin in earnest.

Rab and his father corresponded weekly; to Ann he wrote separately, the weekly 'mail' arriving in India with the boat. A letter from each of the children was expected in the delivery, and if there was no letter from Rab, Monty would scold him in his Sunday letter with a comment such as 'No letter from you last week. I expect you were settling in.'[21]

There was real warmth in their writing, but on each side it was suffused with a formality alien to Ann. Yet the formality is shaded with a persistent cheerful manner, with Monty's corny sense of humour and a deep, man-to-man affection for his son. He shares news and opinions; he lets his frustrations with India show. He is never quite indiscreet, but he is able to talk to Rab on occasion as if he were a junior colleague whom he could help with a leg-up. It is an engagingly loving friendship. Censorious but deeply affectionate, Monty clearly missed having his elder son around.

'Rabbito mio', he frivolously opens one letter, signing it with his charming formula 'Best of luck, old man, and love from Dad'.[22] When Rab was preparing for the Tripos, Monty was full of advice randomly

---

19 Butler, *The Art of the Possible*, p. 10.
20 Ibid.
21 Trinity: Butler Papers, RAB, A65.5 Monty to Rab, 12 February 1925.
22 Trinity: Butler Papers, RAB, A65.9, Monty to Rab, 9 March 1925.

dropped into letters. 'Don't work up to the last hour', he advises, and
'To be fresh is worth much'.[23] Charmingly, he recognised his occasional dogmatism and pomposity, particularly when he spoke about
money, which was often. When Rab was about to go up to Cambridge,
for example, he pronounced *ex cathedra*:

> *Mon Lapin … I should, I suppose, take the occasion to do the heavy father, but
> I will spare you that. Whilst I was at Cambridge my dad paid all bills from
> College and doled me out £5 at a time, sometimes £10 on my giving him an
> account. I am running you on different lines and putting you on your own,
> and do so with confidence.*[24]

Money was often the subject of Monty's letters, but not because he was
obsessed by it or because he was tight-fisted. He simply was not very
good at it. He repeated to Rab several times in letters that his allowance
would be paid, that he had given instructions to Lloyds Bank. When
Rab was at Cambridge Monty wrote to Rab, confessing that he would
like to have more money so that 'he could have all the clothes he wants
and then he would never again wear a darned sock'.[25] Later in his career,
as retirement approached, financial issues were quite beyond him and he
set aside the figure of *paterfamilias*, asking Rab simply and directly for
his advice regarding his pension and where he and Ann should live.[26]

Rab's letters home during his Marlborough years convey the impression of studied indifference, even cynicism about the school's values.
Much of that cynicism is affectation, the mandatory lack of enthusiasm for all success. Clearly Rab wanted to succeed – he mentions in
his memoir that he played cricket for his house, quite an achievement
without a functioning right arm. He also passed top of his year in the
Corps' Certificate A, the first rudimentary test of understanding of
military matters and tactics.[27]

---

23 Trinity: Butler Papers, RAB, A65.16, Monty to Rab, as the Tripos approaches, 5 May 1925.
24 Trinity: Butler Papers, RAB, A65.220, Monty to Rab, 21 September 1921.
25 Trinity: Butler Papers, RAB, A65.1, Monty to Rab, 11 November 1924.
26 Trinity: Butler Papers, RAB, A65.311, Monty to Rab, 23 March 1935.
27 Trinity Butler Papers, RAB, A70.1, Rab received congratulations from Sergeant-Major G.
     Barnes, 20 January 1921.

Unsurprisingly, there is a wide disparity between the gentle mockery of sports, of the Corps and Field Day and his evident pride at having succeeded. Such was the ethic of public schools at the time: everything was 'rather a bore' and it was singularly bad form to strive to succeed. He may have taken this wry detachment too far – as he did later in his political career – for his housemaster wrote to Monty decrying Rab's lack of ambition.[28]

While Norwood's reforms were coming into effect, Marlborough was only gradually emerging from the sports-dominated, Philistine stereotype of a Victorian public school. Rab, in common with most boys of ability, was in the Classical stream, yet his knowledge of the classics remained woefully deficient and he had reached the fifth form before he was able, 'providentially', to switch to modern languages. This also may have struck his housemaster as symptomatic of that supposed lack of ambition. The brightest boys were guided to read classics in preparation for *Literae Humaniores* at Oxford or the Classical Tripos at Cambridge; the least intellectually endowed were guided to Geography and Economics. It was supposed that the former would enter the Whitehall corridors of power, while the latter would farm their estates. Somewhere between the two disciplines lay history and modern languages, the academic fare of the 'average' boys. In abandoning classics, Rab was deviating from the pre-ordained course for a boy of his ability.

Despite his distrust of Marlborough's methods, Rab had the greatest respect for Norwood. From Marlborough Norwood went to Harrow as headmaster in 1926 and ended his career as president of St John's College, Oxford in 1946. One cannot help but wonder if the Butlers, with their powerful Harrovian connections, eased his passage from the Wiltshire Downs to Harrow on the Hill. There is certainly no doubt that Rab greatly esteemed the Master, for in 1941, when Rab was President of the Board of Education, he appointed Norwood[29] to chair a committee that produced a comprehensive report on curriculum and examinations in secondary schools.

---

28 Trinity: Butler Papers, RAB, A67.
29 By then Sir Cyril Norwood.

As a teenager, immured as a boarder in the narrow, closed world of public school, Rab chafed at its anti-intellectual bent. He became a prefect early, despite his lack of athletic prowess. In his last year, studying modern languages, literature and history, he embarked on a course of study that remained of interest to him throughout his life. In December 1920, he left Marlborough and, having tentatively decided on a career in the Foreign Office, resolved to 'learn French properly', setting off for Abbeville to lodge with a *curé* and to acquaint himself with French classics – La Bruyère and Corneille in particular – at the local Collège Courbet.[30]

In his memoirs, Rab describes the dawning realisation that he had narrowly missed being called up during the First World War. Aged almost sixteen when the Armistice was signed, he was ineligible for service, a duty from which his weak right arm would in any case have exempted him. Early in the war, his cousin Charles Sorley had been killed, one of the 59,247 casualties in the disastrous Battle of Loos,[31] but, in common with many of his schoolmates, he was able to view the war as an abstraction, a horrific event taking place somewhere else.

At the Wick school he 'simply noticed that the masters were leaving, in several cases never to return'[32] and after his cousin's death, during his time at Marlborough, he became more conscious of the war's devastating toll. It was probably in Abbeville, early in 1921, however, that the reality of the carnage became vividly clear. London, the target of bombers, doodlebugs and rockets in the Second World War, was relatively untouched by bombardment between 1914 and 1918. It was the Valley of the Somme that had seen the greatest slaughter of the British Expeditionary Force. Abbeville, between Amiens and the mouth of the Somme, had been behind the French and British lines, but a short distance to the east, between Bapaume and Peronne, the

---

30 A *collège* in France is a middle school for children from the *sixième* to *troisième* grades, between the ages of eleven and fifteen. Rab's classmates, therefore, were all at least three years younger than him.

31 For a chillingly dispassionate account of Loos and the 'dud show' that caused Sorley's death, see Graves, *Goodbye to All That* (Harmondsworth: Penguin Books, 1960), p. 141.

32 Butler, *The Art of the Possible*, p. 8.

British and the French had suffered over 600,000 casualties between July and December 1916.

Two years after the end of the war, when Rab arrived in Abbeville, towns across France were building memorials to their dead and Abbeville had launched an appeal to raise 90,000 francs for an impressive memorial by Louis Leclabart, a sculptor from Amiens. Although the memorial was not finished until 1923, when it was unveiled by Maréchal Foch, the appeal was in full swing during Rab's stay. It was an emotional time to visit the Somme.

Writing later of this period, Rab admits to feelings of claustrophobia and nostalgia, feelings heightened by visits to Abbeville railway station. The father of his particular friend at the *collège* was the signalman, and Rab would visit the signal box to watch the express trains from the Channel ports 'swaying on the points after gliding through the free fast run of the bloody valley of the Somme'.[33] The trains provided a link with the outside world and Rab, lonely and confined in an introverted, provincial town, longed for contact 'with home and with the wider world'.

For what 'home' did he feel nostalgia? He had been away from India since 1911. His recollections of boarding school betray no hint of homesickness, yet, quite suddenly, at the age of eighteen, he fell prey to missing home. The admission probably reflects how close he had grown to relatives in Britain from both the Smith and Butler sides of the family during his schooldays.

The most vivid portraits that Rab paints of relatives in his school years are of his uncle Cyril, Monty's eldest brother, who 'had his estate and guarded his rich collection of Chinese treasures and modern pictures',[34] and of Sir James Dunlop Smith, his mother's brother, 'Uncle Dunlop', who lived with his sister, Aunt Minnie, in Ovington Square. In this 'comfortable house' there gathered on Sunday evenings 'those of the Indian Princes who were in London … [talking] in Hindi

---

33 Ibid., p. 13. In fact, Rab's geography was faulty as the main railway line through Abbeville lies 100 kilometres to the west of the battlefields.

34 Ibid., p. 12.

with Uncle Dunlop – deep voices making a soft thunder – and though sombre in khaki uniform, they were magnificent-looking men'.[35]

Both these uncles made a deep impression on Rab; the one wealthy and eclectic, the other exotic and well-connected in Whitehall. Each makes a stark contrast to the description of Rab's father recorded in 1938 by Henry ('Chips') Channon, Rab's friend and Parliamentary Secretary at the Foreign Office:

> *I am getting to know Rab ... Yesterday I met his parents. His father is a fat little fellow of sixty, but Lady Butler I thought a grand old girl, rather overdressed, grey and not a day over 58. She is tall, jingles when she walks, worships Rab, who – and this is the most charming quality that I have observed in him – could not resist showing off to his impressed parents.*[36]

Monty Butler had a highly successful career in India, rising to be Governor of the Central Provinces in 1925, recipient of numerous honours, including a CB (1916), a CBE (1919) and a knighthood (KCSI, 1924). Yet that sensitive and perceptive observer Chips Channon dismisses him as 'a fat little fellow of sixty' and in Rab's written account he is colourless beside his brother Uncle Cyril.

Breaking with the Butlers' academic tradition, Cyril had not attended university but had made his fortune in the City. He had also married an heiress, Mary Pease, known in the family as 'Aunt May', and he used their combined wealth to indulge his love of modern art. Rab draws a picture of Bourton as 'a home for painters', where 'Wilson Steer was in the dining room' and 'Sickert and McEvoy filled in the gaps'. In addition:

> Augustus John left endless paintings, many of his high women, along the first-floor passages. Tonks, who was then head of the Slade, had

---

35 Ibid., p. 9.
36 Rhodes James, *Chips: The Diaries of Sir Henry Channon* (London: Weidenfeld & Nicolson, 1967). Diary entry for 23 November 1938, pp. 178–9.

pride of place with a cat playing with a necklace in the library, and a birdcage in the hall. He was frequently there for weekends.[37]

Despite his obvious admiration of Uncle Cyril's affluent and cultured style of life, just before Rab left Marlborough he wrote to his parents, apparently sneering at his father's brother. 'Although you make money in business', he wrote, 'the idea of the Diplomatic and HM Service appeals to one as finer somehow than being an individual on one's own wearing a dark grey suit and butterfly collar and knowing the purlieus of the City by heart.'[38]

There is, perhaps, a hint of envious and unjustified superiority in this letter. Cyril Butler was manifestly not a man who knew only 'the purlieus of the City'. A collector of Ming and Tang horses and bowls, a generous patron of the arts, and Chairman of the Contemporary Art Society, Monty's eldest brother personified many of the virtues that Rab admired. Possibly Rab was 'preaching to the choir', expressing emotions that his father would share, sneering at the lack of sense of duty of the City financier. It is a curious letter, as Bourton had been Rab's English home and there is no other evidence that he felt anything but the greatest respect for Uncle Cyril and Aunt May.

Whatever may have been Rab's thoughts on wealth, Bourton and 25 Ovington Square were the houses that the eighteen-year-old Rab referred to as 'home'. Uncle Cyril and Uncle Dunlop, possibly more than Monty, were influential role models in his teenage years and traces of their influence on Rab's actions recur in his future career. It is small wonder that the signal box at Abbeville station failed to maintain its initial excitement.

Although Rab was on the best of terms and stayed in touch for years after with Jean and Evelyn Vernier, his hosts in Abbeville,[39] in 1921 he was anxious to leave that sombre northern town. To his relief, he was able to exchange Abbeville for more congenial lodgings in August but, between his two spells in France, he returned to England in June to sit

---

37 Butler, *The Art of the Possible*, p. 12.
38 Trinity: Butler Papers, RAB, D48.2. Letter from Rab at Marlborough, 27 November 1920.
39 Trinity: Butler Papers, RAB, A74 and A75 *passim*.

for the Pembroke College, Cambridge entrance scholarship. His five months in northern France had served him well, for he excelled in the French papers and was awarded an exhibition.[40] Having passed one milestone by winning an award at his father's old college, Rab returned to France to round out the summer.

Probably through an introduction from his uncle Cyril, Rab had been engaged by Baron Robert de Rothschild to tutor his son Alain.[41] This involved not a tiny *curé*'s lodging with a hot bath in a tin tub just once a week,[42] but accommodation in the family's summer house at Benerville, near Deauville, for the month of August. In September, Rab and his charge decamped to the Château de Laversine at Saint-Maximin, a massive Renaissance palace, originally built for Comte Vasco de Souza and substantially rebuilt by Gustave de Rothschild, Robert's father, after he bought it in 1874.

The task of instructing the eleven-year-old Alain appears not to have been too demanding for, as Rab diplomatically recalled, 'Alain had no intention of spending his vacations over-working.'[43] For Rab, the aspiring diplomatist, the summer was most valuable for the contact it brought with a privileged and sophisticated, not to say enormously wealthy, French family.

Nonetheless, Rab was not immune to the prejudices of his time. A descendant of parents with long lines of Church of England and Presbyterian ministers in their family trees, he was staying, for the first time, with a notable Jewish family – prominent bankers, famous for their philanthropy. His Protestant upbringing and its exclusive nature are expressed in a letter to his mother: 'Money here is in everything you see or touch, but if they take a taxi, they would argue with the man if too much … To call them the "nouveau riche" or "Jew type" would be rot, but they certainly keep a firm hold of it.'[44]

---

40 An exhibition, a minor scholarship, had a value of about £20 annually in 1921.
41 A possibly apocryphal story told by the Rothschilds is that they received so many applications for the tutoring position that they put all the letters from acceptable candidates in a wastepaper basket and threw them from the top floor of the château. Rab's letter hit the ground first.
42 Trinity: Butler Papers, RAB, D48.3. Letter from Rab in Abbeville, 22 January 1921.
43 Butler, *The Art of the Possible*, p. 13.
44 Trinity: Butler Papers, D48.4. Letter from Rab in Benerville-sur-Mer, 20 August 1921.

Again, as with his letter to Monty the previous November, we see Rab expressing views that he may or may not have held, but which were familiar themes to men and women of his parents' generation. Anti-Semitism was automatic among the English professional classes; France had recently been rocked by the Dreyfus affair and systematised anti-Semitism in the French General Staff.

Rab was possibly commenting on a characteristic that he knew would appeal to his father. Monty was notoriously thrifty, thrifty in the Victorian ethic, in which thrift was a cardinal virtue[45] – a trait that is clear from letters to his son – and Rab may have merely used an unfortunate phrase to express it. Nonetheless, the phrase stands out; it would not be the last time that Rab's racial views were, at best, questionable.

Whatever the reason for Rab's unfortunate phrase, he greatly enjoyed his stay and was deeply impressed by the intellectual and financial abundance he encountered. 'One thing quite certain,' he wrote to his mother, 'is that there is nothing in this house and family that I would wish to scoff at.'[46] The enjoyment was, apparently, mutual, for Rab was invited back the following year, more as a welcome guest than as a tutor. In the meantime, leaving Château de Laversine in September 1921, he returned to England for his first year as a Cambridge undergraduate, reading Modern and Medieval Languages.

---

45 He was not badly off by the standards of his time, leaving £33,413.7s 1d at his death in 1952 – the equivalent of £840,000 today.
46 Trinity: Butler Papers, D48.4. Letter from Rab in Saint-Maximin, 3 September 1921.

CHAPTER 2

CAMBRIDGE, 1921–25

When Rab graduated from school to Cambridge, he had more than normal freshman nervousness. Cambridge was his home ground as the Butler family had connections in half a dozen colleges. On the other hand, he was entering his father's old college with Monty's censorious eye constantly upon him. Every 'good chit' and black mark that was noted against his name would, without doubt, reach Monty's ear. He also had his father's achievements to equal or, preferably, to exceed, and that was a tall order.

Rab had chosen Pembroke, principally because it was Monty's old college. Certainly it was not Rab's idea of an intellectual paradise; writing of his 'great friend Willie Wolfson', he gives a bleak picture of contemporary Pembroke:

> Willie was a Russian who had been rescued from the revolution by the British Navy at Novorossiysk. He had aristocratic leanings and political views several miles to the right of mine. But thrown into Pembroke among rowing blues, rugger blues, cricket blues, and other hearties who would knock over your mug of beer as soon as say 'good morning', the charm and elegance of Willie's intellect, manners and appearance constituted an oasis of college civilization.[1]

Rab decided early that the wider field of the university was the more important arena in which to excel. During his first two undergraduate

---

1   Butler, *The Art of the Possible*, pp. 15–16.

years, he continued to aspire to the Diplomatic Service; a good degree and success in the Cambridge Union were important assets to support that ambition. Accordingly he applied himself in those two arenas and in his memoirs we hear nothing of any other activity in his first two Cambridge years. His focus was clear: to earn a first-class degree in Part I of the Tripos in June 1923 and to become president of the Union before he went down a year later. In achieving those objectives, he would emulate his father's success.

Within a month of his arrival, he made his first speech in the Union. By accident or by design, he spoke immediately after his cousin J. R. M. ('Jim') Butler, historian and Fellow of Trinity,[2] who argued that British troops should be removed from Northern Ireland. Rab forcefully propounded the opposite view in a speech described in the *Cambridge Review* as 'a good maiden'.[3] Rab gleefully wrote to his father that he had 'leapt up after Jim' and that he had been 'quite a success' as he 'got several people to realise who I was'.[4] After this auspicious beginning he rapidly established himself in Union debates and made his first platform speech the following May, when he was commended for his delivery.[5]

At the end of his first year, Rab performed adequately in 'Mays', the Cambridge preliminary exams, taking a Second and maintaining his status as an exhibitioner. Since the results of first-year examinations had no effect on the level of his final degree – which would be determined by his performance in Parts I and II of the Tripos – he was far from uncomfortable with his first year as an undergraduate. Doubtless his father wanted more, but Rab left England to revisit the de Rothschilds at their country home with a perfectly creditable academic year behind him.

Aged nearly twenty, Rab had grown into a handsome young man. Trim and spruce, smartly if unfashionably dressed and with something

---

2   James Ramsay Montagu Butler, Fellow of Trinity, was son of Henry Montagu Butler, former Master of Trinity. From 1947 to 1954 he was Regius Professor of Modern History at Cambridge. He is best known for his work as editor of *Grand Strategy*, the British official history of the Second World War. He was knighted in 1958 for his contribution to the comprehensive six-volume series.

3   *Cambridge Review*, 11 November 1921.

4   Trinity: Butler Papers, RAB, D48.4, 8 November 1921.

5   *Cambridge Review*, 19 May 1922.

of a military bearing, he radiated confidence and purpose. A strong jaw and languidly perceptive eyes added a certain sensitivity to an air of solidity and determination. The combination proved attractive to Diane, the teenaged daughter of Baron de Rothschild, who developed an embarrassing 'crush' on him and sent him worshipping letters when he returned to England.[6] The summer passed without incident but proved to be his last summer with the family. He was not invited back to Benerville.

Halfway through his second year, however, he found himself, for the first time, in a romantic liaison with more serious implications. In February 1923, his cousin, Kathleen Smith, daughter of his mother's brother, the Principal of the University of Aberdeen, visited Cambridge, staying with her cousins, the Sorleys.[7] Rab and Kathleen saw each other frequently during February and by early March they were inseparable. During her visit, Kathleen wrote Rab a letter of tangible warmth and closeness. She wrote in a feathery style, skipping from the Asquith–Lloyd George split, to affection to her father's sermon on Sunday, to Rab in Pelican Court in Pembroke. Little substantive was said, but she wrote with the hint of a possessive air.[8]

That visit to Cambridge had a profound impression on Kathleen. She wrote three letters to her mother during the visit, entranced by the aura that surrounded Rab – good-looking, intelligent men, the Union and its politics, balls and dancing, lavish teas in undergraduates' rooms, Rab's speech, strenuous beagling. Everything was wonderfully exciting and at the centre of it all was Rab.[9]

The first letter describes the outing of the Cambridge beaglers, 'a ripping looking set of men', mostly Etonians, who formed Rab's coterie. These 'splendid friends', she told her mother, comprised 'the biggest wigs' in Cambridge, including two cousins called Macpherson. She went to the Pitt Ball with the 'Butler-Macpherson set' who endlessly

---

6   Trinity: Butler Papers, A72, Diane de Rothschild to Rab, October to November 1921.
7   William and Janetta Sorley, parents of Charles Sorley (see Chapter 1). 'Uncle Will' was a Fellow of King's and was Knightsbridge Professor of Philosophy at Cambridge from 1900 to 1933.
8   Trinity: Butler Papers, RAB, A2.1, Kathleen Buchanan Smith to Rab, 18 February 1923.
9   Trinity: Butler Papers, RAB, D57.1, D57.2 and D57.3, 24 February, 1 March and 9 March 1923.

discussed Rab's chances of being elected secretary of the Union. Kathleen was drawn into this speculation and was excited by the prospect.

A highlight of the visit was the descent of Sir Geoffrey and Lady Butler to tea in Rab's rooms. Kathleen, herself from an academic family, understood the significance of a visit from a Fellow of Corpus Christi College and future Member of Parliament, even if he was Rab's relative. Kathleen was impressed by how Sir Geoffrey was respected and liked by undergraduates while Lady Butler was 'unusual'. 'I gather the whole Butler clan sit on the edge of their chairs when she's around', she wrote, 'and wait with stunned faces for bricks to fall.'[10]

Rab was deliberately vague about Kathleen in letters to his parents,[11] but he was clearly more than a little in love. Mysteriously, the affair burned out as rapidly as it had ignited and only from the aftermath can the depth of his feelings be gauged.

In early March, Kathleen wrote to Rab's mother two letters that betray a clear sense of ownership.[12] Yet, by 11 March, they had parted, a parting that Rab evidently saw as final. In an elliptical letter to his mother, Rab tried to describe the unfamiliar emotion that had engulfed him. He and 'K' – as he habitually referred to Kathleen – had parted after a visit to Ely, whence she returned to Scotland by train, in a 'perfectly calm' manner. It is a curious letter, full of imperfectly expressed ideals, stressing that 'recriminations have passed' and that he and K had come to a *parce que c'est toi, parce que c'est moi* understanding.[13] Despite Rab's insistence to his mother that he and Kathleen were 'going forth on a higher and better quest' and that he had 'a greater appreciation of Beauty and [felt] much surer', it is clear that he was puzzled and morose at the abrupt end to his first serious emotional commitment.

Since Rab avoids the subject in his memoirs and since his letters to his parents are far from explicit concerning his emotions or intentions, there is no cut-and-dried explanation for the abrupt end to the month-long liaison. It appears that for both Rab and Kathleen the

---

10 Lady Butler (*née* Elizabeth Levering Jones) was from Philadelphia and was known for her American directness.
11 For example, Trinity: Butler Papers, D48.6, 19 February 1923.
12 Trinity: Butler Papers, D57.6 and 7 March 1923.
13 Trinity: Butler Papers, D48.6, letter of 11 March 1923.

attraction was sudden, powerful and puzzling. Kathleen was two years older than Rab and also his first cousin. Those two factors might have been enough to undermine the liaison. If, as it seems, Kathleen was ready for marriage and Rab, an impecunious undergraduate, obviously was not, then their parting should come as no surprise. Such an explanation also helps to explain why Rab apparently felt that their decision not to pursue the liaison was somehow the more noble course.

In the same letter to his mother, he wrote of the support that the Sorleys, Uncle Will and Aunt J, had given him. They had 'looked on with great mercy and compassion as I whirl in my vortex'. Rab manifestly was missing home, speaking to his mother of 'the need to bridge the distance'. She had returned to India with Iris during the long vacation at the end of his first year, leaving Rab, the oldest child, *in loco parentis*, responsible for his younger siblings Dorothy and Jock, both of whom were now at school in England. He had adult responsibilities and probably felt qualified to possess adult emotions. The logical conclusion of those emotions was, however, something that he was quite unprepared to consider. His ambitions were clearly definable and achievable only if he knuckled down. When he did so, he was elected secretary of the Union in June and in the following month earned first-class honours in the first part of the Tripos.

Quite suddenly, Rab became an adult, a substitute for his absent parents, required to handle his own finances within his £300 annual allowance from Monty.[14] Periodically Rab complained to his thrifty father that his allowance was inadequate, that it did not allow for much expenditure during vacations. Monty remained unmoved by his son's entreaties, although he did send Rab £10 as a congratulatory prize for his First. With the result came the award of a Pembroke scholarship, worth £80 a year.

Rab's financial position improved with the award – not beyond the dreams of avarice, but enough to allow a summer abroad in July and August. Although he maintained then, and repeated in his memoirs, that

---

14 This apparently small amount had the buying power of about £14,000 at today's values. Provided that Rab stayed with family outside Cambridge terms he should have been able to live quite comfortably.

his plans were to join the Diplomatic Service, he also wrote baldly that
in 1922–23, 'Politics and the Union claimed an increasing amount of
my time.'[15] That is the first that we hear of Rab, the aspiring politician,
and, while he may have wished for a career in politics, it can have been
no more than a dream; he had not the financial resources to attempt
one. Meanwhile, the Cambridge Union was a useful ladder to any profession and would be especially so if 'something came up' that allowed
him to opt for a political career, but in the meantime he continued to
equip himself for life as a diplomat. He would use the summer to learn
German.

Rab begins his account of his Cambridge years with the summer
of 1923. He left England for the Krems Valley in Upper Austria,[16]
where – quite by chance as the family he first chose decided to sell
their house – he stayed with an aristocratic family, fallen on hard times
since the First World War and living in exile from Germany. Count
von Stolberg-Stolberg, his wife Prinzessin Regina Reuss zu Weida
and their four children, excluded from the Stolberg-Stolberg seat at
Wernigerode in the Harz Mountains, were living and farming outside
Krems. Rab joined them for the summer as a paying guest and 'got
much more than he bargained for'.[17]

In one long, evocative paragraph, Rab describes his stay with the
Stolberg-Stolbergs. Mixed into the narrative are several emotions.
First, as with the de Rothschild family, he was obviously susceptible to
the charms of aristocracy. Second, there is empathy for the distressed
circumstances of exiled nobles, cast out of post-war Germany for no
fault of their own; underlying this empathy is the clear suggestion
that Germany and Germans had been harshly treated. Third, Rab had
passed from the callowness of the boy who visited Abbeville to become
a young man able to see a mother of four children as a sentient, intelligent being who could be understood as more than simply a symbol
of a different generation. Fourth, there is the clear suggestion that Ola,

15 Butler, *The Art of the Possible*, p. 15.
16 Rab stayed in the Krems Valley under the foothills of the Alps in Upper Austria, not to be
    confused with Krems on the Danube in Lower Austria.
17 Butler, *The Art of the Possible*, p. 14, which is also the source for the following paragraphs.

the sister of the princess, whom Rab met at the Reuss family seat at Ernstbrunn, figured large in Rab's emotions.

Rab was enchanted by the Reuss family and its traditions. Ennobled in the twelfth century by the Holy Roman Emperor Heinrich VI, they had repaid the compliment by naming all male offspring 'Heinrich'. Regina took Rab to meet her brother Prinz Heinrich XXIV, but Rab's account makes it clear that their younger sister Ola was the greater attraction. Rab and Ola 'explored the castle and the woods ... climbed the great Kremsmauer and found fire lilies on the heights ... visited Vienna and tasted the inflation that was then raging'.

He learned the language easily and spent an idyllic summer, happily exploring Austria with a young woman whose destiny, as a German *Prinzessin*, would never be linked with his. He returned to England with the fondest respect for the family that had shown him such hospitality and, it is clear, with the greatest sympathy for Germans who had been made to pay a high price at Versailles. Writing of that summer nearly fifty years later, moreover, he betrays nostalgia for a love affair that could only last a summer. It is the first period of his life since India that he appears to view with any sense of wistfulness.

If the younger princess captured Rab's romantic emotions, Regina Stolberg-Stolberg was no less important to him. Rab had by then spent two years at Cambridge, was engaged in a running battle with his father about his future, was surrogate father to his siblings in England, had fallen in and half out of love with Kathleen in the spring and, he now confessed to his hostess, was desperately lonely.[18] Regina became a close friend, an elder sister and *confidante* for Rab; that closeness clearly helped him to master the German language, which he spoke with feeling and with style. When Rab wrote to thank her for her hospitality that autumn, Regina replied with amazement that his letter was not merely written in German, 'it was more than wonderful; it was German'. She felt pride that he had captured the spirit of the German language so completely.[19]

---

18 Trinity: Butler Papers, A81.10 and A81.14. Letters from Regina Stolberg-Stolberg to Rab, 27 July 1925 and 9 April 1926.
19 Trinity: Butler Papers, RAB, A81, Regina Stolberg-Stolberg to Rab, 19 September 1923.

From Austria Rab continued his skirmishing correspondence with
Monty, who now suggested that Rab pursue an academic career as a
Fellow of Pembroke. This prospect appealed to him not at all.[20] Rab
envisaged himself 'mixing with great and interesting people'. From the
vantage point of Austria he imagined himself involved in 'the rever-
beration and interclash of nations'. To live and work in the narrow
confines of a small Cambridge college, even if a Fellowship were offered him, appalled him:

> *Dad I must do something active, something which is going to help the world
> of today and not that of yesterday … Pembroke dons are sleek and affable and
> content themselves with saying that the modern world is dirty. It may be, but
> there is much to be done.*[21]

Along the way, he assured Monty, he would be 'glad to be able to
fulfil your wish for a three-year Cambridge and President of the
Union thrown in'.[22] The Diplomatic Service remained his goal; the
stay with the Stolberg-Stolbergs confirmed his belief that there were
international wrongs to be righted, as he said to Monty – 'much to be
done'. Secure in that ambition, he returned to Bourton and thence to
Cambridge.

In Rab's account of his life, he treats his third year at Cambridge as
a period of relative ease. 'My studies were not such as to alarm me. I
had decided to stay up for four years in all', he wrote, 'partly to avoid
taking a second tripos too soon and partly because of the likelihood
that I would be President of the Union during 1924.'[23] *Prima facie*, that
simple statement is plausible. It is also only partly true. On 17 July, he
had written to Monty, indicating with some pride that he would spend
just three years on his degree. At that time, moreover, he was almost
certain to be president of the Union; having been elected secretary at
the end of the previous academic year, his elevation would be virtu-

---

20 Trinity, Butler Papers, D48.6, 15 July 1923.
21 Ibid.
22 Trinity, Butler Papers, D48.6, 17 July 1923.
23 Butler, *The Art of the Possible*, p. 15.

ally automatic. The decision to stay up for a fourth year was taken in December 1923 for reasons that Rab apparently decided to conceal.

He returned to Cambridge in October 1923 to begin reading History for Part II of the Tripos. Early in the year he joined the Conservative Association (CUCA), of which his uncle Geoffrey was president. Sir Geoffrey, a man with 'a singular capacity for squeezing an extravagant infectious humour out of the most unpromising situation',[24] was the author of *The Tory Tradition* and was about to be elected to Parliament in December 1923. A progressive Conservative, he treated CUCA as 'a regular school for young Conservatives of ever growing value to the party'.[25] Rab soon became an officer of the Association, adding this to his duties as secretary of the Union.

Sir Geoffrey treated his nephew as his *protégé*. Rab, in awe of the range of his uncle's activities, reconsidered his future. Sir Geoffrey's rooms in Corpus offered 'lavish entertainment' and 'celebrated people' who passed through Cambridge. Rab retained a vivid memory of meeting Winston Churchill as his uncle's guest.[26] By nature a Tory, under Sir Geoffrey's influence Rab began to see the Union as a platform for partisanship and to treat debates as a training ground for the cut and thrust of the House of Commons. The 1923 election saw Stanley Baldwin's Conservatives emerge with the most seats but no majority in Parliament; the Labour Party with 191 seats and Asquith's Liberal Party with 158 held a combined lead of ninety-one over the Tories. The first Labour government was formed under Ramsay MacDonald; more than ever, it appeared, the Tory Party needed to project itself as a reformed party that could attract young voters.

The Cambridge Union during that period was neither overwhelmingly conservative nor overwhelmingly liberal. Results of debates show that the House did not regret the French occupation of the Ruhr in 1923 and welcomed the recognition of the Soviet government.[27] Prominent within the Union were Patrick Devlin and Rab's friend Geoffrey

---

24 Bury, *The College of Corpus Christi and of the Blessed Virgin Mary: A History, 1822–1952* (Cambridge: C.C.C, 1952), pp. 240–41.

25 Ibid., p. 242.

26 Butler, *The Art of the Possible*, p. 15.

27 Cradock, *Recollections of the Cambridge Union* (Cambridge: Bowes & Bowes, 1953), p. 114.

Lloyd, both Tories; and Selwyn Lloyd and Michael Ramsey, both Liberals. As incoming president, Rab set about bringing prominent men from politics and the arts to speak at the Union. He cast his net ambitiously wide, with varying results.

He wrote to Rudyard Kipling, inviting him to debate the relative noxiousness of the two 'isms'. Kipling was unable to come but he proposed a broader horizon – that all 'isms' are wholly damnable. 'It seems to me', he replied to Rab, 'that there might be the makings of a really spirited evening in this.'[28]

He had no more success with Winston Churchill, whom he invited with no strings attached. 'As regards subject', he wrote, 'I would prefer to leave that to you.'[29] Churchill was obliged to refuse the invitation because 'the Westminster election threw [his] literary and other work so much in arrears that ... it was quite impossible ... to add to his public engagements for the next few months'.[30] His greatest *coup* came in the Easter term of 1924, when Stanley Baldwin appeared at the Union to debate the motion 'That this House has the highest regard for Rhetoric'.[31]

By then Rab's immediate future had dramatically changed. During the Michaelmas (autumn) term, he combined his newly assumed activities for the Conservative Association with the apparently contradictory determination to have the Union affiliate with the National Union of Students (NUS). This was almost certainly an initiative proposed by Sir Geoffrey, a 'modern' Tory, and, predictably, it was fiercely opposed by the 'diehards'.[32] Affiliation to the NUS was a cause that Rab passionately espoused and whose urgency was caused by the imminent general election.[33] By early November, he had succeeded in securing affiliation but had clearly overtaxed himself. On 6 November, he wrote to his parents, telling them of his victory, but lamenting,

---

28 Trinity: Butler Papers, RAB, C6.12, 8 May 1924.
29 Trinity: Butler Papers, RAB, A18.3.1. Much later Martin Gilbert found the letter of invitation in the Chartwell Archives and returned it to Rab.
30 Trinity: Butler Papers, RAB, C6.13.
31 Ibid., p. 115; Butler, *The Art of the Possible*, p. 16.
32 Cradock, *Recollections of the Cambridge Union*, p. 119. Essay by R. A. B.
33 The election took place on 6 December 1923.

I wish I could get away from all this, and I will do. It's just the continual
presiding and being present – all of it compulsory. I want to have time when
life isn't a continual vista of jumps and exams and after Cambridge I'm de-
termined to stop the avalanche and say 'What's the hurry?'[34]

There was another element introduced to Rab's life during that term. Late in the summer, after his return from Austria, two friends from the Wick school had taken Rab to Stanstead Hall in Essex, the home of the Courtauld family, to meet their cousin Sydney Courtauld, a lively and independent-minded young woman, and an undergraduate at Newnham College. Directly after the start of the Michaelmas term, Sydney invited Rab to tea in Newnham on 21 October. Rab maintained the friendship, betraying little to his parents but referring in a letter to 'the cheerful Sydney Courtauld up at Newnham'.[35] Yet, by the time of Rab's twenty-first birthday on 9 December, Sydney had felt able to throw a birthday party for him at the Carlton Hotel.[36]

This was more than the act of a 'cheerful' acquaintance; it implied a greater intimacy than Rab admitted to, either in letters home or in his memoir. It suggests that Sydney, at least, predicted a future beyond casual friendship. During three months, if that is so, Rab, in addition to embarking upon a serious relationship with Sydney, had involved himself in politics at the urging of his uncle, undertaken a crusade to bring the Cambridge Union into the NUS, campaigned for the Tories in the December election, fulfilled his duties as secretary of the Union (despite wishing that his presence was not compulsory) and begun a course of study for his final degree in a totally different discipline.

The confluence of all these events and pressures took their toll on a young man, emotionally pampered by his mother, who had thus far taken schoolboy challenges in his stride. From purely undergraduate concerns Rab was projected onto a far larger stage, involving potentially life-changing decisions – all at a time when his primary responsibility

---

34 Trinity: Butler Papers, RAB, D48.6, letter from Rab to his parents, 24 October 1923.
35 Ibid., letter from Rab, 6 November 1923.
36 Trinity: Butler Papers, RAB, D48.6, letter from Rab to his parents, 12 December 1923. Interestingly, he makes light of Sydney's involvement, attributing the generosity to her family. Howard, *RAB*, p. 23*n*.

was to the Tripos. By November, his college had decreed that he be put under the care of a doctor[37] and, during the Christmas vacation at Bourton, he suffered a collapse severe enough for his uncle Cyril to send him to a specialist in Bristol. The latter insisted that Rab desist from any challenging academic work. Instead, he should content himself with general studies in the academic year 1923/24. This would bring him a BA, but if he sought an honours degree, he would need to return to Cambridge for a fourth year.

There was a further consideration. Sydney was the only child of Sam Courtauld, one of the most successful and wealthy industrialists in Britain. Rab would have been inhuman not to consider how marriage to Sydney would dramatically alter his financial position, almost certainly permitting him to devote himself full-time to politics. Paradoxically, this will have added another pressure to the cauldron of doubts that burned in the autumn of 1923 as he pondered whether he had done the right thing in checking the development of his closeness with Kathleen. Conforming with the *mores* of the 1920s, Rab will have asked himself whether it would be 'quite the thing' for him, if he were to marry Sydney, to rely on her wealth to pursue a political career. No matter how emotionally committed he was, the accusation would be made, in the unforgiving catechism of his era, that he had 'married for money'. From the perspective of a 21-year-old undergraduate, these were impossibly weighty questions.

There is no record of how Rab reacted to what was, in all particulars, a nervous crisis. Modern psychology is more specific in defining causes and effect, avoiding expressions like 'mental breakdown' or 'nervous breakdown'. In 1923, when psychiatrists were contemptuously referred to as 'trick cyclists', the confluence of pressures that brought Rab to a standstill produced a result that men of his generation regarded as something to be stoically endured, a source of shame if one succumbed. In explaining the standstill to his father, the sense of failure must have been particularly strong. Not only had Rab failed to emulate

---

37 Howard, *RAB*, p. 22.

his father's success in three years; Monty would, as a result, have to meet the cost of another year at Cambridge.

The immediate outcome for Rab was a release from the 'avalanche' that he had described to his parents in November. He was able to build on his Austrian summer by taking a course in German; he 'attended Sir James Frazer's lectures on the masterpiece of anthropology *The Golden Bough*, and looked in occasionally on lectures on philosophy'. He later chuckled to recall a course on weather, 'attended by sporting young men in very large-squared plus-fours, usually with their arms around a young woman's waist and accompanied by retrievers'.[38]

Further diversion was provided by beagling with the Trinity Foot and South Herts Beagles of Cambridge University. This hunt went out on Monday, Wednesday and Saturday afternoons during winter. They met at the Pitt Club at 12.30 or 1 p.m. and spent autumn and winter afternoons pursuing the hare across Cambridgeshire and Hertfordshire. Kathleen urged Rab to participate to keep himself in shape.[39]

His intellectual life was equally full. As secretary of the university French Club, now president of the Union, and dutiful member of his college literary societies, he was characteristically industrious. At one point he gave two papers in four days, one to the College Martlets Society, *Little by Little or the World as School*, on 3 March 1924, and one to the Pembroke College Historical Society, *The Pattern of French Diplomacy*, on 6 March. These tended to the abstract, following the style of *La Génie Française*, a paper he had given to the Martlets on 30 October 1922.[40] The relief from the demands of his degree course must have been novel; Rab filled the time with a multitude of different activities.

Were it not for Rab's decision to go up for a fourth year, none of these diversions could have been fitted into the timetable with which he rounded out the 1923/24 academic year. His wide-ranging pursuit of non-academic activity prompted *Granta*, the university magazine, to feature a profile of him on 25 April 1924. The light-hearted, gently

---

38 Butler, *The Art of the Possible*, p. 15. He preserved among his papers a certificate that he had successfully attended a course on 'The Weather'. Trinity: Butler Papers, RAB, C1.

39 Trinity: Butler Papers, RAB, C130.

40 Trinity: Butler Papers, RAB, C3.5, 9 and 11.

mocking article referred to 'the romantic side of his character, disguised ever so carefully when you meet him' and commented that he was 'president of everything – except the Chess Club and the Cheese-Eaters'.[41] A possibly apocryphal story tells of undergraduates organising a parade in which they carried placards bearing the slogan, 'Rab – unfair to the rest of us'.[42]

Through his uncle Sir Geoffrey Butler he was also able to put himself about a bit among senior members – at Pembroke and at Corpus Christi, his uncle's college. By the time he took his degree in May 1925 he was on familiar terms with many Fellows, professors and Heads of House, as the sheaf of letters of congratulation shows. Sir Geoffrey had gone to some lengths to ensure that his nephew extracted the maximum benefit from his undergraduate years. To make and develop these connections took time, and the academic year of 1923/24 allowed Rab that luxury.

By the time that Baldwin came to Cambridge as a platform speaker in the first Union debate that Rab presided over, on 11 March 1924, Rab was under greatly less pressure. Baldwin spoke against the motion 'That this House has the highest regard for Rhetoric'. His fundamental position was that 'to tell the truth needs no art at all, and that is why I always believe in it'. 'When we come to big things', he argued, 'we do not need rhetoric. Truth, we have always been told, is naked. She requires very little clothing.'

The House was evenly divided and Rab, in the Union tradition, gave his casting vote for the motion. On the following morning,

> …the Prime Minister asked to be taken early to the train so that he might rummage among the books new and secondhand on the bookstall. He bought a shocker for me, and told me that intellectualism was a sin, and would lead a young man to a fate worse than death. I have always remained a devoted disciple.[43]

---

41 *Granta*, vol. 33, p. 740.
42 Trinity: Butler Papers, RAB, G37.39.2.
43 Cradock, *Recollections of the Cambridge Union*, pp. 115–6. The book by P. G. Wodehouse was scarcely 'a shocker', but it was undoubtedly lower-brow than Rab's normal consumption. Mollie, Rab's second wife, recalled in her memoir that Wodehouse's humour was somewhat wasted on her husband.

Baldwin had been an undergraduate at Trinity, Cambridge between 1885 and 1888, graduating with a third-class degree.[44] It must have given him enormous pleasure, from the lofty perch of a Prime Minister, to tease the over-earnest Rab, desperate to secure his double first, about the danger of intellectualism. Whether it was a serious warning or a good-natured jibe, it was a comment that Rab was never to forget.[45]

Despite this prime-ministerial advice, Rab retained his serious mien in his youth; he admitted that at the Union he 'was never able to make a speech of unrelieved humour'.[46] He served his term as president; he was able to enter the examination hall without undue stress. He took a second-class degree in German, thus earning a BA, but there was never any doubt in his or Monty's mind that more would be required. Rab's year of relative ease was at an end. His father was not slow to remind him of this, writing:

> So you are a BA 30 years after me and 130 years after your great grandfather. On thinking it over, I take comfort in the 2nd ... The experience of your third year will surely produce a 1st in your fourth. Directly you are yourself again, you must get down to it.[47]

Not unnaturally, Monty, recently knighted, now wanted his son to come home to India for the long vacation. Rab, equally naturally, was reluctant to do so, and could offer a sound reason for avoiding the homilies that he feared would be heaped on him. As president of the Union, he was invited to join a debating team that over seven weeks toured universities in eastern Canada and the eastern United States.

The prospect of such a jaunt did not sit well with Monty, and Rab spent much of July arguing with his father. At the end of the month, just before leaving on the debating tour, he made his decision clear,

---

44 Baldwin had come into contact with Henry Montagu Butler, first at Harrow, where he had clashed with the headmaster, and at Cambridge when Rab's great-uncle was Master of Trinity.

45 Butler, *The Art of the Possible*, p. 18. Anthony Howard suggests that Rab elaborated on the story in later years (*RAB*, p. 24). That may be so, but the nub of the tale, that the Prime Minister with a third-class degree gently teased the aspiring politician on the railway platform in Cambridge is vivid and plausible.

46 Butler, *The Art of the Possible*, p. 17.

47 Trinity: Butler Papers, RAB, A65, letter of 7 July 1924.

asking Monty to 'make due allowance for this rotten health' and for 'a somewhat important event to me'.[48] Kathleen Smith had just announced her engagement.

Since their parting ways in March they had continued to write to each other and Kathleen believed that their closeness could lead to a more permanent attachment. At Christmas-time in Scotland, thinking of Rab in his room in Pembroke, she wrote him a letter full of the memory of her visit in February. She wrote of her family, a warm, charming picture of their meeting for Christmas, drawing Rab into her milieu. She talked of coming in from a walk on the shore to find a letter from Rab letting her know that he reorganised his room, moving his desk closer to the fire. 'When I came in from sunshine on the wide sea and golden dunes – there was your letter. How right that was – it made our surroundings meet – and from leaving the low boom of the North Sea breakers I heard from your room.'[49]

A week later she wrote again, a beautiful romance in her phrasing. Everything is subtly shaded and intimate: 'Happy Happy Christmas to you Rab dear. That wish of mine means a lot – and it's the loveliest thing to wish.'[50] In January 1924, she wrote twice, imagining Rab in his room above the Pelican, reporting that the first yellow daffodils are out – 'they mean loveliness and promise for the months ahead – and I send this meaning to you. Prosper, K'.[51] When the Labour Party won the general election she crowed that 'Your man [Baldwin] is out and my man [MacDonald] is in.' She chides Rab for saying that 'the end of the world has come when Labour start a-governing. They'll put a lot of hard work and intelligence into it.' 'Good luck – the best of it – love the term – go a-beagling Saturdays and keep fit – greet all my haunts for me, K'.[52]

Through the first half of 1924 she continued to write, flitting between personal and political subjects, chiding him for his Toryism, nostalgic for her visit to Cambridge, the sunlight across those wide

48 Trinity: Butler Papers, RAB, D48.7, letter of 30 July 1924.
49 Trinity: Butler Papers, RAB, A2.2, 15 December 1923
50 Trinity: Butler Papers, RAB, A2.3, 23 December 1923.
51 Trinity: Butler Papers, RAB, A2.4, 13 January 1924.
52 Trinity: Butler Papers, RAB, A2.5, 18 January 1924.

Grantchester fields, the big spires of Ely Cathedral and the firelight and shadows in Rab's timbered room. 'I wonder if it's centuries ago or just the other day – my Cambridge time. Life spreads out and we learn – how we keep learning – and in the end we find – must find – understanding. And all this seems to put time out of place.'[53]

On Easter Sunday she wrote from the Isle of Arran, eager to share with Rab the joy of a day's climbing, yet asking him obliquely where their friendship was leading, ending with 'Goodbye', a word she had vowed never to use. 'You can push a whole philosophy of life into one long day's climbing,' she wrote, following it with a glorious description of the Western Isles. She is once again the sparkling romantic. Then she describes climbing – the thrill, the 'wonderful rests full-length in the heather'. There is a sensuousness in everything she describes. She proposes coming to Cambridge as 'I want to hear the President of the Union at a certain university town and wander its ways again. Tell me what you think. Goodbye, K'.[54] That suggestion, it seems, was never taken up.

In June she wrote twice, the second time complaining that Rab had put riddles to her that she could not answer.[55] For Kathleen, the decision was a straightforward one; for Rab, two years younger, there was less urgency. A month later, she lost patience and made her choice, writing to Rab:

My own dear Rab, I've done it. I'm going to marry G. P. Thomson ... I look back to the pleasant days when there were no awful decisions – no crossing of one's desire – and I smile to think how one took for granted all life must be like that ... I thank God for every experience of these last years. After all, they have brought me to life and given me, for all the pain, something so much bigger. GP's love is wonderful. He knows and understands so well all the tossing and the storms ... En avant as ever and the best go with you, K.

PS: Will you tell your mother – I have so many letters to write. The world in general will know in a week. Please without fail let me know when you leave for the States and when you get back. Goodnight, never goodbye, K

53 Trinity: Butler Papers, RAB, A2.7, 29 February 1924.
54 Trinity: Butler Papers, RAB, A2.9, 20 April 1924.
55 Trinity: Butler Papers, RAB, A2.11, 21 June 1924.

Just before she and Thomson married in September she wrote Rab a touching 'what might have been' letter, thanking him for a painting of Notre Dame, presumably his wedding present to the pair.[56] Rab was about to leave for his debating tour; his life was still circumscribed by the university and by his own ambition.

Meanwhile, Sydney Courtauld had gone down from Cambridge with a II.2 (a lower second-class degree) and Rab had visited her and her parents on at least two occasions. It is unclear how close they had become, but in one letter home Rab wrote, 'I miss someone to share my interests with,'[57] a wistful reminder of how close he and Kathleen had been.

After learning of her engagement, Rab wrote to Monty that he would 'go to America in order to fulfil a commitment and return a free man in every way'.[58] This opaque comment hints at his regret that his affair with Kathleen had cooled, suggesting somewhat pessimistically that she was irreplaceable. He certainly avoided plunging in with Sydney 'on the rebound' for when he eventually contacted her in December she was somewhat arch in her response, referring to his silence and wishing him 'good luck with the Tripos' five months away.[59]

In the interval, Rab set off for North America while Sydney spent the late summer and autumn in Rome. The debating tour lasted a little over a month. The three Cambridge men, Rab, A. P. Marshall of Gonville and Caius, and Gerald Sparrow of Trinity Hall, set off with the princely sum of £610 between them, arriving in Nova Scotia on 19 September. The itinerary was demanding, with twenty-two debates spread over thirty-six days and visiting Halifax, New Brunswick, Montreal and Toronto in Canada. Crossing the border into the USA, they stopped at Cornell, Syracuse, Hamilton University, Colgate, Vassar, Columbia, Princeton and Swarthmore on their way south to Washington for an evening at George Washington University. They then headed north again, visiting Yale, Mount Holyoke, Harvard,

---

56 Trinity: Butler Papers, RAB, A2.14.
57 Trinity: Butler Papers, RAB, D48.7, letter of 23 July 1924.
58 Trinity: Butler Papers, RAB, D48.7, letter of 30 July 1924.
59 Trinity: Butler Papers, RAB, A9, letter of 24 December 1924.

Dartmouth and Bates College in Maine before sailing home on 25 October.[60]

The motions debated involved issues that were viewed differently from British and American perspectives. On five occasions – at Colgate, Vassar, Columbia, Princeton and George Washington – the teams debated 'That modern democracy is not consistent with personal liberty', a motion guaranteed to arouse American passions. Another favourite, debated at Bates, Mount Holyoke and Swarthmore, was 'That all countries should recognise the present Government of Russia'. At Yale, in a foretaste of a Cambridge Union debate the following term, the less politically charged motion 'That we pity our grandchildren' was at issue. Outside the debating halls the three watched an American football game at Princeton, were well entertained wherever they went and used their available time for hurried sightseeing.

Press interest followed them throughout and praised the style and quality of English rhetoric. Rab won plaudits from the *Montreal Evening Star* for 'excell[ing] in quick rapier work duelling, for in his armoury he carried the weapons of humour, raillery and satire, which are so effective in debate'. In Toronto, the university's paper *The Varsity* praised the Cambridge team as 'scholars of merit and wide experience', demonstrating 'a brilliant standard of debating'.[61] For his part, Rab wrote a somewhat arch letter to the *Daily Princetonian* that 'American college men, like English undergraduates, are chasing a good time and not the almighty dollar, from what I have seen of them.'[62]

Rab was intrigued by the difference in debating technique between the British team and their American counterparts. The British spoke extempore, in contrast to the Americans and Canadians, who

> sat with a team of nine – three speakers, three librarians and three train-
> ers. The job of the trainers was to see that the speakers had a good
> steak before the debate and to watch over their health. The librarians sat
> with card indexes behind the speakers and, if moved, passed a card with

60 Trinity: Butler Papers, RAB, C10.
61 Trinity: Butler Papers, RAB, C10.34.
62 Trinity: Butler Papers, RAB, C10.51.

an apt quotation for immediate use. These varied from the classics to Lloyd George's latest utterance. It was not surprising that with all these ministrations the opposition speakers were somewhat stilted.[63]

Returning from the tour, Rab went up to Cambridge for his fourth year. After two years of French and a year of relatively undemanding work, he now undertook History and International Law for his final degree. Monty had written to him after his third-year exams, making the point – of which Rab would have been well aware – that 'You can't do your history on what you know already, like your French.'[64] Rab had important support from his uncle Geoffrey, who had done extensive work for a book on international law and allowed Rab to see his notes.[65]

That Rab was not in contact with Sydney during the Michaelmas term of his final year is probably an indication of his resolve to be fully prepared for the Tripos. When he wrote to her at the end of the term she responded in a formal, slightly chiding fashion, revealing her willingness to make the first move, but leaving the way open for retreat:

> *Dear Rab,*
>
> *A letter was certainly far more appreciated than a snow storm would have been. The last I heard of you was in America with your portrait in all the illustrated press. I am glad it was a success and amusing ... Is the tripos to be history again? Thank heaven I've not got to take another ... If you are in London about January 5th I shall be at 14 Vicarage Gate. I don't know when term begins but I daresay you will have gone up ... All good wishes for the New Year, especially with the tripos.*
>
> *Yours, Sydney E. Courtauld*[66]

After the two had re-established contact in December, their friendship grew rapidly. In January 1925, Sydney moved into her own flat in

---

63 Butler, *The Art of the Possible*, p. 17.
64 Trinity: Butler Papers, RAB, A65, letter of 7 July 1924.
65 *The Development of International Law*, published in 1928.
66 Trinity: Butler Papers, RAB, A9.1, Sydney to Rab, 24 December 1924.

Kensington – an unconventional move in the 1920s for a young woman of twenty-two – and in April she wrote a mischievously irreverent letter, suggesting that she would soon be in Cambridge and concluding cheerfully: 'You will probably see me up in the course of the term – distinguishing mark – claret coloured coupé picking off pedestrians in K[ing's] P[arade]. Yours, Sydney'.[67]

Two weeks later she wrote again with dates that she would be in Cambridge. Since the Tripos was then just weeks away, her wanting to see him at that point suggests a new closeness in their friendship, although she did allow Rab an escape route: 'I shall be in Cambridge from p.m. of 22nd to the 25th. Is there any likelihood of seeing you? Don't hesitate to say if you want to be a hermit. I shan't be offended. [Then authoritatively] My suggestion is … Yours ever, Sydney E. Courtauld'.[68]

In the event, Rab was determinedly preoccupied with his work and, although they were able to meet, he was, understandably, less than a solicitous host. He had even cut the Union from his weekly schedule, proposing just one motion on 1 December 1925, 'That this House, believing the prosperity of England to be on the wane, has grave fears for the happiness of its grandchildren'.[69] Nonetheless he found himself able to tear himself away from his desk for lunch with the persistent Sydney. She, understanding his focus and carefully avoiding any hint of possessiveness, wrote to him from London, 'It was very nice seeing you on Saturday', then scribbled in haste, 'Good luck all this week with everything. I shall hope to hear from you when it is all over – not until. Yours, Sydney.'[70]

Rab was determined to excel in the Tripos, partly to emulate Monty and partly because he had now decided on a career. He had a yearning for politics, but not the private income to support it; the Foreign Office was an acceptable second-best in his view, but this too perturbed Monty, who felt that the Foreign Service also

---

67 Trinity: Butler Papers, RAB, A9.3, Sydney to Rab, 20 April 1925.
68 Trinity: Butler Papers, RAB, A9.4, letter of 11 May 1925.
69 Trinity: Butler Papers, RAB, C7.45.
70 Trinity: Butler Papers, RAB, A9.6, Sydney to Rab, 25 May 1925.

required a sizeable private income and urged caution. Rab had heard from the Foreign Office on 3 May 1923 that he was 'suitably qualified for admission to the competitive examination for appointment to the Foreign Office and Diplomatic Service'.[71] He now talked it over with his uncle Geoffrey, who felt strongly that he should take the exam.[72] The first thing, however, was to make the very best of the Tripos and, perhaps, take a Fellowship in the short term, if one were offered.

From his brief account of his final year's work, it is obvious that his research in his special subject, Peel's second ministry, was extensive and deep. So much so that he was able to recite the names of MPs on each side of the division over the Irish Coercion Bill. Rab developed great admiration for Peel, his resolution in the face of opposition and his determined integrity in pursuing a policy over the Corn Laws that, he was quite aware, would result in his defeat. Rab's recognition of the hazards of splitting the party stayed with him throughout his own political career.

His preoccupation with the Tripos caused a second illness, this time simply physical. As Rab recalled,

> As the examination approached my health deteriorated for the second time in a year and I got jaundice. Ashley Clarke ferried me out to see his father, a doctor in Norfolk. He said that I must take the exam in spite of my illness and recommended moving to stay with the beloved Oliver Priors,[73] taking champagne twice a day and some special pills.[74]

Will Spens, the Senior Tutor at Corpus, and his uncle Geoffrey attempted to dissuade him from sitting the exams but Rab brooked no further delay and, in the event, performed remarkably. In the examination hall he found Peel 'quite congenial' and excelled in the international

---

71 Trinity: Butler Papers, RAB, C1.4.

72 Trinity: Butler Papers, RAB, A10.1, Geoffrey Butler to Rab, 23 March 1925.

73 For two years Rab was fortunate to have as his tutor Professor Oliver Prior, a Fellow of St John's who had recently become Professor of French. Rab recalls in his memoir that 'his wife became a lifelong friend and they looked after me on many a vital occasion'. Rab thus added Prior and his wife Camille to the families that provided a home from home in his early years.

74 Butler, *The Art of the Possible*, pp. 17–18.

law paper. With the sudden clarity that comes with deep knowledge of his subject, halfway through the time allotted he was dissatisfied with his answers. Tearing up everything he had written, he wrote answers to six questions, essays that placed him first in the university.

Immediately after the examination he was 'bundled off' to a Scottish spa by his mother, who had returned to England to be available, if needed, during the Easter term. It was at Strathpeffer that he learned his results and received the offer from Spens of a Fellowship at Corpus Christi.[75] This was on a temporary basis and did not tie Rab's hands for long. Despite the disdain with which he had treated Monty's suggestion of an academic career, he immediately accepted.

From the various young women in Rab's life came characteristic messages of congratulation. From his sister Iris came a suitably irreverent cable: 'Alleluia sing to Jesus will it be Corpus genius turns my dear fellow Iris'.[76] Sydney was ever practical, writing, 'It's perfectly splendid that you've pulled it off so well. I knew you would but I was afraid that perhaps it might have been a 1-2 after that beastly jaundice … I think I am as glad as anyone will be over it. Yours, Sydney.'[77] Kathleen, now Mrs G. P. Thomson, tended, as ever, to the superlative in her message, 'How you can get better with the finest mind in the world?'[78]

From India, Monty wrote to congratulate Rab, arranging for a further £10 to be credited to his bank account for his 'fine effort'.[79] Rab, his future employment secured, now perhaps for the first time envisaged a life free from the constraints of his family. Deciding against a visit to India in the remaining two months of the long vacation, he accepted an invitation from Sydney and her parents Sam and Lilian Courtauld to spend two weeks of August with them on the fjords north of Bergen. He sailed to Norway to join Sydney, her mother and Sir John Atkins, a family friend, for a much-needed holiday that was to change the foundations of Rab's life and permanently alter the opportunities open to him.

---

75 Trinity: Butler Papers, RAB, A162.1.
76 Trinity: Butler Papers, RAB, B1.11.
77 Trinity: Butler Papers, RAB, B1.24.
78 Trinity: Butler Papers, RAB, B1.48.
79 Trinity: Butler Papers, RAB, A9, letter of 21 June 1925.

CHAPTER 3

NEW HORIZONS, 1925–29

If either Rab or Sydney envisaged that their friendship would evolve into marriage, it was Sydney who had that foresight. When Rab's close friendship with Kathleen Smith came to an end, he wrote to his mother that he was no longer a Puritan. He seems to suggest that previously he had no experience of affairs of the heart and that he could, for the first time, imagine himself emotionally involved. There had been the summer in Austria when he had tender feelings towards Ola Reuss zu Weida, and in August 1925, by his own account, he spent time with Sydney and 'the romance of the fjords helped to develop into love a friendship which had started in Cambridge'.[1]

In contrast to the passive Rab, Sydney had chided him for his silence the previous December; it was she who proposed that she visit him in Cambridge in May; it was her invitation to Norway that brought the two together, 'to go on expeditions down the fjords in a paddle-steamer'.[2] Sydney was a forceful and determined young woman who, throughout her life, applied herself energetically to the task in hand. If it was her intention to bring to a head the friendship between the two, she succeeded, for on their return to England they had decided to marry.

In typical fashion Rab avoids overt emotion when he describes the reaction of Sydney's mother:

---

1 Butler, *The Art of the Possible*, p. 19.
2 Ibid.

My future mother-in-law, a formidable Irish-woman, appeared to accept me for two reasons: first, that I was a member of the Carlton Club; and second, that when carving I could make a partridge do six.[3]

With the approval of Sydney's parents assured, the couple now went about securing the assent of Rab's parents, who had been told little of the developing match. Monty had been puzzled by the trip to Norway, writing to Rab in July, 'I do not understand whether you are entertaining the Courtaulds or they you in Norway.'[4] Rab had clearly been a hint ambiguous about his friendship with Sydney and given a false impression to his father. Monty, however, seems to have had an inkling of his son's intentions, and urged him not to hurry to be financially independent as he would be happy to continue to finance him for a while. Throughout August and September Monty repeated that Rab's allowance would be paid.

Monty, however, was in India, and the first step was to introduce Sydney to Ann who was spending the summer in Devon. Rab returned first from Norway and hurried to Devon. Sydney celebrated her twenty-third birthday on her way back and travelled down to join Rab and his mother. After the weekend she wrote to Rab that, 'It was so much nicer meeting Lady Butler there than it would have been in London where everyone is rushed.'[5]

Her letters suddenly take on a more authoritative tone – at least towards Rab. 'I think it is terribly important that you sleep properly,' she wrote. 'Don't get bored but do take care of yourself at Bourton.'[6] She mixes frivolous anecdotes – how she was arrested for contempt of court as she failed to respond to a summons for a traffic offence while they were in Norway – with authority – the plan for decorating Rab's rooms in Corpus – to the romantic – 'Yesterday was a special day and left me very happy.'[7] She began to write almost every day, alternating lectures with endearments and signing with Rab's pet name for her, 'Love, Jeannot'.

3 Ibid.
4 Trinity: Butler Papers, RAB, A65.25, Monty to Rab, 12 July 1925.
5 Trinity: Butler Papers, RAB, A9.9, Sydney to Rab, 8 September 1925.
6 Ibid.,
7 Ibid.

'The most important thing in front of you is this fellowship,' Sydney wrote in October, 'and to get the most out of it I don't think you should hold it for less than two years. You'll see as you get into it but I don't want you to hurry anything because of me.'[8] They had become very close very quickly and to cement their family Sydney's dog Raider became the object of their joint affection, almost like their child. Rab would feed Raider from the table when he visited Sydney in London; Raider accordingly pined for Rab when he was away. Letters flowed between London and Cambridge with details of lectures, news of Raider and plans for the future.

At first Rab told his father little of his intentions. When he did, Monty was much relieved as he had sensed that something was in the air. 'I am glad you wrote, old man', he replied, somewhat muddled and unsure quite what to say, 'as it makes it so much easier to have no secrets.'[9] When, a week later, Rab told him that Sam Courtauld had provided for Rab to receive £5,000[10] tax-free for life, he was stunned and wrote with charming ingenuousness, 'I am amazed at the generosity of the treatment you are to get. You have learnt to manage money on a small scale and will not lose your head, I know, over the big scale.'[11]

Rab's financial position – and therefore his options for his future career – had been changed beyond the cautious Monty's most optimistic hopes. Monty was impressed by Rab's descriptions of his fiancée and even more disposed to take her to his heart when Rab sent him a photograph of Sydney. He replied as though both he and Rab were adventurous young bucks. 'Young fellow my lad, you are in luck and no mistake.'[12]

During his time as a Cambridge undergraduate and his close association with his uncle Geoffrey, Rab had begun to aspire to a career in politics. That had not been a realistic ambition with an annual allowance of £300 from Monty. It took Rab and Sydney a very short

8   Trinity: Butler Papers, RAB, A9.17, Sydney to Rab, 14 October 1925.
9   Trinity: Butler Papers, RAB, A65.39, Monty to Rab, 7 November 1925.
10 The equivalent of £250,000 *per annum* in 2014.
11 Trinity: Butler Papers, RAB, A65.40, Monty to Rab, 16 November 1925.
12 Trinity: Butler Papers, RAB, A65.54, Monty to Rab, 13 February 1926.

time to decide that a Corpus Fellowship was not to feature large in their future. Rab prepared to leave his residential post at Corpus at the end of the 1925/26 academic year. He and Sydney would 'go round the world for a year as a preparation for entering public life'.[13]

Predictably, Monty was not without a view in the matter and, equally predictably, his view was shaded with disapproval. He was delighted that Rab would at last be revisiting India and he urged them, whether they went east or west, to spend Christmas in Nagpur.[14] As the day of the wedding drew closer, Monty became palpably excited. It had been a long time and now he lectured Rab as an old India hand to a novice, spelling out exactly what clothes he should bring.[15] (He had given the same detailed advice in 1924, when Rab was planning a visit that never happened.)

Rab's biographer notes that 'it was now taken for granted, even by Sir Monty' that Rab would have guaranteed admission to the House of Commons.[16] Rab certainly had the academic credentials and the ambition. Those assets, combined with the wealth and influence of the Courtauld family, it was universally assumed, would ease his passage to a safe seat. Even so, Monty was able to disapprove of 'this all-the-world-in-a-year stunt'.[17] He made this clear to Rab in a letter whose untypically illogical reasoning arouses the slightest suspicion of jealousy on Monty's part.

On the premise that 'no one nowadays can expect to get preferment in politics until he is well over 30', Rab's father suggests that he see the world piecemeal, rather than in one tour, writing:

> *If you exhaust the world by the time you are 25, you will fret at the long waiting ... You will find it a great help, I am sure, to have fresh fields to explore each year or every other year until the time comes for you to take office in some Ministry.*[18]

---

13   Butler, *The Art of the Possible*, p. 20.
14   Trinity: Butler Papers, RAB, A65.59, Monty to Rab, 24 March 1926.
15   Trinity: Butler Papers, RAB, Monty to Rab, 5 April 1926.
16   Howard, *RAB*, p. 32.
17   Trinity: Butler Papers, RAB, A65, letter of 13 February 1926.
18   Ibid.

The letter is revealing, not only for the light it casts on Rab's father's view of the correct order of things and the decencies of expecting gradual preferment, but also because it is clear that, even before their wedding, Rab and Sydney had decided on Rab's future career in politics and were preparing to invest time and money immediately to equip him.

Rab laid the foundations of that career by writing a number of articles about India, a step that perturbed his cautious father. Monty wrote a restraining letter to register his own position:

> I am not keen on your continuing to write articles about India. If you are to do justice to them you would have to get in touch with the politicians and really study the issues, and this might embarrass me and uncle H[arcourt]. Anything you write would be interpreted as having our support.[19]

Amid Monty's mixed delight and concern, after much fuss over wedding presents, amid excited preparations in Nagpur, the capital of the Central Provinces, for the return of the son and heir, Rab and Sydney were married at noon on 20 April 1926 in St Mary Abchurch, a charming Wren church off Cannon Street. It was a quiet affair because of Sam Courtauld's dislike of press intrusion. Rab's parents were absent in India and unable to attend.[20] Edmund Pearce, the Master of Corpus, officiated; Geoffrey Butler, Fellow of Corpus, was best man. The church itself was granted to Corpus by Elizabeth I; thus Rab married into a wealthy family in a service that underscored his new position as a Corpus don. After the service and a family luncheon at the Ritz, the newlyweds were driven to Cambridge in the Courtaulds' Rolls-Royce.

Before they could set off on their world tour, however, Rab needed to fulfil his commitment to Corpus. This does not seem to have been particularly demanding, save that, as a junior lecturer, he drew the short straw of giving a lecture at the unpopular hour of 9 a.m.

---

19 Trinity Papers: A65.53, Monty to Rab, 8 February 1926.
20 Trinity: Butler Papers, RAB, C1.69.

Combining his Tripos subjects, he lectured on Modern French History, specifically the Third Republic. In the context of Cambridge in the 1920s, this was a daringly 'modern' subject as the Third Republic was born with the collapse of the Second French Empire and defeat in the Franco-Prussian War of 1870–71. It was riven by faction after the First World War and, arguably, under weak leadership in the inter-war period, failed to provide the moral certitude to resist German expansion and aggression. It is interesting to speculate how Rab's analysis of the Third Republic may have influenced him a dozen years after he left the Corpus Senior Common Room.

At the end of the academic year, Rab resigned his residential Fellowship, becoming a supernumerary Fellow. He and Sydney donated a 'handsome Directoire clock for the Combination Room' at Corpus[21] and readied themselves for their world tour. This involved a thorough preparation both in the seeking of introductions and the choice of reading material. Rab had met Leo Amery, the Secretary of State for the Colonies, at a conference of British Empire students in July 1924 and invited him to speak at the Union.[22] This meeting emboldened him to call on Amery to ask him for introductions along their route. Amery obliged and the couple were equipped with contacts qualified to give them an accurate picture of contemporary conditions in Australia, New Zealand and Canada.[23]

Reading Rab's account of his preparation for the trip tends to encourage support of his father's objections. He was taking a great deal in with a single swallow. This, of course, had been the tendency that caused his nervous collapse in late 1923. It must have been an enormous temptation for Rab, a young don, to make the grandest possible tour. He had connections through Monty to the India Office and to the Secretary of State for the Colonies; his uncle was firmly established among Conservative Party intellectuals; he had an influential patron in his father-in-law, willing to speak for and to subsidise Rab's political career; not least he had a new wife urging him to quit the

21 Bury, *The College of Corpus Christi*, p. 260.
22 Trinity: Butler Papers, RAB, C13.5.
23 Butler, *The Art of the Possible*, p. 20.

backwaters of academe and begin scaling the political ladder. The differences between Rab's and Sir Monty's approach to a political career became clear early in Rab's and Sydney's trip, when they sailed for Bombay aboard SS *Rampura* on 17 September and visited Rab's parents in India.

It had been fifteen years since Rab had left India for the Wick school. During that decade and a half Monty had risen to be president of the legislative council of the Punjab in 1921; to be secretary to the government of India in the department of education, health and lands in 1922. In 1924 he was appointed president of the council of state, and in 1924 he became Sir Montagu Butler, Governor of the Central Provinces. Systematic reward for continued effort contrasted strongly with the rapid advancement that Rab appeared to seek with his assault on all fronts of foreign and Commonwealth affairs.

During the three months that Rab and Sydney spent in India, principally at Nagpur, Rab discussed his future with his father. It was not a meeting of minds, as Rab recorded:

> I studied and enjoyed his patient methods of administration and his subtle intrigues with Congressman Tambe. But about my own political future he seemed to have some very strange views, which we discussed in lonely mountain walks at Pachmarhi. He thought that it was not in my line to take strong personal executive decisions. My forte was to be friends with all, impartial and diplomatic. He was in favour of my entering Parliament, but only for the purpose of becoming Speaker.[24]

Whilst Sir Monty failed to recognise the extent of Rab's ambition – a trait that few of his later colleagues failed to spot – he did identify one of his son's shortcomings that was to become equally recognised by his critics in the years ahead. Most notably, however, Sir Monty invested Rab with his own judicial nature in his imagination, failing to see his son's burning desire for power. While Sir Monty was urging him to aim to be Speaker of the House of Commons, Rab was developing

---

24 Ibid., p. 21.

an ambition to be a Cabinet minister or Viceroy of India.[25] While Sir
Monty, possessor of 'his patient methods of administration', was casting
Rab as a worthy and recognisable functionary, Rab imagined himself as
the King's *alter ego*, guardian of the jewel in the Monarch's crown.

By early April 1927, after visiting Uncle Harcourt, then Governor of
Burma, Rab and Sydney were in Adelaide, en route to Melbourne and
Sydney, where Rab had introductions from Amery to an ex-Premier
and future leaders of Australia. He expressed to Geoffrey Butler his
high opinion of South Australian wine and promised to bring back
some bottles for the Corpus High Table.[26]

After the eastern cities of Australia they visited a sheep station
before heading on to New Zealand. From there they sailed to Fiji
and the Society Islands, Samoa and Honolulu, and on to Vancouver,
where they were due to arrive on 25 July.[27] Both Rab and Sydney were
working hard, preparing Rab for a run at a parliamentary seat. They
recorded films of their travels to show in a suitable constituency on
their return. 'We have really worked hard and used every moment,' he
wrote to Geoffrey. 'Sydney is working too.' Sydney, obviously, was destined to be a political wife as he wrote in the first person plural, 'In all
modesty we start our political novitiate and cross the bridge from the
academic to the political.'[28] Not only was Sydney a willing participant
in Rab's plans for a political future; she was at least as ambitious for
her husband as he was for himself. The *Newcastle Journal* later quoted
Sydney as saying at their wedding, 'I'll make him Premier.'[29]

When Rab and Sydney arrived at Sooke Harbor on the southwest
tip of Vancouver Island in July 1927, they found two letters waiting for
them, indicating that William Foot Mitchell, the Conservative MP
for Saffron Walden, was considering retirement. At the age of sixty-
eight, he was looking ahead to an election to be held before October
1929; if he was to step down, he wanted to allow his successor time to
become acquainted with the constituency before that election.

25 Ibid., p. 20.
26 Trinity: Butler Papers, RAB, D4.4.
27 Trinity: Butler Papers, RAB, D4.3.
28 Trinity: Butler Papers, RAB, D4.4.
29 *The Newcastle Journal*, 10 December 1954.

Foot Mitchell had spoken to Geoffrey Butler in the House of Commons in order to sound him out about Rab's qualifications to succeed him. According to Geoffrey,

> He then said he had been approached by a Mr Courtauld with reference to one whom he thought I might know. Might he ask me some questions? These he did. He then told me something about the constituency – it is largely agricultural, it is very large and, therefore, makes a good deal of demands on any candidate.[30]

The second letter was from William Courtauld, Sydney's second cousin who lived in the Saffron Walden constituency at Halstead. He wrote to Rab that he had 'just seen Foot Mitchell' who had told him that, if his health permitted, he would stay until the general election, that he thought the local Conservative Association would consider Rab favourably, and that Rab should contact him immediately once he'd returned.[31] He added that it was essential for Rab to have a house in the constituency and that he would need to spend about £1,000 annually on subscriptions, charities and the like. Clearly neither Mitchell nor William Courtauld envisaged any difficulty in Rab's being adopted by the party.

The dates of the two letters are intriguing. In his letter of 20 June, Sydney's cousin wrote that he had 'just seen' Mitchell, while Geoffrey Butler wrote on 14 June that Mitchell had been approached by 'a Mr Courtauld', who had then approached Geoffrey for a reference on Rab. The dates suggest that someone, possibly Sydney's father Sam Courtauld, first mooted the idea to Mitchell, thereafter leaving negotiations to William. In the interim, Mitchell spoke to Rab's uncle. In due course, after speaking to Geoffrey, Mitchell reported back to William.

This sequence seems most plausible. Sam, the *paterfamilias*, makes the first approach in early June, speaking to Mitchell himself in order to bring maximum pressure to bear; Mitchell, suitably awed,

---

30 Trinity: Butler Papers, RAB, A10.5, Geoffrey Butler to Rab, 14 June 1927.
31 Trinity: Butler Papers, RAB, A13, letter of 20 June 1927.

approaches Geoffrey Butler before 14 June and, after receiving a good report, speaks, as instructed, to William Courtauld. Courtauld then writes on 20 June that he has just seen Mitchell. If that was the sequence of events, the Courtauld family was certainly combining to look after Rab's interests.

Something went awry in the process of communication, as Sam Courtauld wrote to Rab, reproving him for not keeping him fully informed. He did, however, affirm his support, stressing:

> *I also told [the agent] that I was in no way opposed to the idea myself, but had always approved of your intention to go into parliament and was prepared to help you in any way short of taking an active part in any campaign. That I cannot do as I am not a convivial party man.*[32]

It might have been expected that this news would impel him to return home with all haste and present himself to the constituency association. Yet he and Sydney, despite having admitted to some weariness and a desire to return home, continued with their original travel plans, heading east across Canada in leisurely fashion and returning from Quebec aboard SS *Empress of Australia* on 31 August.

That leisurely return was soon replaced by eighteen months of diligent apprenticeship to the trade of politics. The constituency of Saffron Walden, the largest in Essex, was, as Geoffrey Butler had described, agricultural, containing three market towns of some size: Saffron Walden itself, Dunmow and Halstead. In common with many East Anglian agricultural communities, it took pride in its Liberal tradition and since the redistribution of seats in 1885 had been held by a Liberal for thirty-six of the intervening forty-two years, never being won by a Labour candidate. When Rab returned to meet the local Conservative association, therefore, although Mitchell had held the seat for the Tories since 1922, it was by no means a safe seat.

The nature of the constituency, the diminishing appeal of Baldwin's 'Safety First' policy, unreceptiveness of East Anglian farmers to the

---

32 Trinity: Butler Papers, RAB, A14.1, Sam Courtauld to Rab, 1 July 1927.

growing Labour Party[33] – all these factors contributed to Rab's selection and subsequent success at the polls. Because it was not a safe seat there was no competition for the job; Rab was the lone candidate, and, given the growing appetite for change from the Baldwin ministry, it was politic for Saffron Walden to introduce a young man with no association with the past. Those two considerations acted in Rab's favour during the process of selection. Despite 'considerable doubt about my tender age and attainments',[34] Rab was unanimously selected at a Saturday afternoon meeting on 26 November to represent the Tories at the next election.[35]

Soon after, Rab contacted his friend Geoffrey Lloyd, a Cambridge contemporary from Trinity, who had contested the seat of Southwark South East while still an undergraduate. Lloyd, like Rab, had been a member of Geoffrey Butler's circle of young Conservatives at Cambridge. One biographical essay records that his early years at Cambridge were devoted to 'hunting, drinking and punting' until he was 'reclaimed to seriousness' by Rab's uncle.[36] He became Private Secretary to Hoare in 1926 and worked closely with Chamberlain and Baldwin. Rab and Lloyd had kept up their friendship since Lloyd went down in 1924; now Lloyd replied to Rab, telling him that he had mentioned his name to Baldwin,[37] who well remembered their meeting at the Cambridge Union. By the time that the election was held, therefore, Rab's name was known to the leaders of the Tory Party.

Rab applied himself to learning his new trade – 'as systematic a task as learning French at Abbeville'.[38] He and Sydney promptly honoured their undertaking to the association by acquiring a house at Broxted. From this base the personable young couple criss-crossed the county. From his earliest days in politics he was greatly assisted by Sydney, whose energy at the hustings became legendary. Visiting two

---

33 As recently as 2010, the antipathy of the constituency to the Labour Party was shown in a general election in which the results were: Conservative 30,155; Liberal Democrat 14,913; Labour 5,288.
34 Butler, *The Art of the Possible*, p. 22.
35 *The Herts and Essex Observer*, 27 November 1927. Cited by Howard, *RAB*, p. 36.
36 *Oxford Dictionary of National Biography*, citing Devlin, *Taken at the Flood*, p. 47.
37 Trinity: Butler Papers, RAB, A115.
38 Butler, *The Art of the Possible*, p. 22.

or three of the constituency's eighty villages each week, they held an
evening event, showing films of their recent tour of the Empire, followed by a visit to the local pub. Mixing with the villagers, showing
films that 'interested the villagers much more than political speeches',[39]
he presented himself as a man of wide experience despite his youth.

He also showed an appreciation of local issues when he seized
cannily on the question of the application of import duties to barley.
Sending to every working-men's club in the constituency a cask of beer
'brewed within the Division', he indicated that he would work to put
an end to the illogical system whereby hops were subject to import
duties whereas barley was not. Clearly the protection of barley, too,
would be beneficial to the local farmers.

Along the way, Rab became entranced by the beauty of his adoptive
constituency. At the western end of Constable country, boasting ar-
chaic village names such as Sibil Hedingham and Colne Engaine, the
countryside seemed to Rab to be 'ready to be painted', and his delight
with 'the happy seat' emerges clearly from his memoir.[40] It proved to
be an enchantment that lasted and which was mutual, for Rab represented Saffron Walden for thirty-five years.

The election year of 1929 began auspiciously for Rab and Sydney, as
their first son, Richard, was born on 12 January. Monty and Ann were
ecstatic at the arrival of their first grandchild[41] and Ann bubbled over
in a chatty letter to Rab. As with many grandparents, this was the first
grandchild ever to be born: 'I am so happy darling. Sydney and you
are clever to have this nice Richard and I will write to her forthwith. I
think Richard is a darling and so is Sydney and so are you.'[42]

As the election approached, Monty was analytical, encouraging
and supportive in his letters, astutely analysing Rab's performance.
His opinions are surprisingly objective on a subject likely to occasion
violent partisanship. What seems to have given him, a lifelong civil

39 Ibid.
40 Ibid., pp. 22–3.
41 Trinity: Butler Papers, RAB, A65.180.
42 Trinity: Butler Papers, RAB, A67.7, Ann to Rab, 14 January 1929.

servant, most satisfaction is that election to the constituency of Saffron Walden, in Monty's view, meant 'a safe seat for life'.[43]

Monty's and Rab's excitement at the beginning of Rab's political career was tinged with sadness just before the May election. Geoffrey Butler, whose health had deteriorated since 1927, died on 2 May at the tragically early age of forty-one. He had been Parliamentary Private Secretary to Sir Samuel Hoare at the Air Ministry since 1925 and the two had become close friends. Hoare remembered him warmly in his memoirs:

> I never had a better friend than Geoffrey, nor an adviser who gave me wiser guidance. Those who were with him at Cambridge or in the House of Commons will never forget his delightful wit, lively imagina- tion and unsurpassed talent for making friends, particularly amongst the young ... His last words to me when I visited him on his death- bed were: 'Look after my young nephew Rab, and help him in his political career.'[44]

Geoffrey's influence on Rab – as uncle, academic colleague and Presi- dent of the Cambridge University Conservative Association – had been enormous. His last words to Hoare did not go unheeded and Hoare's patronage of his nephew brought Rab his first ministerial ap- pointment three years later. Even as Rab prepared to fight his first parliamentary election, Geoffrey was convinced that Rab had a formi- dable future ahead of him, and it was a great blow to Rab that his uncle did not live to see him launched on his journey.

Several factors had come to Rab's aid when he met the selection committee of the division. Other considerations were equally ben- eficial when Britain went to the polls on 30 May. Rab describes the national mood succinctly:

> It was not that there was anything particularly wrong. What was evi- dent was a lack of initiative and a general sense that it was time for a

---

43 Trinity: Butler Papers, RAB, A65.203, Monty to Rab, 6 June 1929.
44 Lord Templewood (Sir Samuel Hoare), *Nine Troubled Years* (London: Collins, 1954), p. 71.

change … a feeling that the Tories were persisting on too traditional lines and this gave an opportunity for the Labour Party.[45]

His analysis was accurate in both particulars and the opportunity was seized by Labour, who gained 136 seats to finish with 287, short of an overall majority but with a lead of twenty-seven over the Tories. Rab, having no association with the existing Tory government, did not suffer from the desire for change. Moreover, the 1929 election 'marked the Indian Summer of the old Liberal Party'.[46] David Lloyd George, making a last attempt to revive his party's fortunes, had appropriated Labour's policies, publishing a pamphlet titled 'We Can Conquer Un-employment'. This created the climate for the 'Indian Summer' and the Liberals benefited greatly in the traditional strongholds, the 'Celtic fringe' and East Anglia.

This 'last throw' by Lloyd George helped Rab immeasurably. In the teeth of a national swing of 3.7 per cent to the Labour Party the seat was secured by the habitual disinclination of local voters towards Labour. Instead, such defections from Tory ranks as took place were to the Liberals. The result, therefore, was quite out of line with the national result. Rab won 13,561 votes while the Labour and Liberal candidates were almost level with 8,642 and 8,307 respectively. Rab was home with a majority of 4,919.

45 Ibid., p. 23.
46 Adelman, *The Decline of the Liberal Party 1910–1931* (London: Longman, 1982), p. 58.

CHAPTER 4

A FOOT ON THE LADDER,
1929–32

The 1929 election marked the effective demise of the Liberal Party and the resolution of the electorate into the now familiar shape of Conservative and Labour, roughly evenly split. Each received over 8 million votes. The election also brought a Parliament made up of more full-time politicians than ever before, with only ninety-six company directors; for the first time, moreover, Trades Union leaders did not constitute the majority of Labour members.[1]

Baldwin resigned as soon as the results were known and Ramsay MacDonald took office for the second time on 5 June. Very soon the government was faced with the dominant issue of the election: unemployment. MacDonald appointed a team of four – J. H. ('Jimmy') Thomas, George Lansbury, Tom Johnston and Oswald ('Tom') Mosley – to address the problem.

On 30 October, Rab made his maiden speech in the Commons. Predictably, he chose an agricultural subject. In a Private Member's Motion, Sir Edward Iliffe urged prevention of the dumping of German cereals. Rab spoke of his visit to north Germany earlier that year and reported that 'the situation in German agriculture has been practically as bad as that in British agriculture, and the situation in countries where there is a protective tariff, such as Switzerland or Australia, is very often just as bad.' Protection was no remedy for Britain's troubles.[2]

---

1 Taylor, *English History, 1914–1945* (Oxford: Clarendon Press, 1965), p. 342.
2 Hansard, 30 October 1929, vol. 231, col. 202.

It was a non-partisan speech, agreeing that agricultural depression was caused by world conditions, stressing the consequences of unemployment in his constituency and calling for an international conference on prices and the gold standard. It was not a daring or wildly creative address, but it received general approval from *The Times*, which singled out Rab and E. F. Wise, the Independent Labour Party candidate for Leicester East, for 'impressive' maiden speeches.[3]

Meanwhile, the government's unemployment team failed to agree on a policy. Mosley and Thomas locked horns until Mosley 'saw no more of Thomas than was necessary' and 'got on with the job of working out, within the departments, what seemed ... the real policy necessary to deal with unemployment'.[4] The upshot of Mosley's work was a set of proposals known as 'The Mosley Memorandum'. Radically different from conventional economic wisdom, it proposed planned foreign trade and expansion financed by credit, a basket of creative and progressive proposals that affronted Philip Snowden, the Chancellor of the Exchequer. When the Labour Cabinet rejected his proposals in May 1930, Mosley resigned.

Whilst this split in the Labour ranks was political manna for the Tories, Mosley was the only minister to put forward innovative ideas to solve the problem of unemployment, the adoption of which might fulfil the election pledge of MacDonald's government. After his resignation, Mosley spoke derisively in the Commons of the government's indecisive economic policy. He had begged the Cabinet to make up its mind how much it would spend on unemployment, how much money it could find, and then allocate the money constructively. No such system had been adopted, but 'departments have come crowding along, jostling each other with their schemes, and, like bookmakers on the race course, the man who can push the hardest, make the most noise and get through the turnstile first, gets away with the money.' It was vital, Mosley argued, to decide how resources would be allocated in any national reconstruction.[5]

3   *The Times*, 31 October 1929, p. 14.
4   Mosley, *My Life* (London: Nelson, 1968), p. 234.
5   Hansard, 28 May 1930, vol. 239, col. 1363.

On the previous day, Harold Macmillan, a Tory who had lost his seat in the 1929 election, wrote to *The Times*, regretting the criticism that Mosley had received for making proposals that attempted to honour the government's election promises. In a letter liberally peppered with irony – a letter that Rab ironically described as 'magisterial'[6] – Macmillan expressed his disgust with a system that treated election promises in such cavalier fashion. His letter falls into three parts: first, an attack on the 'Elder Statesmen of the Socialist Party' for their myopia, and amazement that the media had followed suit; second, a criticism of the previous Baldwin government for 'pledges and promises [that] were either negative or self-contradictory'; and third, an ironic and somewhat disingenuous questioning of the 'game' of politics:

> *It may be that the sound and traditional English system is just as I have described; that we are always to have a party of the left, speaking and obtaining office by means of extravagant promises which only its most naïve supporters expect to see fulfilled, alternating with a party of the right, which will for ever operate an equally effective and perhaps more subtle technique, fighting its elections on the basis of a programme which is either self-contradictory or obscure, confident that when it has obtained power it cannot hope to emulate a more inspiring example than that of the reactionary immobility of parties alleged to be progressive. I suspect that this is the real way the game ought to be played. Only, if these rules are to be permanently enforced, perhaps a good many of us will feel that it is hardly worth while bothering to play at all. Sir Oswald Mosley thinks the rules should be altered. I hope some of my friends will have the courage to applaud and support his protest.[7]*

Rab, together with three colleagues, Lord Lymington, Harold Balfour and Michael Beaumont, collectively known as 'The Boys' Brigade',[8]

---

6   Butler, *The Art of the Possible*, p. 26.
7   *The Times*, 27 May 1930.
8   Viscount Lymington, MP for Basingstoke; Harold Balfour, MP for Thanet; Michael Beaumont, MP for Aylesbury. All three, like Rab, had entered Parliament in the 1929 election.

immediately wrote to *The Times* a letter that was printed on the following day:

> Sir,
>
> We have read with interest and some surprise Mr Harold Macmillan's letter published in your issue of today. When a player starts complaining 'that it is hardly worth while bothering to play' the game at all it is usually the player, and not the game, who is at fault. It is then usually advisable for the player to seek a new field for his recreation and a pastime more suited to his talents.[9]

In his memoir, Rab comments that the brief reply 'caused chuckling in the Whips' Office'.[10] That may be true, but it had a greatly more far-reaching result. This early political 'Rabism', none too subtly suggesting that Macmillan had chosen the wrong career, was not forgotten. Twenty-six years later, Macmillan, in a speech to the Conservative 1922 Committee, neatly turned Rab's sabre thrust around in an exchange that contributed to the thwarting of Rab's ambitions.[11]

Rab seems insensitive to the fact that he had insulted Macmillan profoundly. Instead, writing in 1971, he seemed still to be proud of the neat manner in which he skewered a political colleague. Perhaps he felt that Macmillan, who had failed to be re-elected to Stockton-on-Tees in the 1929 election, was fair game as he was no longer in Parliament. Perhaps Rab was unaware of how malicious his comment must have appeared to its target. The most conspicuous aspect of the exchange is that Macmillan, choosing to criticise most severely the Labour Party and the media who rushed to debunk Mosley, had made a valid point that Rab and his friends ignored in the interests of taunting a dissenting colleague.

Coupled with Rab's casual dismissal of Macmillan is his judgement of Mosley. 'It is surprising', he writes, 'to look back and remember how

---

9   *The Times*, 28 May 1930.
10   Butler, *The Art of the Possible*, p. 27.
11   On 22 November 1956. See below, Chapter 15.

seriously Mosley was taken forty years ago.'[12] This comment is as un-generous as the barb aimed at Macmillan. By the time Rab wrote that comment, Mosley had been disgraced, imprisoned, effectively exiled and was living outside Paris. He had originally joined the Labour Party because of his dissatisfaction with the Conservatives and, after repeated efforts in 1930 to persuade the Socialists to adopt his anti-unemployment measures, he left the Labour Party. Thereafter his story is one of disillusion and folly.

In 1930, however, Mosley's proposals showed great clarity of thought and contained elements of economic policy later propounded by Keynes. Rab gives him no credit for that foresight, nor does he give any quarter to Macmillan for acknowledging that disregard of election promises constituted deception. Instead we see Rab and his colleagues, pleased with their attack, presumably because Macmillan had the gall to recognise a virtue in an opponent, an opponent moreover who had the impudence to suggest that Baldwin's ministry of 1924–29 had been anything but perfect. Whilst Rab may have made some points with Baldwin, this early Rabism, like many of his later *bons mots*, returned to haunt him.

Rab was displaying orthodox Baldwinism in this gratuitous thrust as Macmillan was showing early signs of slipping dangerously to the left. The failure of several progressive Tory candidates to gain re-election was deplored by *The Times*, the *Daily Telegraph* and *The Spectator*. The *Daily Mail*, however, predictably, accused Baldwin's government of being crypto-socialists and gleefully urged that no parliamentary seats be kept for 'semi-Socialists such as Captain Macmillan'.[13] Duff Cooper, too, came in for criticism from the right when he and Macmillan were derided by the *Saturday Review* as 'only Socialists in disguise'.[14]

The Conservative Party underwent fundamental self-analysis after losing the 1929 election. There was a schism not only between left and right but along the lines of age. In fact, Baldwin's front bench was not

12 Butler, *The Art of the Possible*, p. 27.
13 *Daily Mail*, 22 June 1929. Cited by Macmillan, *Winds of Change* (London: Macmillan, 1966), p. 232.
14 *Saturday Review*, 29 June 1929.

excessively geriatric with ten Cabinet ministers under sixty,[15] but it gave the impression of being a group of reactionary, over-cautious time-servers. The slogan of 'Safety First' and a policy of 'safeguarding' and imperial preference created the impression of a party wedded to outdated doctrine.

Nonetheless, the 26-year-old Rab did not hesitate to throw his lot in with Baldwin. We can only speculate how he saw the succession over the next decade. Chamberlain at sixty was Minister of Health and the likely successor; Amery, aged fifty-six, also had a following in the party. Rab, who had worked for a few months with Hoare, may well have identified him, aged forty-nine, as the eventual leader of the Baldwinites. Through Hoare he had met Chamberlain; his acquaint-ance with Baldwin dated back to the Cambridge Union debate of March 1924. He had at least a passing acquaintance with Leo Amery and he had met Edward Wood (Lord Halifax) in Ottawa. Naturally enough, it was with these established insiders that he allied himself. It would have required an extraordinary second sight to have predicted what the decade of the 1930s would do to the Tory hierarchy. Like Baldwin, Rab opted for safety first.

There was, however, a growing restlessness and a developing anti-Baldwin movement. As early as 1924, Lord Beaverbrook had written to Sir Archibald Salvidge that

> As far as I can make out nearly all Baldwin's ex-colleagues are profoundly dissatisfied with him. The exceptions are Amery from self-interest and Chamberlain from stupidity ... The Party will simply jog along in the bad, mad, sad old way.[16]

Beaverbrook's antipathy to Baldwin developed into overt hostility over the Empire Crusade, a cause that he adopted passionately, publishing a manifesto, *Empire Free Trade*, in October 1929. Its underlying premise was that:

15 These were Leo Amery (b. 1873), Lord Birkenhead (b. 1872), Winston Churchill (b. 1874), Sir Philip Cunliffe-Lister (b. 1884), Sir John Gilmour (b. 1876), Sir Samuel Hoare (b. 1880), Sir Douglas Hogg (b. 1872), Lord Eustace Percy (b. 1887), Sir Arthur Steel-Maitland (b. 1876) and Edward Wood (later Lord Halifax, b. 1881).
16 Taylor, *Beaverbrook* (New York: Simon & Schuster, 1972), p. 221.

The foodstuffs we need in this country could all be raised either on our own soil or in the British Dominions, Colonies and Protectorates. The coal, machinery and textiles that the increasing populations of our new territories overseas demand could be supplied by the mines and factories of Great Britain and its dominions.[17]

Beaverbrook began his crusade in the hope that he could control Baldwin; only when he realised the impossibility of that did he begin to plot to remove him. Rab, motivated largely by his determination to stick with Baldwin but also by distaste for Beaverbrook, whom he described as 'green and apeish',[18] remained firmly in line, despite the defection of the other three members of the 'Boys' Brigade'.

Beaverbrook found an ally in Lord Rothermere and the two press barons waged a fierce campaign to remove Baldwin from the Conservative leadership, for which Beaverbrook strongly backed Churchill. Deeply distrusted by Tories and Liberals alike, Churchill led attacks on Baldwin in the Commons and, Baldwin suspected, was angling to revive the old coalition between Liberals and Tories, led by Lloyd George and himself.[19]

During the autumn of 1930, dissatisfaction with Baldwin's leadership spread within the party; the success of Vice-Admiral Taylor, an Independent candidate backed by Beaverbrook, in the South Paddington by-election on 30 October further undermined Baldwin's authority. By January 1931, that authority was again challenged when Churchill resigned from the shadow Cabinet over constitutional concessions to India. Chamberlain recorded in his diary that

> the question of the leadership is again growing acute ... I am getting letters and communications from all over the country ... I cannot see my way out. I am the one person who might bring about S. B.'s retirement, but I cannot act when my action might put me in his place.[20]

---

17 Ibid., p. 267.
18 Trinity, Butler Papers, RAB, D48.14; diary note for 4 November 1929.
19 Macmillan, *Winds of Change*, p. 237.
20 Diary entry for 23 February 1931. Cited by Feiling, *The Life of Neville Chamberlain* (London: Macmillan, 1947), p. 185.

As Chairman of the Party, Chamberlain spoke to the Tory leaders and recorded that 'everyone, I think, except Willie Bridgeman,'[21] was of opinion that S. B. would have to resign'[22]. When it was announced on 1 March that Sir Ernest Petter would stand as an Independent in the St George's by-election – the prospective Conservative candidate having withdrawn on the grounds that he could not support Baldwin – it seemed that Beaverbrook might succeed in forcing Baldwin's resignation. Indeed, Baldwin himself saw no other option. Chamberlain, summoned to Downing Street, noted that 'S. B. has decided to go at once' and the editor of *The Times* prepared an editorial leader announcing 'Mr Baldwin withdraws'.[23]

Bridgeman persuaded Baldwin not only to stand fast but to take the fight to Beaverbrook and Rothermere. The by-election thus became the battlefield on which the question of Baldwin's leadership would be decided, an event that Macmillan described as 'one of the most extraordinary episodes in recent political history'.[24] Duff Cooper 'stepped into the breach with admirable courage' and, despite his friendship with Beaverbrook, fought a campaign in which he savaged him and Rothermere.

Rab, a mere freshman backbencher, was not privy to the intricacies of the struggle at the top, but the issue of loyalty to Baldwin was freely discussed. Along with Baldwin loyalists and anti-Beaverbrook forces, he threw himself into the fray to support Cooper – and, therefore, Stanley Baldwin. Macmillan saw the by-election as a coalescence of 'Society' behind Baldwin to thwart the bounders who were attempting to oust him. 'Meetings were held in every drawing room, as well as in every local hall and school,' he recorded. 'Excitement grew daily to a fever pitch.'[25] Baldwin warmed to the fight, shaking off his despondency of a fortnight before and attacking the press barons in a rousing speech on 17 March. 'What the proprietorship of these papers is aiming

---

21 The former First Lord of the Admiralty.
22 Feiling, *The Life of Neville Chamberlain*, p. 185.
23 Ibid., p. 186.
24 Macmillan, *Winds of Change*, pp. 237–8.
25 Ibid., p. 238.

for', he declared, 'is power without responsibility – the prerogative of the harlot throughout the ages.'[26]

Rab's first two years in Parliament had not been uneventful. Neither had they been what he expected. Coinciding with the lowest point of Baldwin's prestige in the party, they revealed to the young Member for Saffron Walden the tectonic shifts beneath the assured surface of Conservative policy. As he wrote to Sir Monty, Baldwin's enemies were like 'the hosts of Midian who prowl and prowl around'.[27] Palace plots were not to Rab's taste; his loyalty to Baldwin was absolute. He joined the forces of Society supporting Duff Cooper and attempted to attend a Beaverbrook meeting but was denied entry. After a strenuous and vitriolic campaign, he had the satisfaction of seeing Cooper win the by-election with a majority of 6,000 and of having done his part to salvage the position of his leader.

Rab's year-long Commonwealth tour must have seemed a remote and irrelevant indulgence as he surveyed the political scene in 1931. He had no wish 'to be a sniper or a schemer',[28] yet this seemed to be a mandatory activity as his senior colleagues danced to the music of ambition. Amid the internal struggles of those two years, there was, however, one issue to which Rab could make an informed and valuable contribution. The divisive question of the future of India, delicately shelved since 1919, had been brought back to centre stage just five months after the 1929 election. On 31 October, the Viceroy, Lord Irwin,[29] publicly announced that India's constitutional advance should lead naturally to assumption of Dominion status.

On 27 June 1929, Irwin returned to England for mid-term leave. The election the previous month had brought William ('Wedgie') Wedgwood Benn to the India Office, a development that Irwin welcomed, as he 'was always rather a friend of mine in the House of Commons,

---

26 The phrase, probably the most famous Baldwin quote, was suggested to him by his cousin Rudyard Kipling.
27 Trinity: Butler Papers, D48.14. Letter of 4 March 1931.
28 Trinity: Butler Papers, D48.14. Letter to his father, 26 August 1931.
29 The names and styles by which Lord Irwin were known tend to be confusing. Born Edward Frederick Lindsay Wood, he was known as Lord Irwin from 1925 to 1934. In 1934 he became the 2nd Viscount Halifax on the death of his father, a title he held until 1944, when he became the 1st Earl of Halifax.

and I have no doubt I will get on with him'.[30] Irwin felt that the exclusion of any Indian representatives on the Simon Commission of 1928 had been a serious error causing deep resentment in India, and that Britain should make a gesture to restore faith among Indian leaders.

This desire to meet Congress leaders half way conflicted with the prevailing mood among the Tories. Ironically, a Conservative aristocrat was more in tune with the mood of the new Socialist government than with his party colleagues, who urged imprisonment of Gandhi and the Congress leaders together with a policy of repression. During July and August, Irwin explored with the Labour Cabinet the holding of a round-table conference that would bring together representatives of Britain, British India and the Indian Princes. At the same time, he argued, there should be a statement of the intention to move gradually to the granting of Dominion status. Monty, unsurprisingly, was among Irwin's critics, writing to Rab that 'He is now looked on as a weak, well-meaning Viceroy, who had not the courage of his convictions.' Like many an India hand nearing retirement, he felt that 'the new order' was allowing India to slip towards legitimised anarchy. 'My advice has not been listened to', he lamented, 'whence most of the trouble.'[31]

On 25 September, the Cabinet accepted the substance of Irwin's proposals, subject to certain qualifications as to how this should be announced. Irwin accordingly returned to India and issued a Gazette Extraordinary on 31 October. Raising the question of Dominion status, it announced the government's intention to hold a round-table conference. The announcement in equal measure renewed Indian confidence in British intentions and produced a firestorm in the Tory Party.

On 5 November, Lord Reading led an assault on the government in the Lords, principally for acting unilaterally before the report of the Simon Commission was released. Speaking of the use of the term 'Dominion status', he admitted that 'he took objection at once to the use of the term'. In due course India might reach 'responsible government,

---

30 Hickleton Papers: *Correspondence with Viscount Halifax*, p. 256. Cited by Birkenhead, *The Life of Lord Halifax* (Cambridge, MA: Houghton Mifflin, 1966), p. 268.
31 Trinity: Butler Papers, RAB, A65.115, Monty to Rab, 17 June 1932.

then full responsible government and a Government which would really be formed on the basis of Dominion Governments'. But to speak of Dominion status before the report of the Simon Commission would be premature. His proposal, essentially, was to stall for time and not mention 'Dominion status' at all.[32]

This disingenuous position was maintained by Tory diehards and the first round-table conference was scheduled for November 1930, even as Irwin was being compelled to use repressive force to maintain order. Not surprisingly, the conference was boycotted by the Congress Party, many of whose leaders were by then imprisoned. The futility of the first conference impelled Irwin to reach an accord with Gandhi and Congress to enable a second, more meaningful, conference to be held.

On 5 March 1931, the Viceroy and Gandhi reached agreement whereby, in return for the release of political prisoners, Congress would participate in the second conference and restrain from the civil disobedience movement they were conducting. For the imperialists in Britain, the very act of negotiating with Gandhi was repugnant. Churchill, explaining his resignation from the shadow Cabinet, expressed his disgust graphically:

> It is alarming and also nauseating to see Mr Gandhi, a seditious Middle Temple lawyer, now posing as a fakir of a type well known in the East, striding half-naked up the steps of the Viceregal Palace, while he is still organising and conducting a definite campaign of disobedience, to parley on equal terms with the representative of the King-Emperor.[33]

Since 1926, Sir Monty had been advising Rab to avoid becoming involved in the affairs of the subcontinent. 'No one in England is the least interested in India and never will be,' he erroneously cautioned his son.[34] Now, according to Lord Eustace Percy, Baldwin in private

---

32 Hansard, House of Lords, 5 November 1929, vol. 75, col. 376.
33 Winston Churchill: Address to the Council of the West Essex Conservatives, 23 February 1931.
34 Trinity: Butler Papers D48.12. Letter from Sir Montagu Butler, 3 February 1926.

could talk of little else.[35] He placed enormous trust in Irwin, trust that Rab wholeheartedly shared; for Rab Irwin's term as Viceroy was 'the greatest episode in a varied and distinguished career' and his pact with Gandhi 'both realistic and right'.[36]

During the summer of 1931, Rab could regard Indian affairs from an objective distance. The problem was firmly in the lap of the minority Labour government and he was able to speak frankly to Monty about the state of opinion in Britain. In his memoir he paid lip service to Churchill's resignation, referring to it as 'a tragedy' in the future Prime Minister's career. He regarded Simon with the same cool objectivity, agreeing with Baldwin that his proposals, in the finest traditions of British rule, were 'not enough and that if we were to keep India within the Commonwealth, we must be prepared to go further and faster'.[37]

Events of the summer and autumn were to remove the luxury of dispassionate judgement, however. On 24 August, Macdonald, frustrated by his government's failure to deal with the spreading economic crisis, offered his resignation to George V. Requested by the King to remain as Prime Minister, he immediately formed a 'National Government', an action that was viewed as gross betrayal by the Labour Party, who promptly expelled him, and which offered the Conservative Party the opportunity to avenge their defeat of two years before. By October, the Tories had forced a general election. The Conservatives won 470 seats in a massive victory; MacDonald remained in Downing Street, but the huge Tory majority in the Commons decisively altered the balance of power.

As part of the formation of the National Government in August, Sam Hoare took office as Secretary of State for India. At that point the second round-table conference was due to start in two weeks and Hoare was immediately under pressure to assemble his team. Now in a position to fulfil his promise to Geoffrey Butler, Hoare invited Rab to be his Parliamentary Private Secretary, an offer which Rab, despite repeated cautions from Sir Monty about the irrelevance of India and

---

35 Butler, *The Art of the Possible*, p. 38.
36 Ibid., p. 40.
37 Ibid., p. 42.

the dangers of being dragged into an endless wrangle, was happy to accept. Monty, in spite of his concerns, was delighted with the appointment, writing to congratulate Rab, 'Now you have got your foot on the ladder.'[38]

In this capacity Rab was present at the second round-table conference, the only session attended by Gandhi, the sole representative of Congress. During the three months of the conference Rab had an opportunity to observe Gandhi closely and to speak to him at length in October. The conference itself ended without resolving underlying problems – specifically the position of minorities within India. The inability of different minority groups to reach agreement was, of course, precisely the deadlock that the right wing envisaged.

For Rab, the experience was sobering; having been born in India, son of a provincial Governor, he felt himself especially qualified in matters affecting the subcontinent, a qualification that Gandhi forced him to question. Gandhi put it to Rab that the British were capable of great self-deception and of 'lulling ourselves into the belief that we were doing the right thing by Congress'. Rab frankly admitted that he was motivated by idealism, rather than by the realities of Indian politics.[39]

Gandhi's observation to Rab neatly summed up the difficulties that faced liberal-leaning British. The self-deception, rooted in paternalism, that he attributed to them was something of which Rab was himself guilty. The failure of other British statesmen to grasp the extent of the gulf between Indian nationalists and even the most progressive British representatives was to colour relations between Britain and India for a further fifteen years. The Indian delegations returned home, conscious that they would now be dealing with a more Conservative government. Were there any doubt on that score, the arrival of Lord Willingdon as Viceroy to succeed Irwin reinforced their apprehensions about the road to Dominion status.

The second session having ended in failure, Gandhi returned to India and a different Viceroy; Lord Willingdon emphatically did not

---

38 Trinity: Butler Papers, RAB, A65.151, Monty to Rab, 23 September 1931.
39 Butler, *The Art of the Possible*, pp. 43–4.

share Irwin's view of Gandhi or the Congress Party. 'You I know see something in him,' the new Viceroy wrote to Irwin,

> *but I have never been able to discover it, and to my mind it is his combination of qualities that makes him really dangerous. I have never been able to discover anything in him but a little* bania [merchant] *who is the most astute and opportunist politician I have ever met.*[40]

Nor was Sir Monty impressed by Gandhi. Before the second round-table session he wrote to Rab that 'all this slobber over him disgusts me'.[41] Indeed, he embodied the characteristics of diehard Tories, writing to Rab that 'There is nothing like a cut across the buttocks for checking religious emotion – I have ordered whipping for the low class people caught at this game.'[42]

In the October election Rab's majority increased dramatically after the Liberal candidate stood down and urged his supporters to vote for Rab. With a majority of over 16,000, his position in his constituency was secure and he felt able to accept an invitation to join the Indian Franchise Committee on a four-month-long tour of India early in 1932. This involved leaving his position as Hoare's PPS but offered Rab the chance to advance himself in his own right. His relations with Hoare, moreover, were somewhat uncertain as the Secretary of State had urged Rab to continue as his PPS after the election but had promptly introduced a second PPS to the India Office.

Rab had no illusions about Hoare's ambition; nor did he delude himself that he felt any great sentiment for or loyalty to Rab. In a chillingly dispassionate portrait of Hoare he sums up his impressions of the Secretary of State:

> He would sit in his 'Empire' library, and before the light of one steely electric fire, he used to work out the roles ... for his friends and associates

---

40 Hickleton Papers: Lord Willingdon to Lord Irwin, 10 January 1932. Cited by Birkenhead, *The Life of Lord Halifax*, pp. 317–8.
41 Trinity: Butler Papers, RAB, A65, letter from Sir Montagu Butler, 28 July 1931.
42 Trinity: Butler Papers, RAB, A65, letter from Sir Montagu Butler, 13 August 1930.

to play. I was amazed by his ambitions; I admired his imagination; I shared his ideals; I stood in awe of his intellectual capacity. But I was never touched by his humanity. He was the coldest fish with whom I ever had to deal.[43]

It was clear in 1931–32 that the question of the Indian constitution and possible Dominion status would remain a controversial – and central – issue for some time. That being the case, even if it entailed stepping off the ladder that he had so recently stepped onto, the opportunity offered by the Indian Franchise Committee might position Rab in the forefront of an influential progressive movement and greatly increase his personal visibility. Accordingly, he did not hesitate; on 14 January 1932, he and Sydney sailed for India.

During the four-month tour, Rab was greatly impressed by the Committee's chairman Lord Lothian, the recently appointed Under-Secretary of State for India. The principal recommendation of the Committee was that the electorate be increased from 7 million to 36 million with qualifications based on property and education. Rab later wrote that 'commentators regarded our work as being unusually distinguished for its liberalism'.[44] After receiving the Committee's report, together with reports from the Federal Finance Committee and the Indian States' Inquiry Committee, Hoare addressed the government's future policy in the Commons.

'The time has now come', he opened, 'when the government must make a number of important decisions upon Indian policy, and must take this Committee into their confidence as to their intentions.' There was no doubt that change was imminent, and he asked for Members' help in surmounting 'in a practical and sensible way, the obstacles that still stand in the path of constitutional development'.[45]

Rab's membership of the Franchise Committee might have passed relatively unnoticed into history but for the resignation from the government in September of the two remaining Liberals, Sir Herbert Samuel

---

43 Butler, *The Art of the Possible*, p. 57.
44 Ibid., p. 45.
45 Hansard, 27 June 1932, vol. 267, col. 1485.

and Sir Archibald Sinclair, over the decisions on tariffs and imperial preference reached at the Ottawa Conference. Those two Cabinet resignations were soon followed by the resignation of Lord Lothian.

Hoare now had to find a new Under-Secretary to take Lothian's place and, with the third session of the round-table conference scheduled to open in mid-November, he had no time to train a novice, but needed someone who understood something of Indian problems, as he later wrote:

> I felt that if I was to succeed, I must have as a colleague an Under-Secretary who both knew me and my methods of work, and even more important, what to avoid in dealing with the very susceptible Indians ... I saw the ideal Under-Secretary in my Parliamentary Under-Secretary, Rab Butler.[46]

At first, Hoare encountered resistance from the Conservative whips, who pressured him to take on a more experienced Under-Secretary who could 'read a written answer with a pleasant manner and evade awkward supplementary questions in the House of Commons'.[47] At twenty-eight years old, with little parliamentary experience, Rab was a neophyte by comparison with Lothian, a veteran member of 'Milner's Kindergarten'.[48] Hoare persisted, however, and urged Baldwin to appoint 'someone capable of grasping every detail of a very complicated subject, and that the only possible choice was my Parliamentary Private Secretary, Rab Butler'. Baldwin, despite not then being aware of Rab's qualities, fell in with Hoare's demand and prevailed on MacDonald to ratify the appointment.[49] Not quite in the manner that Rab had envisaged it, his gamble of January had paid dividends. Without the committee experience under his belt, Rab would not have been considered for a junior ministerial post by the wily Baldwin or the beleaguered MacDonald.

---

46 Templewood, *Nine Troubled Years*, p. 71.
47 Ibid., p. 72.
48 The collective term 'Milner's Kindergarten' refers to the group of civil servants who served under Lord Milner in South Africa after the Boer War, a training that started many on successful careers.
49 Templewood, *Nine Troubled Years*, p. 72.

CHAPTER 5

ASCENT, 1932-37

Rab's relations with his father were, on the whole, formal and dutiful – reflecting respect rather than agreement with Sir Monty's *obiter dicta*. Yet it must have given Rab pleasure to have entered the government before his thirtieth birthday, which his father had told him was impossible, and to have addressed an issue in which, according to Sir Monty, was of no interest to anyone in England. Far from being a dead issue, moreover, India's progress to Dominion status promised to be a very live topic indeed.

Live, certainly, but not without attendant risk. Ranged against Indian reform was the reactionary element of the Tory Party, led by Churchill, who was indefatigable in opposing the attenuation of Empire, maintaining that opposition until India's independence in 1947. India, according to orthodox Conservative doctrine, was little more than a creation of the British Raj. To speak of extending self-government to a subcontinent that for centuries had been riven alternately by war and savage tyranny was an absurdity, a fanciful, unrealistic tenet of Liberals and Socialists motivated by doctrine, unable to face the disagreeable truth that self-government would reignite religious and racial discord that only British rule had abated. Once that rule was relaxed, they argued, Hinduism and Islam would drive the subcontinent into violent civil war with resultant carnage on an unimaginable scale.

To progressive Tories, such attitudes were outdated, inaccurate and a cloak for imperialism. The movement towards self-government, fanned by the loss of 50,000 Indians fighting on Britain's side in the First World War and the massacre at Amritsar in April 1919, had gathered momentum. The emergence of educated leaders such as Gandhi and Nehru was a clear signal of Indian determination to influence and ultimately to control Indian destiny. Rab, in common with the progressive minority of the Tory Party, was convinced that India's evolution was inevitable. He was also conscious that he was putting his head above the parapets. At the age of twenty-nine, showing worrying signs of liberalism, a marked man on account of his new-found wealth, an intellectual in a party that was more at ease with hunting and shooting than with Cézanne and Manet, he knew that caution was essential.

He was under no illusions about the passions that the proposed Government of India Bill would stir. For him, however, the appointment was more than a simple promotion; it was a marked step upwards towards the intellectual élite of the Tory Party, a leap towards formulation of policy. He was already a frequent contributor of papers and memoranda to the newly formed Conservative Research Department (CRD); involvement in the framing of the Government of India Act would further enhance his status. His jubilation at the appointment was expressed in his description of the India Committee as 'probably the best that we could possibly have had'.[1] After his disillusion with the sniping and scheming of his first two years in Parliament, he was now working with a group whose integrity and collective intellect he admired. He was moving in exalted company.

The third round-table conference achieved nothing and was followed by a period of unnatural calm, described by Rab as one of 'suspended animation'. It was clear that there would be concerted opposition to the proposed Federation of India but unclear how forces would be aligned. Hoare and Rab were acutely aware of the danger that 'doubts and suspicions' could easily split the Conservative Party.

When the government published a White Paper in March 1933, there followed a three-day debate on the proposed appointment of a Joint Select Committee to consider every aspect of India's future government. Rab spoke for the government on the third day and subtly communicated to the House his own background in India and the

---

1 Butler, *The Art of the Possible*, p. 46.

sense of danger inherent in the factional manoeuvring. Knowing that his speech would be followed by Churchill, he used the metaphor of the Indian jungle to set the scene:

> Many a time I have sat in the jungle in Central India watching a bait, in the form of a bullock or calf tied to a tree, awaiting the arrival of the lord of the forest, and put there as a trap to entice him to his doom. On this occasion, I have exactly the same feelings as those of the miserable animal whom I have so often looked upon in that position, and, if I compare myself to that bait, I may compare my right hon. Friend the Member for Epping [Mr. Churchill] to the tiger. I hope that hon. Members and the right hon. Gentleman himself will remember, however, that there is waiting for the tiger a pair of lynx eyes and a sure and safe rifle to ensure his ultimate fate.[2]

Rab spoke for thirty-six minutes, an accomplished performance, addressing complex issues but stressing that 'This plan is not born of expediency or fashioned in haste, or the result of any political compromise. As we have worked upon it, we have come to know and to believe in our hearts that it is the best.' His speech was well received both by the public and by parliamentary colleagues and Rab received a full postbag of congratulatory letters.[3]

When Churchill spoke, the thrust of his argument, punctuated with colourful oratory, was that Britain was proposing 'the definite decline, and even disappearance, of our authority in India, which proclaim our disinteresting ourselves in the welfare of its people and our readiness to hand over, after 180 years, India's fortunes to Indian hands'.[4] He stressed Britain's responsibility for the '100 million new human beings' in India, who 'are here to greet the dawn, toil upon the plains, bow before the temples of inexorable gods'. It was a cleverly conceived reproach, designed to appeal to the public rather than to the House of Commons. By invoking paternalism and deeply ingrained benevolent

---

2 Hansard, 29 March 1933, vol. 276, col. 1011.
3 Trinity: Butler Papers, RAB, F1.
4 Hansard, 29 March 1933, vol. 276, col. 1035.

racialism, Churchill repositioned the battle outside parliamentary debate – where the government carried its motion with a massive majority – and, Rab recorded, 'caused considerable damage, not only to the party, but to the implementation of the Government of India Act once it had finally been passed'.[5]

From the House of Commons the battleground shifted to the constituencies where, in a bizarre confrontation, the two factions waged a propaganda war. Churchill and his supporters mobilised first through the creation of the India Defence League in April. This 'league', launched in June 1933 and supported by twenty-eight peers, fifty-seven MPs, two former Governors and three Lieutenant-Governors of Indian provinces,[6] was a pressure group of right-wing imperialists that appealed to British responsibility for protecting all segments of Indian society. Its operations were funded by the Duke of Westminster, Lady Houston and sundry Indian princes.

A gullible public, susceptible to the paternalistic argument that only under British care could India move towards self-government, was easily persuaded that it was in the interests of Indians that power be retained in British hands. This proposition astounded Rab, and in letters to his parents he described the logic as that of the contention that the fox enjoys the hunt as much as the hunters.[7]

The government's response, for which Rab, in collaboration with Hoare, was largely responsible, was the creation of a rival pressure group, the Union of Britain and India (UBI). He became 'very busy' with UBI business[8] during the first half of May, culminating in the Union's launch on 20 May. Propaganda activities of this blatantly government-sponsored group were Rab's responsibility; the difficulty that he encountered was the reluctance of even liberal Conservatives to become embroiled in an intra-party squabble, particularly one in which Churchill was a protagonist. 'Winston', Rab records, 'made the party organisation his principal target and wrought a good deal of

---

5   Butler, *The Art of the Possible*, p. 48.
6   Stewart, *Burying Caesar* (London: Weidenfeld & Nicolson, 1999), pp. 164–5.
7   For example, Trinity: Butler Papers, H45, letter of 9 April 1933.
8   Butler, *The Art of the Possible*, p. 51. Bodleian: *Davidson Papers*, MSS Eng. Hist. c.561/13.

havoc.'[9] To widen the UBI's exposure and impact Rab worked with the Marquess of Dufferin and Ava to create a newspaper as an organ of UBI propaganda.[10]

The campaign confronting the government was emotive and crude, but none the less effective for that. Hoare lamented that a highly complex issue – the Bill was to contain 473 clauses – was incapable of being presented as succinctly as the India Defence League's 'attack of headlines and campaign slogans'.[11] Sir Monty may have been strictly accurate in maintaining that no one in Britain was interested in India, but the issue of Britain's imperial responsibility was a very effective tail with which to wag the dog.

For Rab, appalled at the notion of two sides within the party organising conflicting meetings, the experience was depressing. This depression was enhanced by a growing disenchantment with Hoare, whose political integrity he was beginning to doubt. In a letter to Lord Brabourne[12] he bemoaned the state of the party:

> *I find myself more out of sympathy with Conservative principles than I have been for some time, although the tendency has been growing. At our last party conference the audience would have been a credit to the zoo or wild regions of the globe. No ray of enlightenment shone on a single face except the shining pate of Sir Henry Page Croft who has the merit of looking fairly well groomed.*[13]

This disillusion in no way diminished Rab's dedication to the passage of the India Bill. The report of the Joint Select Committee was published in November 1934 and in February 1935 the Bill eventually made its way into the House of Commons. In a BBC broadcast Churchill attacked it in a memorable flight of oratory:

---

9   Ibid.
10 Trinity: Butler Papers, RAB, F1.16.
11 Butler, *The Art of the Possible*, p. 51; Bodleian: *Davidson Papers*, MSS Eng. Hist. c.561/13.
12 Formerly Micky Knatchbull, his former colleague in Hoare's office, who had been elevated to the peerage and appointed Governor of Bombay.
13 Butler, *The Art of the Possible*, p. 53. RAB to Lord Brabourne, 5 October 1934.

Sir Samuel Hoare has thrust upon Parliament the most bulky Bill ever
known. If it was as luminous as it is voluminous, it would indeed command respect. But what is this India Home Rule Bill? I will tell you.
It is a gigantic quilt of jumbled crochet work. There is no theme; there
is no pattern; there is no agreement; there is no conviction; there is no
simplicity; there is no courage. It is a monstrous monument of shame
built by pygmies.[14]

To the last he maintained the position that it was a betrayal of India,
unworthy of the great traditions of Empire. At the Third Reading of
the Bill in June he distinguished between the alleged intransigence
and bias of senior ministers and the role played by Rab. Challenging
the former, he lamented the manner in which the Bill was being presented, that the Bill was not a good one, 'but that it would be a good
thing to put it through and get it out of the way'.

In characteristic Churchill style, however, he felt able to pay a tribute to David Margesson, the Chief Whip, and to Rab, whose tireless
work had brought the Bill to its Third Reading: 'The Secretary of
State has had the support of several able colleagues on the front
bench – and particularly the Under-Secretary, who has distinguished
himself greatly and has established a Parliamentary reputation of a
high order.'[15]

Churchill continued to have great respect for Rab, despite differences over India. Soon after Rab was appointed a junior minister,
Rab wrote to Churchill, wishing him a speedy recovery from illness.
Churchill responded in typical fashion, both congratulating Rab on
his office and sounding a note of caution. 'Although, as my views
are very much those of your uncle', he wrote, 'we shall probably
find ourselves opposed in debate, I trust our personal relations will
remain upon the agreeable footing to which you have raised them.'[16]
In maintaining good diplomatic relations with Churchill, Rab was

---

14 *The Times*, 30 January 1935, p. 14. Churchill insisted that he said 'sham' and not 'shame'.
15 Hansard, 5 June 1935, vol. 302, col. 1911.
16 Trinity: Butler Papers, RAB, G1.15. WSC to Rab, 7 October 1932. The uncle to whom Church-
    ill refers is Rab's uncle Sir Harcourt Butler.

covering all bases. Despite his loyalty to Baldwin and Chamberlain and his expressed contempt for the 'glamour boys' of whom Churchill was the senior member, he took care not to alienate the man who, if war broke out, would be a strong contender for the leadership.

Two days after the Third Reading of the Bill, Baldwin took over from MacDonald as Prime Minister. The latter, increasingly hamstrung, both physically by declining health and politically by his expulsion from the Labour Party, became Lord President of the Council. Conservative control of the National Government was absolute as the opposition front bench included just two Members, George Lansbury and Clement Attlee, with any experience of government. The Labour Party, bitterly divided and in disarray, suffered four years of parliamentary discomfort, while the remarkable career of Stanley Baldwin entered its final phase with his third spell in Downing Street.

As part of the government's reorganisation, Hoare was moved to the Foreign Office and Rab had the responsibility for the final stages of steering the India Bill through Parliament. This he managed with efficiency and considerable diplomacy, earning praise from all shades of the Conservative Party and respect from political opponents. Rab himself was most pleased by a tribute from Churchill, who spoke of his contributions as 'cogent, terse, informative, well-reasoned' and commented that, if he took up law as a career, his oratory would guarantee success.[17] Viscount Dunglass, later the Earl of Home, at the time a first-term Member, attributed the success of the Bill as much to Rab as to Hoare.[18]

Rab was acutely aware of the shortcomings of the Bill, specifically the impossibility of imposing a British form of democracy on such a diverse population. 'The Government of India Act', he wrote in hindsight, 'was vastly complicated by the characteristics, physical and political, of the Indian subcontinent.'[19] He saw with clarity that Federation was essential but that such a development would be resolutely

---

17 Butler, *The Art of the Possible*, p. 58.
18 Lord Home, *The Way the Wind Blows* (London: Collins, 1976), p. 50.
19 Butler, *The Art of the Possible*, p. 59.

opposed by the Princely States. Without their agreement, the issue of democracy was academic. He thus piloted a Bill which, while admirable in its intent, was destined to be unworkable. With some misgivings he accepted plaudits but was pessimistic about peaceful progress towards self-government.

While Rab was occupied with Indian affairs, Sir Monty was becoming increasingly dissatisfied with his role on the subcontinent. He began to send Rab hints in 1932, writing, 'I wish I was done with India' but adding 'I feel also that at any moment I may be wanted in India.'[20] At the age of sixty, as Rab's political career showed signs of flourishing, Monty was impatient to return to England; financially, however, he feared that retirement would pose a challenge. He was becoming cantankerous, alarmed at the direction of the government's India policy, equally alarmed at the prospect of life on a government pension in a country with which he was out of touch. A satisfactory solution eased his departure from India when he was appointed Lieutenant-Governor of the Isle of Man. In August 1933, he finally returned to Britain and took up his new appointment. Rab worked assiduously with Sir Claude Hill, the outgoing Governor, to make all necessary arrangements on his father's behalf.[21]

Rab's standing within the party was, at this point, delicate. His position at the India Office, a remarkable first step on the ladder for a man under thirty years old, could, he knew, be attributed to nepotism. His handling of the India Bill had marked him out as a future star, potentially a party leader. He will have been aware that he must tread carefully, scrupulously observing the established Tory hierarchy, while at the same time maintaining his growing reputation as a 'new', progressive Conservative. To continue his ascent without alienating at least one section of the party would require considerable tact and diplomacy.

These skills were further tested when Hoare was appointed Foreign Secretary in June 1935 and was succeeded at the India Office by

---

20 Trinity: Butler Papers, RAB, A65.116, Monty to Rab, 3 July 1932.
21 Trinity: Butler Papers, RAB, F2.

Lawrence Dundas, the 2nd Marquess of Zetland. A former Governor of Bengal and biographer of Lord Curzon, Zetland was

> a slightly dandified figure who looked as if he wore a corset; his voice was rather unattractive and his delivery somewhat pompous. Indeed as a speaker he had little ability either to make his subject attractive or to hold the attention of his audience, all of which disadvantages were underlined by an irritating gesture he made by a jerking movement of the head repeated continuously.[22]

To Rab, Zetland was 'too punctilious to be informal and too strait-laced to be communicative'.[23] An imperialist, albeit more liberal than extremists of the Conservative Party, he firmly believed in safeguards to check the ascendancy of Congress and was determined to impose his authority and personality on the India Office. Whilst Rab was the spokesman for his department in the Commons, the new Secretary of State made it clear that his Under-Secretary had strictly limited access to his office. Requests for an appointment needed to be made in advance and in writing. When Rab approached him for advice on how he might improve the sensitiveness of his political antennae, Zetland replied curtly, 'Read my books.'[24] It was not a situation that appeared promising to an ambitious young politician, anxious to make his own mark. For two years, Rab chafed at these restrictions, developing a growing restlessness, cautiously surveying the political landscape, aware that Baldwin's dominance of the party might be coming to an end, but hesitant about his own future moves.

In July, Baldwin demonstrated his gratitude for Rab's handling of the India Bill by paying a weekend visit to the Butlers in their constituency, staying for the weekend at their new home, Stanstead Hall. Rab rightly saw the visit as a significant endorsement and was alarmed when one of the Butlers' dogs bit the Prime Minister. To his surprise

---

22 Jenkins and James, *From Acorn to Oak Tree: The Growth of the National Trust, 1885–1994*, p. 77. Cited by Woods, *Oxford Dictionary of National Biography*.
23 Butler, *The Art of the Possible*, p. 61.
24 Ibid.

and delight, Baldwin 'said calmly, "I quite understand how you feel; I want to do that to every supplementary question in the House at this time of year."' Once again, as at Cambridge a decade before, Baldwin reserved his political advice until he took leave of Rab at Kelvedon railway station. 'I am so glad to have seen you at home in the country', he said. 'You must go on coming down every weekend. Life in the country makes you see things whole and will enable you, like me, to steer between Harold Macmillan and Henry Page-Croft; then you will be on the path to Leader of the Conservative Party.'[25]

Rab's loyalty to Baldwin was absolute and tinged with deep affection. Baldwin's tenure of power, however, was coming to an end and the star of Neville Chamberlain was in the ascendant.

Rab, frustrated by the systematised apathy of the India Office, was impatient to move to a post that offered him scope for initiative and, reasonably enough, he saw the Foreign Office as the most promising stage. He raised the issue with Monty who shuddered to contemplate the minefields that Rab would have to negotiate, advising him not to accept an Under-Secretaryship at the Foreign Office if it were offered.[26] Rab, doubtful about returning to work with Hoare, looked beyond his former chief's tenure. If Baldwin's position were secure and Chamberlain positioned to take over in two or three years, Rab would be comfortable if Halifax were to become Foreign Secretary. As so often, Rab saw the potential benefits while his father saw only the dangers. For the moment, at any rate, the question became academic when Anthony Eden rather than Halifax succeeded Hoare in December. As it eventually turned out, on this occasion Sir Monty's natural caution proved to be more on the mark.

The last two years of Baldwin's ministry, the period of Rab's impatient service at Zetland's India Office, were the most controversial of the Prime Minister's career. In rapid succession came the general election of November 1935, the Hoare–Laval pact that allowed Mussolini a free hand in Abyssinia, Hoare's resignation, Hitler's reoccupation of

---

25 Butler, *The Art of the Possible*, pp. 29–30.
26 Trinity: Butler Papers, RAB, A65.315, Monty to Rab, 25 May 1935.

the Rhineland, and, the final act of Baldwin's career, the events leading to the abdication of King Edward VIII in December 1936. Meanwhile, in the background, periodically at centre stage, rumbled the arguments over Britain's rearmament. Baldwin survived those turbulent two years but at the cost of his health. He handed over his office to an impatient Chamberlain on 28 May 1937.

In those two years Rab played a minor role. By his own admission, he was restless but, after his triumph of 1935, he had no opportunity to affect events. The spectre of war was abhorrent to him; the issue of rearmament, however, seems to have passed him by – as it passed by the majority of the Conservative Party. Only from Churchill and his associates were dire warnings heard. In Rab's own memoirs, the last two years of Baldwin's premiership pass without comment. After a paragraph dismissive of Zetland he moves without interruption to Chamberlain's decision to transfer him to the Ministry of Labour.

Throughout his career Rab valued party loyalty as the cardinal political virtue. Born to a tradition of the Civil Service, from which one never resigned, an astute observer of Peel and the potential risk of dividing the party, now becalmed in the India Office while the focus of the government shifted to Germany, Italy and Abyssinia, he surely felt a sense of frustration. When Hoare was forced to resign and Eden succeeded him at the Foreign Office – the youngest Foreign Secretary in almost a century[27] – he must have imagined that his ascent had been checked. Eden, while five years older than Rab, was of his generation, thirty years younger than Baldwin. For the new Foreign Secretary it was an elevation to the position of Crown Prince, a position described by Eden himself as 'not necessarily enviable in politics'.[28]

Between the generations, however, lay the prospect of Chamberlain's Ministry. When he succeeded Baldwin in 1937 he was quick to remove Rab from the India Office and to give him exposure to home affairs in the role of Parliamentary Secretary at the Ministry of Labour. Whilst

---

27 At thirty-eight years old, Eden was the youngest man to hold the office since Lord Granville in 1851.

28 Eden, *Full Circle* (London: Cassell & Co, 1960), p, 266. Eden uses the expression to describe his return to government in 1942 after believing in 1938 that he would never hold office again. 'The long era as crown prince', he wrote, 'was established.'

the appointment had the appearance of a demotion, Rab describes this as 'an apprenticeship for future office' and such was almost certainly Chamberlain's intention. Baldwin himself had appointed Eden with the equivocal comment that 'It looks as if it will have to be you', after commenting that Austen Chamberlain, Neville's half-brother who aspired to the job, was 'gaga'.[29] Relations between Eden and Chamberlain were not to be easy.[30] The new Prime Minister, suspicious of Eden, was looking to the likely succession a decade in the future.

An irony of that succession is that Eden, when he became Prime Minister in 1955, had no experience of home affairs; almost his entire time in government had been spent at the Foreign Office. This, among other factors, caused the failure of his government and his undoing. In posting Rab to the Ministry of Labour, Chamberlain planned to equip Rab in the area of domestic affairs that had caused the greatest human difficulties in the 1930s. There was a real danger that Rab would acquire the label of an 'India man' and a spell working on less exotic issues would be a useful apprenticeship. Chamberlain, with his background in local government, was himself apprehensive and ill-informed about international relations – Churchill famously remarked that he viewed foreign affairs 'through the wrong end of a municipal drainpipe'. The new Prime Minister saw the appointment as an essential step in Rab's evolution into a future party leader.

In the event, of course, the cataclysmic shift in the Tory leadership decisively destroyed any influence that Chamberlain held in 1937. Rab willingly accepted the Prime Minister's offer and joined Ernest Brown at the Ministry of Labour. An unglamorous appointment, it brought him experience of the running of an important department, in which the counsel of Sir Thomas Phillips, the Permanent Secretary, was invaluable. For nine months, Rab applied himself to the business of learning about regional development and the wider issue of unemployment.

---

29 Eden, *Facing the Dictators* (London: Cassell & Co, 1962), p. 316.
30 For example, over the speed of rearmament (*Facing the Dictators*, p. 437); over the purpose of Lord Halifax's visit to Berlin (Ibid., pp. 512–3); over relations with the United States (Ibid., pp. 553–4) and Chamberlain's dismissive attitude towards FDR (Ibid., pp. 558–9).

During January 1938, Eden, increasingly marginalised in Cabinet, laboured to impress on Chamberlain and on Sir Thomas Inskip, the Minister for Co-ordination of Defence, the importance of lining up Britain, France and the United States against Hitler and Mussolini. When Roosevelt offered to summon the entire Diplomatic Corps to the White House on 22 January in order to work out tentative proposals to reduce international tension, Chamberlain dismissed the idea as 'vague' and continued his attempts to reach accord with the dictators. Over the following month, the gulf between Chamberlain and Eden widened over what Eden regarded as craven subservience to Mussolini. On 20 February, Eden, together with Under-Secretary Viscount Cranborne and Parliamentary Private Secretary J. P. L. Thomas, resigned.

Eden's resignation realised the scenario that Rab had envisaged in 1935, bringing Halifax to the Foreign Office; along with Eden, checks on Chamberlain's policy of appeasement were removed. Halifax, a member of the House of Lords, needed an able and versatile mouthpiece in the Commons, a role that Chamberlain, assisted by a competent Under-Secretary, was prepared to play. On the Wednesday following Eden's resignation, Rab was having dinner alone in the Commons when he saw David Margesson, the Chief Whip, dining with Lord Halifax. The pair were pointing towards him, clearly discussing him 'in earnest conversation'. Correctly guessing that a job offer was being spoken of, Rab was not surprised to be summoned by Margesson the following day and told that Halifax wanted him as his Under-Secretary. Chamberlain, the Chief Whip assured him, would be in touch.

With some trepidation as 'both Halifax's predecessors had been unseated in untimely fashion – Hoare ignominiously, Eden voluntarily – and Halifax himself was known to have accepted the succession with great reluctance',[31] Rab accepted Chamberlain's offer. He thus moved from the relative calm of the Ministry of Labour into the eye of the brewing European storm.

---

31 Butler, *The Art of the Possible*, p. 62. Halifax described his experience as Viceroy of India, saying 'I have had enough obloquy for one lifetime.'

CHAPTER 6

APPEASEMENT, 1938–39

Lord Halifax chose Rab to succeed Cranborne largely because of the interest in Indian affairs and the 'progressive' views that they shared. Halifax, Viceroy from 1926 to 1931, was impressed by Rab's handling of the India Bill and valued that experience in his Under-Secretary. As Chamberlain pointed out, Rab would be the sole Foreign Office Minister in the Commons and would shoulder considerable responsibility.

In his memoirs, Rab contrasts his 'political duty' with 'political advantage',[1] but there can be no doubt that the offer was extremely attractive. Not only would it place him close to the Magic Circle, it would also position him among Chamberlain's potential successors. At sixty-eight, the new Prime Minister could look forward to at least one term of office, possibly longer; in that time Rab could substantially advance in the Tory hierarchy. With Eden temporarily out of the running and Halifax in the House of Lords, he had a unique opportunity to earn a Cabinet post – even, perhaps, as Foreign Secretary in a future reshuffle – and thus emerge as the obvious heir apparent if Chamberlain remained in office.

As for opportunity, foreign affairs were at the forefront of public concern. Rab surely calculated that he, the visible minister in the Commons, could parley two or three years' experience into a Cabinet post while using the carapace of the highly respected Lord Halifax to deflect any criticism of policy. Baldwin may have rejected Eden's

---

1 Butler, *The Art of the Possible*, p. 62.

suggestion that Halifax become Foreign Secretary in 1935 on the grounds that a peer would not be acceptable,[2] but Halifax provided substance in Chamberlain's new Cabinet. Since his return from India in 1931, no post had fallen vacant without Halifax's name being mentioned as a possible successor.[3]

Thickening the shell under which Rab could operate was the new Foreign Secretary's patent moral decency. Shortly after Rab's appointment, he received a letter from a Church of England minister stressing that 'Nobody can say that this is a defeat for idealism with Lord Halifax and you in the saddle now.'[4]

Idealism in 1938 meant belief in the quest for peace. In short, appeasement. This idealism originated in collective guilt after the Treaty of Versailles, which imposed heavy penalties and reparations on Germany. The treaty had been reached despite grave differences between the victorious nations in an atmosphere described with cynical realism by Sir Robert Vansittart, later Permanent Under-Secretary at the Foreign Office. Speaking of the French attitude, he wrote:

> Once proud of their strength, they thought now only of security and knew that their chance would not return; France had been ruined by a bully and did not mean to let him off. Britain was not yet part of the Continent, the United States was still far and, unless you had seen something of both France and Italy, you would not have guessed how little they thought of each other. France passed for hysterical because she knew her own mind too emphatically, and because at least three nations thought that they had won the war single-handed.[5]

British attitudes combined this guilt with a suspicion that France after 1919 was a weak reed. Soon after the First World War, Sir Douglas Haig spoke prophetically to the 13th Earl of Home, Alec Home's father, 'Mark my words, Home,' he prophesied, 'the French have

---

2   Eden, *Facing the Dictators*, p. 316.
3   Roberts, *The Holy Fox* (London: Weidenfeld & Nicolson, 1991), p. 46.
4   Trinity, Butler Papers, B11. Cited by Roberts, *The Holy Fox*, p. 50.
5   Lord Vansittart, *The Mist Procession* (London: Hutchinson, 1958), p. 207.

been bled white in two wars. They can never again be trusted as a reliable ally.'[6]

Distrust of France was heightened by fears of a French lurch to the far left. Communism in France was in its infancy in the 1920s. The *Parti Communiste Français* had been formed in 1920 but it remained aloof from the mainstream of the French left for several years. There was widespread complacency. The war was over; the German menace had been overcome, albeit at huge cost; reparations had been imposed on the German aggressor; everything could return to business as usual. Gaston Doumergue, President of France from 1924 to 1931, was a radical who came to power through the *Cartel des Gauches*, committed to curbing a resurgent Germany. His term as President had seen no fewer than four Prime Ministers in three years until Raymond Poincaré of the *Alliance Démocratique* came to power in 1926.[7]

With suspicion of France grew sympathy for the Weimar Republic. With the Kaiser safely exiled, a legend grew that ignored Germany's invading and ravaging Eastern Europe. Instead, as Weimar struggled to pay reparations, those reparations were relaxed and, when National Socialism triumphed in 1933, that sympathy was transferred to the Nazis. The genesis of National Socialism, the victors' conscience whispered, was a direct result of the punitive clauses in the Treaty of Versailles.

Thus appeasement, a desire for peace, embodied the morally laudable notion of forgiveness. It occupied the moral high ground. To Halifax, a devout high-church Christian, forgiveness was explicit in Christian belief. To Chamberlain the pragmatist, it was merely a question of establishing what Hitler's Germany demanded and reaching terms that would avoid a breakdown of the peace; merely a matter of rectifying errors of Versailles. Everything was negotiable.

Such were the attitudes of the Tory Party leaders when Rab accepted his new post, and from the outset he was in accord with them. Three days after his appointment he called at the German Embassy and professed his wish for 'a close and lasting relationship with

---

6   Lord Home, *The Way the Wind Blows*, pp. 43–4. Sir Douglas Haig became Earl Haig in 1919.
7   This thumbnail sketch of the French political landscape first appeared in Jago, *The Man Who Was George Smiley: The Life of John Bingham* (London: Biteback Publishing, 2013), pp. 38–9.

Germany',[8] from which the German diplomats concluded that Rab
had 'no prejudices' against Germany.[9] Throughout the build-up to the
Munich conference, German diplomats regarded Rab as sympathetic
to their cause. In June 1938, Helmuth Wohlthat, Goering's Commissioner for the Four-Year Plan, met Rab and reported that he was well
disposed towards Germany. Rab told Wohlthat that Britain was 'ready
to treat the Sudeten German question … in accordance with German
wishes'.[10] As late as May 1941, Rab was seen by Berlin as a potential
intermediary in peace overtures to Britain.[11]

One of Rab's first actions was to appoint a Parliamentary Private
Secretary and, at the suggestion of David Margesson, the Chief Whip,
he made a fortunate choice.[12] Fortuitous, certainly, for Rab's biographers, as he appointed Henry 'Chips' Channon, a diarist whose astute,
sensitive comments about his minister illuminate Rab's years at the
Foreign Office.[13]

In the first week of March, Rab invited Channon to be his PPS,
immediately telling him that he must abandon his homburg and
wear a bowler hat, as the homburg was 'too Edenesque'.[14] As they
talked, they 'suddenly became friends' for Channon realised that Rab,
although 'a dull dog', was 'without prejudices, very alert, extremely
able and sensible; in fact the ideal man for his none too easy job'.[15]
So began a political collaboration and a friendship that lasted until
Channon's death twenty years later. As the world inched closer to war,
it is Channon's diaries that give the most perceptive insight into Rab's

---

8   Gilbert and Gott, *The Appeasers* (Boston, MA: Houghton Mifflin, 1963), p. 78.
9   *Documents on German Foreign Policy*, Series D, vol. 1, 128. Cited by Gilbert and Gott, op. cit.,
    p. 79.
10 Gilbert and Gott, op. cit., p. 128.
11 Rab is described in a memorandum to Hitler from Albrecht Haushofer, a foreign policy
    adviser to Hess, as 'no Churchill or Zion advocate'. TNA: KV2/1685. Memorandum of 12 May
    1941.
12 Butler, *The Art of Memory: Friends in Perspective* (London: Hodder & Stoughton, 1982,
    pp. 50–51.
13 Channon's diaries are not always flattering to Rab, who attempted to delay their publication.
    He refers to them with a typical Rabism, commenting that the only thing that upset him
    about Channon's account was his dim view of Rab's clothes. Butler, *The Art of Memory*, p. 53.
14 Such fastidiousness concerning symbolism of accessories was typical of Rab. After Chamber-
    lain's fall he never appeared in public carrying an umbrella.
15 Rhodes James, *Chips*, pp. 148–9. Diary entries for 4–8 March 1938.

relations with the appeasers. They demonstrate simply that Rab went to greater lengths to accommodate Hitler than any other member of Chamberlain's government.

In the early days of their friendship it was Rab's dispassionate, unprejudiced approach to issues that most impressed Channon. He brought to problems an analytical mind free of pre-conceived policy, tinged perhaps with a certain *odium generis humani,* as Channon observed: 'Rab is a curious chap, my charming chief; with the brains and the ability of a super clever civil servant, but completely unprejudiced. He ... looks upon the whole human race as mental! His years of experience with the East are of value to him now.'[16]

Rab had been at his new post for less than two weeks when Hitler annexed Austria on 12 March. This was not his first violation of the Treaty of Versailles – the occupation of the Rhineland and the German military build-up had long exercised Churchill – but it was the first overt sign of the Führer's territorial appetite. Chamberlain requested from the Chiefs of Staff a report on the strategic situation after the *Anschluss,* and received the alarming opinion that the 2,500-mile German–Czech frontier was indefensible.[17]

Over the following days, the House of Commons was 'full of intrigue' as Chamberlain came under mounting fire from 'the insurgents' – Churchill, Duff Cooper, Eden – and Rab was closeted with Chamberlain and Halifax, planning the government's response. This was to be delivered in the Commons on 24 March. In the days leading up to the debate, the three worked together until the early hours in drafting and redrafting Chamberlain's statement.[18]

Chamberlain's view, backed by an appreciation of the Chiefs of Staff, was that Britain was powerless to help Czechoslovakia. He wrote to his sister Ida:

You have only to look at the map to see that nothing that France or we could do could possibly save Czechoslovakia from being overrun by the Germans.

---

16 Rhodes James, *Chips*, p. 151. Diary entry for 12 March 1938.
17 Butler, *The Art of the Possible*, pp. 64–5.; Rhodes James, *Chips*, p. 150. Entry for 12 March 1938.
18 Rhodes James, *Chips*, p. 152. Diary entries for 21 and 22 March 1938.

> *... The Austrian frontier is practically open; the great Skoda munition works*
> *are within easy bombing distance of the German aerodrome, the railways*
> *all pass through German territory, Russia is 100 miles away. Therefore we*
> *could not help Czechoslovakia – she would simply be a pretext for going to*
> *war with Germany ... I have therefore abandoned any idea of giving guar-*
> *antees to Czechoslovakia, or to France in connection with her obligations to*
> *that country.*[19]

Chamberlain's private view, however, was not one that he could express in the Commons. To fashion his conclusions into an acceptable presentation of policy, long sessions with Halifax and Rab were necessary. The resultant statement that Chamberlain made in the Commons debate, an hour-long exposition of government policy, bears the clear stamp of Rab's reasoned approach, an almost academic analysis, leading to the conclusion that 'We still intend to employ ourselves, and to urge others to employ, the methods of reason and diplomacy rather than those of menace and of force.'[20]

Distinguishing between the government's 'attitude' and its 'policy', the Prime Minister clearly defined the parameters of appeasement. 'I cannot imagine', he said, 'that any events would change the fundamental basis of British foreign policy, which is the maintenance and preservation of peace and the establishment of a sense of confidence that peace will, in fact, be maintained.' Peace was in the interests of the British Empire, but that did not mean that nothing would rouse Britain to fight. Treaties, vital national interests, defence of territory and communications – all these, he assured the House, were potential *casus belli*. Above all, Britain would ever defend 'our liberty and the right to live our lives according to the standards which our national traditions and our national character have prescribed for us'.[21]

The Prime Minister's confidence in the League of Nations had been shaken; collective security had failed to prevent war; but the League

19 Neville Chamberlain to Ida Chamberlain, 20 March 1938; Cited by Macleod, *Neville Chamberlain* (London: Frederick Muller, 1961), p. 224.
20 Hansard, 24 March 1938, vol. 333, col. 1413.
21 Hansard, 24 March 1938, vol. 333, col. 1399.

had been given a task beyond its power to fulfil. The *Daily Herald* had stated in a leader that the League had ceased to exist. It might be more effective to deal with a smaller number of nations rather than the 'cumbrous machinery of Geneva' but such an arrangement would 'not differ from the old alliances of pre-war days which we thought we had abandoned in favour of something better'.[22]

Carefully defining conditions in which the government might take up arms, Chamberlain moved to the question of whether Britain should undertake to support France if she were 'called upon by reason of German aggression on Czechoslovakia to implement her obligations under the Franco-Czechoslovak Treaty'. While making it clear that Britain's vital interests would not be threatened in such an event, Chamberlain drew the distinction between legal obligation and the situation that would face Britain and other nations if war broke out: legal obligations would be swept aside; the 'inexorable pressure of facts might well prove more powerful than formal pronouncements'; and other countries would almost certainly become involved, much as they had in 1914.[23]

For that reason 'all the resources of diplomacy should be enlisted in the cause of peace'. At the same time, greater efforts were being made to speed the pace of rearmament and to make Britain 'strong enough to meet whatever call may be made upon it'. That this was happening in other countries would, he argued, 'be a valuable contribution towards international reassurance'.[24]

In structure, sentiment and content it was a superb address. Benefiting from the objectivity that Channon admired in Rab, it addressed not only the *Anschluss* but also relations with Italy, particularly in relation to intervention in the Spanish Civil War. As a lucid statement of a position reluctantly reached by reasonable means it was a masterpiece. As Clement Attlee was not slow to point out in his response, however, while everyone in the Commons would agree that the government's aim was the preservation of peace, there was less than agreement

---

22 Ibid., cols 1401–2.
23 Ibid., cols 1405–6.
24 Ibid., col. 1412.

on the policy to secure peace. 'I thought that right from the start', he charged, 'the Prime Minister was confused in his mind between aims and policies, and having followed his speech out very closely I could not discern anything in it in the nature of a policy which made for peace.'[25]

In Chamberlain's speech we clearly see Rab's hand in drafting, in carefully avoiding the polemic thrusts for which the Prime Minister was noted and arriving at a superbly logical thesis. It was a milestone in Rab's acceptance of the policy of appeasement. The fatal flaw of that policy, of course, was that it presupposed that Hitler was susceptible to reason and inclined to negotiation. So clear and reasoned was Rab's approach that, when he and Channon attended the Assembly of the League of Nations in Geneva six months later, among reasonable and decent men, his arguments were persuasive, as Channon recalled:

> This morning I stole away from the meeting of the Assembly ... and drove Rab to the far side of the lake where we lunched and talked for two hours. He was charming. He thought aloud; told me his creed, displayed his civil service cunning, his way of handling men, his theory that the man in possession when challenged must inevitably part with something though, as he said, it is better to postpone the challenge as long as possible. That is something that these hare-brained Edenites do not understand. As we talked, the lake lapped the shores, and I came to the conclusion that there would be no war, no matter what people said. Rab, too, has implicit faith in Halifax and Chamberlain and agreed with me that both were linked together by an understanding.[26]

Later that evening, at a ball given by Lady Diana Cooper, Rab recited Lamartine's 'Le Lac' as he looked over Lake Geneva.[27] If war could have been avoided by reason and by civilised, cultured behaviour, then Rab would have been foremost among the peacemakers. The sacrifice

---

25 Ibid.
26 Rhodes James, *Chips*, pp. 166–7. Diary entry for 16 September 1938.
27 Butler, *The Art of the Possible*, p. 75; Rhodes James, *Chips*, p. 167. Diary entry for 16 September 1938.

of Czechoslovakia was a contingency that he was perfectly prepared to accept.

The optimistic notion that 'the man in possession when challenged must inevitably part with something' survived a short while longer. Walter Runciman, newly created Viscount Runciman, who 'seemed to have fallen from a page of Dickens and resented his fall',[28] impressed on Edvard Beneš, the Czech President, that, to avoid war, Czechoslovakia must cede the Sudetenland. Chamberlain, persuaded in a visit to Berchtesgaden that Hitler would be satisfied with that outcome, returned to England, confident that his man-to-man meetings with the Führer had avoided war. That form of negotiation, a practical deal between men of business, was something he understood. Shocked by the violence of Hitler's insistence on the cession of the Sudetenland to the Reich, personally affronted by Hitler's truculence, he nonetheless was quite convinced that he knew his man. Thus Chamberlain, the Nonconformist business executive, and Halifax, the moral idealist, willingly assisted by Rab, the donnish historian and ethical logician, set Britain on the course that led to Munich the following month.

Crowds shouting 'Good old Neville' greeted Chamberlain on his return to London. After meeting Daladier and Bonnet, French Premier and Foreign Minister, and explaining that, unless France were attacked, Britain would allow the cession of the Sudetenland as the price of peace, Chamberlain informed Beneš that he needed his consent to the dismemberment of Czechoslovakia to take to his next meeting with Hitler. Against an Anglo-French demand that he tear his country in two, Beneš had little choice. Paris was relieved of its obligations to Prague. London had made it clear that the fate of the Sudetenland was not its concern. Another man-to-man meeting between Chamberlain and Hitler, this time at Bad Godesberg, could now take place, unencumbered by any difficulty from Beneš or Czech Prime Minister Hodža. 'European peace is what I am aiming at,'

---

28 Eubank, *Munich* (Norman, OK: University of Oklahoma Press, 1963), p. 82.

Chamberlain informed newsmen as he prepared to fly to Cologne, 'and I hope this journey may open the way to get it.'[29]

When that hope was thwarted by Hitler's enhanced demands, Chamberlain was baffled and angry. As Macmillan recalled much later,

> He thought you could do business with Hitler and Mussolini ... like businessmen, both of whom trust each other and know the other to be a man of complete integrity. He didn't believe people existed [who say] one thing and do another ... It was pathetic really.[30]

The meeting was not conducted along traditional business lines; Chamberlain had been 'gazumped', but saw no alternative to meeting Hitler's demands and advising the Czechs to do likewise. This despite the fact that the Godesberg demands were greatly more stringent than the original Anglo-French proposals.

Nothing had changed the opinion that Chamberlain expressed to his sister in March. Anglo-French meetings in September, culminating in Munich, did no more than define the basis on which an ultimatum would be presented to Prague. After Chamberlain's return from Bad Godesberg, Halifax instructed Rab to ascertain the Soviet position with regard to Czechoslovakia.[31] Until the last, Rab strove to find some basis on which Britain might deter Hitler, pressing Maxim Litvinov, the Soviet Commissar for Foreign Affairs, and extracting from him on 23 September the vapid assurance that the USSR 'would take action' and 'might desire to raise the matter with the League'.[32]

Even then, as Channon's diary shows, Rab was serenely confident that war could be avoided. The Munich agreements, reached between Germany, France, Britain and Italy, while Czech delegates, excluded from the conference, awaited news of their fate in an adjoining room, persuaded him of the success of Chamberlain's intervention. In the final

---

29 Ibid., p. 155.
30 Harold Macmillan, BBC interview, 30 October 1975.
31 Halifax to UK Delegation Geneva, 1.15 p.m. 23 September 1938, no. 1043, Woodward, *Documents on British Foreign Policy 1919–1939*, Third Series vol. 2 (London: HMSO), p. 480.
32 *Documents on British Foreign Policy 1919–1939*, Third Series vol. 2, pp. 497–8. Cited by Macleod, *Neville Chamberlain*, p. 226. Butler, *The Art of the Possible*, p. 70.

weeks before Munich, policy was decided at inner Cabinet level, but there is no doubt that Rab was fully in line with Chamberlain and Halifax. When, four months after Munich, the German Army marched into Prague, Rab, along with Chamberlain, was shocked at Hitler's duplicity.[33]

Rab's own account of the slide towards war in 1938 is predictably rational and predictably supportive of Chamberlain's posture. He rightly concluded that the Soviet Union 'could not be trusted to wage war in defence of interests that were not bound up with her own security' but avoids the conclusion that the same could be said of Britain – that he, Halifax and Chamberlain had taken a virtually identical position in March 1938 and worked hard to present the Czech crisis as a remote academic issue of no concern to Britain.

As for France, Rab maintains that Bonnet, if not Daladier, worked hard to find an escape route from the treaty binding them to defend Czechoslovakia. Echoing the prevailing opinion that France was decadent and that 'the worm-eaten fabric of French political society' provided no deterrent to Hitler, Rab ignored the unpleasant truth that Chamberlain, Halifax and he catastrophically misjudged Hitler's motive and methods.[34]

In retrospective justification for the policy of appeasement, Rab makes the valid point that, with a year's grace between 1938 and September 1939, Britain was vastly better equipped to fight when the inevitable war broke out. But that is to discount the professed aims of the appeasers – to avoid war. However much Lord Swinton had reinforced the Royal Air Force, however much anti-aircraft and barrage balloon defences had been augmented and radar stations completed, the stark fact remains that since 1936 a series of concessions to Nazi Germany had encouraged Hitler in his belief that the Western democracies would not resist him. Critics of Chamberlain and Halifax advocated resistance from 1933 onward. A. L. Rowse articulates that view, brushing aside the argument that appeasement was justifiable to right the wrongs of Versailles:

---

33 Rhodes James, *Chips*, p. 186. Diary entry for 15 March 1939.
34 Butler, *The Art of the Possible*, p. 72.

The simple truth that I saw at the time and held to unchangeably throughout the '30s was that, whatever concessions were justifiable to Weimar-Germany, no concessions should ever be made to Hitler. This was the right line to adhere to all evidence now proves: hold the ring around Hitler's Germany, and the break will come inside. The generals would certainly have got rid of him if we had not presented him with success after success on a platter.[35]

Inevitably, after the war was won, there were few who admitted to having favoured appeasement in the 1930s. As historian Andrew Roberts shrewdly points out, 'Just as membership of the French Resistance suddenly swelled after VE-Day, so if everyone who professed himself an anti-appeaser in the 1950s had actually been one in the 1930s, the policy could not have lasted a day.'[36] Certainly appeasement was supported by august personages such as Geoffrey Dawson, editor of *The Times*, together with Halifax and Sir John Simon. Undoubtedly there was a right-wing clique of aristocrats who advocated closer collaboration with the Nazis. But there was an equally prominent group of Conservatives, led by Churchill, who rumbled Hitler early on and relentlessly pushed for rearmament after 1933.

Subsequent events have ensured that post-war observers judge that any sane Member of Parliament should have stood up to Chamberlain, that there should have been a score of resignations. To maintain that argument is to overlook the Prime Minister's strong position and the public support he enjoyed. He wanted peace and offered an ostensibly honourable method of preserving it. 'Faraway countries' have frequently been sacrificed in similar circumstances.

For critics of appeasement, Munich has become the defining symbol of Britain's shame. Before Chamberlain flew to Berchtesgaden, Duff Cooper had believed that Hitler was merely bluffing, and on the morning Chamberlain departed he wrote to his sister-in-law Kakoo Rutland:

---

35 Rowse, *Appeasement: A Study in Political Decline, 1933–1939* (New York: Norton, 1963), p. 8.
36 Roberts, *The Holy Fox*, p. 52.

There are now only three horses left in the race: 1. Peace with Honour; 2. Peace with Dishonour; 3. Bloody war. I don't think 1. has an earthly. The other two are neck and neck. If I were betting I should transfer my money continually from one to the other – and I'm not quite sure which I want to win. But if no. 2 wins the Derby you can safely back no. 3 for the Leger.[37]

On 1 October, Cooper resigned, the only minister to register by resignation his disgust with the Munich agreements.[38] Writing to Chamberlain, he admitted that it was 'extremely painful … in the moment of your great triumph to be obliged to strike a discordant note'.[39] When he explained his reasons to the House of Commons he delivered a calm and sombre indictment of the government.

First Cooper acknowledged the popularity of Chamberlain's actions at Munich. Large crowds had packed Downing Street; inside No. 10 there were 'enthusiastic throngs of friends and colleagues who were all as cheerful, happy, glad and enthusiastic as the crowd in the street'. He continued, in words not fundamentally different from those that Rab had used in Chamberlain's March address, to define the principles for which Britain fought wars. After the invasion of Austria, he recalled, he had urged that Britain make a firm declaration of what her foreign policy was. At the time he had been met with the argument that the people of Britain were not prepared to fight for Czechoslovakia. But, he continued, 'the people of this country were prepared for it – resolute, prepared and grimly determined'. The issue was no more Czechoslovakia than it had been Belgium or Serbia in 1914. It was simply the principle for which Britain had fought Louis XIV and Napoleon. 'We were fighting then, as we should have been fighting last week,' he said, 'in order that one great Power should not be allowed, in disregard of

37 Duchess of Rutland Papers, 15 September 1938; cited by Charmley, *Duff Cooper* (London: Weidenfeld & Nicolson, 1986), p. 117.
38 Although Harry Crookshank, Secretary for Mines, went so far as to write and later withdraw a letter of resignation. (Charmley, *Duff Cooper*, p. 130.)
39 Chamberlain Papers, NC 7/11/31/76; Cooper to PM, 1 October 1938; cited by Charmley, *Duff Cooper*, p. 126.

treaty obligations, of the laws of nations and the decrees of morality to dominate by brutal force the Continent of Europe.'[40]

Tracing Chamberlain's progress from Berchtesgaden, through Godesberg to Munich, he pointed out the absurdity of the guarantees that the Prime Minister had given, leaving Britain with 'the additional serious commitment that we are guaranteeing a frontier that we have at the same time destroyed'. In a rousing finale he condemned Hitler for breaking the Treaty of Versailles, breaking the Treaty of Locarno, entering Austria by force before assuring the world that he had no designs on Czechoslovakia. By 'well-timed bluff, bluster and blackmail' Hitler achieved his aims without having to fight. 'The Prime Minister may be right,' he concluded, but

> I cannot believe what he believes. I wish I could. Therefore, I can be of no assistance to him in his government. I should be only a hindrance, and it is much better that I should go. I remember when we were discussing the Godesberg ultimatum that I said that if I were a party to persuading, or even to suggesting to, the Czechoslovak government that they should accept that ultimatum, I should never be able to hold up my head again.[41]

Churchill applauded Cooper's speech as 'one of the finest parliamentary performances I have ever heard … admirable in form, massive in argument and [shining] with courage and public spirit'.[42] The truth, however, as was well known to Chamberlain, was that if Hitler attacked Czechoslovakia, there was nothing that Britain could do about it. As Sir Alexander Cadogan, Permanent Under-Secretary at the Foreign Office, acidly recorded in his diary, 'We must go on being cowards up to our limit but *not beyond.*'[43]

On 4 October, a three-day debate opened in the Commons. Herbert Morrison, effectively the Deputy Leader of the Labour Party, led the

---

40 Hansard, 3 October 1938, vol. 339, cols 31–2.
41 Ibid., col. 40.
42 Charmley, *Duff Cooper*, p. 130.
43 Dilks, *The Diaries of Sir Alexander Cadogan, 1938–1945* (New York: Putnam's, 1972), p. 102. Entry for 21 September 1938.

assault on the government, accusing ministers of maintaining 'a policy of drift', of a 'cowardly, unimaginative and ineffective policy, merely negative, of dodging trouble whenever it came',[44] and of favouring fascism because of their own 'subconscious international class consciousness'. This, he charged, was driving them to the point of being willing to betray liberty and favouring fascism. 'That class consciousness', he argued, 'has now reached the point at which they are even prepared to set aside the interests of their country.'[45]

The thrust of Morrison's attack – that Chamberlain had erred in the manner of his dealings with Hitler and Mussolini, approaching them as a suppliant – led to the accusation that, instead of achieving peace, appeasement had made war more likely. This reduced itself into a dispute along party lines as to the integrity and savvy of the Prime Minister. After eight hours of debate on 4 October and a further seven hours on the following day, Rab wound up for the government.

Placed in the position of defending the Prime Minister, the pace of rearmament, the Munich accords, the future of Czechoslovakia and the assertion that, as a result of diplomacy, war had been averted, Rab employed diversionary tactics. His first approach was to distinguish between public opinion in Britain and international opinion that he had observed 'in the engine room' of the League of Nations in Geneva. Subtly hinting that British sentiments were insular in comparison with the broader sweep of international opinion that he had observed, he asserted that the Prime Minister was held in the highest esteem abroad. Belgium and Switzerland, to name but two nations, had expressed 'their admiration and gratitude for the action of the Prime Minister'.[46]

The issue of the debate, he continued, was whether a different settlement or preferable result could have been achieved. His principal, overriding assertion was that the Prime Minister had been faced with two abhorrent alternatives – either war or a settlement imposed by Germany – and that he had skilfully avoided both. Without any

44 Hansard, 4 October 1938, vol. 339, col. 171.
45 Ibid., col. 174.
46 Ibid., cols 448–9.

attempt at justification of the settlement at Munich, he reverted to the workings of the League and the repetition that the Prime Minister was held in the highest regard by member nations. If the government was to succeed in its task, he chided the House, it was 'important that British public opinion should be firmly behind the Prime Minister and the government in [its] task'.[47] There was a simple choice between settling differences with Germany by consultation and facing 'the inevitability of a clash between the two systems of democracy and dictatorship'. War settles nothing, he concluded. In a series of specious assertions he deftly avoided any defence of Munich, any response to the charge that the government had, by accommodating Hitler, brought Britain to the verge of war. Instead, as he had managed to persuade Channon in Geneva that there would be peace, he avoided the issue of whether Chamberlain, in spite of Belgian and Swiss support, had concluded a shameful pact with the Führer and fed his appetite for further aggression. It was a speech whose tactics were coherent but whose substance was pitifully lacking.

On the following day, after a mere three hours of debate, the House divided on the question-begging motion 'That this House approves the policy of His Majesty's Government by which war was averted in the recent crisis and supports their efforts to secure a lasting peace'. With a majority of 366 to 144, the government was not embarrassed. Of the Munich settlement, no objective analysis was made beyond the assertion that a repetition of the Great War had been avoided. Czechoslovakia had been partitioned and now lay vulnerable to German attack. Chamberlain assured the House that 'Now peace has been secured, and not only for the moment. Now the end of the period of changes and treaties of 1918 can be foreseen and we all hope that a new era will begin in Anglo-German relations.'[48]

For both Rab and Chamberlain, the debate was a triumph of obfuscation, myopia and bald assertion of platitudes. They had confidence that Hitler's appetite extended only to the Sudetenland and that he

---

47 Ibid., cols 452–3.
48 Hansard, 6 October 1938, vol. 339, col. 550.

shared the Prime Minister's faith in the agreements reached. On 30 November, in a speech to 'The Parlour', a dining club that brought political and industrial leaders together, Rab argued that Hitler's strategy was to 'Infiltrate East' and 'Bluster West'.[49] In short, Britain had nothing to worry about. From that speech it is clear that, four months before the invasion of Bohemia, Chamberlain and Rab had reached the decision that Prague must be sacrificed. Once that occurred at dawn on 15 March 1939, Chamberlain admitted in the House that it 'was not in accord with the spirit of the Munich agreement' but stressed that 'The object that we have in mind is of too great significance to the happiness of mankind for us lightly to give it up or set it on one side.'[50]

In his memoirs, looking back over the eighteen months leading up to the outbreak of war, Rab holds firm to the position that Britain's prestige abroad stood high after Munich. In Britain his own position was enhanced when he was made a Privy Councillor in the New Year Honours List. As a reward for his loyalty to Chamberlain and Halifax, it was an honour earned; in the coming months he amply justified their confidence by his performance in the Commons.

The government came under increasing fire, not only over the abandonment of Czechoslovakia but also for its position on non-intervention in the Spanish Civil War and its relations with Italy, whose government was openly assisting General Franco. It fell to Rab to answer – or to deflect – attacks from all sides of the House, and his dexterity in avoiding definitive answers prompted Lloyd George to name him 'the Artful Dodger'.[51] A more sinister note was sounded by Channon who, after lunch alone with Rab at the Butlers' house in Smith Square, recorded that he found Rab 'very sly and subtle. Reserve, reserve all the way is his motto.'[52]

From the moment that Parliament reassembled on 31 January 1939, Rab was bombarded. It seemed that the recess had given Members time to reflect on a wide range of issues and Rab's 'sly subtlety' was called

49 Rab's notes for that speech are at Trinity: RAB, G9.120–22.
50 Hansard, 15 March 1939, vol. 345, col. 440.
51 Butler, *The Art of the Possible*, p. 74.
52 Rhodes James, *Chips*, p. 183. Diary entry for 13 January 1939.

for when, on the following two days, he made thirty-five speeches in answer to questions on every aspect of foreign policy. He managed to be singularly uncommunicative on every front, offering practical lessons in the art of non-response. Replying to Ellen Wilkinson on 31 January, concerning granting belligerent rights to General Franco, he was stolidly opaque.[53] On the following day he was elusively vague in the matter of British casualties in the evacuation of Hankow and Canton.[54]

In the six weeks between the end of the Christmas recess and 15 March, when German troops entered Prague, Rab made 544 speeches and gave thirty-five written answers in the Commons in connection with foreign policy. Whilst many of them were brief and not over-informative, his workload was demanding and support of Chamberlain unwavering.

One of the most remarkable characteristics of Rab's memoirs is the absence of self-justification. There is an apparent frankness throughout his account of his years at the Foreign Office. Nowhere is this more evident than in his almost naïve surprise that both Chamberlain and Halifax became more resigned to go to war after the German occupation of the rump of Czechoslovakia. On 16 March, over lunch at 10 Downing Street, the Prime Minister 'said with resignation, but with our solemn approval, "I have decided that I cannot trust the Nazi leaders again."'[55]

On the following day, Chamberlain spoke to the Birmingham Unionist Association. He repeated his belief that the people of Britain and the Commonwealth had supported his policy at Munich and shared his confidence that war had been averted. But now, for the first time, there was a resolve behind the face of appeasement, a clear message to the Führer that Britain would fight. No greater mistake could be made, he said, 'than to suppose that, because it believes war to be a senseless and cruel thing, this nation has so lost its fibre that it will not take part to the utmost of its power, resisting such a challenge if it ever were made'.[56]

---

53 Hansard, 31 January 1939, vol. 343, cols 41–2.
54 Hansard, 1 February 1939, vol. 343, col. 181.
55 Butler, *The Art of the Possible*, p. 77.
56 Address to Birmingham Unionist Association, 17 March 1939. Macleod, *Neville Chamberlain*, p. 274.

The speech heralded a shift in foreign policy, a shift for which Halifax later claimed credit and which apparently surprised Rab. 'Whence comes the present drive away from the policy of appeasement?' he wrote in his diary.[57] Even then, with Locarno, Berchtesgaden, Godesberg, Munich and the occupation of Prague as testimony to Hitler's continued deceit and aggression, Rab was baffled that the policy of appeasement should be set aside. His ingenuousness is as remarkable as his honesty in recording it.

At this point, as the foreign policy triumvirate surveyed the wreckage of their 1938 policy, a tectonic shift occurred. In spite of his fighting words in Birmingham, Chamberlain continued to hope that Germany could be contained by a triple alliance of Britain, France and the Soviet Union to guarantee the Polish border. Rab dutifully supported Chamberlain. Halifax, 'half unworldly saint, half cunning politician',[58] moved decisively away from the Prime Minister and, given Rab's dedicated hewing to the Chamberlain line, from his own Under-Secretary. When Britain gave an unconditional guarantee to Poland on 5 April, the action was cheered by Parliament and the public. Yet, according to Channon, Rab was 'annoyed that he has not been more consulted over the Polish Guarantee and thinks that Halifax, who is veering away from the Prime Minister, intends to keep him in the background'.[59]

The defection of Halifax was no sudden switch of allegiance. From a high point in November 1937, when he visited Germany, his trust in Hitler and the Nazis had eroded by stages until he began to wage a one-man war in Cabinet to reverse Chamberlain's commitment to appeasement. The visit to Germany was ostensibly at Goering's invitation to attend a hunting exhibition in Berlin and to shoot foxes in East Prussia, Mecklenburg or Saxony. A meeting with Hitler in Berlin was included in the original plan, but this was subsequently modified, and Halifax was invited to Berchtesgaden, a change that required him to travel the breadth of Germany and gave the impression that he had proposed the trip.

57　Butler, *The Art of the Possible*, p. 77.
58　Rab's succinct character description, Ibid.
59　Rhodes James, *Chips*, p. 192. Diary entry for 5 April 1939.

In Berchtesgaden, Hitler and Halifax met for three hours, during which meeting Halifax intimated – to the subsequent astonishment of Eden – that the map of Europe created at Versailles might be adjusted. In Berlin he met Goering, who amused him, prompting him to write: 'But his personality, with that reserve, was frankly attractive, like a great schoolboy ... a composite personality – film star, great landowner interested in his estate, Prime Minister, party manager, head gamekeeper at Chatsworth.'[60]

He also met Goebbels, whom he had 'expected to dislike intensely'. To his surprise, Halifax, conceding that 'it must be some moral defect in me',[61] was impressed. The German leaders had succeeded in first alarming, then charming their guest. Wishing to be candid, Halifax had given Hitler to believe that Britain would permit German expansion in Central Europe. In common with any trusting dupe, deceived by a show of candour, he reacted with moral outrage when he recognised the extent of the deception that his hosts had played on him.

By the time of Chamberlain's flight to Berchtesgaden, Halifax doubted the sincerity of the Nazis and, when the Prime Minister flew to Godesberg, seriously alarmed by the extent of Hitler's demands, he attempted to impress on Chamberlain the importance of securing concessions from the Führer. Stunned at the Prime Minister's conviction that he commanded Hitler's respect and had some influence with him, Halifax saw in the terms demanded at Godesberg the extent of Hitler's perfidy and the dangers of continued appeasement.

At a Cabinet meeting on 25 September, Halifax surprised his colleagues by speaking out against Hitler's demands at Godesberg. Leslie Hore-Belisha, the War Minister, recorded in his diary that 'Halifax gave a fine moral lead',[62] for the first time expressing his doubts that he and Chamberlain were in full accord. From that position he resisted Chamberlain's attempts to bring him back into the appeasers' fold, urging speedier rearmament, demanding that Chamberlain take a

---

60 Halifax Papers: A4.410 3.3. Cited by Roberts, *The Holy Fox*, p. 73; Lord Halifax, *Fullness of Days* (New York: Dodd Mead, 1957), p. 193.
61 Birkenhead, *The Life of Lord Halifax*, p. 373.
62 Minney, *The Private Papers of Hore-Belisha* (London: Collins, 1960), p. 146. Diary entry for 25 September 1938.

tougher stance, notably in his Birmingham speech after the occupation of Prague. By early April 1939, when he urged an unconditional
guarantee to Poland, Halifax was committed to remain in the Cabinet
and to use all his influence to alter Chamberlain's course. Rightly judging that Rab was unlikely to act against the Prime Minister, he ceased
to confide in his Under-Secretary. The extent to which the two had
grown apart during the high noon of appeasement is suggested by the
fact that Halifax made not one reference to Rab in his autobiography.[63]

Judging Rab's actions during this crucial period, Halifax's biographer Andrew Roberts concludes that

> for all his brains in his 1950s and 1960s heyday, it is hard to see Butler
> as a sympathetic figure in the 1930s. He took to appeasement with an
> unholy glee not shared after the *Anschluss* by anyone else in the Foreign
> Office. His extreme partisanship against members of his own party,
> his relish for back-room deals and his almost messianic opposition to
> Churchill make Butler ... seem a thoroughly unattractive figure.[64]

It is hard to disagree with this judgement. Rab, now aged thirty-six,
had assumed huge responsibilities in the Commons and, like some
hothouse flower brought on too quickly, was conscious that he owed
his eminence entirely to Chamberlain. From a post-war perspective
it is difficult to imagine the respect in which Chamberlain was held.
Whatever iniquities have been attributed to him in later years, he acted
throughout with the honest intention of preventing war. That he was
misguided is beyond doubt; that he was sincere, however, is equally
clear, as Halifax readily admitted.[65] In nailing his colours firmly to
Chamberlain's mast, Rab was convinced of the Prime Minister's recti-
tude and certain that other factions within the Tory Party – Churchill,
whom he regarded as a dangerous buccaneer, Eden and his coterie of
'glamour boys' – were more than likely to hurl Britain into the second
continental war in twenty-five years.

---

63 Halifax, *Fullness of Days*.
64 Roberts, *The Holy Fox*, p. 140.
65 Halifax, *Fullness of Days*, pp. 202–3.

Once Rab had accepted appeasement intellectually, he was as resolute in supporting it as Vansittart and his successor, Sir Alexander Cadogan, were in opposing it. Rab felt it was vital to neutralise Vansittart and he wrote to Halifax that his 'concern was to minimise Vansittart's influence among hard-line members in Parliament'.[66] At the outset he was in good company, at one with his boss, the Foreign Secretary. Once Halifax parted company from Chamberlain, however, his own position in the hierarchy became less certain.

Now the name of Halifax as the next Prime Minister was heard around the smoking room. As Halifax had been urging Chamberlain from Munich to the outbreak of war to bring Churchill and Eden into the government, to invite Labour leaders into a non-party administration, the prospect of Halifax in Downing Street was distinctly unappealing to Rab. This would have discredited Chamberlain, brought Eden back to the Foreign Office and terminally disrupted the favourable succession that Rab envisaged. The characteristics that Channon identified in Rab – his ambition, his cunning – persuaded him that his only viable course of action was to follow Chamberlain's lead and make every effort to avoid war. Like Macbeth, he was 'so far stepped in blood'[67] that his course was charted for him.

On 7 April – Good Friday – Mussolini invaded Albania. The Cabinet met on Easter Monday, the first time that they had gathered on a Bank Holiday since the Great War. With the dictators acting in concert, the threat of war was increasingly real. According to Channon, Rab alone remained calm, while Halifax was 'wobbly'.[68] On 13 April, before a Commons debate, Rab walked over to Downing Street with Halifax, who remarked, 'I suppose you are coming to give the PM moral support.' As Channon noted in his diary, 'Halifax is weaned away from Neville now on many points, but Rab, as Alec Dunglass told me, still sees eye to eye with him, and the PM still feels more mentally at home with Rab than with anyone.'[69] By late May

---

66 TNA: FO 800/328. Butler to Halifax, 30 July 1938.
67 'I am in blood stepped in so far that, should I wade no more, Returning were as tedious as go o'er.' Shakespeare, *Macbeth*, Act III, Scene 4.
68 Rhodes James, *Chips*, p. 193. Diary entry for 11 April 1939.
69 Rhodes James, *Chips*, p. 193. Diary entry for 13 April 1939.

1939, he was the only minister to support Chamberlain – as Chamberlain himself ruefully admitted, 'not a very influential ally'.[70]

Indeed, Rab had become Chamberlain's 'blue-eyed boy', according to Channon.[71] During the last four months of peace, his devotion to appeasement remained absolute, a position that he later justified on the grounds that every month without war was a month gained in the process of catching up with Germany. The entire basis of Chamberlain's policy was that the *Wehrmacht* was ready for war while the British Army was not. Yet this was far from the truth. One specially mobilised German division, for example, said in its 'after-action' report that 'units could not have fought for at least two weeks after mobilisation. Soldiers lacked knowledge of their weapons, the division lacked trained officers and NCOs; reserve officers and NCOs were too old, too fat, and rarely met *Wehrmacht* standards.'[72] This was no isolated example. Without trained reserves and the industrial capacity to arm them, the *Wehrmacht* in 1938 was in no position to fight a war simultaneously on two fronts.

Duff Cooper consistently maintained that Germany, despite its efforts to rearm, was not ready for a prolonged war. There were severe shortages of raw materials; the economy was in trouble; Hitler's own generals were opposed to any adventure. Britain, he argued, should have joined France and gone to war with Germany sooner.[73] Oliver Stanley agreed with Cooper that time was on Germany's side.[74]

Nonetheless, the British state of preparedness was 'deplorably inadequate'. Cadogan, reading through his diaries after the war, admitted that during the early months of 1939 the government gave the impression of

a number of amateurs fumbling about with insoluble problems ... We were being swept along on a rapid series of surprises sprung upon us by Hitler with

70 Neville Chamberlain to Hilda Chamberlain, 28 May 1939, Chamberlain Papers 18/1/1101. Cited by Stewart, *Burying Caesar*, p. 365.
71 Rhodes James, *Chips*, p. 197. Diary entry for 9 May 1939.
72 Ubungs-Division XIII A.K. 20 October 1938. NARS T-79/224/000316. Cited by Murray, *The Change in the European Balance of Power: The Path to Ruin, 1938–1939* (Princeton: Princeton University Press, 1984), p. 222.
73 Charmley, *Duff Cooper*, p. 115.
74 Murray, *The Change in the European Balance of Power*, p. 190.

*a speed that took everyone's breath away. He was pursuing his tactic of 'one
by one'. And it was that in the end that drove Chamberlain to take a sudden
and surprising decision to guarantee Poland.*[75]

The cynicism involved in that decision is astounding. Cadogan argues
that for Chamberlain it was 'a signpost for himself', that he 'was committed, and in the event of a German attack on Poland he would be
spared the agonising doubts and indecisions'. Yet, immediately after
giving that guarantee, the government began negotiations with Germany that, if successful, would, in Sir Horace Wilson's words, 'enable
Britain to rid herself of her commitments *vis-à-vis* Poland'.[76] Herbert von Dirksen, the German Ambassador in London, sent a secret
memorandum to Berlin on 21 July 1939, reporting on a conversation
between Wilson and Councillor of State Wohlthat. Wilson, he reported, had said that

> from the point of view of purely domestic political tactics, it was all one
> to the Government whether the elections were held under the cry, 'Be
> Ready for a Coming War!' or under the cry, 'A Lasting Understanding
> with Germany in Prospect and Achievable!' It could obtain the backing
> of the electors for either of these cries and assure its rule for another
> five years.[77]

Rab continued to be deeply involved in the frantic efforts to reach
agreement with Germany, cynically conducted after the Polish guarantee. Since the autumn of 1938, when he arranged lunch at his house in
Smith Square for Erich Kordt, Chargé d'Affaires at the German Embassy, Halifax, Dirksen and himself, he had kept communication open
with the Embassy and now Dirksen even thought of Rab as a possible

---

75 Dilks, *The Diaries of Sir Alexander Cadogan, 1938–1945*, pp. 166–7. Cadogan to Ian Colvin, 20
    January 1964.
76 Dirksen, *Documents and Materials Relating to the Eve of the Second World War* (Moscow: For-
    eign Languages Publishing House, 1948), p. 71.
77 Ibid., p. 72.

direct contact with the Führer.[78] His view was that this would facilitate an Anglo-German agreement that would have enabled Britain

> to extricate herself from her predicament in regard to Poland on the ground that the non-aggression pact protected Poland from German attack; England would be relieved of her commitment. Then Poland, so to speak, would be left to face Germany alone.[79]

The extent to which Rab revealed his views to German diplomats is remarkable. He was in contact with several pro-Germans outside the government who acted as unofficial intermediaries between himself and Berlin. Among these were Ernest Tennant, a friend of Ribbentrop and founder of the Anglo-American Fellowship, and Lord Brocket,[80] also a prominent member of Tennant's group. Collectively, they and like-minded aristocrats conveyed to Berlin the impression that Britain would never go to war over Danzig.

Attempts by Chamberlain and Rab to avoid war, whatever the cost to Poland, continued through the summer. Inevitably, they were conducted in complete secrecy, for, as Wilson indicated to Dirksen in early August, Chamberlain was taking a great risk in negotiating with Germany; if there were a leak, he would be forced to resign. Meanwhile, in desultory fashion, negotiations dragged on in Moscow to conclude an Anglo-Soviet agreement.

Predictably – for Britain had appeared half-hearted in her efforts to reach accord with the Soviet Union – those negotiations came to naught when Ribbentrop, on Hitler's explicit instructions, proposed a non-aggression pact to Molotov. While Channon lamented that 'the Russians have double-crossed us as I always believed they would', Rab

---

78 Dirksen cast around in his mind for a prominent Englishman who could establish direct contact with the Führer – 'a straightforward, blunt and soldierly fellow who at the same time spoke German'. He considered Butler, Ironside, Burgin, Addison, Chatfield. 'But they all lacked something: either they did not know German or fell short as personalities.' Ibid., pp. 177–8.

79 Ibid., p. 187.

80 Lord Brocket was, at least in part, a model for Lord Darlington in Kazuo Ishiguro's novel *The Remains of the Day*. Rab remained friendly to him throughout. Trinity: RAB, G10.48–9.

watched his and Chamberlain's own double-cross of Poland and, on 22 August, the very policy of appeasement collapse.

Britain had given a worthless guarantee to Poland, believing that she would never be called upon to honour it. In France, popular feeling demanded '*Pourquoi mourir pour Dantzig?*' but in Britain, which was 'vitally interested in proving that she honours her political promissory notes',[81] war seemed inevitable in the last days of August. The Cabinet clung to straws as Hitler dictated terms to Warsaw. On 1 September, Danzig declared its incorporation into the Reich; the *Wehrmacht* marched into Poland.

Still Chamberlain vacillated until it became apparent that the Cabinet, the House of Commons and public opinion would brook no further delay in challenging Hitler. After a violent session in the Commons he was warned by David Margesson that postponing the declaration of war would bring down the government. A late-night Cabinet decided that an ultimatum with a two-hour expiry be sent to Berlin at 9.00 the following morning. When Rab went to Downing Street to inform Chamberlain that his ultimatum had received no response, at 11.15 a.m. Chamberlain broadcast that a state of war existed between Britain and Germany. Less than an hour later he told the House of Commons that '[E]verything that I have worked for, everything that I have hoped for, everything that I have believed in during my public life, has crashed into ruins.'[82]

To the far-sighted observer it seemed likely that Rab's career, so promising three years before, had crashed in the ruins of Chamberlain's hopes.

---

81 Dirksen, *Documents and Materials Relating to the Eve of the Second World War*, p. 141.
82 Hansard, 3 September 1939, vol. 351, col. 292.

CHAPTER 7

THE KING OVER THE WATER,
1939–40

It is an obvious truism that war brings opportunities to military officers: the chance for glory, medals, promotion. It is less apparent
that for politicians, too, new gateways open and lasting reputations are
made. Before war was even declared on 3 September, Rab and Chips
Channon were discussing what the future might hold. Rab had hopes
that he might be given a wartime Ministry such as the Ministry of
Information or the Ministry of Economic Warfare. Channon, as usual,
had inside knowledge. On Saturday 2 September, he told Rab, who was
in a 'strangely cheerful' mood, that this would not happen as Chamberlain wanted him to stay at the Foreign Office when war broke out.[1]

By the following week, the government had changed dramatically.
With the appointments of Churchill to the Admiralty and of Eden to
the Dominions Office came the critical moment for Rab to move into
his own Ministry, preferably one with specific wartime importance,
and establish himself for the post-war era. Reasonably enough, he felt
that he had earned that preferment from Chamberlain. Equally reasonably, Chamberlain was reluctant to move Halifax from the Foreign
Office and, for as long as Halifax remained there, he wanted to keep
Rab *in situ*. Again, Channon had excellent intelligence on the subject:

> *Rab is ... disappointed at having been refused the new Ministry of Economic*
> *Warfare. But really, as both David Margesson and Alec Dunglass told me, he*

---

1 Rhodes James, *Chips*, p. 211. Diary entry for 2 September 1939.

is far more needed at the FO as both [Chamberlain and Halifax] so depend
on him. Indeed he is the PM's 'blue-eyed boy'. He ... was considered both for
the Ministry of Information and for Economic Warfare, but in each case the
PM refused to release him from his present important duties. Rab is pleased
but disappointed. Later he will be rewarded.[2]

For the moment, Rab's usefulness to Chamberlain lay in his continuing to play the role of 'Artful Dodger'. This included the task of reassuring the House of Commons that no genocide was taking place in Poland, that there was no conclusive proof that the Germans were bombing anything other than military targets.[3] This, despite evidence from eye-witnesses that the *Wehrmacht* was shooting Poles indiscriminately. 'It is like a shooting party,' Count Raczynski, the Polish Ambassador in London, told Hugh Dalton. 'We are the partridges and they are the guns.'[4]

Sir Edward Grey[5] commented of the First World War that 'as far as Europe was concerned diplomacy in the war counted for little'.[6] This was certainly true for Rab after Hitler launched his attack on France, but in the early days of the 'Phony War'[7] Rab was much occupied in talks with Ivan Maisky, the Soviet Ambassador in London.

In his memoirs, Rab maintains that the British government no longer made any attempt to reach an understanding with Hitler:

The catalogue of catastrophes which began with the subjugation of Poland and ended with the fall of France was indeed punctuated by insidious suggestions – from the Germans, from the neutrals, and from defeatists at home – that we should sue for a negotiated peace. But to the best of my knowledge and belief no one in the British government, and

---

2   Ibid., p. 217. Diary entry for 4 September 1939.
3   Raczynski, *In Allied London* (London: Weidenfeld & Nicolson, 1962), p. 32.
4   Dalton, *The Fateful Years: Memoirs 1931–1945* (London: Frederick Muller, 1957), p. 275.
5   Later 1st Viscount Grey of Fallodon, Foreign Secretary 1905–16.
6   Viscount Grey, *Twenty-Five Years, 1892–1916* (London: Hodder & Stoughton, 1928), vol. 2, p. 159.
7   The expression, 'the Phony War' was used to describe the twilight period between 3 September 1939 and 10 May 1940, when the *Wehrmacht* invaded the Netherlands. In French this period is known as 'le drôle de guerre' and in German as 'sitzkrieg', a play on the word 'blitzkrieg' (lightning war).

more emphatically no one with responsibility in the Foreign Office, ever encouraged the view that we would depart from the path of honour.[8]

On 17 September, the Soviet Union invaded Eastern Poland and ten days later Warsaw surrendered. At this point Rab was actively involved in communicating to Berlin, through the Soviet Union, a formula whereby a settlement could be reached between Britain and Germany. Britain's guarantee to Poland, it was argued, was no longer operative since the Polish borders guaranteed by Britain no longer existed.

Until the moment war was declared on 3 September, Rab and Sir Horace Wilson had put pressure on Poland to make concessions to Germany. On 25 August, Hitler had offered, once there was a 'solution to the problem of Danzig', to 'accept the British Empire'. The response drafted by Rab and Wilson struck Hore-Belisha as 'fulsome, obsequious and deferential'. Instead, the Minister of War argued, the only effective response was to show strength and determination. Under no circumstances should Britain give the impression of hesitation or weakening in its commitment to Poland.[9]

During the few weeks that it took for Germany and Russia to shatter and dismember Poland, it was considered inappropriate to hold peace talks with Germany. Once Poland had been overrun, however, Rab, using Maisky as a conduit, reactivated contact with Berlin. According to Maisky, quoting Rab,

The British government would be ready to make peace even tomorrow if it received assurance that the understanding reached would ensure peace for twenty or twenty-five years. The British government would regard as such assurance a guarantee pronounced by all Powers, in particular the United States and the Soviet Union. In such an event the British government would be prepared, in the event of a lasting peace, to make important concessions to Germany even in respect to colonies.[10]

---

8 Butler, *The Art of the Possible*, p. 81.
9 Minney, *The Private Papers of Hore-Belisha*, p. 220.
10 *Documents on German Foreign Policy*, Series D, vol. VIII, no. 285, Schulenburg to Foreign Ministry, 20 October 1939. Cited by Gilbert and Gott, *The Appeasers*, p. 344.

Not only was the government proposing to accept the demise of Poland; was also willing to make concessions in respect of Tanganyika and the Cameroons. Nor did those concessions require any German surrender of Polish territory, for Rab denied 'in the most categorical manner' that the withdrawal of German troops from Poland was a precondition of peace talks. He maintained that 'the absurdity of such a demand was obvious'.[11] Simply put, it was absurd because the notion of an integral Poland as constituted in 1919 was now out of the question. Cadogan had indicated as much to Giuseppe Bastianini, the Italian Ambassador, but the latter had misunderstood the depth of British betrayal of Poland.[12]

Whilst every German overture was treated with disdain after May 1940, it does appear that Rab's 'memory played him false'[13] when he maintained that Britain never departed from 'the path of honour' in the early months of the war. The policy of keeping Germany sweet, moreover, continued into November.

In early November, an attempt on Hitler's life failed, and widespread concern mounted that he might use this not only as an excuse for housekeeping in Germany but also to launch the expected attack in the West, an outcome acutely feared by Belgium and the Netherlands. On 12 November, Churchill broadcast to the nation on the BBC, making a savage and derisive speech – the first of many of this kind that Britain would be treated to over the following five years. As ever cavalier with the pronunciation of 'Nazi', he lampooned Germany's leaders:

> Nowadays we are assailed by a chorus of horrid threats. The Nazi government exudes through every neutral state inside information about the frightful vengeance they are going to wreak upon us, and they also bawl it around the world by their propaganda machinery. If words could kill, we shall be dead already.

---

11 *Documents on German Foreign Policy*, Series D, vol. 1, no. 375, Weizsäcker memo, 20 November 1939. Cited by Gilbert and Gott, *The Appeasers*, p. 345.

12 *Documents on German Foreign Policy*, Series D, vol. 1, no. 348, Weizsäcker memo, 11 November 1939. Cited by Gilbert and Gott, *The Appeasers*, p. 345. See also *The Cadogan Diaries*, p. 228.

13 An expression used by Rab when Macmillan stated in his memoirs that Rab chose the post of Home Secretary in 1957. Butler, *The Art of the Possible*, p. 196.

Mocking Goering, who had cited German 'humanity' as the reason for Germany's not destroying England, Churchill continued, 'Germany can't bear to do anything to hurt anyone. All they ask for is the right to live and to be let alone to conquer and kill the weak. Their humanity forbids them to apply severities to the strong.'

The speech unleashed protests to the Foreign Office from Dutch diplomats. Rab commented to Jock Colville that Churchill's speech was 'beyond words vulgar'.[14] That comment perfectly encapsulates the polite decorum of 'The Old Order', who abhorred such rhetoric, but whose days were numbered. The notion that Rab might have been appointed Minister of Information – a post subsequently given to Brendan Bracken, one of Churchill's 'gangsters' – that Rab could have been an effective adversary to Dr Goebbels, is fanciful.

The purpose of a Propaganda Ministry is to demonise its opponents, to portray them as bestial, capable of egregious atrocities; a vast and vile vocabulary of vicious racial slurs emerges whenever war erupts. Yet Rab found it 'beyond words vulgar' when Churchill chose to ridicule the leaders of a savage régime with whom Britain was at war. This was destined to be not a war of gentlemen but a war waged against the might of the Third Reich and the Japanese Empire, while Rab, after eleven weeks of war, elected to fight it in the cultured language of the drawing room.

In November, his wrath was directed at Duff Cooper who, from the secure distance of the United States, wrote disparagingly of Chamberlain's dealing with the dictators. 'The motive was not dishonourable,' Cooper conceded. 'The method was not unreasonable.' Chamberlain's error had been to underestimate Hitler's appetite for war. 'His mistake was that of the little boy who played with a wolf under the impression that it was a sheep – a pardonable zoological error, but apt to prove fatal to the player who makes it.'[15]

Rab was outraged by what he saw as Cooper's division of the party in making such comments while he was in the USA. He felt that it

---

14 Colville, *The Fringes of Power* (London: Hodder & Stoughton, 1985), pp. 50–51.
15 Trinity: Butler Papers, RAB, F77.4.

demonstrated a lack of team spirit – even though Cooper had left the team after Munich. This tunnel vision, the greater veneration of party unity than of national security, when Chamberlain's government was about to be driven from office, shows remarkable myopia.

Chamberlain meanwhile was immobilised by gout and there was open speculation among insiders as to his probable successor. Oliver Harvey and Colville saw Halifax as the prime contender 'if things remain quiet', but, if Britain suffered serious military reverses, believed that Churchill would take over. 'God forbid', wrote Colville in his diary.[16] That was a sentiment that Rab at this time wholeheartedly endorsed.

Halifax told Rab that he was confident he could handle the premiership, but that he had no burning ambition to be Prime Minister.[17] Rab felt strongly that Halifax should succeed Chamberlain if the latter were unable to hold the government together. He was able, Rab felt, to gauge accurately both political colleagues and the public. Recording his impressions, he admired the detached judgement that Halifax possessed. 'He has long antennae,' he wrote, 'which feel every movement of the nation and which meet every kind of person.' He was able to read different people accurately, including Churchill, Eden, Labour leaders and young Members of Parliament.[18] Rab was particularly impressed by that talent, one that he believed he shared – which, to some extent, he did. 'The best insight into Halifax's character', he wrote, 'is that he is a Master of Foxhounds. Many of his metaphors are from the chase.'

And still the peripheral flummery of diplomacy wound on. Rab borrowed Channon's house for a covert meeting with Maisky, as Channon records:

Rab asked me today whether Maisky and he could lunch alone at Belgrave Square today for a secret meeting, as he did not want to be seen with him in public. The lunch apparently was a success: I never thought that the Russian Ambassador would ever cross my threshold; I checked up on the snuff boxes on

16 Colville, *The Fringes of Power*, p. 62.
17 Roberts, *The Holy Fox*, p. 199.
18 Trinity: Butler Papers, RAB, F80.98.

*my return but did not notice anything missing. Rab said that his Excellency
is an agreeable scoundrel.*[19]

Two days later the Soviet Union invaded Finland. Had Rab been made
aware of this during his secret luncheon with Maisky? His memoirs
omit any mention of the luncheon or the invasion. The Prime Minister
made a brief anodyne statement to the Commons, privately suggesting that it was not a serious matter, his eye on the diplomatic bonus
that the Soviet Union too might be branded an aggressor. Rab was
sent to Geneva, where the Council of the League of Nations solemnly
expelled the Soviet Union from the League for its act of aggression
against the Finns. Thus ended the twilight league; the twilight war
dragged on.

In early January, the resignation of Leslie Hore-Belisha, Secretary
of State for War, created further friction within the government. Pressured by Lord Gort, the Commander of the British Expeditionary
Force, Chamberlain dismissed Hore-Belisha, offering him the post of
Minister of Information, which he declined. The affair was greeted
with dramatic headlines on 6 January – 'Brass Hats Have Won'; 'Generals Get Their Way'; 'Pushed Out By the Old Gang'[20] – and there was
speculation that this was a move to placate Hitler (Hore-Belisha was
Jewish) and that it was some form of retribution for dragging Britain
into a war because of Nazi oppression of Jewry. The dismissal aroused
Rab's hopes that he might be appointed to his own Ministry, but no
call came from Downing Street.[21]

The dismissal of Hore-Belisha further damaged the image of
Chamberlain and his supporters. An abrasive infighter, Hore-Belisha
had a remarkable knack for antagonising his Cabinet colleagues, and
his departure was not a cause for general regret. The public, however,
saw him as an aggressive reformer of the military apparatus and his
dismissal as a victory for the supporters of a negotiated peace. Whilst
much of the resultant speculation was fanciful, the accusations of

---

19 Rhodes James, *Chips*, p. 225. Diary entry for 28 November 1939.
20 Minney, *The Private Papers of Hore-Belisha*, p. 280.
21 Rhodes James, *Chips*, p. 228. Diary entry for 5 January 1940.

conspiracy among German-sympathisers in government were fanned by the press, to the further discomfort of Halifax and Rab.

Finland reappeared on Rab's agenda later in January when Churchill proposed Operation CATHERINE, an ambitious plan to prevent shipments of iron ore from Sweden, via Narvik, to Germany. Typically, Rab's concern was based on diplomatic rather than strategic grounds and probably prompted by his continuing contempt for Churchill, Chamberlain's most vociferous critic. Rab's reaction was to send a stinging memo, highly critical of Churchill as the inventor of the Dardanelles *débâcle*, to Halifax and Cadogan. In sarcastic vein, Rab conceded that 'a brilliant mind' was behind the plan but linked that mind with the grisly carnage of Gallipoli in 1915–16.

He felt CATHERINE to be 'absolutely wrong' because it infringed Norwegian neutrality; there was a risk of involving Scandinavia in the war before adequate preparations had been made; for the sake of saving three-quarters of a million tons of ore Britain would involve Germany in Sweden, whereupon they could help themselves to all the ore they wanted; it would consolidate Russo-German collaboration by prejudicing Swedish help to Finland; it would dissipate the British war effort which should be principally directed towards France. 'I dislike action for action's sake,' Rab wrote, 'but if we want activity let us help Finland to a greater extent.'[22] Channon advised Rab that he should persuade General Ismay to oppose the plan in the War Cabinet – a proposal that had the desired effect.[23]

It is easy to see Rab's Foreign Office mind at work in this memo. On the carefully arranged chessboard of diplomacy and international relations much that Rab said had validity. In the context of Churchill rising in importance, itching to kill Germans and, once he became Prime Minister in May 1940, driving his Chiefs of Staff mad with insistence on 'action for action's sake' – precisely what Rab disliked – Rab's attitude was diametrically opposed to Churchill's approach to waging war.

22 Trinity: Butler Papers, RAB, G11.12–13, Rab to Halifax and Cadogan, 11 January 1940.
23 Rhodes James, *Chips*, p. 231. Diary entries for 10 and 12 January 1940.

In truth, Rab was still pursuing the possibility of a negotiated peace and was viscerally opposed to any action that might 'provoke' Germany. Much as Chamberlain had believed that Hitler would yield to reason in 1938, Rab believed that moral pressure would dissuade further aggression in 1940. Belligerence from Churchill at the Admiralty might, he feared, derail his attempts to bring Pope Pius XII, President Roosevelt and Mussolini together to exert moral pressure on Hitler.[24]

In late February and early March, the final act of the Russo-Finnish war was played out. On 22 February, Ambassador Maisky approached Rab with a delicately adorned poisoned chalice, as Channon recalled:

> *In the evening Rab came into my room to tell me of the hour he had just spent with Monsieur Maisky. The Soviet Emissary had, it appeared, brought offers of peace: Russia would like an immediate Armistice with Finland, and suggested that England, in the person, if possible, of R. A. Butler, should mediate. A diabolically clever scheme, but Maisky's dove is clearly a vulture, and I hope will be so considered. Rab will report his interview to the Cabinet, and I presume, to the Finns.*[25]

In this 'diabolical' manoeuvre Maisky attempted to stage-manage another Munich. Britain, eager to create an alliance to encircle Germany, would, he calculated, be placed in the position of pressuring the Finns to cede territory to the USSR. Thus the government would be accused of 'another Munich', the effective price for an alliance with the Soviet Union. The offer languished until 12 March when the government announced that it planned to send an expeditionary force to Finland in the event that peace negotiations broke down. Rab was violently opposed to such a move as it might bring the government down without doing anything to help the Finns. Clearly Churchill was behind the suggestion, Rab concluded, pushing Halifax to action, just as he had been campaigning for an alliance with Russia.[26]

On this occasion the government achieved a bloodless propaganda

---

24 Trinity: Butler Papers, RAB, Diary 13 March 1940. Stewart, *Burying Caesar*, pp. 392–3.
25 Rhodes James, *Chips*, p. 234. Diary entry for 22 February 1940.
26 Rhodes James, *Chips*, p. 236. Diary entry for 12 March 1940.

coup, for on the following day the Finns capitulated. Again, Channon was on hand to observe Rab's emotions:

> *The Finnish problem solved itself today with the announcement of the tragic capitulation by the Finns to the Russian terms … The Foreign Office was in a frenzy, but secretly relieved, as our Expeditionary Force, ready to sail, would have had a hazardous task … Luckily Rab's foresight prevented another Munich, which is what we should have been accused of, had we entertained Maisky's proposals: that is certainly not the case this time and our consciences are clear.*[27]

As Rab commented in his memoirs, the government that had created such uncertainty and muddle could not long survive. There was a desperate need for a non-party, National Government that could direct the war through a small, all-party War Cabinet. Whilst Rab, and doubtless Chamberlain himself, were aware of this, they were also aware that the Labour Party leaders were adamant that they would not serve under Chamberlain.

On 9 April, Germany invaded Denmark and Norway. Britain at last responded, sending a force to intervene in Norway. The entire enterprise was a failure; the Germans had occupied Narvik before British ships arrived; British Naval Intelligence had failed to learn anything of what was clearly a long-planned operation. Churchill reported to the Commons on 11 April, an hour-long tale of woe, culminating in optimism. 'Herr Hitler', he believed, [had] 'committed a grave strategic error in spreading the war so far to the North and in forcing the Scandinavian people, or peoples, out of their attitude of neutrality.'[28]

A baffling irony of the Norway operation is that the minister most responsible for urging a campaign that ended in disaster was the man to benefit most from its result. As the month wore on, news of more setbacks and of inexplicably slow action filtered through and the government came under increasing criticism for its handling of the war. On 11 April, *The Times* published a leader, 'Relief for Ministers', making

---

27 Rhodes James, *Chips*, p. 236. Diary entry for 13 March 1940.
28 Hansard, 11 April 1940, vol. 359, col. 746.

suggestions for how the tired old men of the government might be helped by 'alternates' who would lessen their work load. This succeeded in annoying Chamberlain greatly and drawing attention to Churchill's activity, in spite of which he remained challengingly spry. And, at least, Churchill was urging action.

Chamberlain fumed and considered replacing Churchill at the Admiralty. According to Channon, Churchill, aware of this, was making his own dispositions:

> *Today I heard that chagrined by his failure at the Admiralty, he has now thrown off his mask, and is plotting against Neville, whom up to now he has served loyally; he wants to run the show himself: all this was inevitable, and I am only surprised that it did not come before. Winston, it seems, has had secret conversations with Archie Sinclair, A. V. Alexander and Mr Attlee and they are drawing up an alternative Government, with the idea of succeeding at the first favourable moment.*[29]

Chips Channon, devoted follower of Chamberlain and close friend of Rab, is not always the most objective of diarists. He was, however, extremely sensitive to gossip, undercurrents and political plotting. Whilst he probably overstated the importance of plots, there is no doubt that his comments reflect the beleaguered nature of the government during the early months of the war. By the end of April, the Norway venture had become 'terrible, desperate, far worse than the public realises', and talk of 'a cabal against poor Neville' was rampant. By early May, *The Times* was predicting that the two-day debate in the Commons on 7 and 8 May would be 'the most critical which the Government have yet had to face'.[30] The leading article clearly suggested that a combination of Leo Amery, Hore-Belisha, Harold Nicolson and Duff Cooper, along with Churchill, Attlee and Sir Archibald Sinclair, could bring the government down. Rab and Channon accepted for the first time that 'Neville's days are, after all, numbered.'[31]

---

29 Rhodes James, *Chips*, p. 242. Diary entry for 25 April 1940.
30 *The Times*, 6 May 1940, p. 6.
31 Rhodes James, *Chips*, pp. 242–5. Diary entries for 26 April–7 May 1940.

Chamberlain opened the eight-hour-long first day of the debate on 7 May with a tribute to the troops who had fought in Norway, but soon moved onto the defensive. Britain had, he conceded, 'suffered a certain loss of prestige'. Colour had been given to the false legend of German invincibility on land; some discouragement had been caused to Britain's friends, and her enemies were crowing. With startling understatement Chamberlain accepted that 'The news of our withdrawal from Southern Norway created a profound shock both in this House and in the country.'[32]

There followed, as *The Times* had predicted, an assault from the leaders of the Labour and Liberal parties. Clement Attlee led the charge, echoing the Prime Minister's tribute to the fighting men, then turned to the government's conduct of the war. The government would be blind and deaf, he said, 'if they do not realise that there is widespread anxiety among the people of this country … They are not satisfied that the war is being waged with sufficient energy, intensity, drive and resolution.'[33]

The fundamental problem, Attlee charged, was the complacency, not only of the ministers concerned, but of Conservative Members as a group. *The Times* had indicted the Prime Minister for 'his devotion to colleagues who are either failures or need a rest'. In a life-and-death struggle, Britain could not afford to have her destiny in the hands of failures or men who need a rest. The Tories had tolerated men they knew to be failures, he charged. Loyalty to the Chief Whip had overcome their loyalty to the country. 'There is a widespread feeling in this country', he concluded, 'not that we shall lose the war, that we will win the war, but that to win the war, we want different people at the helm from those who have led us into it.'[34]

When Sir Archibald Sinclair shifted to specific criticisms of the tactics employed in Norway, the offensive against the government came from every direction. The Liberal leader had 'heard a very different story' from men returning from Trondheim. He had heard 'several

32 Hansard, 7 May 1940, vol. 360, cols 1074–5.
33 Ibid., col. 1093.
34 Ibid., col. 1094.

examples of deficiencies of equipment'. There had been 'muddle, waste and confusion', which merited a full-scale enquiry.[35]

Even loyal Conservatives found it hard to support the War Cabinet. Brigadier Sir Henry Page Croft, making it clear that this was not an issue of party or personal loyalty, spoke for the majority of Conservative Members, urging 'an entirely new spirit in regard to this war'. Members might stick to their political creed but 'if we do not win this war, all that is gone, and we may become just as much slaves as the people of Poland are ... Let us sink our animosities and encourage the government, instead of indulging in carping criticism day by day.'[36]

When Colonel Wedgwood, Conservative Member for Newcastle-under-Lyme, joined the assault, the Prime Minister's position became untenable. After a brisk summary of the strategic position, Wedgwood concluded simply,

> It becomes obvious that during the last eight months we have not done anything like as much as we ought to have done to meet the danger which is now so obvious to all of us ... We ought to be building far more quickly than we are ... We have wasted these last eight months. Something has been done, but nothing vital.[37]

During the evening it became clear that, under all the parliamentary niceties, support for Chamberlain had ebbed. There was a widespread conviction that a fundamental reorganisation was needed   and that it was imminent. The climax of the first day of debate – indeed, of the entire two-day debate – came when Leo Amery delivered a coruscating attack on the Prime Minister: 'We cannot go on as we are,' he declared.

> There must be a change ... a change in the system and structure of our governmental machine. This is war, not peace ... In war the first essential is planning ahead. The next essential is swift, decisive action

---

35 Ibid., col. 1102.
36 Ibid., col. 1116.
37 Ibid., cols 1122–3.

... Somehow or other we must get into the government men who can match our enemies in fighting spirit, in daring, in resolution and in thirst for victory ... They can be found only by trial and by ruthlessly discarding all who fail and have their failings discovered. We are fighting today for our life, for our liberty, for our all; we cannot go on being led as we are. I have quoted certain words of Oliver Cromwell. I will quote certain other words. I do it with great reluctance ... but they are words which, I think, are applicable to the present situation. This is what Cromwell said to the Long Parliament when he thought it was no longer fit to conduct the affairs of the nation: 'You have sat too long here for any good you have been doing. Depart, I say, and let us have done with you. In the name of God, go.'[38]

The balance of the first day was a *diminuendo*, as the debate wound to the end of the first movement. Arthur Greenwood predicted with foresight that 'If Hitler strikes again, he will strike soon and one wonders whether our plans are ready.' Would Britain be in a position to resist or would the lamentable 'ineffective, disastrous, humiliating' Norway episode be repeated?

By the following afternoon, when the House regathered, the only question discussed was how many Conservatives would vote against the government. Stafford Cripps stressed how far Britain's stock had fallen in the United States after the failure of the Norway campaign and chided Chamberlain for his appeal to personal and party loyalty. 'I never thought that I should be present in this House of Commons', he said, 'when in a moment so grave a Prime Minister would appeal upon personal grounds and personal friendship to the loyalty of the House of Commons. I trust that those revealing sentences which he spoke will show that he is unfit to carry on the government of this country.'[39]

Duff Cooper chose to attack Chamberlain for his bland dismissals of demands for change, contrasting him with Churchill who 'will be defending with his eloquence those who have so long refused to listen

---

38 Hansard, 8 May 1940, vol. 360, cols 1146–7.
39 Ibid., col. 1298.

to his counsel, who treated his warnings with contempt and who re-fused to take him into their own confidence'.[40] When Churchill him-self rose to wind up, it was with the air of a confident, condoling rather than triumphant, gladiator. At last his ambition of leading Britain in wartime was within his grasp. There was magnanimity, together with a seemly statesmanship in his words. He was not advocating controversy. 'Let us keep our hatreds for the common enemy,' he urged. 'Let party interest be ignored ... let the whole ability and forces of the nation be hurled into the struggle, and let all the strong horses be pulling on the collar.'[41]

Rab did not speak in the debate, but as he sat in the House, observ-ing the widening erosion of support for Chamberlain and assessing the implications for his own career, he can hardly have been confident. Not only was his loyalty to Chamberlain absolute (more powerful than his ambiguous loyalty to Halifax), but he saw the rivalry between Cham-berlain and Churchill in stark, black-and-white terms. Chamberlain and his supporters, with whom Rab desperately wished to identify, were the 'sound' men, the decent Tories of the nineteenth-century be-nevolent tradition. Churchill – and, therefore, all his associates, such as Bracken, Beaverbrook, Lindemann – were interlopers, intellectual car-petbaggers. He felt that 'the good clean tradition of English politics, that of Pitt as opposed to Fox, had been sold to the greatest adventurer of modern political history'.[42]

On the following day, there was uncertainty and chaos all over Westminster. It was far from certain that Chamberlain would step down; there was talk of an extensive reconstruction of the govern-ment, hope among the Prime Minister's supporters that Halifax might take over, with Chamberlain as Leader of the House. So unattrac-tive to Rab was the prospect of a Churchill administration that every other possible alternative was canvassed. Every other option, however, was suffused with unreality. A Prime Minister in the House of Lords was unrealistic in a war against dictators; the notion of a National

40 Ibid., col. 1307.
41 Ibid., col. 1362.
42 Colville, *The Fringes of Power*, p. 122.

Government under Chamberlain was never a possibility, so great was the animus accumulated over the previous three years. Channon describes the Mad Hatter's Tea Party atmosphere in Downing Street: 'I went over to No. 10, where a long conversation had been held between Winston, Halifax and Neville each saying to the other "You must be Prime Minister", and each … wanting it for himself.'[43]

Even as the question was batted about between them, it was clear that the Prime Minister would eventually need to summon the leaders of the Labour and Liberal parties. Before the division on the previous day, Hugh Dalton had told Rab that Labour would consider joining a coalition provided that Chamberlain, Sir John Simon and Hoare 'disappeared from the Government altogether'.[44] As requested by Dalton, Rab passed this message on to Halifax.[45] The Labour stance reduced the field to two contenders: Halifax and Churchill. Eventually Chamberlain faced that inexorable truth; Attlee and Greenwood spent forty-five minutes listening to his proposals, ultimately framed in two questions: would the Labour Party join a coalition under Chamberlain, and would they join a coalition led by someone else? As the Labour Party was in conference in Bournemouth, Attlee undertook to consult the Executive and give the Prime Minister an answer the next day.

Predictably, the response was a unanimous 'No' to serving under Chamberlain and a 'Yes' to the second possibility, responses that Attlee telephoned to the Prime Minister before catching a train back to London. Desperate that the second possibility should not involve Churchill, Dunglass pressed Rab to persuade Halifax to step in. Rab doubted the point of pressing, as he had already urged that course. Nonetheless, Rab agreed to make one last pitch, only to find Halifax's office empty. He had left for a visit to the dentist.[46] At 6 p.m. Chamberlain resigned his office and seventy minutes later Churchill accepted the King's commission.

---

43 Rhodes James, *Chips*, p. 248. Diary entry for 9 May 1940.
44 Hugh Dalton, Diary entries for 8, 9 and 10 May 1940. Cited by Pimlott, *Hugh Dalton: A Life* (London: Jonathan Cape, 1985), p. 274.
45 Butler to Halifax memorandum, cited by Birkenhead, *The Life of Lord Halifax*, p. 453. Pimlott, *Hugh Dalton*, p. 274.
46 Colville, *The Fringes of Power*, p. 122; Rhodes James, *Chips*, pp. 249–50. Diary entry for 10 May 1940.

The activity of the day had been frantic, desperate and doomed. The mood of the Commons during the debate of 7 and 8 May, although largely devoid of rancour, had implications that were alarmingly clear. Only a thorough house-cleaning would achieve the desired results, and such a reorganisation was not possible without a non-party government. That, inevitably, meant that Chamberlain could not continue at No. 10 – indeed, when Churchill informed Attlee of his intention to retain Chamberlain in the War Cabinet, the agreement between them almost collapsed.

Four of Chamberlain's most loyal supporters – Rab, Alec Dunglass, Chips Channon and Jock Colville – each of them deeply uncertain of his own future, gathered at the Foreign Office, where Channon produced champagne – almost certainly his treasured Krug 1920 – to toast 'The King Over the Water'.[47]

---

47 'The King Over the Water' was the loyal toast of the Jacobites to Bonnie Prince Charlie, otherwise King Charles III, after the failure of the uprising of 1745. Jenkins, *Churchill: A Biography* (London: Macmillan, 2001), p. 591; Colville, *The Fringes of Power*, p. 122.

CHAPTER 8

BECALMED, 1940–41

On the following morning, *The Times* announced blandly that 'to make possible the formation of a new Government which will command the widest support in Parliament and the country Mr Chamberlain last night had an audience of the King and tendered his resignation as Prime Minister. Mr Churchill then accepted an invitation from the King ... to form a new Administration which will include ministers representing the Opposition parties.'[1] In the next paragraph appeared the more ominous announcement that 'To give the new Prime Minister full freedom of choice all other ministers will resign, although they will retain their offices pending the appointment of the new Government.'

On the same page appeared a Reuters report that 'The Führer and Supreme Commander of the Army has gone to the Western Front to take complete charge of the operations of the forces there.' For Churchill it was doubtless an omen: the clash between Titans, two mercurial leaders, each convinced of his own strategic genius, was ushered in on that day.

Churchill offered Chamberlain a position in the War Cabinet, with difficulty persuading Attlee that this was a prudent step to avoid alienating his supporters, and immediately began forming the inner circle that would direct wartime operations. Rab and Halifax were, unsurprisingly, not part of that group. Rab, Channon recorded, was 'down and depressed'.[2]

---

1 *The Times*, 11 May 1940.
2 Rhodes James, *Chips*, p. 252. Diary entry for 13 May 1940.

It was common knowledge at Westminster that Churchill had offered Chamberlain the Leadership of the House and that Attlee had resisted this. The Labour leaders were determined that 'the guilty men' be purged but the new Prime Minister was acutely aware of the tenuous hold that he had over the Conservative Party and moved with caution.[3]

Once more with hindsight, it is common belief that the entire country was behind Churchill and in favour of dismissing 'the appeasers'. In truth, this was far from the case. The *Daily Mirror* group was one of the few organs of the press to support Churchill wholeheartedly and to urge him to dispose of the men of Munich.[4] Many of the letters that Chamberlain received after Churchill replaced him expressed the hope that 'the game was by no means over'.[5] Rab was among those who wrote to the former Prime Minister and who fervently hoped that recent events could be reversed. He and Halifax continued to hope for a negotiated peace and, with it, a restoration. For as long as the country was at war, however, they recognised that this was unrealistic.

Nominally, Chamberlain was still Leader of the Party, and Rab persisted in his view of Churchill as an interloper. His letter to Chamberlain expressed the hope that he would 'always realise the strength and number of your friends and how much we count on your presence in the Government'. The Tory Party, in Rab's analysis, depended on 'certain virtues and values which those of us, who have been associated with authority since 1931, hold dear, which we are sure you will perpetuate'.[6] Even at this juncture, party unity and allegiance to traditional Tory values dominated his stance. Churchill, fully aware of this, nonetheless moved with cautious delicacy.

On his first day in power, Churchill made the initial eight appointments of his War Cabinet, taking to himself the offices of Prime Minister, First Lord of the Treasury, Minister of Defence and Leader of

---

3   Winston Churchill, *The Second World War*, vol. 2, 'Their Finest Hour' (London: Cassell, 1949), p. 9. Churchill yielded to Attlee's objection and took the Leadership of the House himself.
4   King, *With Malice Toward None: A War Diary* (London: Sidgwick & Jackson, 1970), p. 48.
5   Roberts, *Eminent Churchillians* (London: Weidenfeld & Nicolson, 1994), p. 143.
6   Trinity: Butler Papers, RAB, G37.18; Chamberlain Papers, NC7/11/33/35, 11 May 1949, cited by Roberts, *Eminent Churchillians*, p. 144.

the House of Commons. Chamberlain became Lord President of the Council; Attlee Lord Privy Seal; and Greenwood Minister Without Portfolio. Halifax continued as Foreign Secretary. Ministers of Cabinet rank included A. V. Alexander as First Lord of the Admiralty, Eden as Secretary of State for War and Sinclair as Secretary of State for Air.

Rab spent four nervous days until, on 15 May, Churchill summoned him to the Admiralty, where he was continuing to work. Rab's memory of that meeting, recorded in his memoirs, is particularly vivid:

> He came to the point at once. 'I want you to go on with your delicate manner of answering parliamentary questions without giving anything away.' I said, 'Thank you very much. We have disagreed a great deal in the past; now I shall do my best to serve you.' He bowed very formally. We discussed whether ... he wished me to bring Foreign Office parliamentary questions to him, and he indicated that he would be too busy with other things.[7]

Churchill's response to Rab's question illustrates with clarity his *modus operandi*. On matters that interested him, such as grand strategy, he was relentless in putting his case, often causing fury and frustration to those like General Brooke who resisted or opposed his arguments. If he considered a matter unworthy of his attention, he happily delegated it, yet always retained it in his memory and would suddenly, unexpectedly, demand what results had been obtained.[8] When Rab asked why he had been reappointed, Churchill replied, 'Although we have had disagreements, you once asked me to your private residence.' That, Churchill assured him, 'showed goodwill'. As Rab left his office, Churchill called out cheerfully, 'Halifax asked for you. He seems to get on well with you.'[9]

---

7   Butler, *The Art of the Possible*, p. 85.
8   For an objective and fascinating description of Churchill's *modus operandi*, see Colville, *The Fringes of Power*, pp. 124–8. Colville, at first horrified by Churchill's succession to Chamberlain, became a devoted supporter, describing his premiership as 'one of the greatest administrations which has ever governed the United Kingdom'.
9   Butler, *The Art of the Possible*, p. 85.

On the night of 9/10 May, three German Army Groups[10] invaded the Netherlands, Belgium and Luxembourg in a massive offensive ultimately aimed at France. Sweeping through the Ardennes and crossing the Meuse, Army Group A at the centre drove for the Channel coast. From then until 17 June, when France surrendered, the fighting raged, German troops entering Paris on 14 June. By 3 June, Britain had evacuated 338,226 men from the beaches of Dunkirk[11] in a retreat brilliantly executed against overwhelming odds. On 13 June, Churchill, Beaverbrook and Halifax flew to Tours in an unsuccessful last-ditch attempt to rally the French government to continue the fight. Halifax's biographer is probably correct to suggest that Churchill wanted Halifax beside him to demonstrate that there was no longer any impetus for a negotiated peace[12] and that Britain 'would fight on. She had not and would not alter her resolve: no terms, no surrender. The alternatives for her were death or victory.'[13]

German troops entered Paris on 14 June. Two days later, Paul Reynaud, the French Prime Minister, on whom Churchill counted to stiffen French resistance, resigned. Marshal Pétain assumed control of the government and on 17 June broadcast to the French people that France had applied to Germany for an armistice. Britain now stood alone against Germany, facing a probable German invasion.

On the same day, Rab was taking a break from work in the late afternoon to walk around the lake in St James's Park. Here he met, either by chance or design, Bjørn Prytz, a Swedish industrialist who had been Sweden's Ambassador in London since 1938. The two walked back to the Foreign Office together and, in the course of a conversation (of which Rab took no notes), Rab, according to Prytz, discussed the possibility of Britain's reaching peace with Germany. During their conversation, Rab was summoned to Halifax's office and, again according to Prytz, returned to stress that 'common sense and not bravado' would dictate British policy. That evening Prytz communicated by cable his

---

10 Army Group A (44 divisions under General von Rundstedt); Army Group B (28 divisions under General von Bock); Army Group C (17 divisions under General von Leeb).
11 Dear and Foot, *The Oxford Companion to World War II* (Oxford: Oxford University Press, 1995), pp. 312–13.
12 Roberts, *The Holy Fox*, p. 231.
13 Winston Churchill, *The Second World War*, vol. 2, 'Their Finest Hour', p. 160.

memory of the substance of this conversation to the Swedish Foreign Minister in Stockholm.

Britain's official attitude according to Rab, Prytz informed Stockholm, would be 'that the war must go on, but … that no opportunity for reaching a compromise peace would be neglected if the possibility were offered on reasonable conditions and that no "diehards" would be allowed to stand in the way'. He reported that Rab believed that 'Britain had greater possibilities of negotiation than she might have later on and that Russia would come to play a greater role than the USA if conversations began.'

The message from Halifax, Prytz added, was not to suggest that Britain would accept 'peace at any price'. It was important, he said, as 'it would appear from conversations that I have had with other Members of Parliament that, if and when the prospect of negotiations arises, possibly after 28 June, Halifax may succeed Churchill'.[14]

Christian Günther, the Swedish Foreign Minister, puzzled by the apparent readiness of the British government to negotiate, asked Victor Mallet, the British minister in Stockholm, for enlightenment. Reporting this to Halifax, Mallet commented, 'I told him I was unable to do [this]. He [Günther] realised that it ought to be kept secret unless some further indication were to be given him, but he had been wondering whether Mr Butler's remarks were intended as a hint.'[15]

Rab responded to Mallet the following day on behalf of Halifax, saying that 'Certainly no hint was intended' and suggesting that, regarding the brief conversation between Halifax and Rab, Prytz 'may have exaggerated the importance of … any polite message conveyed to him by way of explanation'.[16]

Details of the exchange between Mallet and the Foreign Office reached Churchill, who promptly wrote to Halifax:

---

14 Tel 723 from Prytz, 17 June 1940, HP39A/XXXIII UDA (Swedish Foreign Ministry Archive). Cited by Thomas Munch-Petersen, 'Common Sense Not Bravado', *Scandia*, band 52:1, 1986. The article by Thomas Munch-Petersen includes all of the documents quoted concerning this matter and references cited are taken from the notes to the article.
15 TNA: Tel 743 from Mallet, 19 June 1940, FO371/24859-N5848/112/42.
16 TNA: Tel 531 to Mallet, 20 June 1940, FO371/24859-N5848/112/42.

My Dear Edward,

It is quite clear to me from these telegrams that Butler held odd language to the Swedish Minister and certainly the Swede derived a strong impression of defeatism. In these circumstances would it not be well for you to find out from Butler actually what he did say. I was strongly pressed in the House of Commons in the secret session to give assurances that the present Government and all its Members were resolved to fight on to the death and I did so, taking personal responsibility for the resolve of all. I saw a silly rumour in a telegram from Belgrade or Bucharest and how promptly you stamped upon it, but any suspicion of lukewarmness in Butler will certainly subject us all to further annoyance of this kind.[17]

When Halifax confronted Rab with Churchill's letter, Rab sent his boss a long, handwritten letter in explanation. Prytz, he was sure, 'did not derive any "impression of defeatism"'. 'It may be', he wrote, 'that I should have entertained no conversation with M. Prytz on the subject of an ultimate settlement. But I am satisfied that I said nothing definite or specific or that I would now wish to withdraw. I am usually cautious in following the leads of foreign representatives. I can see that … I should have been more cautious and I apologise.' Stressing that there must be 'absolute confidence between those whom I serve and myself', Rab put himself in Halifax's hands and awaited his and Churchill's final decision.[18]

Rab's wording is intriguing. He does not deny the words attributed to him, nor does he address the effect that such words might have given. Instead, he comments that he said 'nothing definite or specific or that I would now wish to withdraw'. That, it must be said, gave him a considerable amount of latitude.

Halifax replied to Churchill, saying that he would be 'very sorry if [Churchill] felt any doubt either about Butler's discretion or his complete loyalty to Government policy, of both of which I am completely satisfied'.[19] Churchill, confronted by what could be either the Foreign

---

17 TNA: FO800/322, Churchill to Halifax, 26 June 1940.
18 TNA: FO800/322, Butler to Halifax, 26 June 1940.
19 TNA: FO800/322, Halifax to Churchill, 27 June 1940. Butler, *The Art of the Possible*, p. 81; Trinity: Butler Papers, RAB, G11.80.

Secretary defending his junior minister or, more sinister, an alliance between Halifax and Rab, both seeking a negotiated peace, chose to accept the former explanation. The incident was passed over – but not forgotten by the Prime Minister.

Those are the bare bones of an incident that raises a host of questions – about the accidental encounter between Prytz and Rab, about Rab's intentions, about Halifax's involvement and about Rab's subsequent explanation to Halifax. This issue is, moreover, further complicated by its having occurred on the very day that Paris fell, raising the suspicion that either Prytz or Rab or both wished a message to be passed from London to Berlin.

The obvious initial question is whether the meeting in St James's Park was accidental. The park is a notorious trysting place for meetings that subsequently 'did not take place' and it is quite possible that Prytz, knowing Rab's habits, deliberately 'ran into him' while he took a short walk away from his desk. Equally possible, though less likely, is that Rab arranged the rendezvous. If Prytz did contrive to bump into Rab, apparently by accident, he must have had some motive. That motive was unlikely to have been to extract information on behalf of Germany, for Prytz was an anglophile, educated at Dulwich College, certainly not a German agent or sympathiser.

Once they had met, there was nothing sinister in Rab's inviting Prytz back to the Foreign Office for an informal talk at which no notes were taken. The question then arises whether Halifax coincidentally summoned Rab to his office or whether there was a message that he wished Rab to pass to neutral Stockholm, a suitable conduit for a message to Berlin. The fact that Prytz's message included, in English, the words 'common sense and not bravado', words that very possibly either Halifax or Rab used, suggests that this was the actual phrase that Rab had uttered in his conversation with him. If so, what could these words mean?

On the surface they suggest that Britain's policy would be dictated by *realpolitik*, rather than by determination to soldier on in the face of overwhelming odds. The word 'bravado' suggests an artificial bravery, swagger more than substance, and it is easy to imagine either Halifax or Rab using the word 'bravado' of Churchill in a less than complimentary manner. The balance of probability is that those words were indeed used; the question then arises, from whom did they originate?

Churchill learned of the Swedish cable traffic from routine intercepts and promptly wrote to Halifax commenting that Rab had used 'odd language' and that Prytz had 'derived a strong impression of defeatism'. Halifax showed Churchill's letter to Rab and received an immediate apology, in which Rab wrote, 'You might enquire why … I was reported as saying that "common sense and not bravado would dictate our policy".'[20] Unfortunately, he does not enlighten Halifax as to what that reason was, thus raising the question of whether he was not so gently hinting to Halifax that he was covering for him – that Halifax had used the phrase, that it had been accurately reported, and that it now behooved Halifax to protect Rab, as the *fons et origo* of the whole affair was not Rab but his boss.

Three days after the meeting, Prytz sent a further cable to Stockholm, requesting that his original cable not be sent to Berlin. This is an anomaly as if he had not wanted it passed on, he would surely have mentioned it at the time. The most likely explanation is that between 17 and 20 May either Prytz, Rab or Halifax had recognised the explosive potential of the *verbatim* quote and had intervened to stop its reaching Berlin.

A plausible explanation of the incident is that Prytz did indeed contrive a 'chance encounter' meeting with Rab in order to elicit informally the likely British reaction to the fall of Paris that day. In the course of the conversation between them, Halifax called Rab into his office and, on being told that Rab and Prytz were talking, made an off-hand remark, not untypical of him, that was somewhat contemptuous of Churchill. The neat phrase appealed to Rab and he passed it on *verbatim* to Prytz. It would have been a typical Rabism, albeit a vicarious one. The dig at Churchill would have been perfectly understandable, as Channon, with his habitual nose for plot and gossip, had written in his diary three weeks before, 'I think there is a definite plot afoot to oust

20 TNA: FO 800/322/277, Butler to Halifax, 28 June 1940.

Halifax, and all the gentlemen of England, from the Government …
Sam Hoare warned Rab of this scheme only yesterday.'[21]

Rab's apology to Halifax was almost certainly written for the file
and, in all likelihood, to allow Halifax an escape route if Churchill
wanted heads on a charger. Halifax may have been incensed with Rab
for quoting his comment directly, but as he was – and Rab was – perfectly aware that the words were his, he was placed in the position of
having to protect Rab. Halifax was guilty of making a remark disdain-
ful of Churchill but not implying willingness to make peace. Rab was
not guilty of disloyalty but was assuredly – not for the first or last time
– guilty of gross indiscretion.

Such an interpretation fits with Channon's curious description of
Halifax during this period:

> I reflected on Halifax's character; his high principles, his engaging charm and
> grand manner – his power to frighten people into fits – me sometimes – his
> snobbishness – his eel-like qualities and, above all, his sublime treachery
> which is never deliberate, and, always to him, a necessity dictated by a situa-
> tion. Means are nothing to him, only ends. He is insinuating, but unlovable.[22]

As for Rab's explanation in his memoirs, it is unconvincing and possibly disingenuous. Having described Prytz as 'not a professional
diplomat',[23] he grossly understates the seriousness of the incident by
asserting that 'I certainly went no further in responding to any neutral
soundings than the official line at the time, which was that peace could
not be considered prior to the complete withdrawal of German troops
from all conquered territories. That was common sense not bravado.'[24]
The official line, propounded by Churchill on 4 June, was somewhat at
variance with Rab's interpretation:

> We shall go on to the end. We shall fight in France, we shall fight on the

---

21 Rhodes James, *Chips*, p. 255. Diary entry for 29 May 1940.
22 Rhodes James, *Chips*, p. 256. Diary entry for 3 June 1940.
23 Butler, *The Art of the Possible*, p. 81.
24 Ibid., p. 82.

seas and oceans, we shall fight with growing confidence and growing
strength in the air, we shall defend our island, whatever the cost may
be. We shall fight on the beaches, we shall fight on the landing grounds,
we shall fight in the fields and in the streets, we shall fight in the hills;
we shall never surrender, and if, which I do not for a moment believe,
this island or a large part of it were subjugated and starving, then our
Empire beyond the seas, armed and guarded by the British Fleet, would
carry on the struggle, until, in God's good time, the New World, with
all its power and might, steps forth to the rescue and the liberation of
the old.[25]

Whether Rab was pursuing his own peace initiatives or, more likely,
was merely grossly indiscreet, Churchill promptly reduced his scope of
operation at the Foreign Office. Nonetheless, Rab was a symbol of appeasement and it was politic for Churchill to use him as a mouthpiece
to demonstrate that all Chamberlainite hands were now to the Prime
Minister's wheel. In late 1940, Rab was called on by Churchill to make
two broadcasts on the BBC.

The first of these, on 21 October, was to the Empire and the USA.
Rab painted an optimistic picture, maintaining that America was
growing closer to Britain 'because we are doing our best'. Imperial
policy, he said, was clear: Britain wanted only what was right and fair.
In truth it was a fairly anodyne performance, but that is not infre-
quently the case with wartime broadcasts.[26]

Rab made a second broadcast a few days before Christmas. Once
again, the thrust was simple and emotive, stressing the importance of
the preservation of civilisation based on its underpinning Christian
morality. The response from listeners was overwhelmingly positive.[27]

Two principal considerations influenced Churchill's approach to
foreign affairs at this point. On the one hand, he saw the business
of diplomacy as that of corralling as many countries as possible into
the Allied cause. Pre-eminent among the candidates were the United

---

25 Hansard, 4 June 1940, vol. 361, col. 796.
26 Trinity: Butler Papers, RAB, G11.31, 21 October 1940.
27 Trinity: Butler Papers, RAB, G11.61, 15 December 1940.

States, whose President he wooed assiduously. Thus foreign relations fell decisively into the category of war business that he wished to keep firmly under his own control. He therefore needed to appoint a Foreign Secretary in whom he could repose absolute trust – and Eden was the only suitable minister.

On 12 December, the Marquess of Lothian, British Ambassador in Washington, died and the Prime Minister immediately saw an opportunity to remove his principal critic – and possible challenger – from the mainstream. First he sent Beaverbrook to ascertain how Halifax would receive the offer of the ambassadorship, then on 18 December summoned Halifax to Downing Street to discuss the appointment. Unsurprisingly, Halifax kicked.

Halifax was aware that Churchill's *démarche* was motivated by his wish to restore Eden to the Foreign Office. After expressing his reluctance to Churchill, therefore, Halifax attempted to persuade Eden to go to Washington in his stead, an overture that Eden curtly rebuffed, somewhat sanctimoniously telling Halifax that in wartime one went where one was sent. Churchill, adopting a different approach, pointed out to Halifax the importance of the Washington Embassy if Roosevelt were to be persuaded to bring the United States into the war. Halifax, he maintained, was the envoy whose stature would most convey the importance attached to that process of persuasion. However great Halifax's objections, there could be no ambiguity in the appointment of a former Foreign Secretary to an ambassadorial post. 'The whole story of foreign affairs', Churchill later wrote, 'was at this time fused into one single theme, and this I had in any case to comprehend, and as far as possible shape.'[28]

Typically, Churchill invested his appointment and his departure with pomp: 'In order to clothe the arrival of our new Ambassador, Lord Halifax, in the United States with every circumstance of importance, I arranged that our newest battleship, the *King George V*, with a proper escort of destroyers, should carry him and his wife across the ocean.'[29]

The second consideration was the need to keep the Conservative

---

28 Winston Churchill, *The Second World War*, vol. 3, 'The Grand Alliance' (London: Cassell, 1950), p. 69.

29 Ibid., p. 24.

Party behind him. He was well aware of the feeling of many Members that he and his coterie were gangsters, adventurers, wreckers of the good solid tradition that had put good solid businessmen – Bonar Law, Baldwin, Chamberlain – in Downing Street. In spite of the widespread defection from the party line in the Norway debate, Chamberlain had been received in the Commons with enthusiasm on the following Monday, as Channon recorded: 'After Prayers he [Churchill] went into the Chamber and was greeted with some cheers but when, a moment later, Neville entered with his usual shy retiring little manner, MPs lost their heads; they shouted; they cheered; they waved their Order Papers, and his reception was a regular ovation.'[30]

Well aware of the extent of old-Tory opposition that he faced, Churchill moved with caution in banishing the 'old gang'.[31] Halifax knew that he occupied a pivotal position and, when Churchill had conducted a reshuffle after Chamberlain's resignation in October, he bluntly refused to leave the Foreign Office. Churchill accepted this and initially waited for a more auspicious moment to remove him.

Rab, less symbolic than Halifax, was nonetheless a prominent Chamberlainite and, even after the Prytz incident, retained his position. Once more, Churchill saw little profit in arousing the ire of the knights of the shires, but made sure that Rab's functions were as menial and routine as possible. In his solitary reference to Rab during this period, he later wrote, 'Except in special cases I left the interviews with foreign Ambassadors to the Permanent Under-Secretary, Sir Alexander Cadogan, and to Mr Butler, the Parliamentary Under-Secretary.'[32]

On the night of 18/19 September, Rab's London house was bombed. When he arrived at the Foreign Office, 'shaken, unshaved and untidy', he announced that from now on he would stay with Chips Channon at Belgrave Square. Channon, who lived in considerable luxury – although wartime had compelled him to reduce his complement of

---

30 Rhodes James, *Chips*, p. 252. Diary entry for 13 May 1940.
31 A thorough and perceptive analysis of the attitudes of the Tory Party Members during Churchill's first year in power is 'The Tories versus Churchill' in Roberts, *Eminent Churchillians*, pp. 137–210.
32 Winston Churchill, *The Second World War*, vol. 3, 'The Grand Alliance', p. 69.

household staff from fifteen to six – made all necessary arrangements, and Rab moved into Belgrave Square, accompanied by his red boxes.[33]

On 12 September it became known that Chamberlain was suffering from terminal cancer and in October he resigned the leadership of the Conservative Party, receiving the offer of a peerage and the Garter, both of which he refused.[34] Churchill was fulsome in his gratitude for Chamberlain's loyalty and, when the former PM died on 9 November, gave a powerful and moving tribute to him in the Commons.[35] From the perspective of practical politics, however grave the loss to the government, from the moment of Chamberlain's resignation Churchill was able to consolidate his hold on the party.

On 22 October, Brendan Bracken, now acting openly as the Prime Minister's political Chief of Staff, approached Rab to offer him his long wished-for Ministry as President of the Board of Education. Channon believed that Rab 'secretly coveted' the position,[36] noting in his diary that

> *Rab, with his brilliant intelligence, has many ideas of the new England that will emerge after the war. he thinks that our whole system will be drastically modified and perhaps improved: I only hope that it will be he who is the architect of the reconstruction. Though the post-war new order, I fear, rather bores me, Rab is obsessed by it … I am becoming increasingly attached to Rab and find him fascinating. His perpetual good nature, his shrewdness, his balanced views, and lack of pose and pretence are amazing in one so young.*[37]

While the overwhelmingly important task facing Britain was the winning of the war, and all peripheral Ministries would attract less immediate visibility, Rab was, as Channon noted, far-sighted enough to realise that Britain would be a very different country after the war. If he were able to position himself as one of the architects of that new post-war Britain, he could quickly obtain Cabinet rank and, once

---

33 Rhodes James, *Chips*, p. 267. Diary entry for 19 September 1940.
34 Macleod, *Neville Chamberlain*, p. 297.
35 Hansard, 12 November 1940, vol. 365, cols 1617–21.
36 Rhodes James, *Chips*, p. 270. Diary entry for 22 October 1940.
37 Rhodes James, *Chips*, pp. 268–9. Diary entry for 7 October 1940.

again, be a contender for the leadership of the party. For both humani-
tarian and political reasons, therefore, he was eager to receive a formal
offer from Churchill.

While his house in Smith Square was being repaired and he was
boarded out with Channon, Rab continued to make regular weekend
visits to Sydney and the children in Stanstead. Over one weekend he
was joined by John G. ('Gil') Winant, the American Ambassador,
a former Governor of New Hampshire, who had briefly taught in
Concord. Rab had great respect for Winant's intellect and his grasp
of British politics. The Ambassador, to Rab's surprise, predicted that
Britain would move to the left after the war and urged Rab to go to
the Board of Education. Had he been talking to Bracken? Rab asked.
'No,' replied Winant. 'I thought it out for myself. This is where you can
influence the future of England.'[38]

That offer, however, was not immediately forthcoming and Rab
toiled on at the Foreign Office, certainly chagrined that, while Eden
was away in Cairo during March, it was Churchill and not he who
handled Foreign Office business. The next eight months were for Rab
a period in the doldrums and, despite his damaged arm, Rab, together
with Geoffrey Lloyd, his friend from Cambridge, registered for military service in May 1941. Ernest Bevin, by then Minister of Labour and
National Service, duly reported that two ministers were attempting to
sign up, to which Churchill responded that 'they should not leave their
present important duties, which bring them just as much under the fire
of the enemy as training for the Army'.[39]

On 22 June 1941, the entire shape of the war changed. Hitler launched
Operation BARBAROSSA, the invasion of the Soviet Union. The
Labour Party was jubilant, the British public vastly relieved; even
Churchill, a committed anti-Communist, commented that 'If Hitler
invaded hell I would make at least a favourable reference to the devil
in the House of Commons.'

Churchill was convinced that the German invasion of the USSR

38 Butler, *The Art of the Possible*, p. 87.
39 Howard, *RAB*, p. 88*n*. For Churchill's memo to Bevin, Trinity: Butler Papers, RAB, G13.

would be the war's turning point.[40] This despite the belief of the Chiefs of Staff that Russia would not be able to resist for more than three or four months.[41] If Russia could survive that long, however, then Hitler would not be able to attempt an invasion of Britain before October, by which time weather conditions would make such an operation hazardous. For the first time since May, the atmosphere of crisis was less pronounced.

Four weeks later, on 18 July, Churchill summoned Rab to Downing Street to offer him the Board of Education, an offer that Rab happily accepted. His memoirs portray Churchill 'after his afternoon nap and purring like a tiger'.[42] 'I want you to go to the Board of Education,' he stated bluntly. 'I think you can leave your mark there.' He argued that Rab would be making an important contribution to the war effort and urged him to 'introduce a note of patriotism into the schools'. When Rab replied that he had always looked forward to going to the Board of Education if he were given the chance, Churchill expressed surprise but was delighted at his enthusiasm.[43]

'Come and see me to discuss things,' he concluded. 'Not details but the broad lines.' With this typically Churchillian valediction, Rab left the Foreign Office, trading his post of diminishing influence at the centre for a potentially critical position if Britain managed to survive. Arguably, Churchill had succeeded in winkling the last of the 'guilty men' from a position of influence. On the other hand, Rab had his own Ministry for the first time; he had a measure of independence and, in this 'backwater' of government, would be able to operate without the gimlet eye of the Prime Minister observing his every move.

The period from May 1940 to July 1941 had begun with unspoken mutual suspicion between Churchill and Rab. During the first few months of Churchill's Ministry there was the very real possibility that the Tory Party might relent in its opposition to Chamberlain and bring him back to replace Churchill. That possibility soon evaporated, but

40 Butler, *The Art of the Possible*, p. 89.
41 Danchev and Todman, *War Diaries of Field Marshal Lord Alanbrooke* (London: Weidenfeld & Nicolson, 2001), p. 166. Later comment on diary entry of 22 June 1941.
42 Butler, *The Art of the Possible*, p. 90.
43 There is a story, probably apocryphal, that when Rab thanked Churchill for the opportunity, Churchill replied, 'I meant it as an insult.'

the anti-Churchill faction transferred those hopes to Halifax. When Halifax was safely removed to Washington, Sir John Simon installed on the Woolsack, and Hoare dispatched, not to India as Viceroy as he had wished but to the Madrid Embassy, there were no members of the Old Guard close to the centre of the War Cabinet. Rab could be left to lie fallow while Churchill and Eden conducted Foreign Office business.

Gradually Rab acquired respect for the Prime Minister, fundamentally revising his early impressions, recognising his qualities as vital to Britain's war effort, noting, perhaps with surprise, Baldwin's comment that Churchill was 'our greatest war leader'.[44] Possibly Rab had also undergone some kind of reassessment in his view of himself. His realism of the 1930s had yielded to apparently greater idealism and a different reality by 1941. His attempt to join the Colours in May will have impressed Churchill – although he was not slow to deny the request. Channon's comment that Rab was 'obsessed with the post-war new order' suggests a different man from the 'sly and subtle' Butler that he had observed in March 1939.

The Prytz incident certainly chastened him. He came very close to losing his job and must have recognised that, whether he was acting as an independent agent or whether he obfuscated the truth to protect Halifax, he had acted in clear defiance of government policy. The ease with which Churchill ultimately removed Halifax from the Foreign Office should have demonstrated the folly of continuing to carry a candle for a discredited cause. Ambition alone should, in December 1940, have urged collaboration with the despised 'Glamour Boys'.

Without in any way diminishing his political aspirations, Rab adapted his methods to changed circumstances, blending his idealism, the Butler tradition of involvement in education, and a recognition that he needed to refashion his own image if he were to be in the van of post-war Tory reform. Not perhaps a Damascene moment, but a coming to terms with his own position in a changing party. He had a first-class mind and had rediscovered the idealism that urged him to

---

44 Butler, *The Art of the Possible*, p. 89.

put it to best use. Churchill, a shrewd judge of men, was far too practical to allow that mind to rust in a backwater.

After fourteen months of cautious circling of each other, Prime Minister and President of the Board of Education agreed their truce and willingly worked together. It was not necessarily a love-feast, but, for all the differences between the two, it turned out to be a momentous appointment.

CHAPTER 9

REDEMPTION THROUGH
EDUCATION, 1941–45

Rab's enthusiastic response to Churchill's offer of the Board of Education may have reflected his true feelings, but there were other considerations that influenced him. First, he was eager to have his own Ministry. Second, he was under-employed at the Foreign Office. Having been close to Chamberlain and involved in high policy, his role – imposed on him by Churchill – of 'minder' to foreign diplomats was frustrating. His diary and papers of that period bear witness to his belief that real policy had been hijacked by Churchill and Eden.[1]

Third, and most importantly for the longer term, he was eager for the opportunity to improve his relations with the very people – Churchill, Eden, Beaverbrook, Bracken – on whom he had poured scorn in the Chamberlain era. After December 1941, it seemed certain that Britain would survive and that Churchill and his henchmen would be national heroes; it was desirable for Rab to be one of the inner circle when that came to pass.

For Churchill, too, Germany's invasion of the Soviet Union marked the beginning of a different phase of the war – an auspicious event to be followed, he was confident, by the entry into the war of the United States. Through that long summer, even when successive British military initiatives were crowned with defeat and retreat or evacuation, Churchill believed that time was now on Britain's side. He needed

---

1   See, for example, Trinity: Butler Papers, RAB, G13, Memorandum, Butler to Eden, 2 July 1941, in which Rab somewhat frivolously refers to Eden the matter of extra coupons required by the Duke of Alba, the Spanish Ambassador, to acquire an adequate supply of socks from his hosier.

to plan for the period following the war and, as in 1918, he was aware that the electorate would be impatient for change. It was vital that his government present a radically different image from that of the Tory Party between the wars. He needed new men, young men, capable department chiefs who would facilitate his ambition to lead Britain in peacetime. Rab fitted that mould to perfection, provided he could shed the label of appeaser.

The mini-reshuffle that Churchill conducted on 20 July 1941 was delicately shaded to fit the image he strove to project – a vigorous government, moving with the times, tempered by the necessary experience to 'finish the job' of defeating Germany. For vigour, younger men were promoted: his son-in-law Duncan Sandys as Financial Secretary to the War Office; Hugh Seely (later Baron Sherwood) as Under-Secretary of State for Air; and Brendan Bracken as Minister of Information. For experience, Churchill moved former Cabinet Secretary Lord Hankey to the office of Paymaster General. For party balance, he brought a Labour Member, Ernest Thurtle, as Parliamentary Secretary to the Ministry of Information, along with an Independent (Hankey) and a Liberal (Seely). Richard Law, a 41-year-old Tory, succeeded Rab as Under-Secretary at the Foreign Office.

Cuthbert Headlam, the shrewd Chairman of the National Union, was sceptical about the reshuffle. He was less than impressed with the appointment of Duff Cooper to the Duchy of Lancaster, commenting that 'he has failed in every job he has been given: is clearly incompetent as an administrator, but belongs to the Winston clique'. With Bracken succeeding him at the Ministry of Information and Sandys going to the War Office, Headlam concluded that 'the family and friends are well looked after by Winston in the old, unabashed Whig manner of the eighteenth century'. Rab's appointment was noted, but not commented on.[2]

Part of Rab's eagerness to leave the Foreign Office was due to his mixed feelings about Eden, the recipient of a typically dismissive

---

2   Headlam, *Parliament and Politics in the Age of Churchill and Attlee* (London: Cambridge University Press, 1999), pp. 264–6, diary entry for 21 July 1941.

Rabism. 'Anthony's father', Rab commented, 'was a mad baronet and his mother a very beautiful woman. That's Anthony – half mad baronet, half beautiful woman.'[3] Whether or not Eden was aware of that sobriquet, he threw a dinner party on 5 July as a farewell gesture when Rab moved on, inviting Rab, the Churchills and Max Beaverbrook to his new flat above the Foreign Office. For Rab, this was an important step towards what he saw as his post-Munich rehabilitation, his acceptance into the inner circle of Churchill's party. He moved on to the Board of Education with renewed confidence.

In 1845, Disraeli wrote *Sybil*, a *roman à thèse*, subtitled *Two Nations*, in which he described the great divide that separated the wealthy and the working classes in Britain. Rab had this division in his mind when he resolved that his reform of British education would be radical and comprehensive, addressing the gross inequalities that had long been a shameful aspect of British society, despite periodic proposals to eliminate them. The most recent effort at reform, the Fisher Education Act of 1918, had ultimately failed. Rab took up the fight that Fisher had initiated.

Richard ('R. H.') Tawney, the socialist economic historian, worked in Glasgow before the First World War and was horrified to observe that most boys left school aged between twelve and fourteen and that for over 80 per cent of these the only jobs available were as 'a messenger, milk boy or van boy'. Boys entered these dead-end jobs, only to be dismissed when they were old enough to demand an adult wage.[4] This provided the principal motive for the reforms of the Fisher Act and, in reducing such abuses at least, the Act was largely successful. The outbreak of the Second World War had exacerbated the problem, both at schools, where an increasing number of teachers were called up, and in factories and agriculture, where the need for child labour increased during the war.

The clarion call of Lloyd George in 1918 for 'a country fit for heroes' demanded extensive reform and efforts by central government both to raise the school-leaving age and to introduce training in day

---

3   Cosgrave, *R. A. Butler: An English Life* (London: Quartet Books, 1981), p. 12.
4   Goldman, *The Life of R. H. Tawney: Socialism and History* (London: Bloomsbury, 2013), Chapter 1.

continuation classes until the age of eighteen. Local education authorities were charged with ensuring that extended education and training
was provided and they were given power to enforce attendance. Additionally, they were to be able to provide scholarships to cover costs for
children who passed an examination to attend fee-paying secondary
schools. The school-leaving age was raised from twelve to fourteen and
employment of children under the age of twelve outlawed.

Resistance to the Act, predictably, came from three of the pillars of
the Conservative Party – industrialists, landowners and the church. As
a result of their opposition, combined with the economic downturn of
the 1920s and 1930s, many of the provisions of the 1918 Act never came
to pass. A generation later, Rab surveyed the state of British education,
the faltering minor advances that had been made since Fisher's far-
reaching proposals and, very early in his tenure, resolved that nothing
less than root-and-branch reform would satisfy the electorate; as in
1918, a people emerging from a horrific war expected significant and
permanent improvements in living conditions and social services.

The permanence of the chasm that Disraeli had described in 1845
was brought home to inhabitants of rural areas by the evacuation of
children when Britain's cities were threatened with bombing in the
early days of the war.[5] The majority of evacuees were sympathetically
received by their country hosts, who were happy to offer hospitality as
their contribution to war service.[6] There were others, however, 'whose
arrival in the English countryside was greeted with pity and disgust.
Who were these boys and girls – half-fed, half-clothed, less than half-
taught, complete strangers to the most elementary social discipline
and the ordinary decencies of a civilised home?'[7]

When Rab took on his new brief, schools in rural areas were

---

5   Operation PIED PIPER handled the evacuation of over 3.5 million children, of whom
    many returned to cities after the Blitz. Others spent the entire war away from their
    homes.
6   The arrival of children from Birmingham in a quiet rural village is the background to Evelyn
    Waugh's satirical novel *Put Out More Flags*. A family of three apparently parent-less children
    become objects of terror in the surrounding county – and a powerful weapon in the hands of
    an unscrupulous billeting officer.
7   Iremonger, *William Temple, Archbishop of Canterbury* (London: Oxford University Press,
    1948), p. 569.

stretched by a paucity of teachers; a 'double-shift' system was in operation, but, in spite of every effort, almost 1 million children were
receiving no education at all.[8] Middle-class England was shocked by
the persistence of 'two nations' and there was widespread shame at
the failure of the British system to educate the 'citizens of tomorrow'.
Public opinion was overwhelmingly in favour of an overhaul of the
entire educational apparatus.

In contrast to the shameful condition of state schools stood the
public schools, symbols of privilege, the object of hatred by their enemies at a time when, 'though engaged in a death struggle with Hitler,
England was seething with plans for reform of the Public Schools'. In
the words of one contemporary social historian,

> The most likely solution – if there is to be one at all – would be one
> in which the Public Schools would take state money and accept state
> interference in order to bring into their ranks the best elements of the
> working class, would reform in the direction of liberal working-class
> aims, and yet would remain at least semi-independent boarding schools,
> emphasising training for leadership.[9]

The stark contrast between the extremes of British society was violently at odds with a growing belief that, after the struggle for political
equality had been won by the Representation of the People Act of 1918,
the Second World War would usher in reform to create, if not economic parity, at least parity of opportunity. At the heart of that social
faith was the conviction that educational reform was a vital first step.

This theme was taken up by Britain's religious leaders early in the
war when Cosmo Lang, Archbishop of Canterbury, together with
William Temple of York, Cardinal Hinsley, Archbishop of Westminster, and Walter Armstrong, the Moderator of the Free Church
Federal Council, wrote to *The Times*, asserting that 'the present evils

---

8   Although Rab, in answer to a question in the House of Commons, maintained that only 1 per
     cent of children were receiving no education. Hansard, 31 July 1941, vol. 373, col. 1527.
9   Mack, *The Public Schools and British Opinion*, vol. 2, p. 459. Cited by Dancy, *The Public Schools
     and the Future* (London: Faber & Faber, 1963), p. 15.

in the world are due to the failure of nations and peoples to carry out the laws of God'. Along with the five basic principles for the ordering of international life urged by Pope Pius XII, the letter associated 'five standards by which economic situations and proposals may be tested':

- Extreme inequality in wealth and possessions should be abolished;
- Every child, regardless of race or class, should have equal opportunities of education, suitable for the development of his peculiar capacities;
- The family as a social unit must be safeguarded;
- The sense of a divine vocation must be restored to man's daily work;
- The resources of the earth should be used as God's gift to the whole human race, and used with due consideration for the needs of the present and future generations.[10]

Such a letter, equating education with the resources of the earth, 'God's gift to the whole human race', demonstrates the sacrosanctity bestowed on education by religious leaders. Whilst they shared a broad estimate of its importance, however, Rab was to discover that their views differed substantially in detail.

Rab's forebears included several social reformers and educationalists. Two Butlers had been headmasters of Harrow School and one had been Master of Trinity College, Cambridge. Yet his experience of the educational system at the grassroots was negligible. James Chuter Ede, the Parliamentary Secretary at the Board of Education, commented acidly that Rab was unfamiliar with the exact nature of elementary schools when he arrived at the Board's offices in Kingsway.[11] Ede, a Socialist, Unitarian and former teacher, to whom Rab acknowledged a great debt of thanks,[12] was precisely the experienced hand needed to help him steer an ethical yet practical course between the obstacles in his path. Immediately upon his arrival at the Board, Rab wrote to

---

10 Letter to *The Times*, 21 December 1941, p. 5.
11 BL: *Ede Diaries*, Add MSS 59690, entry for 15 August 1941.
12 Butler, *The Art of the Possible*, p. 93. Ede was subsequently Home Secretary in Attlee's government.

Ede at the House of Commons, proposing a meeting. 'I shall rely very much on your experience,' Rab wrote. 'I am convinced of the opportunity we have to give the educational system of the country a real helping hand, so let us go forward together.'[13]

In Ede's record of the meeting there is a perceptible sense of caution, but Rab 'invited [him] to talk over any matters on which [he] wished to express a view'[14] and a mutual confidence rapidly developed. Very soon Rab became convinced that his efforts should be directed to reform more radical than Churchill envisaged. When he found himself torn between adhering to the Prime Minister's directive not to introduce divisive policies in wartime and pursuing the fundamental changes that he believed were necessary, it was Ede's resolve that was instrumental in keeping Rab on track.[15] Ede was also a vital link between the Tory minister and the Labour leaders – Attlee, Ernie Bevin and Greenwood – who supported Rab during the three years it took for him to make the Education Act a reality.

By the time that Rab arrived at the Board of Education, the need for educational reform was widely accepted by department officials and by the public. Under the direction of the Permanent Secretary Sir Maurice Holmes and the Deputy Secretary Sir Robert Wood, senior officials had discussed and agreed on a number of proposed reforms which they included in the 'Green Book', published in the month before Rab's arrival.[16] These had been foreshadowed in March by Rab's predecessor Herwald Ramsbotham, speaking to the Lancashire branch of the National Union of Teachers in Morecambe. He and senior officers of the Board were addressing the question and working towards introducing legislation to implement reform. He was looking for the school-leaving age to be raised to fifteen as soon as possible, day continuation classes up to the age of eighteen, and – a remoter objective – secondary or post-primary schools extended so that 'in due

13   BL: *Ede Diaries*, Add MSS 59690, entry for 22 July 1941.
14   Ibid.
15   BL: *Ede Diaries*, Add MSS 59692, entry for 30 January 1942.
16   Board of Education, *Education after the War*. It was known as 'The Green Book' for its green cover.

course all boys and girls up to the age of sixteen can be furnished with an education suitable to their various tastes and capacities'.[17]

The timing of raising the school-leaving age, Ramsbotham continued, 'depended largely on how soon the damaged schools could be repaired or replaced'. There would be 'a colossal rebuilding programme, but he hoped that our homes and schools would be given a high degree of priority'. In short, he committed the cardinal sin, in the Prime Minister's eyes, of introducing into public debate issues capable of dividing the National Government in wartime by speaking of legislation. For this tactical error he was removed from the Board and 'kicked upstairs' as Viscount Soulbury.

Churchill made it clear to Rab on his appointment that his principal responsibility would be to handle evacuation. 'You will move poor children from here to here,' he told Rab, moving imaginary children across his blotting pad.[18] Suitably cautioned, Rab at first moved slowly, asserting in a Written Answer in the Commons that a memorandum circulated to local education authorities, teachers and churches was merely a basis for the discussion of educational problems of the future, not an official statement of government policy.[19]

Ramsbotham had arranged to meet a deputation of church leaders on 15 August and Rab, somewhat ambitiously, decided to keep the appointment. Encouraged, perhaps, by the sentiments expressed by the prelates in their letter to *The Times* the previous December, he underestimated how jealously the Anglican Church guarded its position in the educational framework. Only since 1870 had central government been responsible for providing primary education, when William Forster, Vice-President of the Council, introduced a Bill for national primary education. From the outset the proposed Bill reeked of compromise, when Forster outlined guiding principles: duty to parents, to constituencies, to taxpayers. Care must be taken 'not to destroy the existing system in introducing a new one'.[20]

---

17 *The Times*, 17 March 1941, p. 2.
18 Butler, *The Art of the Possible*, p. 90.
19 Hansard, 31 July 1941, vol. 373, cols 1563W–1564W.
20 Hansard, 17 February 1870, vol. 119, col. 443.

In the intervening years a dual system had developed with state schools and church schools co-existing uneasily. No matter that the number of church-run schools had declined, or that the fabric of those schools themselves was deficient, or that in many cases just one teacher handled all primary instruction. The prerogative to manage its own schools was not one that the Anglican Church intended to surrender. As for Catholic schools, enrolment had increased, but the problems facing the Catholic Church and the church's proprietorial views were substantially similar.

Knowing some of this background and having been cautioned by Ede of the potential obstacles, Rab was greatly encouraged by the co-operative attitude of the deputation – which included Cosmo Lang and William Temple, current and future Archbishops of Canterbury. A former minister at the Foreign Office, he felt confident that he had the diplomatic skills required to negotiate an acceptable formula that balanced technical and religious instruction in schools across Britain. Armed with this confidence, he set off for a fortnight's holiday, during which he reflected on the issues facing him.

On his return he sent Churchill on 12 September a letter 'stressing the need to adapt the educational system to present social requirements'.[21] The Prime Minister's response was immediate and categorical. He refused to contemplate a new Education Bill while the war continued. He refused to speculate on what new facilities the country would be able to afford at the end of the war. He wanted no discussion of the future of the public schools. Rab's brief, he repeated, was to get the schools working as well as possible in wartime and to contribute to the war effort by offering technical training to provide munitions and radio workers. Party politics were taboo for the duration of the war and Rab's plans raised these 'in a most acute and dangerous form'. To Rab's further dismay, Sir Maurice Holmes, the Permanent Secretary at the Board, meekly accepted Churchill's veto on reform as absolute.

Rab, however, was determined that he and Chuter Ede would put their stamp on the Board[22] and 'basing myself on long experience with

---

21 Butler, *The Art of the Possible*, p. 94.
22 BL: *Ede Diaries*, Add MSS 59690, entry for 22 July 1941.

Churchill over the India Bill, decided to disregard what he said and go straight ahead'.[23] Shrewdly reckoning that he could frame a Bill that avoided controversy and which would be acceptable to all parties, he at first proposed to form a Joint Select Committee to bring the issue of educational reform into the open, an idea promptly rejected by both the Prime Minister and Attlee.[24] Undeterred, Rab resolved to move stealthily, albeit decisively, to achieve his goal. Sure of the support of Attlee, Bevin and Morrison for the principle of reform, he believed that he could avoid division within the National Government; flexible as to the future of the public schools, confident that he could hammer out an acceptable formula regarding religious instruction, he embarked on a three-year-long crusade to put a genuinely reformist Act on the books.

The proposals of the Green Book, which would form the substance of talks with local education authorities, teachers' unions and other educational bodies, were intended to be kept under wraps. The book, however, was 'distributed in such a blaze of secrecy that it achieved an unusual degree of publicity'.[25] Thus, in October, in a Written Answer to the Commons, Rab felt able to enter into details. His Written Answer set out the range of issues that he was resolved to address:

- The raising of the school-leaving age. Should there be exemptions after fourteen?
- The need for re-defining elementary education.
- The need to review the method of the distribution of children at eleven to the different types of secondary school.
- The contribution that might be made to maintaining the mental alertness and physical welfare of young people; to the improvement of their vocational training, and the development of social and recreational interests, by a system of part-time day continuation schools to the age of eighteen.

---

23 Butler, *The Art of the Possible*, p. 95.
24 BL: *Ede Diaries*, Add MSS 59690, entries for 16–17 September 1941.
25 Smith, *To Whom do the Schools Belong*, p. 155. Cited by Jeffreys, *The Journal of the Historical Association*, vol. 69, 227, October 1984, p. 417.

- The relation of the Youth Service to such development.
- The need for an improved and extended system of technical, commercial and art training and closer relations between education and industry and commerce.
- The need for equality of opportunity for students to attend universities.[26]

As Rab points out in his memoirs, the Green Book also proposed the 'abrogation in the secondary schools of the ban on denominational religious instruction imposed by ... the Act of 1870' and this would have led to a clash with the church schools which were responsible for education, not to the age of eleven but to the age of fourteen. Rab spent the winter of 1941–42 working on both the lay and religious aspects of his plans for the proposed Bill. It was becoming clear to him and to Ede that the responsibility for religious instruction was going to be the principal difficulty to circumvent and Rab decided to deal first with lay questions.

One such question concerned the public schools, many of which were in financial difficulty and 'in danger of extinction'.[27] Rab took the view that the question had a disproportionate explosive capability – that is, that the subject was capable of raising the heat of discussion in a manner vastly greater than the issue's relevance to the reforms that Rab proposed. Accordingly, he decided to tackle that potentially divisive issue once the general outlines of his reforms were more clear. His approach, he resolved, would be first to deal with the state schools, second with the church schools, and third to appoint a committee to study if and to what extent the public schools could form part of the broader system.

The principles for that system would be that the state provide elementary education until the age of eleven and secondary education for all over that age. The school-leaving age would be raised, initially to fourteen, and later to fifteen or sixteen. There should be more practical training and a system of apprenticeships, leading to 'a practical form

---

26 Hansard, 23 October 1941, vol. 374, cols 1937W–1939W.
27 BL: *Ede Diaries*, Add MSS 59691, entry for 20 October 1941.

of continued education, later to be known as County Colleges'.[28] The guiding principle was that the state provide education that embraced 'training suited to the talents' of individual students. Within those parameters, substantially those of the Green Book, he would address separately the roles of church schools and public schools.

Those were the broad principles that Rab presented to the National Union of Teachers in a conference on 9 April 1942. With some pride, he recorded in his memoirs that the president of the Union applauded them as 'the most progressive ever outlined by a President of the Board of Education'. The first milestone of his proposed reforms had been reached.

Chuter Ede provided invaluable support during the winter months. Initially suspicious of Rab, believing that he had merely been shunted onto a branch line for the duration of the war, Ede was impressed by his determination, particularly by his resolve to pass a wide-ranging Act and not simply to apply a sticking plaster to individual contentious issues. In February he was able to demonstrate the extent to which his admiration for Rab had grown.

Churchill summoned Ede to Downing Street at noon on 4 February. Before keeping the appointment, Ede met Rab, who told him that Churchill would offer him a Parliamentary Secretaryship in another department, a move that Rab did not welcome. Ede replied that if Churchill demanded a move in the interests of the war effort, he would have to obey his orders, but that he would try to influence him, if Churchill allowed him to speak, that his best work would be done at the Board.[29]

When Ede was shown in to see Churchill, he learned that it was proposed to send him to the Ministry of War Transport. Ede respectfully declined the offer, saying that he was committed to the practice and administration of education. There were 'delicate negotiations over religion and the public schools in hand'. To bring in another person at that stage would necessitate starting over again.[30] To Ede's surprise and

---

28 Butler, *The Art of the Possible*, p. 96.
29 BL: *Ede Diaries*, Add MSS 59692, entry for 4 February 1942.
30 Ibid.

delight, Churchill accepted the decision – once Attlee had endorsed it – saying that he knew that Ede wanted only to serve the country. Rab later commented that Ede was 'probably the only man who had refused to move from the Board' and that even more impressive was that he was 'the only man who had successfully defied Churchill's desire to move him from one post to another'.[31]

In their first year of working together at the Board, Rab and Ede made significant progress. In October 1941, in co-operation with Lord Woolton, they initiated a drive for additional milk and lunches in schools, resulting in provision of milk for 3.5 million children and doubling the number of school lunches to over 700,000. In spite of wartime shortages, this initiative led to dramatic improvement in children's health. In the same month, they established a committee under Sir Cyril Norwood, formerly Master of Marlborough, to report on secondary schools and the examination system. Recognising the need for trained teachers, Rab appointed the Vice-Chancellor of Liverpool University to chair a committee to look into the recruiting and training of teachers.[32] Additionally, he set about reforming curriculum far beyond the rudimentary content generally offered, introducing courses in the current affairs of Britain's allies, the Soviet Union and the United States, as well as physical training, music, drama, handicrafts and domestic science.[33]

In June 1942, he announced to the Commons an initiative of the utmost importance. Recognising the 'growing feeling that there is some advantage in the corporate life of [boarding schools], which should be made more widely available', he set up a body under the chairmanship of Lord Fleming 'to work out a plan under which the facilities of a boarding-school education might be extended to those who desire to profit by them, irrespective of their means'. The choice of Fleming, he told the House, was made because, being a Scot, he 'was not wedded by previous association to any type of schooling in England'.[34]

---

31 Ibid.
32 Hansard, 16 June 1942, vol. 380, col. 1412.
33 *The Times*, 17 June 1942.
34 Hansard, 16 June 1942, vol. 380, col. 1416.

Overall, Rab was proud to report to Parliament,

> To have succeeded, as we have done, in retaining the normalcy of the
> lives of nearly 5 million children during the course of the war, a war very
> often over our own soil, means that we have, at one and the same time,
> husbanded our greatest national asset, maintained the national morale –
> and I think the morale of the parents has been exceptionally important
> in this time – and we have assisted the war effort.[35]

One week after Rab's successful presentation of his plans to the National Union of Teachers, William Temple, Archbishop of York, was
installed as Archbishop of Canterbury. For Rab this was a consummation devoutly to be wished; it is doubtful if it could have been better
arranged by Providence to facilitate educational reform, for Temple
and Rab were, in President Truman's memorable phrase, 'two halves
of the same walnut'.[36] One description of the Archbishop illustrates
clearly the qualities that would prove to be valuable once Rab and he
joined forces:

> The clarity and speed with which he wrote memoranda or answered let-
> ters were … outstanding. There have been more convincing philosophi-
> cal theologians, more effective social reformers, greater preachers, more
> single-minded ecumenists, but no one who combined all these skills to
> so high a degree and who so steadily matched his leadership with the
> hour. His ceaseless activity on so many fronts was possible only because
> of a remarkable inner calm, a prayerfulness, cheerfulness and lack of
> pomposity which all who encountered him experienced.[37]

In their backgrounds, too, the pair were well matched. The new Archbishop, himself the son of a former Archbishop of Canterbury, was
at Balliol at the turn of the century and, like Rab at Cambridge, had

---

35 Ibid., col. 1403.
36 Rab's engaging portrait of Temple and his contribution to the 1944 Act are in Butler, *The Art*
    of Memory, pp. 143–63.
37 *Oxford Dictionary of National Biography*, 'William Temple' by Adrian Hastings.

been President of the Oxford Union. Like Rab, he had taken a double first and, immediately upon graduation, had been appointed to a Fellowship.[38] Once again in common with Rab, he had resigned his Fellowship to follow another direction – in Temple's case to be ordained – and had risen rapidly in the church, becoming Bishop of Manchester at the age of thirty-nine. From 1910 to 1914 he had been Headmaster of Repton School. A Socialist at Oxford, he had been a member of the Labour Party until 1925, prone to provoke more reactionary colleagues both at Queen's and at Repton. In 1942, while Rab was putting the finishing touches to his initial proposals for educational reform, Temple published *Christianity and Social Order*, his vision of how Anglican theology should co-exist within a more egalitarian post-war society. An independent thinker, he had questioned orthodox Christian doctrine – specifically the Virgin Birth and the physical resurrection of Christ – which had led the Bishop of Oxford to express his reluctance to ordain him in 1908.

Once engaged, Temple was as tireless as Rab in urging reform, relentless in his focus on central issues rather than a slave to established practice. His response to colleagues who objected to the raising of the leaving age was typically direct: 'I am putting this very crudely, but I believe that our Lord is much more interested in raising the school-leaving age to sixteen than in acquiring an agreed Religious Syllabus.'[39]

As a tactic to engage Temple, Rab focussed not on any issue of syllabus but on the more practical question of the physical condition of the church schools. The Church of England had built few schools since 1918 and had been closing them at an average rate of over seventy each year. Remaining schools were in poor shape, and Temple himself acknowledged that the church was bound to emerge as the loser in a confrontation between church and state. The main business of the church in the 1940s, he maintained, was 'not surely to be fighting a rearguard action in perpetual retreat till we are driven off the field by the competition of the resources of the state, but to take care

---

38 Temple's Fellowship was at Queen's College, Oxford.
39 Iremonger, *William Temple*, p. 575.

that we are interpenetrating with our influence all that the state itself is doing'.[40]

What, then, should the state do? Rab and Chuter Ede discussed this question and arrived at a possible solution that could be offered to church schools of all denominations. Schools could elect to be either 'aided' or 'controlled'. An 'aided' school would retain the right to appoint teachers and to decide on the nature of religious instruction. The local education authority would be responsible for teachers' salaries and the school's running expenses, but school managers would bear the responsibility for bringing the school's facilities up to a required standard. For such alterations and improvements they would receive a grant from the state, amounting to 50 per cent of the cost.

In a 'controlled' school the powers and responsibilities of the local education authority would be more comprehensive, including all running expenses and teachers' salaries, together with the appointment of teachers. Religious instruction would be according to an agreed syllabus.

When Temple and a few colleagues met with Rab at the Board of Education in early June, Rab stressed once more the physical decay into which the church schools had fallen, pointing out their age and the number that were on the government's 'black list'. Refusal to cooperate with the Board, Rab argued, would be to do a disservice to children. Temple, impressed by the figures quoted, undertook to urge his clergy to accept the agreed syllabus and to allow the great majority of church schools to adopt controlled status. Whilst this was not yet a clear victory for Rab, it was a significant step forward.

There remained the Nonconformist churches and the Catholic Church; each had its own individual objections to Rab's proposals. For the Catholic clergy, with principally urban congregations, the obstacles were doctrinal, in that Catholic schools formed a basic part of religious observance; and financial, in that the cost of restoration of more than twelve hundred schools was beyond the church's budget. For the Nonconformist communities there was the abiding concern that

---

40 Ibid., p. 571.

in the rural areas, where their congregations flourished, the alliances between Tory squire and Anglican vicar were, in their view, reactionary and sinister. In many villages, moreover, the only school available was the Anglican school, and this created resentment for non-Anglicans.

When Rab received 'a very formidable' Free Church deputation on 6 October 'with light touches he put the conference in a very good humour', stressing his two *desiderata*: first, that 'schools should reach a reasonably high standard physically and educationally'; second, that 'a reorganisation which had been hanging about … must be completed and made nationwide within a reasonable time of the appointed day for the raising of the school leaving age to fifteen'. Rab and Ede were 'closely questioned on the details and it became clear that the principal fear of the deputation was about the consultations between LEAs and managers over the appointment of Head Teachers'.[41] Overall, Rab was pleased with the mood of the meeting and felt that he 'had not let the Church of England down'. Ultimately, his policy in dealing with Free Church groups was to encourage them to reach a compromise with the Church of England.

Despite holding two meetings, over which Temple presided, the Free Churches and Anglicans were unable to reach agreement, and the Nonconformist grievances persisted. Fortunately, reason prevailed; the virtues of the Board's proposals were so patently progressive and sound that no effort was made by the Free Churches to impede the progress of the Bill.

Rab's dealings with the Catholic Church, by contrast, were met with concerted opposition. At a meeting with a Catholic delegation on 15 September, Rab, by prior agreement with Temple, indicated the terms of the preliminary agreement with the Church of England. The reaction was unpromising as the option offered to the Church of England, viewed from the Catholic perspective, contained nothing new. The church would continue to pay for the upkeep of its schools, while Catholic parishioners would continue to pay rates and local taxes for the upkeep of local schools that they would not feel able to use.

41 BL: *Ede Diaries*, Add MSS 59694, entry for 6 October 1942.

Whether or not the local schools were supported by the state or by the Anglican Church, or jointly by both, was immaterial.

The reaction of the Catholic Church leaders was worsened by their perception that Rab had agreed the substance of his proposed educational reforms in advance with Temple and that

> by the time Mr Butler got round to consulting them the main terms of the Bill were already clear ... Mr Butler had already worked out the entire scheme for fitting in the Catholic schools at this point, although it would be two years before the Bill was passed through Parliament ... The Catholics were left to the end of the line![42]

A small committee was established by the Catholic hierarchy to negotiate with the Board of Education and other interested parties. This included Archbishop Peter Amigo, Bishop of Southwark, and it was to him that Rab wrote, proposing the principle of 'aided' schools on 6 September.[43] Arguing that the demand of Cardinal Hinsley, Archbishop of Westminster, that 'the Catholic schools should be within the national system of education' was inconsistent with the Catholic claim for exceptional treatment, Rab was confident that the proposed 50 per cent grant would be accepted by the Catholic bishops.

He had reckoned without the Cardinal's political adroitness, however. In his State of the Union speech of January 1941, President Roosevelt had spelled out what came to be known as 'The Four Freedoms': freedom of speech, freedom of worship, freedom from want and freedom from fear. Since then, in August 1941, Churchill and Roosevelt had met at the Atlantic Conference in Newfoundland and reaffirmed their commitment to human rights in the post-war world in the Atlantic Charter. The Cardinal, therefore, sounded a topical note when he wrote to *The Times*, stressing the unique situation of Catholic schools in the educational system. The freedom of conscience of all, he wrote, must be protected. Catholics, a minority largely from

---

42 Clifton, *Amigo: Friend of the Poor* (Leominster: Fowler Wright, 1987), p. 102.
43 The full text of that letter is quoted by Clifton, *Amigo: Friend of the Poor*, pp. 211–14.

the poorer section of the community, had 'a special claim for fair play, especially from any and every party or group that professes to uphold the ... rights of minorities'. Catholic schools 'should receive equal treatment with other schools if there were to be 'equal opportunity for all'. No equal opportunity would exist for a minority, 'saddled with extra and crushing financial burdens because of their definite religious convictions and because they cannot accept a syllabus of religious instruction agreeable to the many'. The letter ended magisterially. 'We emphatically repeat', the Cardinal wrote, 'that we are convinced that no political party will seek to or be able to set at naught the respect of British people for the rights of minorities.'[44]

Strictly speaking, British Catholics were not being denied any of the 'Four Freedoms' that Roosevelt had articulated. No matter; with American entry into the war after Pearl Harbor came the British canonisation of the President, and the mere suggestion that the state was violating any principle that he embraced was dynamite. Rab had been outmanoeuvred – a fact brought home to him forcefully when Churchill cut the letter from *The Times*, affixed it to a piece of cardboard and sent it to Rab with the terse message, 'There you are, fixed, old cock.'[45]

This episode depressed Rab deeply, although he had never seen the total acquiescence of the Catholic Church as a *sine qua non* of an Education Bill. Nonetheless, absence of overt dissent was vital if he were to circumvent the veto that Churchill had placed on divisive legislation in wartime. In November, Rab wrote to Temple, expressing his concern that 'If all the main partners do not solve this question together on this occasion – however patient we may have to be – I rather wonder who will find a way out ever.'[46]

In typical Butler vein, lighthearted and detached, he relates in his

---

44 *The Times*, 2 November 1942, p. 5.
45 Butler, *The Art of Memory*, p. 159. Anthony Howard notes that this blunt message was how Rab later related the story but that in a minute dated 3 November 1942 he referred to a telephone call from Churchill, who told him bluntly, 'You are landing me in the biggest political row of the generation.'This minute is at Bodleian: R .A. Butler's files on Education Bill, RAB 2/2. See Howard, *RAB*, p. 129 and note. Also, Butler, *The Art of the Possible*, p. 100.
46 Iremonger, *William Temple*, p. 571.

memoirs his attempts to find a Catholic leader with whom he might reach some form of agreement. For the balance of 1942 and through much of 1943 he continued these efforts, achieving little and reaching the conclusion that the Church of Rome was 'hydra-headed'.[47] When Archbishop Amigo replied negatively to his letter in November, Rab asked to see him in person. He was shown in to see the fully robed Archbishop in a room overlooking the ruins of Southwark Cathedral and politely asked why he had come. A drive to meet the northern Catholic bishops at Ushaw College outside Durham yielded a fine *gigot d'agneau* and much red wine for dinner, followed by a solemn visit to the chapel to view a magnificent ivory figure on the High Altar – but no measure of agreement. 'We were all filled with a certain awe, which was no doubt intentionally administered,' Rab recorded. 'Chuter Ede told me he thought he was going to faint.'[48] Despite a positive response to his speech at Ushaw from the Bishops of Salford, Lancaster and Liverpool, no real progress was made, and Rab proceeded to draft his Education Act with the issue of Catholic schools unresolved.

Rab's concerns were augmented by apathy – even outright opposition – from many of his own party. When he and Ede discussed how education might be referred to in the King's Speech to be delivered on 11 November, Rab complained that 'the Conservative Party was at sixes and sevens. Its members … spent their time in the Smoke Room consuming expensive drinks and intriguing.'[49] He railed against the stupidity he encountered in the 1922 Committee, many of whose members wanted 'Old Toryism', whatever that might be. The country, he maintained, was massively in favour of educational reform. Yet the King's Speech contained the briefest of references to education. Churchill, Ede recorded, 'thought that we would fail, but [Rab] was not downcast'.[50] He modified his tactics, circulating a paper on education to his colleagues on the Lord President's Committee. This line

---

47 Trinity: Butler Papers, RAB, G15. Diary entry for 9 September 1943.
48 Rab's record of his peregrinations to find 'one man of dignity and reliability with whom one can perpetually be in touch on a personal basis' are described in laconic style at *The Art of the Possible*, pp. 105–6.
49 BL: *Ede Diaries*, Add MSS 59694, entry for 26 October 1942.
50 BL: *Ede Diaries*, Add MSS 59694, entry for 11 November 1942.

of advance was preferable to tackling Churchill, and Rab believed he would have a Bill drafted and introduced around Easter 1943.[51]

There was speculation during the autumn as to who would succeed Lord Linlithgow as the next Viceroy of India. Channon, ever with his ear to the ground, recorded that the 'waiting list, apparently, is Lord Greene, Rab, Bobbety Cranborne, Miles Lampton, Oliver Lyttelton, Sam Hoare'.[52] During November, Brendan Bracken called on Rab to float the idea that, when Lord Linlithgow retired,[53] Rab might succeed him. This was a curious suggestion on Churchill's part, as, had Rab been appointed, there would have been fundamental disagreement between Viceroy and Prime Minister concerning the path to independence. In the event, it suited Churchill's military strategy to shuffle generals between the Middle East Command and India. General Wavell was already Commander-in-Chief in India, and when Churchill replaced General Auchinleck with General Alexander in the Middle East, he moved Auchinleck to India as C-in-C and appointed Wavell Viceroy.[54] This made sense for a number of reasons; a more difficult question concerns Rab's reaction to Bracken's suggestion.

On the first page of his memoirs Rab wrote wistfully, 'If there is one long-standing political ambition whose non-fulfilment can still give me the sharpest of pangs, it is that I never became Viceroy.'[55] In the context of the years 1942 to 1947, it is hard to take that statement at face value. It was by no means certain that Churchill, aged sixty-eight in November 1942, would remain – or wish to remain – in Downing Street at the end of the war. There would be an election soon after the war ended, the outcome of which was equally uncertain, and Rab had severe doubts about the suitability of Eden as Churchill's successor.

---

51 BL: *Ede Diaries*, Add MSS 59694, entry for 7 December 1942.
52 Rhodes James, *Chips*, p. 336. Diary entry for 21 September 1942.
53 The Marquess of Linlithgow eventually retired on 1 October 1943 after seven years as Viceroy.
54 All three generals subsequently became Field Marshals (Wavell on 1 January 1943; Alexander on 4 June 1944; Auchinleck on 1 June 1946) but in late 1942 all three held the rank of General and are referred to as such.
55 Butler, *The Art of the Possible*, p. 1. In 1944, Sir Alan ('Tommy') Lascelles wrote: 'I like Rab; he has plenty of ego in his cosmos, and not a vast deal of humour, but he is very able, and sincere. The Viceroyalty is clearly his ultimate goal.' Diary, 10 February 1944. *King's Counsellor* (London: Weidenfeld & Nicolson), pp. 200–201.

We know from the diaries of Chips Channon that Channon saw Rab as extremely ambitious and that he was widely perceived as a possible Leader of the Party in peacetime. It is almost inconceivable that, within a few days of his fortieth birthday, he would have considered a move from the mainstream in favour of a prestigious but ultimately peripheral post. Since the office had been created in 1858, the list of Viceroys was a panoply of aristocratic names, of whom none, with the exception of Halifax, were ever in contention for the premiership.

His own account of events suggests that he refused the putative offer – an account supported by a handwritten draft of a letter to Bracken that was probably never sent.[56] It would have been folly for Rab to have abandoned his proposed Education Bill at this point, however great his frustration with the Catholic bishops. Education was his path back into the hierarchy of the party and, equally important, into the public eye. It is unlikely that he considered accepting such an offer, even if it was made; at all events, Churchill changed his mind and withdrew the offer.

By 1947, India had been granted independence, an outcome that Rab had foreseen and which he supported wholeheartedly. His comment that it caused him 'the sharpest pangs' not to have been Viceroy has a romantic ring but is far from the truth. When Bracken mooted the possibility, Rab's ambitions were more for political power than the pomp and grandeur attached to a largely ceremonial post. It is hard to take seriously the suggestion that, fully engaged with education in November 1942, he considered any course other than bringing to fruition what he had begun. During November it was decided that Linlithgow would stay on for another year as, according to Channon, 'Winston will not invite Rab to be Viceroy, and the Cranbornes, Sinclairs and Devonshires have all, after reflection, turned it down.'[57]

The New Year brought distress to Rab and his family. His younger brother Jock, resisting all attempts to dissuade him from leaving a 'reserved occupation' in the Home Office, had enlisted in the RAF. He

---

56 Trinity: Butler Papers G14; draft letter dated 19 November 1942. Anthony Howard believes that it was never sent. Howard, *RAB*, p. 131.
57 Rhodes James, *Chips*, p. 346. Diary entry for 6 December 1942.

completed his training and, on his first operational flight, was killed when 'icing' on the wings caused his plane to crash on takeoff. Rab, who in his Cambridge days had been as much a surrogate father as a brother while his parents were in India, was devastated.

It was not in Rab's nature to betray deep emotions and he maintained a stoic manner, taking one day from work to attend Jock's funeral in Essex. Ede, hearing of the accident, had written a letter of condolence to Rab and Rab thanked him for the kindness, adding that 'what [Ede] had written about consolation helped his father recover from the shock'.[58] The conversation immediately turned to individual Catholic leaders and local government finance. Death in wartime is unaccountable, illogical, inevitable. Rab accepted the shock, then turned to his work as a carapace for his grief. He would do so again a decade later.

Later that month he spent a long evening with Channon, 'discussing old days, the political set-up, the possible re-birth of the Conservative Party and his own chances of both the premiership and the Viceregal throne'. It is as if Rab were taking stock of his life and his future as he went into training for the most important fight of his career. Channon's impressions at this point are revealing:

> *I do not think that he is advancing: in fact, he is contracting ... And Rab has such obvious defects ... is lacking in imagination ... and so simple in his way of life as to be almost irritating. Yet he has great gifts too – shrewdness, calm judgement, and ambition. But he is* au fond *a civil servant. I hinted much of this to him tonight, and he was depressed thereby, and has now gone to bed.*[59]

It was a depressing landscape that Rab surveyed. Churchill, accepting the need for reform, objected to his methodology. The Tories, as a group, opposed reform. The Viceroyalty had been tentatively offered, then withdrawn. No definitive agreement had been reached with the Churches. He had provisionally set Easter 1943 as the date to present his Bill. Now that deadline was just three months away.

---

58 BL: *Ede Diaries*, Add MSS 59695, entry for 13 January 1943.
59 Rhodes James, *Chips*, p. 349. Diary entry for 25 January 1943.

By January 1943, the military situation had changed dramatically. On 8 November 1942, the Allies launched Operation TORCH, the invasion of North Africa, the first major Anglo-American offensive. From 14 to 24 January, Churchill and Roosevelt met at the Casablanca Conference and announced to the world that they demanded nothing less than Germany's unconditional surrender. On the Eastern Front, General von Paulus and the German Sixth Army were surrounded and cut off at Stalingrad. The ultimate defeat of Nazi Germany was assured.

From Rab's tactical perspective as he prepared his Education Bill, there were both bonuses and drawbacks in the changed mood in Britain. On the one hand, the talk of post-war reform assumed a new reality. On the other hand, as the main political parties looked forward to a resumption of party politics, Churchill's hold on the coalition was weakened, a development that he was determined to resist. Rab recognised the need to move even more diplomatically in his presentation of his reforms to all parties. It would require dexterity to satisfy the Labour Party that there would be more than temporary window-dressing in his proposals and a certain selectivity in his approach to his Conservative colleagues.

That selectivity resulted in the tactical decision to remove the incendiary issue of the public schools from his reforms. In July 1942 he had appointed Lord Fleming to 'consider means whereby the association between the public schools … and the general educational system of the country could be developed and extended'. Rab allowed the committee to proceed at its own pace and not to provoke the right wing of his own party by 'tinkering' with the public schools. It was not until July 1944 that Lord Fleming's Committee delivered its report.

Rab had an opportunity to reward Ede for his continuing support when, on 24 April 1943, the Rev. W. A. E. Austen wrote to tell Rab that Ede had been up at Christ's College, Cambridge but, having no money, had been unable to stay up to complete his degree. Austen suggested that Rab arrange for him to receive an honorary degree, which Rab undertook to do. He contacted the Vice-Chancellor, Dr Venn, the son of John Venn of Venn Diagram fame, who obtained agreement to confer an honorary MA on Ede.[60]

Rab immediately agreed to Austen's suggestion but impressed on him that this must be their secret. Indeed, he mentioned nothing to Ede, who wrote to Rab on 6 June 1943 to say how much he had enjoyed visiting Cambridge and spending an afternoon with Rab's father, by then Master of Pembroke College. Although Rab had kept the secret, Ede wrote, 'I have no doubt that it was your generous thought which welded the chain of events leading to Friday's ceremony.'[61] Rab handled the matter with typical kindness and sensitivity. Not only did he recognise how much the degree would matter to Ede; he also sensed that Ede, if he knew that Rab were expending effort on his behalf during wartime, would feel acute embarrassment and possibly back away from accepting the degree.

Curiously, Rab's efforts in education were greatly assisted by the proposals for social security of the Beveridge Report, published in December 1942. Conservatives were disturbed at the expected cost of implementing Beveridge's programme; even Bevin accepted that no government would simply implement his proposals without knowing the eventual bill, while Cherwell's concern was that the Americans might feel that they were subsidising Socialist measures in Britain.[62] Kingsley Wood, the Chancellor of the Exchequer, told Rab that he would prefer to spend money on educational reform than 'throw it down the sink with Sir William Beveridge'.[63] This had to be balanced with Ede's warning that 'something on account' needed to be offered in social policy. The *legerdemain* of the '1918 trick' was fresh in Socialist memories.[64] Rab, paradoxically, was more sure of support from the Labour Party than from his own party, particularly after Bevin intervened to secure permission from the Lord President's Committee for Rab to proceed with the drafting of a Bill.

With a certain caution Rab adopted 'a thoroughly democratic way

---

60 Trinity: Butler Papers, RAB, G15.41–2, 10 May 1943.
61 Trinity: Butler Papers, RAB, G15.50, Ede to Rab, 6 June 1943.
62 Gilmour, *Whatever Happened to the Tories* (London: Fourth Estate, 1998), p. 17.
63 BL: *Ede Diaries*, Add MSS 59694, entry for 16 September 1942.
64 BL: *Ede Diaries*, Add MSS 59695, entry for 27 November 1942.

of proceeding, publishing the government's proposals in advance and taking account of the reactions to them in the Bill'. A White Paper[65] was published and, finally, on 29 July 1943, 'Rab introduced his famous Education Bill, or rather presented it in its preliminary stages.'[66]

'We shall retain in our system a diversity of choice, while attempting at the same time to fuse the parts and weld them into an organic whole,' he opened. Then, in a fitting analogy, he compared the existing system to a schoolboy's jacket:

> It has done wonderful service, and much maternal care has been lavished upon it, but there are certain signs that it is becoming out of date. The sleeves are running far up the arm. The tell-tale let-down of material will barely cover the expanse of anatomy allotted to it. Stains, rents, patches and tears appear in various parts, and the shine on the nap makes one reflect on the need for change. It is not surprising, since the tailoring of this particular jacket was done in 1870, when our elementary system was designed to retain children in school up to the age of ten years.[67]

The government proposed 'a radical reconstruction of the whole scheme'. Rab presented the proposals of the White Paper: nursery schools provided by local authorities from the age of two; compulsory education from the age of five; raising the school-leaving age to fifteen and, later, to sixteen; free secondary education for all children; and compulsory part-time education until the age of eighteen for young people already in work. The number of technical colleges would be increased – there were, he said, only 379 in the whole country – and these would be 'the universities of industry', offering both technical and general education. Meanwhile, he added, the future of direct grant schools would await the report of the Fleming Committee.

Speaking of the dual system, he denied the accusation that 'our schools are Godless and that our teachers are pagan', and explained

65 Cmd.6458, published on 16 June 1943.
66 Rhodes James, *Chips*, p. 374. Diary entry for 29 July 1943.
67 Hansard, 29 July 1943, vol. 391, cols 1826–7.

the principles of 'aided' and 'controlled' schools – incurring later in the debate the accusation that in failing to abolish the dual system altogether the government had shirked the issue. Moving to the supply of teachers, Rab stressed the importance of improved teacher training, 'perhaps the most vital matter for the future of education'. This question would be entrusted to an inquiry chaired by the Vice-Chancellor of Liverpool University, which would report 'at a not impossibly distant date'. Building to a ringing peroration, Rab concluded,

> I believe Parliament has a double responsibility; first, to the generation which is winning this victory to assure them that a plan for the future world will go through, and, second, to the children to provide them with a chance to live in that future world. Thus Parliament may become a link between two generations. May we prove worthy by taking the first step on the road to educational reform this week. Let us see that in our time we have achieved something. We have got rid of the antiquated structure and reconstructed it. We have removed some of the impediments to the proper fusion of the efforts of church and state. We have made it possible for children to be looked after up to eighteen by care and supervision and we have induced a new love for those spiritual values which makes the human personality. If we can say that, we shall have fortified the character of the individual, and right action will flow from right character. If we can achieve right character in our rising generation we can say that in this time of strife we have ensured the fulfilment of our hopes.[68]

On the following day Ede wound up for the government succinctly, declaring that 'the government cannot but be pleased with the general reception this scheme has had in the House. We recognise that on broad general lines we have secured a greater measure of approval for our proposals than I believe has been given to any education measure that has ever been brought before the House.'[69] The one criticism he

---

68 Hansard, 29 July 1943, vol. 391, cols 1826–45.
69 Hansard, 30 July 1943, vol. 391, col. 2034.

detected was that the reforms were not being implemented quickly enough. The religious issues had not derailed the Board's proposals; the question of the public schools had been deferred. Rab's skilful drafting, combined with what Channon described as his 'unostentatious manner', had set the context. He had spelled out the ideals and Ede, ex-teacher and Board of Education veteran, had added the substance.

When the proposals were debated in the Lords, Archbishop Temple complimented the Board and its president on having offered 'for the first time, the hope of a complete national system'. He then requested that three points be considered: first, 'that in the controlled schools ... there will be genuine security that the special religious instruction required by the trust deed shall be given by a member of the staff approved by the foundation managers'. Second, that the grants for building repair should be increased to 75 per cent; and third, that 'there should be readiness to provide new denominational schools to come, when built ... if in any locality 80 or 90 per cent of the population sufficient to fill the school signify their desire for a school of that character'.[70]

Rab was understandably alarmed that, at this critical stage, Temple was applying pressure with the unspoken threat that the Anglicans might now make cause with the Catholic Church, which could sink the entire enterprise. When the Archbishop explained his actions, however, Rab conceded that the unexpected manoeuvre was 'ingenious in effect for it forestalled further ... demands from the high Anglicans'.[71]

At the end of 1943, Rab received grateful thanks from the teaching profession when an educational journal praised his considerable achievement in formulating the Education Act:

> The publication of the new Education Bill has given a notable start to the coming year, and education rightly takes its place at the forefront of the government's plans for social reconstruction. It is no mean achievement for a nation to prepare for these advances in social policy while still engaged in critical phases of the war against Nazi oppression.[72]

70 Hansard, 4 August 1943, vol. 981, cols 1005–6.
71 Butler, *The Art of Memory*, p. 161.
72 *Teachers' World*, 29 December 1943; Trinity: Butler Papers, RAB, L6.2.

Rab was now a celebrity, the target of cartoonists, dramatically thrust into the public gaze as a reformer. He was asked by a literary magazine to list his favourite books. The list is a typical Rab construction, designed to demonstrate his breadth of knowledge and interests. His choices were:

Winston Churchill	*My Early Life*
Charles Dickens	*The Pickwick Papers*
H. W. Freeman	*Joseph and His Brethren*
J. A. Froude	*Caesar*
Apsley Cherry-Gerard	*The Worst Journey in the World*
Thomas Hardy	*Far From the Madding Crowd*
James T. Morier	*Hajji Baba of Istaphan*
Arthur Quiller-Couch (ed.)	*The Oxford Book of English Verse*
R. L. Stevenson	*Treasure Island*
W. M. Thackeray	*Henry Esmond*[73]

In early 1944, when planning for the invasion of Northern France was filling newspaper columns, on the day that General Eisenhower designated General Bradley to command the US forces on D-Day, the Education Act was sufficiently newsworthy for a newspaper to publish a cartoon with the caption 'Ragging the Head'. Rab was drawn standing in front of a blackboard on which was written '2+2=4' and 'C-A-T spells CAT in Anglican, Roman Catholic, Nonconformist and any other religion'. The presence of the cartoon on 17 January, when issues of world-shattering importance were taking place, illustrates how deeply Rab's educational reforms were cared about and discussed in Britain.[74]

As the war entered its final phase with the preparations for the Normandy Landings, speculation began as to who would succeed Churchill. It is interesting that Churchill was seen by many correspondents as strictly a wartime leader and there was a wide assumption that, even if the Conservatives were returned to power, a new Prime Minister

73 Trinity: RAB, G16.2.
74 Trinity: Butler Papers, RAB, G16.29. *Evening Standard*, 17 January 1944.

would enter Downing Street. *The Recorder* treated Eden as heir apparent, but touted Rab as an outside possibility: 'Here is a fine mind and an astute one … His drawback is that as a speaker he lacks passion … He has a political philosophy which goes deep, but his appeal is to the mind, not to the emotions.'[75]

Another newspaper published its odds for the succession. Interestingly, Eden was not mentioned and the odds were shown as:

2–1   Sir John Anderson
5–1   Oliver Stanley
10–1 Rab Butler
20–1 The Field

The article added the rider that after Rab's handling of the Education Bill in the Commons the odds against him might have shrunk to 7–1.[76]

This public awareness of educational reform and lionising of its architect helped the passage of the Bill through Parliament on 15 December 1943, when it had its First Reading, and during the two-day debate at its Second Reading in January 1944. On that occasion, Rab, confident that he had satisfied all financial objections from the Catholic community, raised his head to the distinguished Strangers' Gallery, where the new Archbishop of Westminster was watching the progress of the Bill, and mischievously quoted a stanza from the hymn 'God Moves in a Mysterious Way':

> Ye fearful saints, fresh courage take;
> The clouds ye so much dread
> Are big with mercy, and will break
> Fresh blessings on your head.[77]

Two weeks after the Second Reading, Rab addressed the 1922 Committee, the potentially hostile group of Tory backbenchers. Channon,

---

75 *The Recorder*, 19 February 1944; Trinity: Butler Papers, RAB, L7.1–2.
76 *The Record,* 4 March 1944; Trinity: Butler Papers, RAB, G16.85.
77 *Daily Telegraph,* 20 January 1944.

who had attended specially to hear Rab, was impressed by his 'shrewd speech', commenting that 'It has made him known to the country as a whole, and may well make him Prime Minister one day.'[78]

Headlam took quite the opposite view about Rab's future, recording that

> Rab Butler attended the [1922] Committee and talked about education. He spoke well but did not disclose much about his proposed bill – people however seemed quite pleased with what he said: he has a certain following in the House, but I have never heard anyone talk of him as a prospective leader ... there is more in him than there is in Anthony Eden – but unfortunately he has little or no glamour and perhaps, too, is a little too careful about making a false step. If you want to get to the top (and I believe Rab is ambitious) one has to take risks some time or other.[79]

All seemed set fair for the Bill to make its way through Committee, through its Third Reading and onto the Statute Book until, on 28 March, it suffered an unexpected reverse. Thelma Cazalet Keir, the Conservative Member for Islington East, moved an amendment that there should be no differentiation between men and women in teachers' pay awards. With an alliance of Tory reformers and Labour Members supporting the amendment, the National Government was defeated by 117 votes to 116. Rab had argued that it was not the business of the government to overturn the machinery employed by the teaching profession. When the defeat was announced, he slammed his papers into his briefcase and stormed out of the Chamber.

'The situation is serious', Channon recorded, 'and might herald the break-up of the coalition. I am so sorry for poor Rab.'[80] Rab himself was incorrectly reported as being prepared to offer his resignation to Churchill. But both he and Channon reckoned without the doughty determination of the Prime Minister, who was not going to see a good

---

78 Rhodes James, *Chips*, pp. 385–6. Diary entry for 2 February 1944.
79 Headlam, *Parliament and Politics in the Age of Churchill and Attlee*, diary entry for 17 March 1943, pp. 360–61.
80 Rhodes James, *Chips*, p. 390. Diary entry for 28 March 1944.

Bill founder. Survivor of periodic votes of confidence throughout the war, commenting that the Lord had delivered his enemies into his hands, he determined to 'rub the rebels' noses in their mess'.[81] On the following day, Churchill put down a Motion of Confidence; the government prevailed by a massive margin of 425–23. Rab had support from all sides of the House: Bevin threatened to resign if Rab's position was undermined; Ede stated his intention of resigning if Rab were forced out. The crisis was over; Churchill commented that to bring in the issue of equal pay for women was like putting an elephant into a perambulator, and the Bill went to its Third Reading.[82]

Churchill's personal identification with the successful passage of the Act was typically canny. Having been opposed to the introduction of any Bill that might divide the government in wartime, he had observed the attention that the Act was attracting and doubtless saw how such a reform would assist him to stay in office once the war was over. Hence the *volte-face* and the vigour with which he now helped Rab bring his proposals to fruition.

At the Third Reading, Members vied with each other to congratulate Rab and Ede. Towards the end of the debate, Sir Edward Campbell concluded his encomium with a tribute to Rab:

> We called the old Act the Fisher Act. How are we going to remember this Bill? Shall we not call it the Butler Act? ... I want to congratulate both the ministers, and I am perfectly sure that this Bill, which is now receiving its Third Reading, will be very successful and very useful to the country.[83]

Thus the 1944 Education Act became the Butler Act. Rab himself, while delighted with the renown and public recognition it brought him, was realistic in seeing the Bill as 'codifying existing practice, which always seems to me to be the hallmark of good legislation'.[84]

---

81 Butler, *The Art of the Possible*, p. 121.
82 Trinity: Butler Papers, RAB, G16.90.
83 Hansard, 12 May 1944, vol. 399, col. 2247.
84 Trinity: Butler Papers, RAB, G15, 37.

That is not undue modesty: the sonorous ideals – parity of opportunity, parity of esteem – indissolubly linked with his name had already been incorporated in the Green Book proposals prepared before he went to the Board of Education. The Bill itself, moreover, was crafted with a warier eye on the Tory backbenches than on the Labour Party.

The fact remains, however, that to Rab belongs the considerable kudos of having brought the Bill to pass. Determined that proposals for educational reform should not languish as they had in the past, he worked tirelessly to see them come to fruition. It was gratifying to be cast in the role of the one true Tory reformer at a time when reform was in the air. The right wing of his own party might view him as a milk-and-water Socialist but he had ceded enough to the right for the Bill to pass. He had also established himself across the country as a man of principle, a man to watch. And he had a visionary Bill associated with his name.

On 3 May, Churchill cabled Rab, 'Pray accept my congratulations. You have added a notable Act to the Statute Book and won a lasting place in the history of British Education'[85] and, on 10 August, when the Act received the Royal Assent, the Ministry of Education came into being with Rab as the first minister.[86] When the 'caretaker' government took over in 1945, Rab and Chuter Ede received a warm farewell from an educational journal:

> Educationalists generally will regret that the changes in the government preclude the continued association with the Ministry of Education of Mr R. A. Butler and Mr J. Chuter Ede. Their period of office has been one of the most notable in the history of British education.[87]

This sentiment was echoed on the following day when the magazine *Education* ran a headline 'EDUCATION'S SEVERE LOSS' and praised Rab as a 'powerful yet temperate minister'.[88] The teaching

---

85 Trinity: Butler Papers, RAB, G16.179.
86 Trinity: Butler Papers, RAB, G16.183.
87 *The Schoolmaster*, 31 May 1945; Trinity: Butler Papers, RAB, L6.4.
88 *Education*, 1 June 1945; Trinity: Butler Papers, RAB, L6.5.

profession generally tends to the left in politics. That Rab, a stout Conservative, should receive praise from two official mouthpieces of the profession is a remarkable tribute to his pertinacity and principles in piloting the Bill into law.

CHAPTER 10

RESHAPING THE CONSERVATIVE PARTY, 1945–51

O n 21 March 1943, the Prime Minister broadcast on the BBC, spelling out the government's general proposals for reform once Germany and Japan were defeated. It was a comprehensive agenda, at the centre of which was 'A Four-Year Plan for England'. After cautioning his audience that the war might drag on for longer than they thought and having fenced himself around with warnings that no government could 'bind themselves or their unknown successors … to particular schemes without relation to other extremely important aspects of our post-war needs', he moved first to the shape of the post-war world and, next, to the future of Britain.

Weaving together the strands of winning the war and creating a better Britain thereafter, Churchill associated the Conservative Party, and in particular himself, with long-standing attempts at social reform. He spoke of his 'friend Sir William Beveridge', declaring himself to have been 'lieutenant' to Lloyd George, the 'prime parent of all national insurance schemes'. From the perspective of the Labour Party, the Prime Minister was simply hijacking Labour proposals and, in an assumption that Greenwood described as 'staggering', suggesting that the coalition government would remain in power to implement them.

By the autumn of 1944, in Churchill's words as the end of the war was imminent, 'the odour of dissolution was in the air'.[1] It was clear that the coalition government was in its last session. There was talk of

---

1   Hansard, 31 October 1944, vol. 404, col. 667.

an election in July or an election in October. Rab, convinced that there was a strong case for maintaining the coalition at least until Japan surrendered, argued that time was needed to put the Conservative case to the electorate. Without support within the party hierarchy, however, Rab's advice was ignored. After a meeting at Downing Street, at which Rab had predicted that an early election would be a disaster, Beaverbrook told Rab, 'Young man, if you speak to the Prime Minister like that, you will not be offered a job in the next Conservative government.' 'That doesn't really affect me,' Rab replied, 'for if we have an early election, there is not going to be a Conservative government.'[2]

Rab's advice was met by pathological resistance of the diehards to any form of Socialism and the general conviction that the Prime Minister's prestige would suffice to attract support from a grateful electorate. Trading on his position as the personification of Britain's resistance to Hitler, Churchill projected Tory plans for reform as sensible and adequate, while suggesting that the Labour Party, impelled by dangerous doctrine, went beyond the pale. This was the substance of the manifesto that the Tories published, capitalising on Churchill's popularity and titled 'Mr Churchill's Declaration of Policy to the Electors'.

On 23 May, Churchill offered King George VI his resignation and, four hours later, at the King's invitation, formed a new 'caretaker' government. During the war, Ernest Bevin had served as Minister of Labour and National Service. With the break-up of the coalition, this post was now awarded to Rab. It was an important appointment, whose centrality was underscored in the manifesto, which said of the Four-Year Plan, 'Already a beginning has been made in carrying it out, and the Education Act for which our new Minister of Labour is greatly respected is already the law of the land.'

Doffing his cap to the Labour Party, Churchill noted that Rab would have the responsibility for implementing 'the demobilisation proposals … which Mr Bevin has elaborated with much wisdom'. The message was clear. Yes, the Labour Party comprised many well-intentioned

2 Butler, *The Art of the Possible*, pp. 126–7.

men such as Bevin, but so did the Tories. Just a few months ago Rab, the Minister of Education, had piloted a progressive Bill into law. A purple passage, including a deft thrust at Labour, described Rab's aims and achievements. The objective, he declared, was 'to provide education which will not produce a standardised or utility child, useful only as a cog in a nationalised and bureaucratic machine, but will enable the child to develop his or her responsible place, first in the world of school, and then as a citizen.' A Conservative government must aim 'to produce the good citizen of tomorrow. Technical education, at all levels, must be greatly extended and improved.' In summary: 'No system of education can be complete unless it heightens what is splendid and glorious in life and art. Art, science and learning are the means by which the life of the whole people can be beautified and enriched.'[3]

If the Conservative Party was going to fight an election on a platform of social reform, its poster child was to be Rab Butler, architect of the 1944 Butler Education Act. His prestige and his value to the Tories was greater than ever before.

In many respects – foreign policy, the United Nations, the need for domestic reform, the urgency of building new homes – the Conservative and Labour manifestos were remarkably similar. The principal doctrinal difference was over the issue of state control but, at root, the issue was a question of trust. Aneurin ('Nye') Bevan best captured the mood of the electorate with his book *Why Not Trust the Tories?*, published in 1944. The thrust of his attack was simple: as in 1918, so in 1945; the Tories would look after the wealthy. Voters should not fall for the sales talk. The overarching criticism of Tory policy that he posed was simple: 'Why should we trust you to do in the future what you would not use your power to do in the past?'[4]

The Labour cause was greatly aided – in what many observers considered the greatest blunder of the 1945 election – by Churchill's assertion that to elect a Labour government would be misguided because

---

3   Conservative Party 1945 election manifesto, para. 12, 'Education'.
4   Bevan, *Why Not Trust the Tories?* (London: Gollancz, 1944), Chapter 1, '1918. After the Armistice'.

a Socialist policy is abhorrent to British ideas of freedom … Socialism is inseparably interwoven with totalitarianism and the abject worship of the state … Socialism is in its essence an attack not only on British enterprise, but on the right of an ordinary man or woman to breathe freely without having a harsh, clumsy, tyrannical hand clapped across their mouth and nostrils. [Labour] would have to fall back on some kind of Gestapo, no doubt very humanely in the first instance.[5]

Despite his last-minute doubts during the post-war Potsdam Conference,[6] Churchill was confident that his prestige alone would suffice to win the election for the Tories. In listening to the blandishments of wartime cronies such as Beaverbrook, Bracken and Cherwell, he allowed himself to be deceived. Younger ministers – Rab and Macmillan, for example – had grave doubts about whether Churchill's wartime eminence would smoothly translate into a mandate to govern in peacetime. Even they, however, were astonished by the extent of the 1945 reversal. Labour gained 239 seats to gain a majority of 182 over the Tories. The first majority Labour government was voted into office in a massive rejection of Tory promises.

Since 1929, there had existed within the Conservative Party a shadowy group known as the Conservative Research Department (CRD). Founded during Baldwin's premiership, it was the brainchild of Neville Chamberlain and from 1937 to 1940 functioned to a great extent as Chamberlain's private office, supplying material for his speeches, vetting possible candidates for Parliament, acting as a 'think tank' for policy initiatives. When war broke out in 1939, the department was closed, and the director and many of his staff moved on to create the Films Division of the Ministry of Information. For the duration of the war, under a National Government, organisations devoted to partisan policy research were effectively disbanded in the interests of unified effort.

---

5   *The Listener*, 7 June 1945. This became a popular, if unworthy theme of the election. Bevin was so disgusted by the 'Gestapo' imputation that, when Rab arrived at the Ministry of Labour to take over from him, he refused to show him round, called for his hat, and walked out.

6   Lord Moran, *Churchill, Taken from the Diaries of Lord Moran* (Boston, MA: Houghton Mifflin, 1966) pp. 295, 297, Diary entries for 19 and 20 July 1945.

Nonetheless, both parties kept a watchful eye on trends that would affect policy after the war, and in July 1940 the Tory Party Chairman Sir Douglas Hacking approached Rab and requested him to handle research 'with a view to adjusting the Party's outlook to the radically different trends of thought which prevail at a time like this'.[7] Rab, a natural choice for the task, combined the intellectual ability and practical experience necessary to develop and employ an effective think tank. When Hitler invaded the Low Countries and France, however, there was little time for developing proposals for the post-war party, and it was not until the following year that Rab was able to spend time at the department.

In May 1941, the General Director of the party wrote to Rab, inviting him to chair 'a small, high-powered and representative committee … to examine the whole question of post-war policy'.[8] The efforts of the Post-War Problems Central Committee (PWPCC) were sporadic during the war and, in July 1943, Rab, fully occupied with his Education Bill, resigned. He was replaced by David Maxwell Fyfe, whose interests lay more in propaganda than policy.

In August 1944, the Third Reading of the Education Bill behind him, Rab returned to the chairmanship of the PWPCC. During this period, with limited resources, inadequate staff, and, above all, less than enthusiastic support from Churchill, whose interests were more in foreign policy and defence than domestic issues, the committee received little leadership from the top. Moreover, Churchill's intimates in government – Beaverbrook, Cherwell, Oliver Lyttelton – were viewed as his cronies rather than as sound party men.[9] The committee was treated as peripheral and was scarcely in a position to influence Tory policy. Only after the 1945 election did the Conservative Research Department regroup and begin the daunting task of re-establishing the Tory Party on solid foundations. Rab was promptly appointed chairman – a sound appointment from a public-relations perspective, as he, more than any other senior Conservative in Parliament, presented to

7   Ramsden, *The Making of Conservative Party Policy* (London: Longman, 1980), p. 96.
8   Ibid., p. 97.
9   Gilmour, *Whatever Happened to the Tories*, p. 14.

the public the image of moderate social reformer. His task, as he saw it, was not to 'lay down Party policy but ... [to] help to provide the necessary material on which long term policy could be based'.[10]

It was vital to his efforts that the CRD's product be acceptable both to forward-thinking party intellectuals and to the proponents of 'Old Toryism' who had so infuriated him over education. He turned to David Clarke to write *The Conservative Faith in the Modern Age* and to Quintin Hogg to write *The Case for Conservatism*.[11] Rab later wrote that 'These books were written at an early stage under the aegis of the Research Department so as to restore the whole faith and philosophy of the Conservative Party.'[12]

Rab's analysis of Churchill in 1946 is revealing. He distinguishes between 'the constructive part of his mind', which 'always dwelt more naturally on the international scene than on bread-and-butter politics', and 'his formidable powers of exposition and debate', which were employed in oratorical assaults on his opponents, rather than on positive policy.[13] It is as if the Prime Minister considered it rather vulgar to have to express why he and his party should be elected; as if the necessity to make reasons clear somehow invalidated the candidate. This, combined with the reluctance to outline policy as it gave his political opponents a target to shoot at, made him wary of any publicly expressed domestic philosophy or policy.

Rab, by contrast, was impressed by the efforts that the Labour Party had expended in propounding their policies. Herbert Morrison, Home Secretary in the wartime coalition, had been an active propagandist and, as Rab recorded in his autobiography, the results in 1945 were influential in convincing him that the Tories needed to adopt the same tactics if they were to capture the ideological high ground.[14] It was not enough simply to rant against nationalisation and to assume that the electorate would calmly agree. It had not been enough in 1945 for the Conservatives to invoke 'the living unity of the British people, which

---

10 Ramsden, *The Making of Conservative Party Policy*, p. 106.
11 Both were published in 1947.
12 CRD (N) File, 'Notes for Lord Butler's Memoirs', p. 13. Cited by Ramsden, op. cit., p. 108.
13 Butler, *The Art of the Possible*, p. 133.
14 Ibid., p. 129.

transcends class or party differences' and to declare that 'upon our power to retain unity, the future of this country and of the whole world largely depends'.[15] Splendid oratory that might have been. A reasonably intelligent audience, however, could be forgiven for pointing out both that it was not the case, and that they had heard such rhetoric throughout the six years of war.

For Rab, the natural starting point was to ask why his party had lost the election. Clement Attlee, asked a similar question, why Britons had rejected Churchill, replied simply, 'They didn't; they rejected the Tories.'[16] It was that simple truth – a truth Churchill was unable to accept – that Rab set out to reverse at the next election. In a speech in March 1946, he expressed his doubt that 'many independent electors without party affiliation voted for doctrinaire Socialism', speculating that 'many were misled because a positive alternative was not put before them with sufficient fervour'. 'That, he said, 'makes it all the more important today for us to preach what our faith really is'.[17]

The shift from propaganda to philosophy was precisely the kind of task for which Rab's academic mind was suited. In a memorandum prepared for one of the last meetings of the Post-War Problems Committee, eschewing doctrine in a vacuum, he set out the principles by which the department should operate and the methods by which it could be most effective.

The purpose of a party Research Department was entirely practical, he argued. Its function was to gather ideas from a number of sources, sift through them and deliver to the party leadership material that might be used in an election programme. The decision on what to use lay with the leadership; the responsibility of providing it lay with the Research Department. Initially the size of the staff would be limited, so the most reliable and thorough individuals were called for. Their role would be to sift ideas according to four criteria: congruence with

---

15 Conservative Party 1945 election manifesto, para 1.
16 Williams, *A Prime Minister Remembers* (London: Heinemann, 1961), pp. 8–9; Granada Historical Records, *Clem Attlee*, p. 27.
17 Speech of 30 March, 1946. Earl of Kilmuir, *Political Adventure: The Memoirs of the Earl of Kilmuir* (London: Weidenfeld & Nicolson, 1964), p. 161.

Conservative philosophy; practicality; acceptability by the party; relevance to a real need.[18]

Of the four criteria, the third was possibly the most testing; the Prime Minister himself had a marked aversion to fashioning detailed policy. 'When an opposition spells out its policy in detail,' he lectured Rab, 'the government becomes the opposition and attacks the opposition which becomes the government. So, having failed to win the sweets of office, it fails equally to enjoy the benefits of being out of office.'[19] To avoid spelling out policy in detail, however, resulted in a collection of abstracts – 'liberty with security; stability combined with progress; the maintenance of religion, the Crown and Parliamentary Government' – which Churchill mixed together when he spoke in Edinburgh in April 1946.[20]

This was precisely the kind of oratory that Rab was determined to avoid. His first task, as he saw it, was to assemble a team who would not be satisfied with high-flown generalities in nineteenth-century clothing, but who would bring an aggressively modern approach to Conservative philosophy, refashioning it to meet the needs of post-war Britain at least as well as the Labour Party.

Central to the revival of the CRD after the 1945 election was David Clarke, who had been involved in the department since 1935. When Ralph Assheton, the Party Chairman, requested Clarke to staff a separate Secretariat to prepare information and briefs for the Parliamentary Party, Clarke recruited three exceptional and widely divergent young men, each of whom nursed his own political ambitions: Reginald Maudling, Iain Macleod and Enoch Powell. Maudling, with a First in 'Greats' from Merton, assumed a cultivatedly languid, almost sybaritic air that concealed an acute grasp of philosophy and economics. Macleod, a graduate of Caius, Cambridge, was a collaborator in the

---

18 Butler, *The Art of the Possible*, pp. 138–9.

19 Ibid., p. 135.

20 Churchill's speech has been compared with the paean to imperialism sung by Disraeli, when he intoned that 'there is another and second great object of the Tory Party. If the first is to maintain the institutions of the country, the second is, in my opinion, to uphold the empire of England' in a speech at the Crystal Palace in 1872. Hoffman, *The Conservative Party in Opposition 1945–51* (London: MacGibbon & Kee, 1964), p. 140.

development of the Acol system of bridge bidding and, before the war, had played bridge professionally. Powell, a former Fellow of Trinity, Cambridge and Professor of Greek at the University of Sydney at the age of twenty-five, had ended the war as a 33-year-old brigadier. None of the trio was a conventional thinker; they had arrived at embracing Conservatism by different routes, but each believed passionately in the necessity for forward-thinking Tory government in post-war Britain.

For the CRD itself, Clarke sought members who had no ambitions to enter the Commons, as they would be most needed in the periods leading up to elections. His first recruits were Michael Fraser and Peter Goldman, a duo who, with Clarke, David Dear and Geoffrey Block, 'provided ... the Department's experience and continuity, the solid foundation of its research work over the next fifteen years and more'.[21]

Two further reforms were implemented after the 1945 election: the appointment of an Advisory Committee on Policy and Political Education (ACPPE), and the creation of the Conservative Political Centre (CPC). To the ACPPE, Rab recruited members among whom were 'some of the brighter people of the party', who 'have not been condemned to follow the narrow party track and would help us with a wider outlook'.[22] The CPC was designed to further political education in schools and colleges. To direct this body he recruited Cuthbert ('Cub') Alport, a fellow alumnus of Pembroke who, like Rab, had been President of the Cambridge Union. Rab and he saw the CPC as 'a kind of Conservative Fabian Society which would act as a mouthpiece for our best modern thought and attract that section of the post-war generation who required an intellectual basis for their political faith'.[23]

Rab's first goal, once his impressive team was assembled, was to get the party 'facing in the right direction before it made firm commitments'.[24] He was moved to action, however, by the mood at the 1946 party conference in Blackpool, at which the party leaders were pressed for more precise formulations of Conservative industrial policy. When

---

21 Ramsden, *The Making of Conservative Party Policy*, p. 105.
22 Ibid., p. 106.
23 Ibid., p. 107.
24 Gilmour, *Whatever Happened to the Tories*, p. 33.

an Industrial Policy Committee was formed, Rab was appointed its chairman, and a group that included three future Chancellors of the Exchequer and three future Cabinet ministers was assembled. Industrial policy was at the heart of the political debate in 1946, and this was reflected in the calibre of the group.[25]

Just as Rab had exceeded his brief in 1942, when he resolved to propose a full-scale Education Bill, so four years later did he raise the ante by transforming a policy statement into *The Industrial Charter*, a wholehearted attempt to reposition Tory policy in the social landscape of the post-war period. To achieve this, Rab recognised the importance of carrying both wings of the party and, as with the search for consensus over education, he oversaw exhaustive efforts to canvass the opinions of industrialists across the country. For a 'Charter' to be acceptable – and to become the basis of policy on which to fight an election – considerable weaving together of policy strands would be required. As a result, the document went through several drafts before the final version was complete. In this version, 'Butler's hand [was] clearly revealed in the wording.'[26]

The fundamental premise of *The Industrial Charter* was that the Tories had forfeited their position as the natural government of the moderate centre in wartime conditions and, rightly or wrongly, by the perceived indifference of the party to the economic crisis of the 1930s. The Charter should, therefore, state in unequivocal terms a policy that would recapture that moderate centre – the very group that Attlee was struggling not to alienate as he was urged to move further to the left.

At the same time, the Charter needed to gain acceptance across the entire Tory Party and, therefore, a certain amount of ritualistic Socialist-bashing was mandatory. In the context of the immediate post-war period, harking back to six years of co-operation, the final document was a masterpiece, a carefully crafted statement of Tory policy.

The first section of the charter draws the battle lines with clarity: 'We wish to substitute for the present paralysis, in which we are experiencing the worst of all worlds, a system of free enterprise, which

---

25 The future Chancellors were Rab, Macmillan and Derick Heathcoat-Amory; the future Cabinet ministers were Oliver Lyttelton, David Maxwell Fyfe and David Eccles.
26 Hoffman, *The Conservative Party in Opposition 1945–51*, p. 147.

is on terms with authority, and which reconciles the need for central direction with the encouragement of individual effort.'[27]

Having painted a picture of paralysis, the charter addresses four issues: economic values, the present crisis, the place of government in a free society and, in a cascade of Tory principles, the workers' charter. It is arranged, with a care that testifies to Rab's technique, in the manner of a symphony, four movements of different tempo, building to a resolution of discord, a reasoned conclusion.

The first movement is full of optimism as it enumerates the values that Conservatism holds dear: opportunity; the balance between tasks and rewards; assurance of steady employment; the status of individual personality; restoration of freedom of choice; confidence in the future; greater reward for greater responsibility; fair reward for initiative.

From the sunlit hilltop, the second movement passes to the Slough of Despond. In 1914, every person in Britain was owed about £100 by overseas debtors. Now each person owes overseas creditors the same sum. The malaise of 'Socialism' stalks the land, as 'the Socialist Chancellor has not kept the right balance between inflation and deflation', and the people suffer under 'the crushing level of expenditure by the Socialist Government'. Thus, referring to the Labour Party as the 'Socialists', Rab doffs his cap to the right wing of his own party.[28]

The third movement allows rays of light to penetrate the Stygian gloom of Socialism. There is a need for co-operation; controls must be removed, for 'Controls breed like rabbits'; the heavy weight of taxation which discourages extra effort, the expansion of enterprise, must be alleviated. As for nationalisation, it will not all be reversed. There will be selectivity, sensible caution.

The up-beat final movement trumpets the general rights championed by the Tories: security of employment; the incentive to do the job well and to get a better one; status as an individual, however big the firm or mechanical the job may be. Then, in a final favour handed to the Conservative right, the trumpet of Toryism is heard, as, 'We must

---

27 Conservative and Unionist Central Office, *The Industrial Charter*, p. 3.
28 Ibid., p. 9.

bring back into large-scale industry the personal contact and interest at present found most strongly in the small firm.'[29]

Rab later recalled that 'Peel's Tamworth Manifesto made a rallying point for Conservatism in much the same way as our Charters made a rallying point. And I was definitely aware of the need to copy the Tamworth Manifesto not in its content which was dated but in the type of document it was.'[30] At first sight grandiloquent, Rab's comparison has more than an element of truth. Had the Tories not attempted in 1947 to adapt to conditions not greatly different from those of 1834, the position of the Labour Party, guided by Attlee and Bevin to centre left, would very possibly have been solidified for a decade.

The Charter was released on 11 May to a generally positive reception. Predictably, it was criticised by *Tribune* in an article that gleefully predicted that before the year was out the Butler Charter would split the Tory Party as it had not been divided for half a century. From the right wing there was the equally predictable reaction that it had not gone far enough, that it was a compromise – and, therefore, might achieve the same result. *The Times* took a broad view of the Charter in the context of the role of the opposition:

> This statement is the first and indispensable step in the Conservative campaign to establish the national alternative. It is only a beginning ... The statement is in a sense the first contemporary essay of the Conservative Party in the art and science of Opposition outside of Parliament. It is urbane in manner and humane in tone. If it occasionally seems to take a somewhat rosy view of the consequences of its proposals, without insisting too much on the sterner realities which will face this country in any event, that is the way of Oppositions. Labour was certainly no exception in the past.

The article commended the Charter for not 'setting out to jettison present policies with all speed' and, instead, seeking 'to make them more efficient, more economical and much less restrictive'. On the

---

29 Ibid., pp. 28–33.
30 CRD (N) File, 'Notes for Lord Butler's Memoirs', p. 13. Cited by Ramsden, op. cit., p. 112.

question of 'fair shares', which had served the Labour Party well in 1945, it noted that 'The Conservative Opposition does not deny fair shares but insists upon individual opportunity and incentive; the stress is upon liberty.' Since the Conservatives accepted 'the present range of social services, the special place of trade unions in the community, and the responsibility of the state for providing the conditions of high and stable employment', even though the emphasis was different, the Charter contained eminently equitable proposals. Indeed, the article added, 'There is no item in this part of the programme which any politician in any party would oppose. This is as it should be.'[31]

In spite of an apparently enthusiastic response from Churchill, who placed Rab at his right at a shadow Cabinet dinner at the Savoy, the former Prime Minister gave no public endorsement to the Charter until after its publication. At that point he offered a somewhat Delphic endorsement, approving the spirit of 'honest and progressive realism' in which it had been written, and referring to it as 'a broad statement of policy to which those who are opposed to the spread of rigid socialism can now rally'. It was left to the party conference at Brighton in October to adopt the Charter as party policy. Even then, as Reggie Maudling later recalled,

> I was working for Winston on his concluding speech to the conference and we came to the topic of the Industrial Charter. 'Give me five lines, Maudling', he said, 'explaining what the Industrial Charter says.' This I did. He read it with care, and then said, 'But I do not agree with a word of this.' 'Well, sir,' I said, 'this is what the conference adopted.' 'Oh well', he said, 'leave it in', and he duly read it out in the course of his speech, with the calculated coolness which he always accorded to those passages, rare as they were, which had been drafted by other people, before he went back to the real meat of his own dictation.[32]

When the Charter was overwhelmingly adopted by the conference delegates, Churchill, his fears of a party schism overcome, summoned

---

31 *The Times*, 12 May 1947.
32 Maudling, *Memoirs* (London: Sidgwick & Jackson, 1978), pp. 45–6.

Rab and Sydney to his hotel suite, where he congratulated Rab warmly and called for quantities of Pol Roger.[33] For Rab, the adoption of the Charter was a signal success. He could now with some confidence maintain that he had the Tory Party 'facing in the right direction' and that he had created the precedent for future policy statements. As Macmillan summarised the document, 'The Socialists are afraid of it; Lord Beaverbrook dislikes it; and the Liberals say it is too liberal to be fair. What more could one want? Was ever a child born under such a lucky star?'[34]

Between May 1947 and March 1949, the CRD released six more publications, which Rab in his memoirs refers to collectively as 'The Charters'.[35] The culmination of this process was the publication in July 1949 of *The Right Road for Britain*, a document that evolved as the basis for the Conservative manifesto when Attlee called an election for February 1950. Rab notes that 'none of these statements was attended by the political excitements of *The Industrial Charter* or can be said to have achieved a comparable impact. But they had a cumulative effect in robbing the Labour Party of its favourite parrot-cry, namely that the Conservatives had no policy.'[36] For that reason alone, to appreciate the impact of Rab's tenure at the CRD, it is worthwhile to examine briefly the nature and content of the publications.

The Industrial Charter was more than a fair deal for factory workers; it was aimed at a far broader constituency. This was less true of the succeeding publications, each of which had a smaller and more specific target audience. In April 1948, David Maxwell Fyfe published his essay *Monopolies*, not, as might be expected from the title, an attack on private monopolies, but an indictment of state ownership, of 'natural' monopolies created by the government. 'The Socialists', he wrote, 'have created new monopolies each so vast and so bureaucratic an

---

33 Butler, *The Art of the Possible*, pp. 148–9. Pol Roger was Churchill's favourite champagne from the first time he tasted it in 1908. To this day he is commemorated by the producers who name their best quality champagne *Cuvée Sir Winston Churchill*.

34 In a speech at Church House, Westminster, 14 June 1947.

35 These, together with *The Industrial Charter* and *The Right Road for Britain*, were bound together and issued by the CRD as a book with the grandiose title *Return to Greatness*.

36 Butler, *The Art of the Possible*, p. 149.

organisation that they have not only reproduced on an enormous scale the dangers of monopolies of all kinds but have passed beyond the limits within which sound and efficient administration is practicable.'[37]

In June 1948, *The Agricultural Charter* was released. Using the same research procedures as *The Industrial Charter*, this was a comprehensive work that stressed Britain's need to feed the population and to reduce dependence on imported foods. This was of vital importance, the Charter stated:

> We are determined to bring home to the overcrowded population of our islands the grave danger of real food shortages, which might well lead in times of emergency to the risk of starvation. That is why we are resolved to give home agricultural production the highest priority, and to introduce a sense of urgency, of continuity and of certainty into policy.[38]

The Labour government, Rab charged, failed to grasp this urgency and were instead pursuing a policy of appropriating land for new towns. There must be safeguards against a rapacious government. There must also be an agricultural workers' charter. This would guarantee three general rights:

- Status as an independent individual;
- Incentive to do the job well and opportunity for advancement;
- Security of employment.[39]

In February 1949 came *The Conservative Policy for Wales and Monmouthshire*, written almost entirely by Enoch Powell and published simultaneously in Welsh. This urged the creation of a Cabinet post, a Minister for Wales, together with radical improvements to roads, water, electricity and housing.[40] In the same month appeared *A True Balance*, a report on 'Women's Questions', delivered to the Conserva-

---

37 Conservative Political Centre, *Monopolies*, April 1948.
38 Conservative and Unionist Central Office, *The Agricultural Charter*, p. 5.
39 Ibid., p. 22.
40 Conservative and Unionist Central Office, *The Conservative Policy for Wales and Monmouthshire*, February 1949, pp. 11–12.

tive and Unionist Women's annual conference, but aimed at a far wider audience. Underlying the publication was Rab's conviction that, while the majority of manual workers saw Labour as the working man's party, that was less true of working women.[41] A targeted appeal to women might produce positive results in the privacy of the ballot box.

The freedoms proposed for women seem archaically quaint to the modern reader – that Breach of Promise laws should be abolished; that a woman had a right to know her husband's income; that women might be admitted to sit in the House of Lords – but these were considered radical proposals in 1948. Once again the Labour Party came in for criticism: the Conservative Party believed that people should be able to choose whether to own or rent their homes, whereas 'the Socialist policy was precisely the opposite'.[42]

Two other publications rounded out the series: *Essays in Conservatism* in March and *Imperial Policy* in June. In two years Rab had co-ordinated statements of policy, carefully chosen for their appeal to a segment of the electorate, each of which painted the Labour government in the worst possible colours. In their approach to state ownership they were creating far worse monoliths than Capitalism; in agriculture they were too busy with their policy of new towns to recognise the real danger of starvation; the shameful condition of unrepresented Wales did not concern them; the oppressed role of women was more evident to Conservatives than to Socialists. In each case a large section of the electorate would, it was hoped, be attracted by the Tories' humanity, set in stark contrast to the unfeeling bureaucracy of Socialism. At no point, it is true, did the word 'Gestapo' reappear, but the suggestion of rigid totalitarianism was a permanent backcloth.

The timing of the offensive was fortuitous. The austerity imposed by the Labour government – 'fish and Cripps' in the memorable phrase of Harold Macmillan[43] – had become oppressive, and there seemed no end to economic gloom and increasing state control. Churchill

---

41 A point made by Ross McKibbin, 'Labour Vanishes', *London Review of Books*, 20 November 2014.
42 Conservative and Unionist Central Office, *A True Balance*, February 1949, p. 7.
43 Macmillan, *Tides of Fortune*, p. 167.

crowed that 'the complete failure of nationalisation is apparent … the experiment has cost us dear'.[44]

The build-up to the publication of *The Right Road for Britain* was masterly. The CRD pamphlets were, to some extent, 'preaching to the choir', but they were aimed at precisely the centrist voter that the Tories felt they had lost in 1945. Successively, farmers, women, the Welsh, imperialist patriots and intellectuals had been appealed to; an olive branch, moreover, had been extended to the right wing of the party, to Sir Waldron Smithers, for example, the Member for Orpington who had described Rab as 'pink'. Smithers might be, in the words of John Boyd-Carpenter, 'an extreme Tory out of a vanished age',[45] but he was by no means the only Tory who saw in Rab's policy statements a dramatic and dangerous shift to the left. Rab went a considerable distance towards placing the party 'on the fairway of modern economic and political thought'.[46]

By 1949, with an election certain before July 1950, Rab and his team at the Conservative Research Department had set the stage for a comprehensive paper that would evolve into the manifesto in that election. From his original posture of resistance to any declaration of policy, Churchill, greatly appreciative of the repeated attacks on 'the Socialists', entered the production of the master document with gusto. *The Right Road for Britain* engaged him enough for him to write a brief Ciceronian foreword.

The premise of the manifesto was that 'Britain stands at the crisis of her history'. After two world wars she needed to 'find in the second half of the twentieth century an assured foundation for those spiritual qualities and that national well-being which are now imperilled'. The country needed 'firm faith and practical policy to match the stern tests of the hour'.[47]

---

44 Randolph Churchill, *Europe Unite* (London: Cassell, 1950), pp. 343–5. See Gilmour, *Whatever Happened to the Tories*, p. 35.

45 Boyd-Carpenter, *Way of Life: The Memoirs of John Boyd-Carpenter* (London: Sidgwick & Jackson, 1980), p. 79.

46 Letter from Rab to Lord Woolton, 7 March 1949. Ramsden, *The Making of Conservative Party Policy*, p. 134.

47 Conservative and Unionist Central Office, *The Right Road for Britain*, July 1949, pp. 6–7.

Having laid out the issues facing Britain, the paper states baldly that the Labour Party had failed, that 'it is trying to create a completely Socialist Britain' and that 'If present policies are pursued to their logical conclusion, property with its rights and duties will be destroyed, management will be left without initiative, the trades unions will cease to be independent and local government will become a rubber stamp.'[48]

This apocalyptic outcome could be avoided, the booklet argued, if Britons could return to the unselfish atmosphere of wartime and become once more 'a family of free and energetic individuals helping one another in misfortune, spiritually alive, rich in the infinite variety of social organisms and communities … Thus, inspired by our glorious history, shall we create a national solidarity which binds us all together.'[49] That this was a virtual election manifesto was shown in the conclusion to that section that distinguished between 'the Socialist illusion' and the practical nature of Conservative belief. The stark implications of the choice were laid out in terms that showcased Rab's cerebral approach and Churchillian oratory. In one dynamic paragraph, the paper contrasted a paradise of freedom and personal choice with a purgatory of oppressive government, social conflict, multiplied restraints and the enslavement of the workforce to national monopolies.

This virtuoso performance was followed by specific policies, stressing the security of the individual, the Conservative Party's support for the Trades Union movement, its rational approach to nationalisation – that the Tories would denationalise where practical but maintain state ownership where it was more efficient.[50] After a reprise of the principal tenets of *The Agricultural Charter* and *A True Balance*, the paper proceeded to appropriate most of Labour's social service policy as its own. Adding to those promises a rousing section on Conservative housing policy, and adducing the 1944 Education Act as proof of its *bona fides*, Rab raised the spectre of Communism and Britain's role as a world leader. After a paean of praise for the Commonwealth, Rab returned to

48 Ibid., p. 8.
49 Ibid., pp. 9–10.
50 Ibid., pp. 23–6.

the spiritual nature of the challenge. 'What Britain needs', he wrote, 'is not only a new Government but a new spirit to meet the crisis of her own destiny. Above all she needs a new vision of the dignity and value of human life.'[51] For good measure, at Churchill's suggestion, an appendix was added, three pages listing 'Our Contributions to the Social Services, 1918–1945'.[52]

The production of the book had harnessed most of the resources of the CRD. An original draft had been prepared by Quintin Hogg; this, reading more like a personal statement than a policy document, was substantially revised by Rab's staff. The proposed alterations prompted Hogg to write to Rab,

> *My poor Rab,*
>
> *Your friends are beyond human aid ... They may be tigers at policy; but the language in which they frame their thoughts is, unfortunately, not the English tongue of our forefathers, and when they write in their queer, pidgin-English jargon, they make no real effort to maintain a coherent or even intelligible argument.*[53]

Rab sought to pacify Hogg without, as Hogg had advised, 'starting again with a clean sheet'. He succeeded in this conciliatory move and himself concentrated on raising the literary standard of the second draft to meet Hogg's standards, an achievement that Hogg acknowledged gracefully. With considerable pride, Rab was able to circulate the final draft to a wide group of senior Tories and, when the book was released on 23 July, it was Rab and his young triumvirate – Powell, Maudling and Macleod – that were credited with its development. In a speech at Wolverhampton, Churchill himself paid tribute. 'Great pains and care have been bestowed on this work by many of my colleagues in the Opposition', he began, 'and by none more than Mr Butler, who has rendered distinguished service, not only to his party, but to his country.'[54]

---

51 Ibid., p. 65.
52 Ibid., pp. 66–8.
53 Ramsden, *The Making of Conservative Party Policy*, p. 137.
54 Butler, *The Art of the Possible*, pp. 151–2.

In the four years since the 1945 election, Rab had added substantially to his reputation. Already marked as a rising star in 1944, by 1949 he had become a force within the party and on 23 July 1949 a massive Conservative rally was held at Stanstead Hall, Rab and Sydney's grand seat in Essex. Five thousand of the Tory faithful attended; Macmillan was the principal speaker.[55]

This ascendancy was underlined by the Canadian political journalist Beverley Baxter, who wrote short sketches of aspiring Tory leaders before the 1949 party conference in Llandudno. Of Rab he wrote:

> Now let the trumpets be muted for we are going to meet the 'Brain' of the party … One of Butler's assets is that he always knows what he's going to say next; one of his liabilities is that he shows it. If only like a good actor he would grope for a word or, with a flash of genius, summon a brilliant phrase from the hinterland of his mind, then would the ranks of Tuscany cheer … His influence in the Party is steadily mounting … Rab does not curry popularity within the Party, perhaps because he has the English quality of shyness.[56]

Less gushing was French reaction to a speech that Rab made in Paris, saying that from the Anglo-French point of view the Atlantic Pact was a transformation of the *Entente Cordiale* into an almost global pact. The notion received a poor reception in France as *Humanité* commented:

> Bref, ce que cet honorable gentleman propose à la veille de la Conférence du Commonwealth britannique … c'est que le peuple de France donne son sang, non plus seulement pour les colonialistes français, mais pour les colonialistes anglais dans le monde.[57]

---

55 Trinity: Butler Papers, RAB, G21.53.
56 *Daily Express*, 5 October 1949; Trinity: Butler Papers, RAB, G21.75.
57 'In short, what this honourable gentleman is proposing on the eve of the British Commonwealth Conference is that the French people give their blood not only for French colonials but for English colonials around the world.' *Humanité*, 9 April 1949; Trinity: Butler Papers, RAB, L17.6ff.

Illustrative of Rab's popularity with the electorate, but guaranteed to raise hackles on the right of the party, was a profile of Rab by Everett Lawson in the *New York Times* magazine in July, describing Rab as

> a sort of young ghost, haunting the right-wing scene, who might easily – by the special sorcery of the intellectual – slip into the running as Conservative Party leader. Butler stands high in Lord Beaverbrook's list of leaders who should not be tolerated at any price, but this is the biggest single brain now changing the face of the Conservative Party ... Butler dreams of a world in which worker, employer, saint, intellectual and capitalist would all join in one synthetic brotherhood, sustained by the humanities and a will to work together for the common good.[58]

Rab must have hoped that not too many knights of the shires read the *New York Times* as the idealistic notion expressed by Lawson would have provoked anti-Socialist apoplexy.

At all events, Rab had succeeded in creating a comprehensive and coherent Conservative policy. He had achieved this in the teeth of fundamental opposition from Churchill – and later from the Chairman of the Party, Lord Woolton, whose relations with Rab became increasingly prickly – and had established himself as the principal arbiter – if not architect – of Conservative policy on which the critical election of 1950 would be fought.

Woolton was not alone in his suspicions of Rab. Older members of the party shared a fundamental distrust of policy and planning, which they regarded as a Socialist vice, and of Rab's reputation as an 'egghead'. Headlam, *doyen* of the old guard, had watched Rab's rise with distaste since 1945, and by 1947 was actively persuading himself that the party could not be led from the left. 'He [Rab] is quite certain that he is one of our leading lights', he recorded, 'and has been successful, so far, in making other people think the same of him,' commenting that

> *He is ambitious and means to be the leader sooner or later. He may be*

– everything is possible in politics – but he never strikes me as having much
personality or go – he is a don and an intellectual – not, I fancy, the type of
man who could inspire a crowd – and so long as 'safety first' is his guiding
principle it is difficult to see him leading a party effectively.[59]

James Reid, the former Solicitor-General for Scotland, shared Headlam's view. Like Headlam, he ranked Oliver Stanley as the most tal-
ented of the younger aspirants and 'as possessing the best brain of the
lot, but does not regard him as a leader – nor does he regard RAB and
Harold Macmillan as possible leaders'.[60]

When there was a debate in the House on the American Aid and
European Payments Bill, Headlam remarked sourly in his diary that
'R. A. Butler (who apparently is a financial expert as well as an expert
on everything else) opened for us.'[61] He maintained his instinctive
antipathy to Rab and distrust of his shaping of policy, commenting
later that year, when the final draft of policy was released: 'I attended a
meeting of northern candidates called to consider Mr Butler's declaration of policy – "The Right Road for Britain" is, if I remember correctly,
the title of this rather tepid little production.'[62]

Nonetheless, in the teeth of visceral opposition from the right, the
stated policy of 1949 was fashioned into a practical and realisable set
of election commitments, a process complicated by the involvement of
Churchill. He, with the whiff of combat at last in the air, insisted on
being involved at every stage of the crafting of the manifesto. Attlee
might distinguish between rejection of the Tories and rejection of
Churchill, but Churchill himself drew no such distinction. He had
been cast out of Downing Street in 1945; he would begin the next
decade as he had begun the last – recalled from the outer darkness to
save Britain once more.

So engaged did Churchill become in the writing of the manifesto,
so combative in his desire to lambast Attlee's government for real and

59 Headlam, *Parliament and Politics in the Age of Churchill and Attlee*, diary entry for 12 February
    1947, p. 487.
60 Ibid., diary entry for 21 September 1947, pp. 521–2.
61 Ibid., diary entry for 27 January 1949, pp. 569–70.
62 Ibid., diary entry for 8 August 1949, p. 599.

perceived iniquity, that Rab eventually protested that, if he were to write one half and Churchill write the other half, the result would be laughable. Eventually Churchill accepted this and restricted his efforts to a modest degree of editing.[63]

The resulting document was a spirited assault on the policies of the Labour Party, delivered with the air of tolerant patience that was now exhausted. Like a parent reining in a wayward child, the Tories reproved the government and accused them of a series of dishonesties. Phrases such as 'they pretended', 'they tried to make out', 'they spread the tale' suggested incompetence overlaid with deception.[64] The accusations built to a simple conclusion:

> During these bleak years Britain has lurched from crisis to crisis and from makeshift to makeshift. Whatever temporary expedients have been used to create a false sense of wellbeing, none has effected a permanent cure. Devaluation is not the last crisis nor have we seen the worst of it yet.[65]

As the election approached, all polls predicted a close result, some putting Labour slightly ahead, some predicting a narrow Conservative victory. In the event, Labour won 46 per cent of the popular vote against 43 per cent for the Tories. Redistribution of constituencies, however, favoured the Tories and they gained ninety seats, leaving the embattled Labour Party with a majority of just five seats. It was not the victory that Churchill had wished for, but it was a significant result nonetheless. As Rab concluded his record of events, 'We produced our policy of enterprise without selfishness. The party had come a long way since 1945.'[66] What Rab modestly omitted to note was that he too had come a long way in those years. The disregarded Chamberlainite shunted to the Board of Education in 1941 had come to personify the caring face

---

63 Butler, *The Art of the Possible*, pp. 152–3. Rab's delightful description of 'policy making with WSC' is preserved in CRD archives and is reproduced in full in Ramsden, *The Making of Conservative Party Policy*, pp. 146–7.
64 *This is the Road*, Conservative and Unionist Party's 1950 Manifesto, paras 6–9.
65 The Labour government had devalued the pound from $4.03 to $2.80 on 19 September 1949.
66 Butler, *The Art of the Possible*, p. 153.

of Toryism in 1944. Over the following six years, he had strengthened his claim to oversee party policy and had established himself in the Tory hierarchy. It seemed inevitable that the government would soon be brought down and that, when that happened, Rab would reap his due reward – a Cabinet seat, perhaps one of the Great Offices of State.

Over the following months, the government ran out of steam. Its Cabinet of old men, many of whom had been under unrelenting pressure since the formation of the coalition in 1940, was further weakened by the death of Ernie Bevin and the ill health of Stafford Cripps.[67] Rivalry between Bevan and Hugh Gaitskell, the outbreak of the Korean War and the government's reaction, the rift between Attlee and Bevan, and finally the violent confrontation between Bevan and Gaitskell over National Health Service charges – which led to the resignation of Bevan and two other ministers – left the Labour Party in ragged disarray. For the most honourable motives but with faulty political acumen, Attlee called an election for October 1951.

Immediately after the 1950 election, Churchill had discerned the possibility of an effective Liberal collapse if another election were to be held in the near future. With under 10 per cent of the popular vote and a mere nine seats, it was unlikely that they would be able to field many candidates in the next election. Accordingly, he suggested to Rab that a study be made of areas where Conservative and Liberal policy overlapped. The purpose, simply, was to find ways in which the Tories could present themselves as more palatable to Liberals than the Labour Party in constituencies where a Liberal candidate did not stand. The principal Liberal *desideratum* was proportional representation, and Rab even went so far as to suggest that some proposals to accommodate this might appear in the next manifesto. This suggestion, anathema to right-wing Tories, ran into serious objections and was shelved before the writing of the manifesto. Churchill's instincts, however, had been correct; in 1951, the Liberal vote shrank to 2.5 per cent of the turnout, a mere 730,000 votes, from which slippage the Conservatives were the beneficiaries.

---

67 Ernest Bevin died on 14 April 1951; Sir Stafford Cripps died on 21 April 1952.

After producing two major policy statements in as many years, Rab saw the need to restate Conservative policy in 1951, but no need to rethink it. Some form of statement would be needed for the party conference in October and this was formulated in *Britain Strong and Free*, on whose drafts was invariably stamped, 'This is not an election programme'. Two new proposals were introduced: a commitment to build 300,000 homes a year and the decision to impose some form of Excess Profits Tax to operate for the duration of the Korean War. The manifesto including both these proposals was in production when, on 19 September, Attlee called an election for 25 October. At this point Churchill intervened, informing Rab that he would prepare a manifesto himself.

The resultant document was pure Churchill. In a little more than 2,500 words he spelled out Conservative proposals with succinct directness. The party might have benefited greatly from having a Research Department, but when the whiff of cordite was in the air, it was Churchill who would lead the charge. As at Omdurman in 1898, so in the election fifty-three years later, the hoofbeats of the cavalry intoxicated Churchill. The 1951 manifesto owed much to Rab's handling of the Research Department since 1945; it owed nothing to him for its drafting. As *Reynolds News* pointed out, 'When it comes to deciding policy there is no nonsense about democracy in the Tory Party.'[68]

The 1951 election added a postscript to that of the previous year, which Churchill had rightly termed 'a momentous election'. In 1950, the Labour Party lost the enormous majority that had brought it to power in 1945; a year later it lost control of the Commons, as the Tories edged past them with a small but workable majority of twenty-six. The demise of the first majority Labour government ushered in thirteen years of Tory rule. Two young Tories of the 1920s – Rab Butler and Harold Macmillan – had contributed greatly to that victory and each was to hold important offices throughout the next thirteen years.

In the late 1940s, during their time in opposition, Macmillan and Rab had become allies as reformers. Rab had succeeded in banishing

---

68 Cited by Ramsden, op. cit., p. 161.

the unwelcome label of 'appeaser' – at least, in the public perception – and had established himself as a forward-thinking domestic reformer on the liberal fringe of the Tory Party with the goal of maintaining and improving Labour's social services, while restoring Britain's economic situation. When the Tories returned to power he enjoyed a considerable lead over Macmillan, a junior partner in social reform.

No one could have predicted in 1951 how their interrelated fortunes would shift and eddy in the next decade.

CHAPTER 11

THE SPECTRE OF MR BUTSKELL, 1951–55

In 1950, the leading three figures in the Tory hierarchy were Churchill, Eden and Oliver Stanley. Stanley, whose ministerial career had begun in 1924, had an independent mind, was not afraid of crossing swords with Churchill, and had worked with Rab on the committee that produced *The Industrial Charter*. Rab described him as 'the acutest brain on the Conservative front bench'.[1] As Chairman of the Conservative Finance Committee, he was the obvious choice to become Chancellor of the Exchequer in a Tory Cabinet. During 1950, however, his health declined and he died on 10 December.

According to Piers Dixon,[2] Rab was confident in late 1950 that he would be appointed Chancellor,[3] believing his only rival to be Oliver Lyttelton. Macmillan confidently expected Lyttelton to go to the Exchequer, and was disappointed with the choice of Rab. 'Before the war I did not know Butler at all', he wrote, 'and certainly was out of sympathy with his views. For he was Under-Secretary at the Foreign Office in the most ignoble period of our history since the days of Charles I and the Treaty of Dover.'[4] Gaitskell speculated that Rab was given the job either because Lyttelton was 'a racketeer' or because Churchill, knowing the job would be intolerable, gave it to Rab, 'whom he dislikes very much'.[5]

---

1 Butler, *The Art of the Possible*, p. 144.
2 Son of the diplomat Sir Pierson ('Bob') Dixon, UK Permanent Representative at the United Nations during the 1956 Suez Crisis.
3 Seldon, *Churchill's Indian Summer* (London: Hodder & Stoughton, 1981), p. 555, note 15.
4 Macmillan, *Tides of Fortune*, p. 497.
5 Williams, *The Diary of Hugh Gaitskell*, entry for 23 November 1951, p. 306.

Eden objected to Lyttelton on the grounds that the appointment would create an unfortunate impression.[6] Thus, in the account of Lord Woolton, no fan of Rab, Churchill 'fell back on Butler'.[7] Rab was summoned to Churchill's home at Hyde Park Gate, where 'Winston was lying in bed puffing a large cigar'. He expressed the appropriate surprise at the offer of the Treasury, which, Churchill said, 'Anthony and I think … had better be with you.'[8]

The 1951 election returned the Tories with a small majority but their percentage of the overall vote remained smaller than that of the Labour Party. Churchill needed, therefore, to present his new Cabinet as attuned to the post-war world, fundamentally different from the image of 'uncaring' Tories of the 1930s. Rab was central to that strategy. As author of the 1944 Education Act, he represented modernity and the breaking down, through education, of outmoded social barriers. He was also the only member of the new Cabinet who had been born after 1900. In a Cabinet largely composed of Churchill's wartime buddies, he played an important role.

Nonetheless, Churchill wanted to be certain that Rab played with his team. Liberal views were all very well in the shop window as long as they stayed there. In the opinion of Churchill's doctor Lord Moran, the Prime Minister was ageing and 'struggling with economic problems … quite beyond his ken'.[9] Macmillan was more critical, writing that 'in reality his general views on economic affairs had not substantially changed from those he had absorbed from his Victorian upbringing. While he was always ready to study new ideas … he was not capable or desirous of initiating new concepts of financial, monetary or economic policy.'[10] Such concepts were simply not of concern to Churchill; he remained in office until his eightieth birthday with the goal of brokering a tripartite treaty between the USA, the Soviet Union and Britain, achieving a lasting peace and winning a Nobel Peace Prize. Both he and Eisenhower, architects of victory in the

---

6   Macmillan, *Tides of Fortune*, pp. 154–5.
7   Bodleian: MS Woolton 3. Diary entry for 22 December 1955.
8   Butler, *The Art of the Possible*, p. 156; Howard, *RAB*, p. 178.
9   Moran, *Churchill, Taken from the Diaries of Lord Moran*, Entry for 30 December 1951, p. 374.
10 Macmillan, *Tides of Fortune*, p. 45.

Second World War, wanted their legacy to be one of lasting peace. The most important offices, central to achieving that goal, were the Foreign Office and Ministry of Defence, both of which were headed by wartime colleagues – Eden at the Foreign Office and, from 1952, Field Marshal Alexander at Defence.

The role of the Chancellor, moreover, had been significantly broadened since 1929 when Churchill was at the Treasury, most recently by Clement Attlee in September 1947. On that occasion, Attlee offered Stafford Cripps the job of 'super-Chancellor', incorporating the role of Minister for Economic Affairs, in order to forestall a *coup* by Cripps and Morrison. Churchill recognised that if he were successfully to fence Rab in, he needed to place an ally at the Treasury.

His first thought was to use Sir John Anderson for the task. Appointed Chancellor both in 1943 and in Churchill's 1945 caretaker government, Anderson was a brilliant administrator, widely respected in Whitehall and 'serenely possessed of the Roman virtue of *gravitas*, a natural moral power exuding from him in the shape of visible dignity and authority'.[11] Twenty years older than Rab, he was not a candidate for the Chancellorship, but could be effectively employed by Churchill to ensure that Rab stayed on the straight and narrow. He accordingly offered Anderson the role of an 'overlord' Minister to the Treasury, Board of Trade and Ministry of Supply, the appointment to be accompanied by a peerage. Anderson accepted the peerage, becoming Viscount Waverley, but declined the post.[12]

Churchill's solution was to appoint Sir Arthur Salter Minister of State for Economic Affairs, explaining to Rab that 'I am going to appoint the best economist since Jesus Christ to help you.' Rab, fully aware of Churchill's intentions, commented wryly in his memoirs that 'Arthur, a very nice man with a record of progressive thought but very many years my senior,[13] was accordingly provided with a high-ranking ministerial title and for thirteen months wrote me numberless

---

11   Wheeler-Bennett, *John Anderson, Viscount Waverley* (London: Macmillan, 1962), p. 384.
12   Ibid., pp. 351–3.
13   Born in 1881, Salter was twenty-one years older than Rab and older than every Cabinet member except Churchill himself.

minutes in green ink with which I did not always agree.'[14] To reinforce the stockade around the Chancellor, Churchill created the Treasury Ministerial Advisory Committee, to which he appointed Lord Cherwell, his most loyal lieutenant in wartime. Cherwell leaned heavily to the right wing of the party and had, with some reluctance, joined the Cabinet as Paymaster General, the position that he had occupied from 1942 to 1945. Curiously, Rab and Sydney continued to live in their house at 3 Smith Square and allowed Cherwell to move into 11 Downing Street, the traditional residence of the Chancellor. This enhanced the impression that he, not Rab, was the minister on hand to offer economic advice to his next-door neighbour. Undeterred by these imposed constraints, Rab, now fifth in the party hierarchy, set about establishing his position with the Treasury officials.

Among the many congratulations that Rab received was a touching note from Leo Amery. 'It seems only the other day', he wrote, 'that you came to confide in me your desire to enter politics and your resolve to qualify for that task by travelling around the Empire. You have arrived, just in time I hope, to save that Empire's financial system from complete disintegration.'[15] Rab soon discovered that Amery's words were not idle.

On his first day in office, Sir Edward Bridges[16] and Sir William Armstrong[17] invited him to lunch at the Athenaeum. Over lunch – or 'what remained of the Club food after the bishops had had their run' – the two Treasury knights impressed on Rab that the country was in dire economic straits, graphically speaking of 'blood draining from the system and a collapse greater than had been foretold in 1931'.[18] The Tories had inherited a balance-of-payments deficit of £700 million and immediate action was necessary to regulate the economy.

When the Cabinet met on the following day, Rab reported this apocalyptic forecast and circulated a memorandum from Bridges, a document that Churchill promptly ordered be sent to Attlee to

14 Butler, *The Art of the Possible*, p. 156.
15 Trinity: Butler Papers, RAB, B15.2, Amery to Rab, 30 October 1951.
16 Permanent Secretary to the Treasury and Head of the Civil Service.
17 Rab's Private Secretary at the Treasury and a future Head of the Civil Service.
18 Butler, *The Art of the Possible*, p. 157.

illustrate the deficit that the Tories had inherited.[19] The spectre of a further devaluation alarmed the Conservative Cabinet and on 7 November Rab described in detail in the Commons the problems facing Britain and the government's proposed solutions.

Central gold and dollar reserves, he informed the House, were being rapidly drained, evidence of a weakening of confidence in sterling. In consequence, the government needed immediately to 'quench any doubts which there may be about the strength of sterling and about our ability in the United Kingdom to manage its affairs effectively'. The balance-of-payments deficit for 1952 was predicted to be between £500 million and £600 million, while reserves at the end of October were below £1.1 billion. Absent a highly flexible domestic economy to adjust to new pressures, the government was forced to take drastic steps to adapt to world conditions, and the deficit with the rest of the non-sterling world needed to be addressed.[20]

The government's long-term objective was expansion and it would reject no plan, however unconventional, to achieve that goal. In the meantime, temporary retrenchment was essential. Imports would be cut immediately by £350 million annually; the amount of sterling allowed for personal overseas travel would be cut from £100 to £50; the bank rate would be raised from 2 per cent to 2.5 per cent.[21] Significantly, Rab assured the House that the government's house-building plan would not be affected as it did not use much steel.[22]

On 29 January 1952, Rab reported to the House on progress. Restrictions and cuts, he stressed, were mere palliatives; expansion and development were the only real lasting remedies. A recent meeting of Commonwealth Finance Ministers had agreed that sterling should be freely convertible and import controls abandoned as soon as possible. The long-term goal must be to 'pay our way', to reduce the deficit with the non-sterling world, and to boost exports. In the meantime, further measures would be necessary: an additional saving of about

---

19 TNA: CAB 128 CC(51) 1.

20 Hansard, 7 November 1951, vol. 493, cols 191–5.

21 Rab had wanted to increase the bank rate to 4 per cent but was dissuaded by Cameron ('Kim') Cobbold, the Governor of the Bank of England, later Lord Cobbold.

22 Hansard, 7 November 1951, vol. 493, cols 197–209.

£150 million in imports; reduction of the travel allowance from £50 to £25; reductions in imported foodstuffs, clothing, furniture, carpets, shoes and toys. The cuts were essential; the money in the till was running out fast, and Britain needed to suffer shortages, and thus allow industry to export more.[23]

That was as far as the Cabinet was prepared to go with 'austerity' measures. Rab encountered opposition on two other proposals: further cuts in rationed foods[24] and on a proposal to reduce the imports of timber.[25] On the latter issue, Macmillan, naturally, was adamant. The Tories had made much of the Attlee government's failure to meet its house-building target and the Tories should not now make the same mistake.[26]

Rab stressed to the Cabinet his determination 'to bring home to the public the gravity of the situation',[27] which he did in a broadcast that day.[28] Describing Britain's plight, he used the same simile that Bridges and Armstrong had employed three months before at the Athenaeum. 'Our lifeblood is draining away', he said, 'and we have got to stop it.' His broadcast received wide applause – from his old patron Sam Hoare, now Lord Templewood, who praised it as 'clear and simple, full of life, and so obviously sincere that it must have carried wide conviction', and from Macmillan, who sent a short, almost perfunctory note from the Ministry of Housing, calling it simply 'a masterly performance'.[29]

In common with Macmillan, Rab must have felt that he was failing to introduce innovative measures that differed greatly from those of his predecessors. The slogan 'Set the People Free' had been central to the Tories' election manifesto; yet he was proposing solutions essentially similar to the post-war measures of austerity for which his party had castigated the Attlee government. It should not be surprising, therefore, that when a 'modern' scheme was proposed, he grasped it eagerly.

---

23 Hansard, 29 January 1952, vol. 495, cols 40–51.
24 This despite support for Rab from Gwilym Lloyd George, Minister of Food. Even a proposal to reduce the weekly sweet ration from six ounces to four ounces was blocked.
25 TNA: CAB 128 CC(52) 8 and (52) 9.
26 TNA: CAB 128 CC(51) 23.
27 TNA: CAB 128 CC(52) 7 and (52)8.
28 The text of the radio broadcast was published in *The Listener*, 31 January 1952.
29 Trinity: Butler Papers, RAB, B16.5, B16.8 and B16.13.

An intermittently recurring criticism of Rab is that he was a fence sitter, a view shared by Treasury officials who grew used to exhaustive discussions of a subject, the apparent arrival at a decision, only to be followed by Rab calling after them as they prepared to leave, 'Of course, nothing's been decided yet.'[30] It was all the more surprising – or testament to his growing frustration – that he immediately embraced ROBOT, a risky plan, but one which, presented as 'freeing the pound', had a certain glamorous appeal for its novelty.

ROBOT, named after its three originators Sir Leslie Rowan, Sir George Bolton and Otto Clarke, was controversial in that it would have restored convertibility of sterling against the dollar, but at a floating rather than a fixed rate. Thus, while the pound would have been 'freed', the plan undermined the basis of the Bretton Woods Agreement of 1944 and was anathema to the United States Treasury. Rab believed that ROBOT, accompanied by deflationary action to strengthen sterling, was vital insurance as 'an external regulator for the balance of payments'; with uncharacteristic daring, he promoted its adoption wholeheartedly. Determined opposition from Cherwell and Salter, however, who warned of disintegration of the sterling area and 'the slippery slope of depreciation', persuaded the more conservative of the Cabinet to reject the scheme.[31]

The timing of that decision had considerable significance. Rab had told the House that 'the interests of the balance of payments … paramount to this country, make it essential to introduce the appropriate Budget at the earliest possible date'[32] and the date of 4 March had been chosen. It was not until the Cabinet meetings of 28 and 29 February that the opponents of ROBOT succeeded in burying the plan. Harry Crookshank, Minister of Health and Leader of the House, told the Commons that Rab would open his Budget a week later than planned.[33]

---

30 Interview with a senior Treasury official, cited by Seldon, *Churchill's Indian Summer*, p. 555, note 23.
31 Butler, *The Art of the Possible*, pp. 158–9. Rab writes with some asperity that 'neither the Prof's private detective agency in economics, fascinating as it was to the Prime Minister, nor Salter's stream of sea-green memoranda would have sufficed to carry the day if the senior members of the government had been of a different turn of mind.'
32 Hansard, 29 January 1952, vol. 495, col. 62.
33 Hansard, 25 February 1952, vol. 496, col. 719.

Behind this opaque and unchallenged statement lay a clash of ide-
ologies within the government. Rab was supported by Lyttelton but
violently opposed by Cherwell, who described it as 'a reckless leap in
the dark' which would have 'appalling political and economic consequences at home and abroad'.[34] Salter and Lord Woolton, Rab's persistent adversary, backed Cherwell in his opposition. Lyttelton lampooned reactionary Tory opinion in a handwritten note passed across
the table to Rab during a Cabinet, 'The water looks too cold to some
of them. They prefer a genteel bankruptcy.'[35]

Rab was treading within the Conservative Party a similar path to
that being trodden by Gaitskell, locked in a struggle with the Bevanites in the Labour Party. Whilst there was little common philosophi-
cal ground between Rab and Gaitskell, each shunned the extreme of
his own party and was loosely termed 'centrist'. From this perceived
resemblance was born the term 'Butskell', coined by *The Economist* to
suggest that Chancellor and shadow Chancellor were proposing essentially similar centrist measures.[36]

When Rab's first Budget was presented to the Commons, he achieved
what *The Times* termed 'a triumph', greeted by 'prolonged ministerial
cheers'.[37] He had worked hard at its construction, creating what he saw
as the form of a Mahler symphony,[38] moving from *Feierlich und gemes-
sen*, through *Stürmisch bewegt* to *Heiter, bedächtig*,[39] sharply contrasting
movements that ended on a note of resonant triumph.

He first stressed the importance of the measures he was taking and
the seriousness of the problems faced. In broad terms, the country
was committed to a large defence programme, with no certainty of
continuing economic support from the United States or any other
NATO Power. At the same time, there was a large and growing United
Kingdom deficit with the non-sterling world, including a formidable

---

34 Timmins, *The Five Giants* (London: HarperCollins, 2001), p. 198.
35 Trinity: Butler Papers, RAB, G24.
36 *The Economist*, 13 February 1954. Both Rab and Gaitskell subsequently worked hard to dem-
    onstrate to their respective parties that there was no substance to the charge.
37 *The Times*, 12 March 1952.
38 Rab's own colourful description. *The Art of the Possible*, p. 161.
39 From 'festive and dignified' through 'stormy and troubled' to 'sunny and deliberate'.

deficit with the dollar area. This caused a dangerous drain on gold and dollar reserves.[40]

At the centre of the solution was the raising of the bank rate, an increase that Rab described as 'a sharp upward movement [that would] show to the world that we not only recognise the very serious situation of the country but are determined to deal with it', however unwelcome the solution. Moving on to government expenditure, specifically on social services, he announced a reduction of over £30 million. This was greeted by an interruption and a complaint of 'Not enough' from Sir Waldron Smithers.[41]

When Rab moved on to the Excess Profits Tax to be imposed, he proposed a rate of 30 per cent of excess profits or 18 per cent of total profits, whichever was the lower. Now, having been attacked by Smithers, he was attacked from the left by an interjection that the rate was 'far too low'. The effect of this, Rab continued, would be that Income Tax, Profits Tax and Excess Profits Levy combined would not exceed 73 per cent of a company's profit. A further tax on distributed profits, however, would discourage payment of dividends.[42]

There followed various minor changes before Rab moved to a substantial increase in tax on petrol – from 10½d to 1s 6d per gallon (an increase of 71 per cent). Addressing food subsidies, Rab 'proposed to bring the food subsidy figure down to a rate of £250 million a year'. Increases in the prices of bread, flour, meat, tea and milk would increase the cost of basic foodstuffs by 12s 6d per week per head of population. For a family with two children these increases would be partially offset by an increase from five shillings to eight shillings per week in the family allowance. There would also be discussions with both sides of industry to make equitable revisions to the National Insurance scheme.[43] War pensions and industrial injury benefits would be increased, costing £10 million and £3 million respectively per year. Pensions for other public servants would also be increased.

There was a need for incentives for the work force, as Britain would

---

40 Hansard, 11 March 1952, vol. 497, col. 1273.
41 Ibid., col. 1286.
42 Ibid., cols 1291–2.
43 Ibid., cols 1295–300.

pull through only by 'increased production and a new spirit of satisfaction in rewards well earned'; but, he said, 'I am convinced that the present weight of direct taxation, particularly on the lower and middle income groups, acts as a very positive discouragement to extra effort.' There would, therefore, be a lighter burden of tax, 'particularly on extra earnings, and thus to encourage people when they put in longer hours overtime or earn more by harder work.'

Rates of tax, moreover, were defective in that 'the starting points of liability [were] too low, the rates of tax … too high and the graduation … too steep'. Accordingly, the single allowance would be increased from £110 to £120, the married allowance from £190 to £210 and the child allowance from £70 to £85. The earned income relief would be increased from the present one-fifth to two-ninths. That, Rab confessed, was as far as he could afford to go in a single leap.[44] The cost in a full year of £228 million would be covered by the revenue from the Excess Profits Tax.

In a rousing finale, Rab orated,

> Solvency, security, duty and incentive are our themes. Restriction and austerity are not enough. We want a system which offers us both more realism and more hope … We must now set forth, braced and resolute, to show the world that we shall regain our solvency and, with it, our national greatness.[45]

The 1952 Budget established Rab as the master of his own house and the government's principal economic officer. He had apparently overcome – or, at least, loosened – the restraints placed on him five months before and now could lay claim to being the 'new broom' that the Tories needed. Unlike Gaitskell, a trained economist, he reached decisions about economics on a matrix of political considerations, although Treasury officials conceded that he generally reached the right decision, albeit by unorthodox means.[46] Channon applauded his performance on Budget Day and noted with pleasure his growing stature

---

44 Ibid., cols 1300–302.
45 Ibid., col. 1305.
46 Seldon, *Churchill's Indian Summer*, p. 156.

as a Parliamentarian. Two of Channon's diary entries from that period illustrate this. On 11 March, he wrote: 'To the House for the Budget ... Rab looking sleek, calm and well ... spoke for nearly two hours, and he was clear, concise, calm, good-tempered. His performance was magnificent. He played politely with the Opposition, who revealed themselves in a really despicable light.'[47]

Two months later, when 'the turbulent Opposition were deflated by Rab's sudden concession of £17,000,000 per annum on Purchase Tax', Channon commented that he was 'the ablest Parliamentarian of our time, cold, courteous, suave and seemingly simple, he outwits everyone'.[48]

That enthusiasm was widespread, not only in Britain but, as Rab was proud to record, internationally. He achieved the remarkable feat of restoring confidence in sterling and a balance of payments surplus while, at the same time, offering real incentives to the industrious. Not only had he shown a remarkable feel for the job, he had overcome the doubts of the Prime Minister while furthering his reputation as a 'modern' Chancellor. That modernism was underscored in July when BBC television aired its first edition of *Press Conference*, a current affairs programme that devoted its first slot to Rab. The producer wrote to him with the dramatic, if self-serving, comment, 'You made history.'[49] By September, he had so grown in stature within the government that, in Churchill's and Eden's absence, it was the 49-year-old Rab who chaired Cabinet meetings.[50]

By 1952, Rab's rehabilitation was complete. He had become Chancellor at a time of crisis in the British economy and had spread calm on troubled waters. On 5 June, he received an honorary DCL degree at Cambridge. Among the other recipients of honorary degrees was Leo Amery, an equivalence that could not have been imagined when Rab approached him in 1926.[51] Three weeks later, along with Dean Acheson

---

47 Rhodes James, *Chips*. Diary entry for 11 March 1952, p. 466.
48 Ibid., Diary entry for 12 May 1952, pp. 468–9.
49 Trinity: Butler Papers, RAB, G24. Letter of 15 July 1952 to Rab from Grace Wyndham Goldie. Howard, *RAB*, p. 190.
50 TNA: CAB 128 CC(52) 80. Today it is accepted that the Chancellor is *ex officio* the second most senior figure in Government. This was not automatically the case in Churchill's constellation.
51 Trinity: Butler Papers, RAB, G25.4.

and Oliver Franks, he received a DCL from Oxford University.[52] A touching note from Violet Bonham Carter at the end of the year accompanied an aquatint of Saint Michael slaying the dragon. 'To Rab', she wrote, 'who has killed so many dragons and has so many more to kill.'[53]

Amid this widespread acclaim, the last months of 1952 brought sadness. On 7 November, his father died of a heart attack. The India that Sir Monty had known and loved had ceased to exist five years before, but he was remembered with affection and respect by the Maharajah of Bhopal and by the Maharao of Kotah, both of whom wrote to Rab of his 'illustrious' father.[54] An obituary in *The Times* praised his 'knack in the handling of men', specifically that 'ardent disciples of the Gandhian cult were turned into loyal supporters through the tonic effect of responsibility for administration'.[55] A memorial service was held in Pembroke College on 15 November. Here also he was remembered with great affection. Oliver Franks wrote to Rab that Monty had been very kind to him when he took over as Provost of Queen's College[56] and one recent Pembroke graduate wrote to tell Rab that 'All who were up at Pembroke in my day held him in high esteem, indeed affection.'[57] Most touchingly, the Queen sent a message of sympathy, referring to her own bereavement when her father George VI had died in February that year.[58]

During that same month, Sydney began to suffer pains in her jaw that baffled dentists and doctors. Although this was of concern to Rab, the discomfort was not initially taken seriously and certainly did not slow Sydney down. Rab was rapidly becoming a national figure and his energetic wife worked hard to support him; in December, the Butlers hosted an extravaganza at 11 Downing Street for all delegates at a Commonwealth economic conference.[59]

---

52 Trinity: Butler Papers, RAB, G25.72.
53 Trinity: Butler Papers, RAB, G25.101.
54 Trinity: Butler Papers, RAB, B19.134.
55 *The Times*, 8 November 1952.
56 Trinity: Butler Papers, RAB, B19.93.
57 Trinity: Butler Papers, RAB, B19.100.
58 Trinity: Butler Papers, RAB, B19.85.
59 Howard, *RAB*, p. 192.

In 1953, a new President entered the White House after General Eisenhower's landslide victory over Adlai Stevenson. Although the Armistice negotiations to end the Korean War dragged on – the Armistice was not signed until 27 July – its worst effects on Britain's economy were over. In February, Rab, Eden and their wives travelled to Washington for talks with Eisenhower and the new administration. In his memoirs, Rab recalls his hope that he and Eden might establish closer relations. 'This', he commented, 'did not happen, since each of us was preoccupied with the mission ahead, and whilst I did not fully realise what he hoped to get out of the new President and Secretary of State, he scarcely began to understand my economic brief.'[60]

Nor were the discussions in Washington more satisfactory. Rab failed to make headway with Eisenhower, who 'gazed at [Rab] in silence' when he mentioned his 'desire to bring the economic links between our countries closer'. Although he developed a good working relationship and personal friendship with George Humphrey, the Secretary of the Treasury, it became clear to Rab that the American administration had an *idée fixe* concerning convertibility and was impatient to see Britain put her house in order.

As *The Times* pointed out, the talks were not, in the proper sense, negotiations; they dealt with specific British proposals, developed at the Commonwealth Conference to make sterling convertible into dollars at some unspecified date. This would necessitate a wider range of sterling exchange rates in early stages, supported by dollar credit either from the US Treasury or the IMF. 'Trade not aid' was the popular phrase for the policy that the Secretary of the Treasury was encouraged to support.[61] For convertibility to be worthwhile, American policy needed to be congruent with British goals and there needed to be full agreement with Commonwealth countries to enable steady progress towards real freedom of trade and exchange.

After the Washington talks, Rab spoke in New York and successfully allayed Republican fears of too close an alliance with Britain. The

---

60 Butler, *The Art of the Possible*, p. 165.
61 The phrase was coined by the *Herald Tribune* on 5 March 1953. The headline read, 'Bold Rab Butler – Britain's Trade not Aid Man'. Trinity: Butler Papers, RAB, L105.

underlying premise of the talks, he said, had been to ensure the effective operation in peacetime of one of the greatest political and military alliances of all time.[62]

How could Anglo-American global objectives now be supported, particularly in the event of a long cold war? Between Eden and Dulles on foreign policy and between himself and George Humphrey on economic matters, a strong personal understanding had developed. After the last war they had not forecast the wrong weather, he said, but had created mechanisms at once too complex and too remote from the comprehension of ordinary men. Good economics need not necessarily be incomprehensible.

Britain had in six years gone from being a substantial creditor nation to becoming a debtor nation to the tune of $13 billion. No country's position had ever changed so greatly in so short a time; yet Britain had honoured and would honour her obligations. Despite the maintenance of compulsory military service and of the largest armoured force in Western Europe, Britain under the Conservatives had made enormous strides and had transformed a debit of over $1 billion in their overseas payments in the last six months of 1951 into a surplus of over $150 million in 1952.

There was, however, a body of right-wing isolationist opinion that saw the Eden–Butler trip as another European invasion of American billfolds. This expressed itself in caustic language:

> Britain only wants everything from the US. Since the close of World War
> II the United States Treasury has contributed $3 billion in foreign aid,
> money taken from the pockets of American taxpayers who are once again
> about to meet the Collector of Internal Revenue. And it still isn't enough.[63]

Rab, quite used to dealing with the right wing of his own party, recognised the cloven hoof of the American heartland as clearly as that of the shires. The presence of Eisenhower in the White House while

---

62 *The Times*, 11 March 1953.
63 *Journal American*, 18 March 1953.

Churchill was in Downing Street was important, but, after the end of Marshall Aid, the building of a clear understanding between Humphrey and Rab was equally vital for the long term. Rab made huge strides to achieve this.

On 14 March 1953, while Rab was visiting Ottawa, the *Daily Express* and the *Daily Mail* reported that, on being asked about the premiership, he replied, 'Only Prime Minister Churchill knows when he will retire. Anthony Eden is Deputy Prime Minister. And I guess those facts answer the question.' Rab's response betrayed a Civil Service mentality, the idea of an automatic stepping up a rung with the retirement of a man at the top. If Rab was answering candidly and not stonewalling – always a dangerous assumption – that response clearly illustrates how he felt in 1953 – and, in a different position, ten years later.[64]

It was almost a month before Rab delivered his second Budget – on 14 April, the first day that Parliament met after the Easter recess. No longer cast in the role of a suppliant, he reported with justifiable pride that the situation was very different from that of a year before.[65] The government's principal achievement, he said, lay in rectifying the adverse balance of payments. The measure of success could be judged by the figures, which spoke for themselves: Britain had moved from a deficit of £398 million on current account in 1951 to a surplus of £291 million in 1952. That surplus, Rab pointed out, was remarkably close to the figure of £300 million that had been regarded as 'stargazing' when he announced it as his annual target.

The battle against inflation too was showing encouraging results. Price controls had been abolished on a large number of articles without resulting in a runaway rise in prices. 'All this', he said, 'has both helped and been helped by that most intangible of all our assets – confidence in our policy and in the pound sterling.'[66] Despite lower revenues and higher expenditures than predicted, he continued, 'If we stand back and look at the developments of 1952 as a whole, we see clear evidence of the success of our disinflationary policies.'

---

64 Trinity: Butler Papers, RAB, L32.
65 Hansard, 14 April 1953, vol. 514, col. 33.
66 Ibid., col. 37.

Yet there was no room for relaxation. Civil Supply expenditure must continue to be reduced; there was an ever-present danger of an increase in defence expenditure. But a step had been taken on the course whereby the government should do less and that the private citizen should be in a position to do more, specifically in housing policy, 'in which private enterprise must play a progressively bigger part and thus proportionately relieve the Exchequer'.[67]

Concerning exports, there had been a move towards freer trade and currencies, but this all took time to produce results. There were increased incentives for industry but these were inadequate. The burden of taxation was too high; no new taxes were proposed; there were reliefs to improve competitive efficiency and to provide incentives for greater effort and increased private saving. Purchase Tax was reduced on several items; Income Tax reduced by 6d in the pound; the benefit of reduction being carried down to the lowest incomes liable to Income Tax. In a closing summary, Rab repeated the call to arms of 1952. 'I have confidence in the response of our people,' he said. 'We step out from the confines of restriction, to the almost forgotten but beckoning prospects of freer endeavour and greater reward for effort.'[68]

Again Channon was impressed both by Rab's speech and its reception:

> Great excitement in the House at Rab's Budget, as he rose this afternoon, and humorously, good-naturedly, unfolded his plans ... It is another step forward on the road to recovery. Rab has recently quietly enhanced his political position and reputation both in the House and in the country ... Rab has had a splendid press and the whole country is relieved and grateful. It thinks his Budget is a masterpiece.[69]

Rab's prestige with the public and with the party was at its height. Whilst Eden clearly was Churchill's heir, Rab had acquired the role of 'the spare', a position that assumed greater possibilities when Eden was admitted to hospital for an operation to remove gallstones. The

67 Ibid., col. 44.
68 Ibid., cols 61–2.
69 Rhodes James, *Chips*. Diary entries for 14 and 15 April 1953, p. 474.

Rab's father, Montagu Butler, c. 1900.
COURTESY OF TRINITY COLLEGE, CAMBRIDGE

Rab's mother, Ann Butler, c. 1901.
COURTESY OF TRINITY COLLEGE, CAMBRIDGE

Rab's younger brother,
John Perceval ('Jock'), c. 1920.
COURTESY OF TRINITY COLLEGE, CAMBRIDGE

Sydney Butler (née Courtauld)
during the world tour of 1926–27.
COURTESY OF TRINITY COLLEGE, CAMBRIDGE

A sketch of Sir Geoffrey Butler, c. 1927.
COURTESY OF TRINITY COLLEGE, CAMBRIDGE

Rab's father, Sir Montagu Butler, in dress uniform, c. 1927. COURTESY OF TRINITY COLLEGE, CAMBRIDGE

Young Member of Parliament, 1929.
COURTESY OF TRINITY COLLEGE, CAMBRIDGE

Rab with his two older sons, Richard and Adam, 1937. COURTESY OF TRINITY COLLEGE, CAMBRIDGE

ABOVE Rab's three sons, Richard, Adam and James Butler, 1937. COURTESY OF TRINITY COLLEGE, CAMBRIDGE

LEFT Sydney Butler with daughter Sarah at a wedding, c. 1947. COURTESY OF TRINITY COLLEGE, CAMBRIDGE

RIGHT Three generations of Butlers at Cambridge. Monty, Rab and Richard with Sydney when Rab received an honorary LLD, 1952. COURTESY OF TRINITY COLLEGE, CAMBRIDGE

With Winston Churchill at St-Jean-Cap-Ferrat, 1955. COURTESY OF TRINITY COLLEGE, CAMBRIDGE

LEFT Arriving at 10 Downing Street for a Cabinet meeting, September 1955.
COURTESY OF PA ARCHIVE / PRESS ASSOCIATION IMAGES

RIGHT Rab at his son Adam's wedding to Felicity Molesworth-St Aubyn at St Martin-in-the-Fields,
October 1955. COURTESY OF PA ARCHIVE / PRESS ASSOCIATION IMAGES

The circus, Rab's preferred form of entertainment. Seen here with his daughter Sarah, c. 1957. COURTESY OF TRINITY COLLEGE, CAMBRIDGE

Before Rab's turbulent installation as Lord Rector of Glasgow University, February 1958. COURTESY OF TRINITY COLLEGE, CAMBRIDGE

Harold Macmillan shooting grouse, c. 1958. COURTESY OF TRINITY COLLEGE, CAMBRIDGE

Rab making a
broadcast in German
for the BBC, c. 1959.
COURTESY OF TRINITY
COLLEGE, CAMBRIDGE

Mollie Butler, as ever
pitch-perfect, at a
political dinner, c. 1960.
COURTESY OF TRINITY
COLLEGE, CAMBRIDGE

A standing ovation
from Cabinet members
after his speech to
the party conference
in Blackpool on
12 October 1963.
COURTESY OF PA
ARCHIVE / PRESS
ASSOCIATION IMAGES

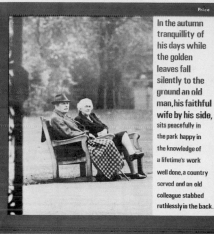

LEFT The cover of *Private Eye* immediately after the 1963 leadership contest.
REPRODUCED BY KIND PERMISSION OF *PRIVATE EYE* MAGAZINE

RIGHT With Dirk Stikker, Secretary-General of NATO, 1963.
COURTESY OF TRINITY COLLEGE, CAMBRIDGE

The Foreign Secretary in the Soviet Union, 1964. COURTESY OF TRINITY COLLEGE, CAMBRIDGE

The Master's Lodge,
Trinity College,
Cambridge. Housing
came with the job.
AUTHOR'S PHOTOGRAPH

The Master of
Trinity, punting on
the River Cam with
Mollie and Susannah
Courtauld, 1965.
COURTESY OF TRINITY
COLLEGE, CAMBRIDGE

Plaque below
Rab's Banner of the
Order of the Garter
in St Mary's Church,
Saffron Walden.
COURTESY OF
SIMON FOWLER

In
beloved memory of
RICHARD AUSTEN
BARON BUTLER
OF SAFFRON WALDEN
K G · P C · C H
1902-1982
whose banner of the Most Noble
Order of the Garter hangs
above

operation was a failure, nearly fatal when the surgeon accidentally cut his bile duct. A second operation was performed on 29 April but was only partially successful, leaving his doctors concerned that he would not recover. Churchill resigned himself to the prospect that 'Anthony may be away for months'.[70] Eden was flown to Boston, where a third operation repaired the previous damage and put him out of danger. It would take six months of convalescence before he could return to the Foreign Office, where Churchill held the fort in his absence.

Churchill's decision to deputise for Eden alarmed his physician. 'You could no doubt do this for a short time as an emergency measure,' Moran told the Prime Minister, 'but to burden yourself with the F. O. for an indefinite period, perhaps for months, is surely not wise.'[71] On 23 June, at the end of a dinner for Alcide de Gasperi, the Italian Prime Minister, Churchill suffered a stroke. At first he refused to allow this to disrupt things and he conducted a Cabinet on the following day, at which, Rab recorded, 'some of us [noticed] that much was wrong'.[72] This assessment was confirmed on 25 June by Rab's niece, Jane Portal, who worked as Churchill's secretary at 10 Downing Street.

Even then Rab was not fully aware of the gravity of the Prime Minister's collapse until, on Friday 26 June, he travelled to Hunstanton to be at the deathbed of his mother. Rab was devoted to her and was puzzled by 'the hardness of expression and apparent forgetfulness of love' that affected her 'in a twilight between life and death'.[73] His visit was cut short by an urgent phone call, requesting his immediate presence at Chartwell, where he was given a letter from Jock Colville. This informed Rab of the seriousness of the Prime Minister's condition, predicting that he would be unlikely to continue in office, and urging him to 'keep the whole matter strictly private for the time being'.[74]

Salisbury was summoned to Chartwell and in a hurried meeting it was agreed that Rab would act as head of the government with Salisbury at the Foreign Office *pro tempore*. At this point, Rab and

---

70 Moran, *Churchill, Taken from the Diaries of Lord Moran*, Diary entry for 24 April 1953, p. 430.
71 Ibid.
72 Trinity: Butler Papers G26, Diary note of 24 June 1953.
73 Butler, *The Art of the Possible*, pp. 168–9.
74 Ibid., pp. 169–70.

Salisbury took a bold decision. Moran and Sir Russell Brain, who were treating Churchill, prepared a medical bulletin: 'For a long time the Prime Minister has had no respite from his arduous duties and a disturbance of the cerebral circulation has developed, resulting in attacks of giddiness. We have therefore advised him to abandon his journey to Bermuda[75] and to take at least a month's rest.'[76]

Rab and Salisbury, on their own initiative, altered the bulletin, omitting all reference to disturbance of the cerebral circulation and substituting 'lighten his duties for at least a month' for 'take a month's rest'. The public was to know nothing of the true state of the Prime Minister's health. The two ministers backed the chance that Churchill would recover. If, on the other hand, he had not recovered – or had died – the repercussions would have been grave.[77]

In the days following his collapse, Churchill repeatedly indicated to his family, his colleagues and to the Queen that he would carry on until the autumn 'when Anthony could take over'.[78] Meanwhile, the public was to be kept in ignorance and the Prime Minister was discouraged from making any public appearances lest he betray his true condition. The deception, surprisingly, was effective.

Between 29 June and 18 August, Rab presided over sixteen Cabinet meetings with no certainty of how things would arrange themselves in the long term. Churchill returned to chair two Cabinets but soon departed, first to Balmoral, then to Beaverbrook's villa at Cap d'Ail, where Rab briefly joined him. He was obsessed with the Margate party conference and that he be sufficiently recovered to make the Leader's speech as scheduled on 10 October. This, perhaps more than anything else, was a goad to the Prime Minister's recovery during that summer. Rab, in his own words, 'went on blithely with my daily companion, the economy'.[79]

---

75 He had planned to meet Eisenhower for a summit in Bermuda.

76 Moran, *Churchill, Taken from the Diaries of Lord Moran*, Diary entry for 26 June 1953, p. 437. TNA: PREM 783/188.

77 The deception that Salisbury and Rab perpetrated after Churchill's stroke had far-reaching implications both for the transaction of government business and for the succession. That aspect of the story is covered in detail in Chapter 9.

78 Moran, *Churchill, Taken from the Diaries of Lord Moran*, Diary entries for 28 June, 30 June, 4 July and 15 July 1953, pp. 441, 448, 464.

79 Butler, *The Art of the Possible*, p. 171.

He took time away from the economy on 21 July to speak to the Commons on foreign affairs. He spoke for fifty minutes, covering much of the globe but failing to inspire.[80] The thrust of the questions put to him by Attlee was to establish when the Prime Minister and Foreign Secretary would be back in harness so that progress could be made towards a summit with the Soviet Union and 'some possibility of the loosening of the tension between East and West'.[81] Churchill was disappointed by Rab's performance, feeling that it was a 'rather tame' sequel to his own earlier proposals for a summit. 'Rab had not held the House on foreign affairs,' he complained.[82] Channon was even less complimentary, writing that Rab's speech had been 'a flop'.[83]

This was not entirely surprising, as Lady Butler, Rab's mother, died on 23 July, aged seventy-six. Rab had been devoted to her and she had retained her faithful, if erratic, interest in his career. This shattering loss, coming so soon after Monty's death, was followed by further distress. The pain that Sydney had first felt the previous November was not responding to treatment and she was disfigured by a sore that began to spread across the right side of her jaw and face. By the autumn, both she and Rab were alarmed that this was no simple infection; in November, she was admitted to Westminster Hospital for what *The Times* described as 'an operation to deal with a mouth infection'.[84] The euphemistic press release did nothing to ease Rab's concerns.

October brought the party conference, a credible and creditable performance by Churchill, and the return of Eden from illness. Rab's *pro tempore* management of the government came to an end. From the thankless task of playing understudy to two absent *prime donne* came diminished responsibility and scant gratitude. By the beginning of 1954, he was concerned that Sydney's condition was not improving, although it was not yet diagnosed as cancer. From the summit of triumph, symbolised by his 1953 Budget, there followed a year and

---

80 Hansard, 21 July 1953, vol. 518, cols 211–27.
81 Ibid., col. 228.
82 Moran, *Churchill, Taken from the Diaries of Lord Moran*, Diary entries for 21 and 22 July, pp. 467 and 469.
83 Rhodes James, *Chips*, Diary entry for 26 July 1953, p. 478.
84 *The Times*, 17 November 1953.

a half of diminished glory and personal anguish. If his critics commented that he had lost the drive, the *élan* that characterised him in his ascendancy, that should come as no surprise.

There was an *intermezzo* amid Rab's concerns in January 1954, when he flew to Australia for the Commonwealth Finance Ministers' Conference. Whilst the conference itself failed to reassure Commonwealth Ministers of the sustainability of sterling ('a damp squib' in forthright Australian opinion),[85] Rab himself emerged as a cogent and coherent exponent of Britain's recovery – a remarkable feat in the context of the previous nine months. He was also appointed a Companion of Honour in the New Year Honours List. January provided a bizarre coda to 1953 – at the same time Rab's *annus mirabilis* and his *annus horrendus*.[86]

Whilst Butskell was not, ultimately, a credible character, his tendency to slide towards the centre was just realistic enough to ring true with the extremes of both the Conservative and the Labour parties. Gaitskell was already at odds with the left wing of the Labour Party, struggling to find a solution to the fissure caused by the Bevanites. For Rab, however, the suggestion in a respected periodical that he shared Gaitskell's economic aims was as damaging as it was absurd. Rab does not deign to refer to Mr Butskell in his memoirs, but even if he lacked substance, Butskell's spectral presence served as a reminder to the knights of the shires that Rab might, at root, be unsound on imperial preference, convertibility, and prey to the 'modern' economics that they heartily despised.

Unsurprisingly in this climate, his third Budget lacked the assurance of the previous two years. Like his second, it opened with a report on the progress made in the previous year. His first Budget had been designed to rectify and strengthen the balance of payments; the second to continue to fortify the overseas position and expand production at home. Taxes had been reduced to increase incentives, but limits had been placed on deliberate expansion. The government had steered a

---

85 *Sydney Sunday Telegraph*, 24 January 1954. Cited by Howard, *RAB*, p. 202.
86 These were the terms that Hugh Dalton, member of the post-war Labour Cabinet, used of the years 1946 and 1947, when the government swung from triumph to crisis and near paralysis.

middle course. That had been successful as in 1953 industrial production reached heights never before recorded in Britain's history.[87]

The balance of payments had greatly improved and would show a surplus of £320 million for the year as a whole. Gold and dollar reserves rose by £240 million during 1953. Exports to North America and Europe had increased. External progress was matched by expansion of production and improvement in living standards. Between January 1953 and January 1954, unemployment fell from 453,000 to 373,000. National Savings had grown, deposits exceeding withdrawals by £40 million between January and April. There were, however, still problems to be faced. Expenditure needed to be rigidly controlled and the national product dramatically increased.[88]

It was an uninspiring budget, delivered without *brio*, and Gaitskell began his attack the following day, judging the proposals 'dull', a word he repeated five times in his opening broadside. Woolton went further in his memoirs, describing it as 'the dullest thing that anyone ever created', but then Rab would have expected no less from Woolton.[89] He himself referred to it as a 'carry-on' Budget in which neither tax increases nor major tax remissions were possible or called for.[90] It had no mass appeal, nor did it endear Rab to his critics in the party.

It was by then six months since Eden had returned from convalescence and, while there had been no clear understanding that Churchill would step down on a certain date, Eden felt that the time for that event was long overdue. Churchill intimated that he would resign when the Queen returned from a Commonwealth tour in May.[91] In March he mentioned June.[92] Pressure mounted in the press, particularly in the *Daily Mirror*,[93] and in April he decided that he would not lead the Tories into the next election[94] – cold comfort for Eden, as no election was due before October 1956. In May he spoke

---

87 Hansard, 6 April 1954, vol. 526, col. 195.
88 Ibid., cols 203–13.
89 Bodleian: MS Woolton 3. Diary entry for 6 April 1954.
90 Hansard, 6 April 1954, vol. 526, col. 218.
91 Moran, *Churchill, Taken from the Diaries of Lord Moran*, Diary entry for 17 December 1953, p. 547.
92 Ibid., Entry for 19 March 1954, p. 565.
93 On 1 April, a *Daily Mirror* editorial titled 'Twilight of a Giant' urged Churchill to resign.
94 Moran, *Churchill, Taken from the Diaries of Lord Moran*, Diary entry for 1 April 1954, p. 567.

of retiring in July;[95] by mid-June he had decided that he would not retire before September.[96] On 1 July, Colville remarked that 'things with Anthony are coming to a head'.[97] Rab appeared bemused, even unconcerned, while his two prominent colleagues grew increasingly distant.

Rab too was frustrated by the Prime Minister's behaviour, particularly as he was more and more at odds with his Cabinet. Churchill saddled him with the unwelcome task of settling the matter of Members' salaries, at the time fixed at the inadequate level of £1,000 a year.[98] During a debate in the Commons, Rab, typically keeping his opinions to himself, committed the government to follow the will of the House.[99]

The Commons voted by 276 to 205 to award an increase of £500, but the Cabinet almost unanimously rejected the Commons' vote, thus negating Rab's support of the increase.[100] Having been isolated in Cabinet over Members' salaries, Rab was again humbled by his colleagues in July. Churchill and Eden, returning from a Washington conference aboard the *Queen Mary*, composed a cable to Molotov, the Soviet Foreign Minister, proposing a meeting in Moscow. This they sent to Rab for onward transmission and, reasonably enough, Rab forwarded it via the Soviet Embassy in London. When Cabinet ministers learned of this they took Churchill to task for not clearing the cable in advance with the Cabinet. Although the Prime Minister, rather than Rab, was their principal target, Rab was left in no doubt that he had exceeded his authority as 'it would have been possible, though very difficult, for him to have contacted the Cabinet at that stage, and he must accept personal responsibility for having decided not to do so'.[101]

Despite fulsome support from *The Economist*, which ran an article proclaiming 'The Miracle has happened – full employment without

---

95   Ibid., Diary entry for 4 May 1954, p. 579.
96   Ibid., Diary entry for 15 June 1954, p. 591.
97   Ibid., Diary entry for 1 July 1954, p. 608.
98   The average wage in Britain in 1954 was £667 per annum.
99   Hansard, 24 May 1954, vol. 528, cols 99–100.
100 TNA: CAB 128/27 CC(54) 39th Conclusions, fols 299–300.
101 TNA: CAB 128/27 CC(54) 52nd Conclusions.

inflation, and this despite the heavy burden of defence, the rising burden of the social services, and some reduction in taxation',[102] the fifteen months since the 1953 Budget, the peak of Rab's prestige, had brought an almost Sophoclean series of setbacks. During the last five months of 1954, he was subjected to greater distress as Sydney's condition deteriorated rapidly. She had accepted for some time, with greater stoicism than Rab, that she would not recover, but by September Rab too finally faced the reality that she had little time left. It was a reality that he kept to himself, telling as few people as possible. After a long year of persistent, intense pain, Sydney died on 9 December, Rab's fifty-second birthday. Among the many letters of condolence to Rab were a telegram and a hand-written note from the Queen. 'I do want to send you one line of deepest and most heartfelt sympathy in your great sorrow. I know what a mortal blow it is to be parted, and my thoughts and prayers are with you and your children at this time of anguish.'[103]

Sydney was a forceful woman who had played a central part in Rab's career. Not by nature a political wife, she had thrown herself into supporting him in every possible way – as diligent hostess, efficient organiser, even as a stump speaker. Rab depended on her for objective and wise counsel, saying of her, 'I would rather listen to my wife on the cost of living than economists. She is at once more polite and coherent.'[104] Her death, in the words of Mollie Courtauld, her cousin by marriage, left Rab 'lonely and bereft'.[105] Rab's reaction was to bury himself in work, as he later recounted ruefully but with some pride.[106] Colleagues observed, however, that after Sydney's death, missing his closest confidante, he seemed less sure of his decisions and actions, that he repeatedly looked for reassurance that he had done or said the right thing. During the early months of 1955, Churchill spent an

---

102 *The Economist*, 3 July 1954; Trinity: Butler Papers, RAB, K24.398.
103 Trinity: Butler Papers, RAB, B24.19.
104 *Daily Express*, 10 December 1954.
105 Mollie Butler, *August and Rab: A Memoir* (London, Weidenfeld & Nicolson, 1987), p. 39.
  Mollie Montgomerie had married August Courtauld, Sydney's cousin. Although she and Rab were not close in 1954, Sydney made the extraordinary prediction that, after her death, Mollie would marry Rab. This occurred after August Courtauld's death in 1959. Ibid., p. 45.
106 Butler, *The Art of the Possible*, p. 176.

increasing amount of time with Rab, who recalls no fewer than 'eight gargantuan dinners with him alone'.[107] The Prime Minister's relations with Eden had deteriorated and, according to Rab's later account, 'in his [Churchill's] last months, he often made funny little advances to me'.[108] However serious those 'advances' were, however, there was no doubt that Eden, if he was fit, would succeed him. That long-awaited event, vociferously urged by the press and confirmed by the Cabinet decision to go to the country on 26 May, finally occurred on 5 April. To the very last, Churchill vacillated, saying to Lord Moran in March, 'If I dug in I don't think they would make me go. But I like Anthony so much and I have worked with him for so long. And he wants to be Prime Minister terribly.'[109]

By then Rab had suffered great loss of face when he announced to the Commons at the end of February that, although the economy was 'fundamentally stronger than it [had] been at any time since the war', it was necessary to 'moderate excessive internal demand and so to match the increase in … exports'. The government was, accordingly, taking prompt action to impose 'certain measures of restraint … to restrict the terms on which cars, wireless and television sets, furniture and a wide range of other consumer goods may be bought by hire purchase'.[110] Inevitably, this announcement was greeted with scorn by Gaitskell and Morrison, who commented on posters liberally displayed around the country claiming that 'Conservative freedom works', 'Should these not now be taken down?'[111] The measures that Rab proposed were to raise the bank rate to 4.5 per cent and impose tighter hire-purchase restrictions. Whilst these were not stringent austerity measures, they called into question the confident, even complacent attitude that the government had maintained since 1953. Had not Rab in 1954 made the bold prediction that a properly run economy would double the standard of living in twenty-five years? Until February 1955, Rab had been held

---

107 Ibid., p. 176.
108 BBC Radio Profile, 29 June 1978. Cited by Howard, *RAB*, p. 210.
109 Moran, *Churchill, Taken from the Diaries of Lord Moran*, Diary entry for 23 March 1955, p. 681.
110 Hansard, 24 February 1955, vol. 537, cols 1453–4.
111 Ibid., col. 1456.

in universally high regard as Chancellor. His wisdom was now more widely questioned.

A month later, as Eden prepared to take over, calling an election for May, Rab delivered his fourth Budget. Remarkably, five weeks before the election, he opened his address with the comment that this was 'a particularly tantalising time, both from the political and economic point of view'.[112] Simply put, Rab was opening himself to accusations that this was to be 'an election Budget' even before such accusations were made.

Rab was partisan from the start, taking a swing at Bevan, who had referred to him as having 'an unprepossessing personality'. Then, uncharacteristically, he claimed personal rather than collective credit for all actions, all improvements:

> In introducing this, my fourth Budget, I have to take account of all these improvements. Can we have them and more, too? How does this Budget fit into a series designed from the beginning to keep up the momentum of our progress? My aim in 1952 was to rescue and fortify sterling. The following year I deliberately gave the incentives needed to encourage effort and the expansion of production. New spirit was infused into industry.
>
> Last year, some people thought that I might have been a little more expansive and a little more expensive. But I am satisfied that what happened justified my decision and my judgement.[113]

To some extent, the Budget is the work of the Chancellor alone, but this paragraph, peppered with 'I' and 'my', went beyond the convention.

In a short speech, Rab spoke of further stimulation of exports through expanded production and proposed a reduction of 6d in the pound on Income Tax as the means of reducing 'the sheer burden of taxation'. This, together with a raising of the threshold for taxation, was the central plank of the Budget.

---

112 Hansard, 19 April 1955, vol. 540, col. 35.
113 Ibid., col. 36.

Reaction from Labour Members was predictably fierce and Conservative approval lukewarm. Curiously, it was attacked on inconsistent, mutually exclusive grounds by the opposition – as both a typical Tory Budget, saving a millionaire with three children £97 a week, and as an election Budget. Perhaps the greatest criticism is that it was an incomplete document – a criticism repeated by Tory Members. Beyond offering sweeteners to voters in the form of a substantial cut in Income Tax, it was a curiously truncated set of proposals.

Most damning is the incompatibility of the February proposals with their effective reversal less than two months later. Rab was giving considerable hostages to fortune and a balance-of-payments surplus. Subsequent events were to demonstrate this clearly and prompt Rab to write later that 'If I had been less scrupulous about the economy I would have retired in May.'[114]

The Budget of April 1955 consolidated antipathy towards Rab among backbenchers and, as ever, Woolton was not slow to suggest to Eden that he replace him. Woolton recorded in his diary that he had urged this on Eden's first day in 10 Downing Street.[115] In truth, Eden needed Rab at the Treasury, at least until the election, as a symbol of continuity and, possibly, was reluctant to add to Rab's woes when he was badly disorientated after Sydney's death.

The balance of Rab's tenure at the Treasury was a low point in his career – both in terms of his morale and his political standing. After a satisfying victory at Saffron Walden and an equally gratifying Tory majority of fifty-nine in the general election, Rab continued as Chancellor, aware that Eden wanted to replace him. After a break in August, spent grouse shooting, and a meeting of the IMF in Istanbul in September, Rab returned to London to learn from Government Chief Whip Patrick Buchan-Hepburn that Eden was proposing a Cabinet reshuffle. Before that, however, there were anti-inflationary measures that needed to be addressed. As the Cabinet had opposed these in June, Rab was compelled to introduce a second Budget in October.

---

114 Butler, *The Art of the Possible*, p. 180.
115 Bodleian: MS Woolton 3, Diary entry for 6 April 1955.

Before that, however, he was to damage his fragile position further. On 18 October 1955, speaking at the annual dinner of the Royal Society of St George, he urged his audience that 'We must not drop back into easy evenings with port wine and over-ripe pheasant.'[116] It is dfifficult to imagine a casual remark more inappropriate to the economic climate – or more tempting for the opposition to seize on.

Rab's fifth and last Budget, delivered after 'wielding the knife continuously for four years', was his most controversial. He opened with a general statement that there was no cause for alarm, that in September the export gap had narrowed, and that the loss of reserves had been halted. The country was suffering from growing pains, he said, and needed restraint 'to enable us to combine internal expansion with external solvency'. But the rise in the Index of Weekly Wage Rates and the increase in distributed dividends forced the government to 'design our policies so that they face up to, and cope with, the danger to the economy – and especially to our competitive power – of a further expansion of incomes and of consumer demand'.[117]

There was too wide a gap in the balance of trade and a decline in gold and dollar reserves, but the continuing high level of demand and the persistent shortage of labour convinced Rab of the 'reason and need to reinforce the restraints which we have so far applied, in order to give the economy, in good time, the degree of relief which it needs and to strengthen the foundations of our balance of payments'. The most controversial measure was the imposition of Purchase Tax on kitchenware, which for some years had been exempt from tax.[118] It was from this proposal that it became contemptuously known as the 'Pots and Pans Budget'.

Once again, we find Rab personalising government measures in a manner that might have been calculated to infuriate his colleagues. In connection with Purchase Tax, he said, 'I must, however, include provisions to deal with two subsidiary matters which are related to the main purpose of the Bill'; of dividend stripping, 'I cannot allow either this practice or this loss to continue.' Equally offensive was his statement,

---

116 *Daily Telegraph*, 19 October 1955.
117 Hansard, 26 October, vol. 545, cols 202–7.
118 Ibid., col. 221.

'Nor am I ready to make up my mind on the permanent alterations in the structure of the tax recommended by the Royal Commission, and so I must do my best within the existing framework of the tax.' One senses Rab's isolation from the Cabinet, that he is standing on his position as Chancellor, asserting himself in the teeth of opposition from his colleagues.[119]

From the opposition front bench Attlee rose to savage Rab in his assessment of the proposals. Rab, he charged, was 'a most temperamental Chancellor of the Exchequer'. From 'the depths of gloom in February, he quite brightened up in April and he is down in the dumps again now.' It was 'very difficult to find any clear policy whatever … He has precious little faith in what he did in February or what he did in the last Budget.'

There was no planning in the national interest whatsoever, he continued.

> The first thing that strikes the present Chancellor of the Exchequer is that anything that is spent in the public interest is less desirable than anything spent in the private interest. If people want to build dog-racing tracks, cinemas, or anything of that kind they will be let off very easily.

Yet anything for the public benefit was to be cut without rhyme or reason. Telephones were now luxuries; money would flow into the pockets of moneylenders while wages would be restrained; young married couples were penalised, despite the expressed Tory wish for a property-owning democracy; there was no attempt to consider what was for the benefit of the country.

Attlee levelled the familiar charge that Rab talked in superficial generalities. As with all Rab's Budgets, he charged, it hit the small man. 'Well,' he concluded, 'they had their time at the last election, and I am afraid that those electors who voted for the Tories will realise now that they are in for the morning after the night before.'[120]

---

119 Ibid., cols 223, 228.
120 Ibid., cols 236–9.

On the following day, Gaitskell delivered a 54-minute-long coruscating attack on Rab. The basic thrust was that everything that the
Chancellor was dealing with in October either was the case or was
predictable in April. An autumn Budget was usually necessitated by
external events of an extraordinary and unpredictable nature. This was
not the case in October. It was dishonest of the Chancellor to pretend
that the April Budget was anything other than an election gambit.
Instead, he charged, the Chancellor had been 'obstinately complacent
… If he had any bad news to give, one could be sure that he would
counteract it by charming, platitudinous sentences of bland optimism.
He is still doing it. We hear it in every other paragraph.'[121]

The country had been 'gravely misled', Gaitskell argued. Rab was
'always an expert in evasion'. 'He uses metaphors very freely' but 'when
we tell people that the roses have to be pruned, they do not think of
themselves as the rose, but as the persons doing the pruning'.[122]

The October Budget, he charged, was 'necessary because the April
Budget – a masterpiece of deception – actively encouraged instead of
damping down additional spending. Now, having bought his votes with a
bribe, the Chancellor is forced – as he knew he would be – to dishonour
the cheque.'[123] In summary, the Budget would not have been necessary if
the April Budget had been an honest Budget. Instead it was cunningly
contrived to appeal to the floating voter. Now, after the election, came the
payoff, in which the rich were catered to and the poor severely harmed.[124]

The Chancellor, Gaitskell concluded, should resign, as his record
as a politician and one-time statesman had been deplorable. He had
'behaved in a manner unworthy of his high office. He began in folly,
he continued in deceit, and he has ended in reaction. He is a sadly discredited minister … Let him lay down the burden of his office, which
he is so plainly unable to carry with credit any longer.'[125]

Later in the debate, Dr Horace King, MP for Southampton, Itchen,
drew the attention of the House to a curious aspect of the Chancellor's

---

121 Hansard, 27 October 1955, vol. 545, col. 393.
122 Ibid., col. 397.
123 Ibid., col. 399.
124 Ibid., cols 405–6.
125 Ibid., col. 408.

speech. 'Naturally', he said, 'it received a hot and hostile reception from this side of the Committee. But what was more surprising was the cold reception it received from the government benches, and the fact that it has been so lukewarmly supported in the speeches delivered during the two days of debate.' The truth was, he continued, that any talk of 'general sacrifice' was irrelevant. The sacrifices were being made by ordinary people while control was being handed to bankers and finance corporations.[126]

More fundamental political issues were not discussed in the Budget debate but were reserved for the following Monday, 31 October, when a Motion of Censure was made by Morrison. That day's proceedings deserve attention, for the Tories, who had remained unresponsive during the Budget debate, coalesced as one to defeat the Motion of Censure, which charged the government with incompetence and neglect in their economic and financial policy, deceit of the electorate for political ends and discriminatory measures.

Morrison opened by stating that the charge involved not only Rab but also the Prime Minister and other ministers. The specific charge against Rab was, first, that he had been proven incompetent in the discharge of his duty and, second, that he deceived the country in the course of the 1955 election. This was not the first occasion that he had deceived the electorate: in 1951 he gave a categorical undertaking not to touch the food subsidies but in his first Budget after the election he slashed them. Referring back to Rab's time at the Foreign Office in 1938–39, he added that Rab was

> expert and highly skilled in not answering Parliamentary Questions … This business of evasion, of promise breaking, of misleading the House and of misleading the country is not right. It is bad and it is to be deprecated. Not only the personal reputation of the Chancellor but … the personal reputation of the Prime Minister, is involved too, because he has given promises and undertakings which are now being broken by Her Majesty's Government.[127]

---

126 Ibid., cols 485–8.
127 Hansard, 31 October 1955, vol. 545, cols 683–5.

Moving to 1955, Morrison remarked that the spring Budget was 'a very, very limited affair', not really a Budget at all. He recalled an article by the financial editor of the *Manchester Guardian* on 20 April, predicting that the inflationary possibilities of the Budget would lead to an increased bank rate and a second Budget. This had been proved true. The spring Budget had no serious economic purpose but placed politics before national interest.

Rab's response was to dismiss both Gaitskell's and Morrison's speeches as 'the trial gallops for the leadership stakes of the Labour Party'. However, when Christopher Soames and Bob Boothby spoke in an attempt to deflect the argument from the issue of government incompetence, Boothby turned his criticism to Rab, saying:

> If the Chancellor of the Exchequer would only hold firm to the true traditions and fiscal policies of the Tory Party, he would have no need to impose fresh taxation. If he had held firm to those traditions, he would have had no reason to impose increased taxation in this Budget; and we should not now be half as frightened as we are of inflation.[128]

In that nice distinction Boothby made it clear that Rab was to be the sacrificial lamb. The sacrifice was noted by Percy Daines, Labour Member for East Ham North, who chided Tory Members for not giving the 'support and moral backing to make it more reasonable for him'.[129] By that point Rab must have tended to agree with him.

Predictably, with Members voting on straight party lines, the Motion of Censure was defeated. But it was Eden's government, not its Chancellor of the Exchequer, that was salvaged from the wreckage. The honour of the Prime Minister had been called into question by Morrison and the tactic of 'circling the waggons' around the leader sadly left Rab exposed on the outside.

Rab now had no illusions about his tenure at the Treasury. He

---

128 Ibid., cols 737–8. Boothby was no fan of Rab. According to Hugh Gaitskell, he openly stated that the Tories' opinion of Rab was one of 'contemptuous disdain'. (Williams, *The Diary of Hugh Gaitskell*, entry for 24 February 1956.)

129 Hansard, 31 October 1955, vol. 545, col. 756.

certainly knew the identity of his chosen successor. He may not, however, have known the full details of the terms that Macmillan had dictated before agreeing to take Rab's job. By the time that the implications of Eden's December reshuffle became clear, Rab had made the most unfortunate decision of his political life.

CHAPTER 12

THE LEADERSHIP, ROUND 1,
1953-55

When Churchill returned to 10 Downing Street in October 1951, eleven years had passed since he first became Prime Minister. Born in 1874, he was approaching his seventy-seventh birthday and colleagues assumed that he would soon hand over the reins to Eden. His standing in the country was unique; no one begrudged the great war leader a short peacetime tenure as Prime Minister before he bowed to the inevitable advance of years and stepped down. Churchill himself indicated that he would remain in office for a year.

Almost immediately, therefore, the question of the succession began to exercise his potential successors. Eden, confident of his position, nonetheless pressed Churchill to appoint him Deputy Prime Minister to legitimise his claim. The appointment of Rab to the Treasury greatly enhanced Rab's standing and Eden, concerned at the attention that the younger man was receiving, sensibly saw the need for him to secure the succession. The Prime Minister, however, resisted Eden's request, arguing that it would infringe on the Monarch's prerogative to appoint his chosen minister to form a Government. That can hardly have been his true reason as Attlee had held the title under Churchill from 1942 to 1945 and Herbert Morrison had held it under Attlee. Churchill himself had set a precedent by appointing Attlee Britain's first Deputy Prime Minister in 1942.

The Prime Minister's stated plan to stay in office for a year – if it was genuine – was revised when George VI died suddenly on 6 February 1952. It would be dereliction of duty, he argued, to desert the new Queen; he would postpone his decision, probably until after the Coronation in 1953.[1]

However assured Eden's succession might appear, there was inevitable speculation around the rise and fall of ministers, the possibility of illness intervening, and, after the 1952 Budget, journalists began to make predictions about the future of the 49-year-old Chancellor. An article in *The Spectator* tipped Rab as the next leader 'if, for any unhappy reason, Mr Eden fell out'.[2] No other likely successor had emerged; the Cabinet was made up of older men, Churchill's long-time associates, most of whom, it was assumed, would yield their Ministries when Eden succeeded.

With Churchill acting as Minister of Defence as well as Prime Minister, the same arrangement as in wartime, the 'inner circle' of ministers comprised Eden (Foreign Secretary), Cherwell (Paymaster General), Salisbury (Lord Privy Seal), Woolton (Lord President of the Council) and Ismay (Commonwealth Secretary), none of them in the first flush of youth. As he surveyed the assembled Cabinet, Rab, at the age of forty-nine, must have felt positively youthful. Eden aside, the inner circle was composed of peers; the only other credible contender for the top job after Eden was David Maxwell Fyfe, Home Secretary and a mere thirty months older than Rab. Maxwell Fyfe had made his reputation as deputy to Hartley Shawcross at the Nuremberg Trials. A brilliant and industrious barrister, he had worked closely with Rab in the drafting of *The Industrial Charter* and was tipped as a possible future leader.[3]

The 57-year-old Minister of Local Government and Planning,[4] Harold Macmillan, was not then considered a contender for 10 Downing Street. Despite his wartime role as 'Viceroy of the Mediterranean', he was not yet a member of Churchill's inner Cabinet and had hoped for a more important brief in the new government. When offering him the job, Churchill shrewdly pointed out that it could make his

---

1   Moran, *Churchill, Taken from the Diaries of Lord Moran*, Diary entry for 21 February 1952, p. 400.
2   *The Spectator*, 23 May 1952.
3   *Daily Mirror* poll of 1954, cited by *Oxford Dictionary of National Biography*.
4   The Ministry was renamed 'Ministry of Housing and Local Government'.

reputation or destroy it. At the 1950 Conservative conference, the ambitious target of building 300,000 homes annually had been enthusiastically adopted; the Minister of Housing would consequently have great visibility and an opportunity to make a name for himself both in the Commons and with the electorate. Macmillan, whose heart had been set on Defence, took a walk with Lady Dorothy[5] around the Chartwell lake and decided to accept the Prime Minister's offer.[6]

In late 1951, Rab could feel well pleased with his place in the constellation. Although not among Churchill's intimates, by virtue of his office he was close to the centre. Since 1944 he had been in the ascendant and was recognised as a key figure in the 'new' Tory Party, one of the principal architects of the election victory. He could afford to bide his time until the ruling group of sexagenarians retired and position himself to succeed Eden, who was five and a half years his senior. If anything were to happen to Eden, of course... well, that remained to be seen. In the meantime, he had the challenge – and the opportunity – of clearing the stables after six years of Socialist economics.

For the issue of after-Eden to make any sense, of course, there was the question of life after Winston. Here there were two dominant issues: the Prime Minister's age and his character. Even before the election of 1951 there were doubts about Churchill's stamina, his continuing interest in his role as leader, and, most worryingly, about his willingness to listen to advice.[7] Sir Leslie Rowan, his Principal Private Secretary during the war, commented that he could no longer remember figures, something he had always been able to do, and that he was walking slowly, like an old man.[8] Lord Moran concluded that 'Winston's mind is only alert when England's security is at stake ... The old appetite for work has gone; everything has become an effort.'[9]

From the day that Churchill took office until the day he stepped down, the various aspirants for his job assessed how his continued occupancy

---

5   Lady Dorothy Macmillan, Harold Macmillan's wife, daughter of the Duke of Devonshire.
6   Thorpe, *Supermac: The Life of Harold Macmillan* (London: Chatto & Windus, 2010), pp. 267–9.
7   Moran, *Churchill, Taken from the Diaries of Lord Moran*, Diary entry for 29 September 1951, p. 366.
8   Ibid., Diary entry for 5 January 1952, pp. 377–8.
9   Ibid., Diary entry for 26 January 1952, p. 395.

of 10 Downing Street affected their chances of taking up residence there. Each brought a different perspective to the complex equation.

In 1951, Anthony Eden stood head and shoulders above his colleagues. He had held Cabinet office before the war, resigned at the 'right' time in 1938, returned to Churchill's wartime Cabinet and accumulated experience of government that his rivals largely lacked. As Churchill's anointed, his position was virtually unchallengeable. With time, of course, others might climb the greasy pole and catch him but, in 1951, he stood alone. The sooner Churchill stepped down, therefore, the better it would be for Eden.

Maxwell Fyfe was unique among the aspirants in having a lucrative career outside politics. He is rumoured to have set himself the ambition of taking silk[10] in his thirties, becoming a government minister in his forties, and reaching the top of the legal profession in his fifties.[11] During the opposition years, he had earned an average of £25,000 annually[12] and could return to the Bar at will. He had already achieved the first two stages of his stated ambition by 1951 and, in the absence of any immediate temptation of greater power, it was time for him to focus on the third stage. By 1954, he had reached that conclusion. Recognising the inevitability of Eden's succession and probably calculating that he might be sixty-five before Eden stepped down, he seized the chance to become Lord Chancellor, taking the title Viscount Kilmuir, in the 1954 reshuffle. In his memoirs, he recalled that 'I might have considered my chances of becoming Prime Minister as a *tertium quid* [a third person of unspecified nature] after the manner of Bonar Law, had not Anthony and Rab been valued friends of mine.'[13]

Harold Macmillan had the most ground to catch up; significantly, in the high-risk job that he took on, he had as much scope as anyone to close the gap. He would have visibility and moral clout in Housing as the Tories had made their housing plans an election pledge, giving his own and the government's goals an identity of purpose. The only

10 'Taking silk' is the popular term for a barrister's being appointed KC (King's Counsel) or QC.
11 *Oxford Dictionary of National Biography*..
12 Approximately £2 million at 2014 values.
13 Kilmuir, *Political Adventure*, p. 233.

worrying proviso for Mac was that things would need to move quickly. Three years older than Eden and nearly nine years older than Rab, he needed Churchill to retire by 1953 and Eden to be in office for no more than one Parliament if he was to have a chance of entering No. 10 before his sixty-fifth birthday. After that, his chance would probably have evaporated. Recognising that he could not possibly supplant Eden in the time available, he could not afford to waste any time in supplanting Rab.

Rab alone enjoyed the luxury of being able to play it long. The longer that Churchill stayed in office, the longer he had to make his mark as Chancellor, the most visible of offices. Equally, Eden and Macmillan would come closer to retirement age with every day that Churchill delayed. If Eden took over in a year's time, the sooner Rab would become his heir apparent. If, on the other hand, Churchill stayed in office for four years and Eden survived two parliaments, Rab would still only be sixty-two. All he needed to do was to perform creditably at the Treasury and keep his name in the news. In the rational world that Rab inhabited, the rewards would naturally follow.

The early months of 1952 altered the alignment of starters and runners. Apart from the death of George VI, a second factor to alter calculations was Churchill's health. In August 1949 he had suffered a stroke in Monte Carlo. On 21 February 1952, he found himself unable to put his thoughts into speech and both he and Moran were concerned that this was the warning of a second stroke. Moran cautioned him that he would 'have to pull out or arrange things so that the strain is less'.[14] On the following day, Moran called on Jock Colville, Churchill's Principal Private Secretary, to establish if it would be possible to reduce the strain, as he had urged. Colville promptly took Moran to Lord Salisbury's office, where the three men discussed the best course of action.

Salisbury's predictable reaction was that the Prime Minister was not able to shed any of his responsibilities and that, therefore, the question was whether or not Churchill could do the work. As the three talked, Salisbury had a sudden inspiration: that Churchill should go to the

---

14 Ibid., Diary entry for 21 February 1952, p. 399.

House of Lords, retain the title of Prime Minister, while Eden acted as virtual PM, leading the House of Commons. Churchill alone had the prestige necessary to hold the office of PM from the Lords and, the three agreed, the only person that could persuade him to take that course was the Queen. Moran and Colville talked the matter over with Alan ('Tommy') Lascelles, the Queen's Private Secretary, but eventually agreed that even the Monarch would not be able to persuade Churchill. Moran continued to press him but ultimately, on 13 March, admitted failure. Churchill was determined to remain Prime Minister and equally determined to do so from the House of Commons.[15]

Fears for Churchill's health, adjourned since February 1952, reappeared on 23 June 1953 when he suffered his second stroke.[16] With Eden out of action for several months and the Prime Minister incapacitated, Rab was pitchforked into a position of unprecedented responsibility and prominence. For four months he was to run the government on a somewhat unconventional and makeshift basis.

If the Prime Minister had died, as his doctor expected, or had been forced to step down immediately, a constitutional muddle would have almost certainly occurred. Colville's opinion was that the Cabinet should recommend to the Queen that she invite Salisbury to form a caretaker government in Eden's absence. In an interview with Anthony Seldon, Colville explained that this was the most sensible option as Salisbury, a close friend of Eden, could be depended upon to step aside when Eden was ready to return.[17] To have appointed Butler, he argued in contradictory fashion, would be unreasonable as he would have to hand over to Eden after a few months. In other words, what held true for Salisbury did not hold true for Rab – a curious logical proposition. The only way that those two statements can be compatible is if it is assumed that Rab would not have yielded to Eden.

Colville's recommended course, moreover, would not have been

---

15 Lord Moran's account of the discussions with Colville and Salisbury are in Moran, *Churchill, Taken from the Diaries of Lord Moran*, Diary entry for 22 February 1952, pp. 400-404, and for 12 and 13 March 1952, pp. 407–8.
16 See Chapter 11.
17 Interview with Sir John Colville, Seldon, *Churchill's Indian Summer*, pp. 87–8 and pp. 537–8, note 40.

popular with Tory backbenchers. Lord Boyle was certain that even a caretaker Prime Minister from the House of Lords would have been unacceptable to the 1922 Committee.[18] Salisbury, therefore, performed a role as an elder statesman in the immediate aftermath of Churchill's stroke, but assumed no caretaker role.

Unless Churchill were to resign voluntarily, no action could decently be taken; his prestige in the country was too great and the party would suffer if it seemed to have carried out a *putsch*. All else is hypothesis. It is, however, significant that at no point does there seem to have been a movement to encourage Churchill to resign in favour of Rab. Instead, the assumption throughout was that the seat had to be kept warm for Eden, whatever the Prime Minister's state of health and however long Eden would be absent.

Three days after his stroke, talking with Moran, Churchill suddenly burst out, 'I'm not afraid of death, but it would be very inconvenient to a lot of people. Rab', he said, 'is very efficient up to a point, but he is narrow and doesn't see beyond his nose. If Anthony were standing by the door there, and I was here, and a telegram was given to him involving a decision, well, in nine cases out of ten we should agree.'[19]

This unsolicited comment seems to suggest that, if he had died, the Cabinet would have had to put up with Rab succeeding him ('very inconvenient to a lot of people') as Eden would have missed the boat, owing to his own convalescence. It also suggests that neither Churchill nor the Cabinet terribly wanted Rab to succeed. As a result, it was accepted by all parties that Rab would stand in until such time as Churchill or Eden or both could return and relieve him. At that point he would meekly step aside.

The episode raises a number of questions. First, there is the question of the alteration of the medical bulletin. Who took the initiative to change it and to give no indication that Churchill might have been rendered unfit to continue? Certainly it was not in Rab's interests that this should be done as, with both Churchill and Eden out of action,

---

18 Ibid., p. 88 and p. 538, note 41.
19 Moran, *Churchill, Taken from the Diaries of Lord Moran*, Diary entry for 26 June 1953, pp. 436–7.

there was a very good chance that he might have become Prime Minister immediately. Instead, he at least acquiesced to changes that were made with Colville's pen.[20]

Second, could Rab have insisted on different treatment? It would have been bad luck for Eden if, through incapacity, he was absent at a critical moment and unable to claim his inheritance. By the same token, it was bad luck for Rab that he was expected to shoulder responsibility for an indeterminate period (it turned out to be October before he was relieved) and then simply revert to the *status quo ante*. Might a more self-promoting, pushy politician have been able to force a better bargain? Rab was, at least, rewarded in the New Year Honours List but could he not have become Prime Minister rather than a Companion of Honour? Would another minister, for example Macmillan, have accepted that arrangement, had he been in Rab's shoes?

This was not a bargain that Rab could have demanded for himself, as that would have appeared grotesquely self-serving. For it to have succeeded there would have had to be a groundswell of support from his colleagues – and that support was not forthcoming. Now – and in the future – there was no strong and vocal pro-Butler party that made its views heard and, as a result, Rab was compelled to allow an opportunity to pass by, an opportunity that a more ruthless opportunist would have used to advantage.

Third, there is Churchill's own attitude. His comment that, whereas he and Eden generally agreed, Rab could not 'see beyond his nose' strongly suggests that the Prime Minister recognised the possibility that Rab might succeed him immediately. It also suggests that he was determined not to allow that to happen and that, whatever doubts he may have had about Eden, he was a more acceptable successor than Rab. If we stretch that point, it is possible that his resolve to keep Rab out may have played some part in Churchill's determination to carry on. It is certainly possible that members of Churchill's entourage, Salisbury for example, wanted the bulletin altered so as to remove the possibility of Rab becoming Prime Minister *faute de mieux*.

---

20 Howard, *RAB*, p. 198.

Lord Cherwell believed that, had Rab demanded the title as well as the responsibility, he could have prevailed.[21] Rab was a conscious conspirator in the decision to conceal the extent of Churchill's incapacity, but it is unclear exactly to what he conspired. In a later radio interview he was magisterially opaque:

> I was forbidden to mention it – forbidden ... I kept quiet at the time because I felt there was something to do with the Crown being involved, in the very early days of the young Queen's accession. The point was that I was the only person who was active, fit and running everything – and I think they felt they should protect Anthony.[22]

Rab, who could be magnificently indiscreet on occasion, went no further than this studiedly vague explanation, and he gave no hint of his personal feelings. There is, however, a clue in his own account of events. In his memoirs he quotes a letter that he received from his friend James Stuart, the Secretary of State for Scotland. Stuart pointed out to him that he was acting Prime Minister, acting Foreign Secretary in the Commons, as well as Chancellor. Those responsibilities added up to quite a burden and Stuart urged him to remember the weight of responsibility that had killed Stafford Cripps.[23]

In the very next paragraph, Rab mentions that he 'heard from Anthony who was in Athens at the conclusion of a yachting trip around the Greek islands'. By the same post he received a letter from Jane Portal, informing him that Churchill was 'in the depths of depression' on the French Riviera. He would be better employed, Rab's niece felt, in working on his *History of the English Speaking Peoples*.[24] The contrast between Rab, over-working himself in London, and his senior colleagues, relaxing at various points in the Mediterranean, is too vivid to be accidental.

As Churchill recovered he once more dug his heels in over resigning. Although he told the Queen that he would retire in the autumn,

---

21 Howard, *RAB*, p. 199 and p. 386, note 69.
22 BBC Radio Profile, 29 June 1978. Cited by Howard, *RAB*, p. 199.
23 Butler, *The Art of the Possible*, p. 170.
24 Ibid., p. 171.

when 'Anthony could take over', and assured Clementine that he would step down in October, he soon added the rider that 'circumstances may convince me of my indispensability'.[25] He accepted that he might never recover but was determined not to make any decisions until September. These postponements seem almost as if he were determined to keep Rab out, particularly after his ineffective foreign policy speech in July. His motives were mixed. He certainly wanted to have 'a shot at settling this Russian business' and he felt that he alone could deal with Moscow. After Stalin's death in March he was insistent that a Big Three summit was now possible and he was desperate to gain the kudos for bringing it about. But he was also increasingly uncertain that Eden would be an effective leader, a concern shared by several of his senior colleagues.[26] Even when Beaverbrook took him to task, warning him that Attlee would attack the government as being full of invalids, he insisted on remaining in place until October. He was aware that to retire while Eden was absent might well hand Rab the top job and he felt 'it would not be fair to Anthony to let Rab take it'.[27]

In October, at the party conference in Margate, Churchill acquitted himself well in the Leader's speech, overcoming concerns that he might not be fully recovered; Eden returned to work and Rab was relieved of his additional responsibilities. He had 'demonstrated that he [was] of Prime Ministerial timber' and, according to David Pitblado, Joint PPS at Downing Street,[28] 'he may be in a better position now than he would be if the PM resigned'.[29] The *status quo* suited Rab reasonably well; nonetheless, in common with Eden and Macmillan, he was anxious to know Churchill's intentions – an anxiety that the Prime Minister did little to ease.

Among Churchill's entourage a concern grew that Eden 'might strike' from sheer impatience. Rab, by contrast, was content to be

---

25 Moran, *Churchill, Taken from the Diaries of Lord Moran*, Diary entries for 28 June, 30 June and 4 July 1953, pp. 441 and 338.

26 Bodleian: MS Woolton, 21.42.

27 Moran, *Churchill, Taken from the Diaries of Lord Moran*, Diary entries for 25 July, 28 July, 5 August 1953, pp. 473, 476, 478.

28 David Pitblado, who had served Clement Attlee as Principal Private Secretary, was joint PPS (with John Colville) to Churchill.

29 Ibid., Diary entry for 8 September 1953, p. 499. Conversation between Moran and Pitblado.

'sitting on the fence with one leg dangling on each side'. 'He likes cricket similes,' Moran wrote. 'He is trying to keep a straight bat, he says. He is not trying to make runs.'[30]

During early 1954 Churchill appeared to favour Rab as a possible successor, despite his relations with Eden. 'Rab is behaving very well', he said to Moran. 'He scorns to play for popularity, just does what he thinks is right.' At dinner on 11 March the Prime Minister spoke frankly to Rab, comparing himself to 'an aeroplane at the end of its flight, in the dusk, with the petrol running out, in search of a safe landing'.[31] This evocative Churchillian prose was, however, not followed by action on the part of the pilot.

Despite such indications of his long-term intentions, however, Churchill remained in place. To Moran he said, 'I shall certainly not retire when any day anything might happen.' Disagreements with the Cabinet, however, prompted Rab, Macmillan and Salisbury to resort to other methods of persuasion. Macmillan decided to call on Clementine and make their view known.[32] Unsurprisingly, he achieved nothing.

By the end of June, Eden was talking openly of resigning unless Churchill stepped down. 'Things are coming to a head,' observed Colville.[33] The Prime Minister criticised Eden for real and imagined faults, using these as a further reason for refusing to budge. Kilmuir and Norman Brook expressed sympathy for Eden and Rab as 'they don't know where they are'. Yet Churchill boasted that 'all the members of the Cabinet have accepted my staying on', adding, 'There won't be any trouble, I think.'[34] If not trouble, there was certainly widespread impatience at the party conference, where MPs made clear their collective opinion that Churchill should resign.

Rab, shattered by his wife's death in December, is less prominent in the counsels of early 1955. Indeed, Macmillan appears to have been the only minister who spoke his mind to Churchill. Eden found it

---

30 Ibid., Diary entry for 11 October 1953, p. 514.
31 Butler, *The Art of the Possible*, p. 173.
32 Soames, *Clementine Churchill* (London: Cassell, 1979), p. 449; Colville, *Footprints in Time*, pp. 253–5; Macmillan, *Tides of Fortune*, p. 537.
33 Moran, *Churchill, Taken from the Diaries of Lord Moran*, Diary entry for 1 July 1954, p. 608.
34 Ibid., Diary entries for 1 July, 30 July and 29 August 1954, pp. 608, 623, 633.

harder and harder to speak to him; the *Manchester Guardian* ran a headline 'Cabinet Urging Premier to Resign'.[35] At the end of March, Rab optimistically reported, 'We've got the fish on the hook, but he hasn't been gaffed yet.'[36] Pressure built until, finally, Churchill accepted the inevitable and it was done. Eden succeeded Churchill and Rab succeeded Eden as Dauphin.

For Rab, the transition was a form of closure. Since June 1953 he had been under enormous strain: from the covert arrangement that gave him circumscribed power and his uncertainty at how best to exercise it; the deteriorating condition and death of Sydney in December 1954; the final heave to detach Churchill from Downing Street; imposition of austerity measures in February; Eden's accession and the imminent election, coupled with the decision to announce a Budget at odds with his February measures. Finally, when he took stock, there was the realisation that his star had not risen during the past twenty months, while Macmillan had consolidated and strengthened his position.

Rab had tried to keep the peace between Eden and Churchill, an increasingly difficult task. Just three weeks before Churchill finally stepped down, Eden, supported by the majority of the Cabinet, led an attack on him, demanding to know his intentions. Rab interjected calmly and rationally. All that mattered, he said, was the question of who would lead the Tories at the next election.[37] Not until Churchill took that final definitive step could anyone be sure. When he did, hosting a farewell dinner party at No. 10, at which the Queen and the Duke of Edinburgh were guests, Eden entered quickly, almost furtively, avoiding the crowd and the journalists who thronged the street. Macmillan, also a guest, played to the crowd, making, one observer believed, 'an early pitch for the succession'.[38]

Rab still had the Treasury, despite Woolton's urging Eden to move him immediately. The new Prime Minister demurred. There were also a Budget and an election imminent and Eden needed apparent stability

---

35 *Manchester Guardian*, 23 March 1955.
36 Bodleian: MS Woolton. Diary entries for 23 and 30 March 1955.
37 Bodleian: MSS Macmillan, dep d20.50. Diary entry for 14 March 1955.
38 Thorpe, *Supermac*, p. 298.

above all. Yet he had already decided that Rab must be moved, telling Robert Carr, 'I can't move Rab from the Treasury, even if in the end it proves the destruction of my Government.'[39] Quite why this might have happened is unclear. One year later, Eden proved himself capable of achieving that result without Rab's help.

In the intervening year, Rab steadily and definitively lost ground, even if his decline was not widely observed. We have seen how his October 1955 Budget was savaged by the opposition[40] and in the last week of October Rab's support within the party evaporated. Luke-warm reaction to the Budget measures from the Tory benches must have been a warning; the extent to which his colleagues rallied on 31 October should not have encouraged him.

On that day, Rab's prospects of becoming Leader of the Conservative Party evaporated. The Tories gave him support when he was assaulted by one after another of the Labour front bench. But their efforts were for party solidarity in the face of a Motion of Censure, not for the defence of Rab. Once Eden, the party, their positions in government were threat-ened, they coalesced as Tories traditionally do. Far better that they should not have had to do so; they held it against Rab that he had put them and the party in that position. Hatreds, resentments and slights surfaced; Rab became the legatee of their doctrinal resentment. He had long been considered too clever by half; now he was a heretic whom they could os-tracise for less envy-filled reasons. The difference between apparent Tory indifference on 27 October and wholehearted rallying on 31 October was remarked on both by Percy Daines and Hugh Dalton who commented:

> We criticised the Budget and the Chancellor's proposals each according to his ability, and he replied according to his ability – sometimes being left very lonely in debate by all the phalanxes of his supporters.[41]

That issue came up again when Harold Wilson, speaking during the Third Reading of the Finance Bill, pointed out that 'at a time when

---

39 Ibid., p. 301.
40 See Chapter 11.
41 Hansard, 31 October 1955, vol. 545, col. 788.

Government changes are said to be in the offing and when, if rumour is right, there are to be a number of vacancies upon the Government Front Bench … hardly an hon. Member opposite has been found to speak in support of the Chancellor of the Exchequer.'[42]

Ten days later, Eden performed his long-delayed reshuffle of the Cabinet, moving Macmillan to replace Rab at the Treasury. On 14 December, Attlee had stepped down from the Labour leadership and Gaitskell had taken his place. Eden's decision had been planned during the summer and, although the reshuffle was seen as a reaction to Gaitskell, it was a quite independent initiative. It was certainly designed to give the impression of 'gingering up' the government and, in that context, Rab's long tenure as Chancellor was bound to end. The curious aspect of the move is that the fresh face at the Treasury was that of Macmillan, eight years older than Rab. Relative age was secondary; Macmillan, after his success at Housing, was perceived as more dynamic, while, according to Treasury officials, Rab had lost his energy and dynamism after Sydney's death. Eden, according to Macmillan, 'felt that Butler, after his four years' unremitting labour, had temporarily lost his grip and needed some respite from the heavy load which he had been carrying. He thought that, of all his colleagues, I would be most likely – from my all-round experience – to be able to carry the burden.'[43]

From December 1955, as Eden came under mounting criticism in the press, both he and Rab made critical errors from which only Macmillan could benefit. Despite his resounding success in the election, Eden soon came under attack as an indecisive leader and for having lost grip;[44] even the *Daily Telegraph* was unenthusiastic, running a headline 'Waiting for the Smack of Firm Government'.[45] This trend culminated in a strident headline in *The Observer* that 'Eden must go'.[46] The barrage of negative articles infuriated Eden and he responded foolishly, issuing an official response from Downing Street that rumours of his

---

42 Hansard, 13 December 1955, vol. 547, col. 1025.
43 Macmillan, *Tides of Fortune*, pp. 696–7.
44 In particular, *Daily Mail*, 3 January 1956; *The Times*, 2 January 1956.
45 *Daily Telegraph*, 3 January 1956.
46 *The Observer*, 9 January 1956.

imminent resignation were 'false and without any foundation whatsoever', a remarkable tactical error.[47] For his part, Rab contributed a
memorable Rabism, promising publicly 'to support the Prime Minister in all his difficulties'.

Rab contributed further to his own decline with an ill-considered
remark in an interview as he was about to depart for a welcome break,
staying at Somerset Maugham's villa on the French Riviera. Fed the
question by a Press Association reporter, 'Mr Butler, would you say
that this is the best Prime Minister we have?' he replied in the affirmative. Not only was the response widely quoted, it was soon distorted
as though Rab had spontaneously volunteered his opinion that 'Mr
Eden is the best Prime Minister we have'. As Rab tartly but accurately
wrote, 'I do not think it did Anthony any good. It did not do me any
good either.'[48]

In November 1955, the *New Statesman* had evaluated the triumvirate
of Eden, Rab and Macmillan and described Mac as 'both the most
brilliant and the least self-assured of the present triumvirate'. 'This',
the article continued, 'explains why the more thoughtful Tories would
like to see him as its leader. But there is little chance that their wishes
will come true.'[49]

By the end of January, Macmillan had become justifiably self-
assured. In three short months both the Prime Minister and the Lord
Privy Seal had gone into steep decline and neither had the necessary
grip on the controls to reverse it. They were descending together and
there was jealousy between them as each or both were criticised in
the press. Clarissa Eden was particularly sensitive to bad press. When
Eden's Press Officer William Clark pointed out that Rab was receiving
more criticism, she retorted that criticism of Rab was justified, whereas
criticism of her husband was not.[50]

In early 1956, the 'Eden Must Go' movement gathered steam but there
was no obvious replacement. Rab's stock remained low, and Macmillan

---

47 *New Statesman*, 14 January 1956.
48 Butler, *The Art of the Possible*, p. 183.
49 *New Statesman*, November 1955, cited by Sampson, *Macmillan: A Study in Ambiguity* (London:
   Allen Lane, 1967), p. 90.
50 Clark, *From Three Worlds* (London: Sidgwick & Jackson, 1986), p. 156.

had not yet had the opportunity to prove himself in any of the Great Offices. Not only was Eden anathema to the left, there was also growing concern in the Conservative Party, as a Labour Party publication pointed out in an article headlined 'Why the Tories Want Eden's Head'.

The Prime Minister was not 'making a go of things', the article argued. He lacked dynamism, was stand-offish and, most importantly, had done nothing to combat rising prices. The Tories were most afraid of a worsening of the economic situation and resultant industrial strife. In this scenario a tougher leader than Eden would be needed to restore equilibrium. Rab was not that man.[51]

Clark suspected that Macmillan was the source of leaks to feed the anti-Eden press, which flared up again in March. Randolph Churchill, the former Prime Minister's son and a persistent critic of Eden, wrote a particularly vitriolic article in the *Evening Standard*, arguing that the time had come for Rab and Macmillan to replace him. Clark went to speak to Macmillan, who expressed disapproval, saying that he would speak to the Prime Minister. Clark 'felt in fact that Macmillan was a bit shifty, and … wondered to what extent he was intriguing.'[52] Nor was Eden alone; Rab too was under attack. A targeted leak appeared in the *Daily Mail* in the summer.[53] Rab, the article hinted, might go to the House of Lords. Rab was quick to deny it emphatically, but the suggestion had been made.

Since December 1953, by contrast, Macmillan had been in the ascendant. From his power base at 11 Downing Street he issued invitations to sherry parties, wooing backbenchers, building his following. By contrast, as one account of these years points out, if Rab 'had asked people to sherry at the Lord Privy Seal's Office, many of them would have been hard pressed to find it'.[54] As Macmillan's visibility waxed, he merely had to wait for one cataclysmic event to derail Eden's government. In the event, he had a mere four months to wait.

---

51 *Socialist Leader*, 14 January 1956; Trinity: Butler Papers, RAB, L53. *Socialist Leader* was the weekly newspaper of the Independent Labour Party, subsequently merged into the Labour Party and renamed *Labour Leader*, published monthly.
52 Clark, *From Three Worlds*, p. 162.
53 *Daily Mail*, 3 July 1956; Trinity: Butler Papers, RAB, L103.
54 Thorpe, *The Uncrowned Prime Ministers* (London: Darkhorse Publishing, 1980), p. 201.

CHAPTER 13

FROM MACMILLAN'S SIDE OF THE NET, 1951–56

As Harold and Lady Dorothy Macmillan walked around the lake at Chartwell after the Conservative victory in October 1951, taking time to consider Churchill's offer, one question was assuredly uppermost in Macmillan's mind: would he be able to parlay his handling of an unglamorous Ministry into a position of prominence that would mark him out as a possible party leader? Ironically, the precedent that he must have considered was that of Rab Butler. Had not Rab done just that at the equally unglamorous Board of Education? Was not Rab even then reaping his reward as Chancellor of the Exchequer?

Three weeks before the election, Brendan Bracken, who seemed 'to be in the thick of things',[1] had told Macmillan that Churchill would stay for twelve to eighteen months, that Eden would go to the Foreign Office and Rab to the Exchequer. What, Bracken asked, would Mac like? Macmillan had hoped for the Ministry of Defence but in 1951, as in 1940, the new Prime Minister initially reserved that office for himself. There was no high-profile slot into which Macmillan could be fitted. The question, simply, was what he could make of Churchill's offer.

The war had ended six years before but post-war austerity persisted. In no sector was this more apparent than in the Labour Party's failure to build the houses promised in 1945. Whilst the Ministry lacked the prestige of the Great Offices of State, the issue of housing was one that commanded public attention and might have enormous repercussions

---

1   Bodleian: MSS Macmillan, dep d9*. Diary entry for 4 October 1951.

at a future election. Macmillan was not slow to appreciate the calculus of power and influence, of visibility and public acclaim. Churchill's offer was the best available; he quickly accepted it.

Within a month he had surveyed the battlefield on which his ascendancy would be built and recognised, long before his future antagonist, that his rise would take place *pari passu* with Rab's eclipse. Rab would be an inevitable, regrettable casualty. Taking Churchill's words in earnest, he worked long hours to set up the machinery of his housing programme: supply and delivery of raw materials; incentives for builders to develop land; and the necessary budget from the Treasury. From the first days he assessed which of his colleagues stood between him and Downing Street, and marshalled his forces accordingly. He fully appreciated the irony that had placed Rab in control of the funds he needed. In the month after the election, he wrote in his diary that 'The Chancellor of the Exchequer gives one the impression of being a bit rattled at the Treasury. Butler is able, conscientious, and has a good sense of humour. But I do not think he has any real grasp of the proportion of things.'[2]

The 'proportion of things' to Macmillan was simply how he would achieve his targets and correspondingly establish his reputation. He recognised that a battle with Rab was inevitable, noting 'I want to build 800,000 houses during the next three years. I should expect to do 230,000 in 1952, 265,000 in 1953, 300,000 in 1954.'[3] A blend of emollience and aggression was employed when Macmillan and Rab met.

In a meeting at the Treasury in mid-December, Macmillan launched an attack on the Treasury officials' plans. 'I made it clear to Butler that I would resign if my plan of working up to 300,000 by 1954 was not accepted,' he recorded. 'So far as Rab can be pinned down (he is a good diplomatist) he seemed to accept this.'[4] Rab was quite farsighted enough to see the implications, 'the proportion of things'. But he had much on his plate, whereas Macmillan had one grand issue, one that he would resign over if he didn't get what he wanted. The two

---

2   Bodleian: MSS Macmillan, dep. d10. Diary entry for 30 November 1951.
3   Bodleian: MSS Macmillan, dep. d10.32. Diary entry for 15 December 1951.
4   Bodleian: MSS Macmillan, dep. d10.34–5. Diary entry for 21 December 1951

men had very different priorities. Whether Rab yielded to Macmillan or continued to resist – thus vitiating an election promise – it was the Minister of Housing who was calling the tune.

When Macmillan presented his housing plan to the Cabinet in December, Rab temporised, proposing that another committee be appointed and another Cabinet Paper presented, recognising 'the political (if no other) need to work up to 300,000'. Churchill asked if Macmillan accepted Rab's view, to which Macmillan replied firmly in the negative, 'as another committee means another month'. 'So we have thrown the double-six,' Macmillan recorded. 'I handed my papers to Norman Brook (Cabinet Secretary) at the end of the Cabinet, so I hope that he will put it in the minutes as the Cabinet decision.'[5] A double-six indeed, as he not only overcame Rab's objections, but established himself as the author of the entire operation.

The word that Macmillan was on the rise spread rapidly. At the end of the year he recorded philosophically in his diary that 'D [Dorothy] tells me that many of her friends think that I have been put into the housing job in order to fail and finish my political career.' Malcolm McCorquodale, the Member for Epsom, had warned her at a luncheon party that 'He must be tough – very tough … For you know who would like him out of the way.' 'All this is very mysterious and to me very unpleasant,' Macmillan wrote. 'It is always said that, in politics, there are no friendships at the top I suppose Eden and Butler are those indicated. But Eden's position is secure, and Butler is so much younger that he can wait.'[6] That entry leaves no doubt where Macmillan envisaged his office might ultimately lead. He set about accumulating as much experience and exposure as he could outside his department, while not letting the housing programme be held up. Creating the image of a man equally at home in foreign as in domestic affairs was to create the image of a Prime Minister in waiting.

Rab's prestige increased substantially during 1952 as a result of his Budget and of the greater trust that the Prime Minister reposed in

---

5   Bodleian: MSS Macmillan, dep. d10.37–8. Diary entry for 28 December 1951.
6   Bodleian: MSS Macmillan, dep. d10.44–5. Diary entry for 30 December 1951.

him, withdrawing the watchdogs that he had posted to the Treasury. Whilst he was forthright in making clear the economies to be practised, however, he was essentially preaching austerity, the same sermon that Cripps had preached five years before. Macmillan's mission, by contrast, was to herald a new dawn, the end of austerity as he relentlessly drove the housing programme to achieve the promised targets. From Rab's perspective, Macmillan's repeated demands for costly and imported building materials, which began as a nuisance, rapidly became a threat.

The threat was made clear in January, when Macmillan launched what he termed 'The Battle of the Capital Investment Programme'.[7] He urged that the Town and Country Planning Act be amended and the 'development charge' abolished, a move that would increase the potential profit for developers. Rab, naturally, resisted this and from January to October 1952 Macmillan continued to press for the amendment. Even as Rab was introducing severe measures – cuts in imports, reduced travel allowances – he was being forced to agree to Macmillan's plans.[8]

While the Chancellor imposed emergency measures, Macmillan incessantly argued in Cabinet that his needs were exceptional and must have priority if he was to achieve the promised 300,000 new homes each year.[9] The promise, a cornerstone of the Tories' electoral appeal, was not one to be broken lightly and Rab was aware of its importance. He was also aware that with each success Mac was improving his stature within the party and with the electorate at large. Voters were able to see Macmillan's energy, legendary during the war but recently dormant, chanelled single-mindedly into obtaining building materials, seeing that they were delivered on time, building new towns (ensuring that the pubs were built first and not last), driving himself and his Ministry officials to achieve the government's targets. Through the first half of the year Macmillan continued to demand the necessary funds,

---

7   Bodleian: MSS Macmillan, dep. d10.46. Diary entry for 1–4 January 1952.
8   Bodleian: MSS Macmillan, dep. d10.59–60. Diary entry for 22 January 1952.
9   Macmillan was also involved in a running battle with Rab over raising the exemption limit for stamp duty on the purchase of a new house.

at the same time assessing Rab's responses, looking for weaknesses, treating every confrontation as symbolic of a more important struggle. At the end of January he commented:

> *I was not so impressed by the Chancellor of the Exchequer today. No doubt he is tired. He seemed not to have a real grip of the situation, and to move too rapidly from one opinion to another. He seems to start firmly, on the basis of the Treasury brief. Then, as the situation proceeds, he is driven to see how thin, unimaginative, and pedantic these briefs often are.*[10]

Reginald Bevins, Macmillan's Parliamentary Private Secretary, recalled Mac's brushes with Rab:

> When there was a bit of a tussle in Cabinet as to whether he wasn't stretching our economic resources by building too many houses, he persuaded Churchill to allow him to argue it out with Rab Butler. Macmillan had, I think, about three nocturnal talks with Rab. I remember the last occasion very vividly. He had a drink with me in the smoking room at about midnight, which was rather late, and then he went off to see Rab and said would I wait for him. He came down at 2 o'clock into the smoking room and bought me a drink and said, 'It's all over Reg, I've got my own way, and I simply report to the Prime Minister that Rab has agreed with me.' Rab was tired, Macmillan had more stamina.[11]

The conflict between Chancellor and Minister of Housing became public knowledge and an article in *The Observer* asked why and how Macmillan won the struggle with Rab: 'The answer is to be found partly in the able personality of Mr Macmillan himself, whose furious enthusiasm and quickness in argument make him a formidable opponent. There even may be a weakness in Mr Butler's own make-up.'[12]

Rab, the article continued, was 'not quite the Iron Chancellor that

---

10 Bodleian: MSS Macmillan, dep. d10.65–6. Diary entry for 24 January 1952.
11 Interview with Thames Television, 1970. Thompson, *The Day Before Yesterday* (London: Sidgwick & Jackson, 1971), p. 96.
12 *The Observer*, 3 August 1952.

the late Stafford Cripps was'. Macmillan concurred, noting at the end of July that

> *The two days' debate on the economic situation has gone badly for the Govt. Butler made a dull, lifeless and academic speech, full of lofty platitudes, but saying and doing nothing to justify the tremendous 'build-up' which the press (stimulated by himself and his propaganda) had given to the occasion. In other words ... a great flop. This was not altogether poor Butler's fault as a week or two ago Churchill had given the impression that a great new policy was to be announced. There is no new policy; it is just Cripps and water as before.*[13]

The battle over the development charge continued fitfully through the summer. Waged in Cabinet it assumed more importance than it deserved, becoming a symbol of 'clout' to both Rab and Macmillan. Rab, typically, was prepared to negotiate a solution, but Macmillan remained adamant that the charge simply be abolished, scorning any notion of compromise. 'Here the Chancellor of the Exchequer has now definitely declared himself,' he wrote,

> *whereas before he had shown a certain degree of hesitation. He is against me and for retaining [the] charge, tho' at a lower rate. He starts at 80 per cent but would go to 60 per cent. This, of course, is the most futile suggestion of all, esp. in the case of arbitrary valuations ... But it sounds a sort of 'compromise' and will probably appeal to the Cabinet. I'm afraid it means another great struggle with Butler and the Treasury at next week's Cabinet.*[14]

In October, Macmillan finally succeeded in detaching Rab's supporters in Cabinet and the development charge was abolished, as Mac had urged since January. 'The Chancellor of the Exchequer did not fight unduly hard for 50 per cent,' Mac noted with satisfaction.[15] This accelerated his programme and by late 1953, amid a fanfare of laudatory

---

13   Bodleian: MSS Macmillan, dep. d12.2–3. Diary entry for 30 July 1952.
14   Bodleian: MSS Macmillan, dep d12.16–17. Diary entries for 13 and 15 August 1952.
15   Bodleian: MSS Macmillan, dep. d12.65. Diary entry for 14 October 1952.

publicity, Macmillan had met his target. Between 1 November 1952 and 31 October 1953, 310,000 houses were built.

Mac was one of the few colleagues that Rab never successfully opposed. Looking back on those two critical years in an interview with Anthony Seldon, Rab wistfully recalled: 'He used to press me like hell … it may have been my fault really … I had been told that I really ought not to have let it through … it was my fault that I didn't realise what a terrific strain on the economy this was.'[16]

Macmillan's tactics had been deft. Reading Churchill accurately, he understood that the issue of housing would bore him and that he would happily leave all the details to Macmillan. Demonstrating the greatest possible contrast with Labour's failed housing programme, on the other hand, would be a priority. Thus Mac from the outset held a trump card.

Nor was he content to hold just one. He assembled a hand of honours and trumps, building the potential to play against all comers. Eden had no experience beyond foreign affairs; by 1951 Macmillan had made and developed extensive European contacts through the Consultative Assembly of the Council of Europe in Strasbourg;[17] in January 1952, he sent Eden a paper on European federation;[18] in August he completed a paper for the Commonwealth Economic Conference.[19] This was not mere inter-departmental competition. This was a brazen statement that Mac was ready to play at the big table. In July he noted in his diary, 'I like both Butler and Eden. They both have great charm. But it has been cruelly said that in politics there are no friends at the top. I fear it is so.'[20]

By the end of 1952, Macmillan had concluded that determination and resolution could carry the day. He became decidedly contemptuous of Rab's tendency to compromise. When Treasury officials produced papers quite at variance with agreed policy, he scoffed that 'Butler, who seemed quite happy with the previous decisions, has equally

---

16 Seldon, *Churchill's Indian Summer*, pp. 258–9.
17 Bodleian: MSS Macmillan, dep d6 and d7 *passim*.
18 Bodleian: MSS Macmillan, dep d10.75. Diary entry for 27 January 1952.
19 Bodleian: MSS Macmillan, dep d12.10. Diary entry for 4 August 1952.
20 Bodleian: MSS Macmillan, dep 11*, 111. Diary entry for 17 July 1952.

happily swallowed the new line.'[21] In the following week, he was even more derisive:

> *I have amused myself by composing a reply to a quite ridiculous letter which I have received, signed by the Chancellor of the Exchequer, but obviously written by one Mr Turnbull of the Treasury. He complains that the building industry is employing more men. But he does not say that productivity has increased by a much larger percentage – nearly double. I cannot understand how ministers can bring themselves to write such letters to their colleagues.*[22]

In the same week, while both Churchill and Eden were absent, he was unhappy that Rab should preside at Cabinet meetings. 'Last time it was the Leader of the House (Lord Privy Seal),' he noted. 'I lunched last week with the LPS, Harry Crookshank. He was much amused at this (which I suppose is the result of a careful intrigue) more especially as there aren't going to be any Cabinets next week, and after that Churchill will be back.'[23] For Macmillan to rise, Rab had to fall – a rational result, because 'The Chancellor of the Exchequer', he said simply, 'has time on his side and can afford to wait.'[24]

Macmillan, by contrast, could not. Nor, however, could he force the pace of change. Throughout 1953, impatient for Churchill to retire and allow Eden to take over, he assessed the relative position of Rab and himself. 'The situation is really fascinating,' he wrote. 'Butler is, of course, playing a winning game. He has, in his side, his comparative youth, his oriental subtlety, his power of quiet but effective intrigue – and the absence of any real competition so well equipped.'[25]

By October, with the success of the housing programme achieved and mentioned in the Queen's Speech in November, Mac set about equipping himself to offer Rab real competition. Focussing on foreign affairs, he was careful not to trespass on Eden's patch, while offering unsolicited papers on Europe and the Atlantic alliance. When Eden

---

21 Bodleian: MSS Macmillan, dep d12.31–2. Diary entries for 1–5 September 1952.
22 Bodleian: MSS Macmillan, dep d12.38. Diary entry for 10 September 1952.
23 Bodleian: MSS Macmillan, dep d12.40. Diary entry for 11 September 1952.
24 Bodleian: MSS Macmillan, dep d12.51–2. Diary entry for 27 September 1952.
25 Bodleian: MSS Macmillan, dep d14.56. Diary entry for 31 July 1953.

finally became Prime Minister in April 1955 and Macmillan succeeded him as Foreign Secretary, he had little time for Rab or for domestic politics. Throughout the spring and summer he was totally immersed in foreign affairs. In October, Eden's determination to move Rab from the Exchequer provided the long-awaited opportunity for a bold pre-emptive bid.

When Eden proposed the move, Macmillan, immediately aware of its implications, reacted with canny and voracious prescience. In an exchange described by Peter Hennessy as 'perhaps the most bizarre correspondence that I have ever read in the National Archives between a senior Cabinet minister and a Premier',[26] Macmillan laid down outrageous conditions for his acceptance of the move. Arguing that as Foreign Secretary he had, under the Prime Minister and Cabinet, overall control of foreign policy, he demanded that he should have similar authority over the home front as Chancellor. In doing so, he not only dictated his future position in relation to Rab but, by the very stipulation, dictated stiff terms to Eden. Mac was that most dangerous animal, an old man in a hurry, but he must have had a shrewd idea that his bid would succeed.

Writing to Eden from Paris on 24 October, three days before Rab's unfortunate announcement of his Budget, Macmillan demanded

> *a position in the Cabinet not inferior to that held by the present Chancellor. As Foreign Secretary, I am head of the foreign front under you as Prime Minister. As Chancellor, I must be undisputed head of the home front, under you. If Rab becomes Leader of the House and Lord Privy Seal that will be fine. But I could not agree that he should be Deputy Prime Minister ... You will realise that the presence of a much respected ex-Chancellor, with all that this implies, in the Cabinet and in Whitehall must somewhat add to my difficulties, however loyal he will try to be. If he were also Deputy Prime Minister, my task would be impossible.[27]*

---

26 Hennessy, *Having It So Good: Britain in the Fifties* (London: Penguin, 2007), p. 377.
27 Bodleian: MSS Macmillan, dep d24*.2–5. Macmillan, like Caesar when he crossed the Rubicon, added the postscript in his diary, '*Alea jacta est*' (the die is cast).

When Eden proposed a compromise whereby Rab, as Leader of the House, chaired Cabinet meetings in Eden's absence, Macmillan continued to press his claim, arguing reasonably that this constituted the substance of Deputy Prime Ministership even if the title were not granted.[28] Eden, however, refused to budge on this issue as he had already given Rab assurances and an official 'batting order' of the party leadership had been circulated. Nonetheless, Mac had extracted a remarkable concession from the Prime Minister and gone some way to consolidating his ascendancy over Rab.

Later that week, reading the English newspapers in Geneva, Macmillan observed with a certain satisfaction that 'the Labour Opposition is working itself up into a great state of excitement, attacking Rab and his "honour". His colleagues (who are often rather bored with Rab's appeal to what is "honourable" in Cabinet) will not be able to avoid a certain amusement.'[29] 'The most damaging thing and the most lasting attack will be on Rab personally,' Macmillan believed – 'that the April Budget, with its tax remissions was a swindle – for the Election. Rab has always rather paraded his virtue (sometimes to the disquiet of his colleagues) so this sort of attack will be very wounding'.[30]

Gaitskell, observing this interplay, later commented that Rab's position had been damaged beyond repair by his 'dishonest' Budget of October. 'There seems to be no doubt', he wrote, 'that Macmillan was not getting on at all well with Eden as Foreign Secretary, and that Tory opinion is rather veering round towards him as the best of the three.'[31]

One of Macmillan's biographers argues that Macmillan became convinced of Rab's weakness with the collapse of ROBOT in 1952 and that thereafter his star was on the wane. Then Rab made a series of mistakes in 1955 from which no salvation was possible. Most importantly, he committed 'political suicide' when he left the Treasury but allowed Eden to marginalise him as a non-departmental minister while he promoted Macmillan in the reshuffle. His five critical mistakes

---

28 TNA: PREM 5/228, Macmillan to Eden, 9 December 1955.
29 Bodleian: MSS Macmillan dep d24*.24. Diary entry for 30 October 1955.
30 Bodleian: MSS Macmillan dep d24*.21–2. Diary entry for 27 October 1955.
31 Williams, *The Diary of Hugh Gaitskell*, p. 422. Diary entry for 16–21 January 1956.

on this analysis were: staying at the Treasury when Eden succeeded Churchill; fashioning an electioneering Budget in April 1955; staying at the Treasury after the May election; introducing the 'Pots and Pans' budget; and accepting the non-departmental post of Lord Privy Seal.[32]

The reshuffle needed delicate handling as it had to satisfy Rab that he was being promoted to Deputy Prime Minister, while reassuring Macmillan that nothing of the sort was happening; and that, as Chancellor, he would be fully in charge of economic affairs. After the reshuffle, Macmillan was positioned at the centre of the Cabinet while Rab lost visibility, marginalised, almost an anachronism. Macmillan's tenure at the Foreign Office had been brief, but he could thereafter point to his holding two of the most important Cabinet slots while Rab was moved out of a position of significance. Momentum was in Mac's favour, and he was confident that he would ultimately be able to manipulate that momentum if the occasion should arise.

When he arrived at the Treasury, Macmillan was shocked by the slide that had occurred under Rab. To appear to supplant Rab's perceived recent inertia with a new dynamic approach was vital, and on 1 January 1956 he circulated to officials *First Thoughts from a Treasury Window*, setting out the economic problems facing Britain and proposing solutions.[33]

It is difficult to imagine a paper better crafted to highlight the differences between the two men. Avoiding academic theory, in language the precise opposite of Rab's new-fangled, hifalutin' schemes like ROBOT, *First Thoughts* is the work of a Chancellor who knew what the man in the street wanted and set out to satisfy him.

To illustrate the economic problems facing Britain, Macmillan used the image of an overflowing bath. Although the plug had been removed, water was flooding over the sides. The householder had three choices: to mop up the water with every cloth available; to turn off one or both taps; or to try to get a bigger bath. Answers were not offered to all the problems, but tangible issues were addressed – utilities, the railways,

---

32 Thorpe, *Supermac*, p. 319.
33 Bodleian: MSS Macmillan, dep c306. This immediately became known in the Civil Service as *What the Butler Never Saw*.

social welfare, especially housing and education. Not all were susceptible to simple remedies, but the new Chancellor made it clear that he
would search for solutions in a sensible and comprehensible manner.

'I would not be afraid of controls', he wrote, 'if limited or clearly
strategic – not control for the sake of control, but because it's sensible in particular circumstances.' The government needed to confront
the trades unions and tackle restrictive practices; to offer incentives
for accepting redundancies. There must be more mechanisation, for
example, introducing ticket machines for trains and buses. 'In general
we must move away from the mediaeval concept which we still have
– that labour is, or ought to be cheap, to the American concept that
labour is bound to be terribly dear and must be used as economically
as possible.' Regarding savings, he stressed the need to 'halt the spectacular fall in the volume of money'. He was opposed to lotteries but
suggested that the Stock Exchange might stimulate a sporting interest
and a chance of winning. 'The masses would get the fun of reading the
Stock Exchange results to see how they were going.'

Such a proposal was pure Macmillan. He distrusted complex solutions and had a special contempt for people whom he considered 'intellectuals'.[34] Echoing Stanley Baldwin thirty years before, he judged
Rab eminently guilty of that sin. He was not afraid of saying, 'I don't
understand. Please explain this to me.' When he took over at the
Treasury he asked his advisers for 'a short paper, very pessimistic, to
make their flesh creep and to use on the Cabinet at an early meeting'.[35]

This direct, common-sense manner was typical of his approach to
problems. In a letter of 5 January 1956 to Lord Chandos, he wrote, 'I
don't like selling exports today and not knowing if I shall get paid for
them.' In the first month after taking over, Mac covered a wide range
of subjects with a wide circle of colleagues, frequenting the smoking
room to talk problems through. The contrast with Rab's donnish, academic approach could not have been more striking. Nor could it have

---

34 He referred to certain Labour MPs as 'rather ill-bred schoolboys', commenting that they were
    'mostly intellectuals' (Bodleian: MSS Macmillan, dep d26.3) and commented that 'It's only
    the Liberal intellectual who is always against his country.' (Bodleian: MSS Macmillan, dep
    d27.36.)
35 Bodleian: MSS Macmillan, dep c306.31.

been accidental. On 8 February 1956 he urged taking the initiative. Don't wait for the opposition, he advised, but put down a substantive motion 'That this House approves the statement by the Chancellor of the Exchequer on the economic situation.' It undoubtedly gave Mac considerable pleasure to suggest this to Rab as Leader of the House.[36]

Thus, by early 1956, the final phases of the three-year process of supplanting Rab were under way. From being a very junior minister in October 1951, Macmillan had advanced significantly, even decisively. When the events of that summer jolted Eden's government, he and Rab were on level pegging.

---

36 Bodleian: MSS Macmillan, dep c306.160. 8 February 1956.

CHAPTER 14

SUEZ: *SCHERZO* AND *ADAGIO*, 1956

Reginald Maudling traced the erosion of Rab's prospects to become leader of the Tories to his actions – and inaction – at the time of the Suez Crisis in 1956. He argues that Rab 'lifted his skirt to avoid the dirt',[1] that Rab's vacillation, tinged with indiscreet disloyalty to Eden, convinced the right wing of the party that he was not to be trusted. In fact, Rab was absent from his desk for much of July, suffering from a virus infecting his inner ear and causing him to lose balance. By the time he returned to a Cabinet meeting on 2 August, entrenched positions had been taken by most protagonists.

Few episodes in post-war British history were more divisive than Suez, and Macmillan, who dramatically and decisively changed his position during the crisis, consolidated his standing, while Rab, who also modified his stance, alienated and ultimately lost the confidence of both wings of the party. Suez provided the first opportunity to compare in a crisis the virtues and strengths of the two contenders to succeed Eden, and the contest's outcome is rooted in the perception of which contender was less associated with the outgoing Prime Minister. Once Macmillan appreciated that, he succeeded in presenting the more resolute face to the Parliamentary Party. As Ian Gilmour wrote in Delphic vein, 'he was thought at least to know his own mind, even if he changed it.'[2] Additionally, by astute handling of his position as

---

1   Maudling, *Memoirs*, pp. 44–5.
2   Ian Gilmour, *Oxford Dictionary of National Biography*, R. A. Butler, para 24.

Chancellor – and by extending his brief to embrace diplomacy and military strategy – Macmillan conveyed an image of broad understanding and control, while Rab's contribution was largely limited to acting as a sounding board within the Tory Party.[3]

The collision course for Britain and Egypt began with the Anglo-Egyptian agreement of October 1954, whereby Britain would withdraw troops from the region in exchange for Egyptian undertakings to uphold the terms of the 1888 Constantinople Convention and to 'guarantee at all times for all powers its free use'. That treaty, negotiated by Eden as Foreign Secretary, infuriated the right wing of the Tory Party and contributed later to Eden's hawkish posture towards Colonel Nasser, the Egyptian President.

Concerned by growing Soviet ambitions in the Middle East, Britain negotiated the Baghdad Pact, creating a 'northern tier' of defence in the region. This move alarmed Nasser, who was convinced that Britain was attempting to re-establish local political hegemony. Predictably, he turned to the Soviet *bloc* and negotiated an arms deal with Czechoslovakia in September 1955. Cannily, he also attempted to solidify relations with the West, approaching Washington for aid to build the Aswan High Dam. In December 1955, John Foster Dulles, the American Secretary of State, announced that the United States and Britain would provide $70 million in aid for Nasser's ambitious project. However, suspicious of Nasser's flirtation with the Soviet Union and of his creditworthiness, Dulles abruptly withdrew the offer on 19 July 1956. A week later, ostensibly to raise revenue to pay for the Aswan Dam, Nasser nationalised the Suez Canal. Rab confessed that this took the British Cabinet completely by surprise.[4]

This constituted a remarkable oversight on the part of the government. Bound up in the question of Suez and Egypt were notions of

---

3   See, for example, in TNA: CAB 134/4107, E. C. (56) 4; E. C. (56) 10th meeting, 3 August 1956; E. C. (56) 8, E. C. (56) 9, and E. C. (56) 11, all on 7 August 1956; E. C. (56) 32, 22 August 1956; E. C. (56) 35, 27 August 1956 and E. C. (56) 41, 5 September 1956. In a little over a month Macmillan circulated ten papers and memoranda to the Egypt Committee, ranging over disparate subjects, demonstrating that not only did he have Treasury officials working diligently and efficiently but also that he was familiar with the broader implications of strategy.

4   Butler, *The Art of the Possible*, p. 186.

British grandeur, Arab nationalism, the pledges of the new (since 1952) republican government of Egypt, anti-imperialist sentiment and, in Washington, fear of growing Soviet influence in the Middle East. Against that background the seizure of that most visible symbol of colonialism was as predictable as the British reaction to its seizure. No less predictable was the concern of President Eisenhower to halt the arms race in the region and bring to an end the simmering Arab–Israeli conflict.[5]

The principal difference between the American stance and that of Britain and France lay in Eisenhower's viewing the affair through the lens of the Cold War, and the conviction of Eden and French Premier Mollet that Nasser alone was responsible for fomenting anti-colonial sentiment in Egypt and Algeria. At a London meeting in March, Mollet saw all the problems of the Middle East, including Soviet expansionism, as the work of Nasser, whom he likened to Hitler.[6] In the same month, when King Hussein of Jordan dismissed Sir John Bagot Glubb, the British commander of the Arab Legion, Eden was convinced that his action was instigated by Nasser and ranted, 'I want Nasser destroyed – not removed, destroyed.'[7] Early in the Suez Crisis he repeated that sentiment, stating bluntly, 'Our quarrel is not with Egypt – it is with Nasser.'[8]

The news of the nationalisation of the canal reached Eden while he was entertaining King Faisal of Iraq and his Prime Minister Nuri Es-Said to dinner at Downing Street. 'Hit Nasser,' advised the latter. 'Hit him hard.' The Iraqi guests departed, tactfully allowing Eden to deal with the crisis and an emergency meeting was held through the night at Downing Street. From the outset Eden favoured the use of force; so outspoken was he during the meeting that the duty secretary warned him that not all those present were bound by the oath of the Privy Council.

From the outset, the Prime Minister viewed Nasser's action as a simple piece of banditry. Egypt should be subjected to immediate

5 Neff, *Warriors at Suez* (New York: Linden Press, 1981), pp. 130–31.
6 Kyle, *Suez* (London: Weidenfeld & Nicolson, 1992), p. 115.
7 Nutting, *No End of a Lesson* (London: Constable, 1967), p. 34.
8 Butler, *The Art of the Possible*, p. 188. Kingseed, *Eisenhower and the Suez Crisis of 1956* (Baton Rouge, Louisiana: LSU Press, 1995), p. 37.

pressure, initially economic pressure and, if necessary, the threat and the use of force. 'The fundamental question before the Cabinet', he said, 'was whether they were prepared in the last resort to pursue their objective by … force, and whether they were ready, in default of assistance from the United States and France, to take military action alone.'[9]

Imitating Churchill's wartime strategy, Eden established the Egypt Committee, a War Cabinet of six members: himself, Salisbury, Macmillan, Lloyd, Home and Monckton. Rab, *de facto* Deputy Prime Minister, was not included as Eden was determined that the Committee not contain any whom he regarded as 'weak sisters'.[10] Early in the crisis Rab was identified as a likely objector[11] and, although he attended some meetings and chaired the Committee in Eden's absence, he was not a formal member of the Committee, which met forty-six times between 27 July and 21 November.

As early as 30 July the group had determined that force would be used. Lloyd informed members of a proposed conference of maritime powers, foreseeing that such a conference would censure the Egyptian government and insist that the canal be placed under international control. 'If Colonel Nasser refused to accept it,' he said, 'military operations could then proceed.' In brief, the conference and its resolutions would be necessary formalities to the predetermined course of action – military invasion.[12]

On the following day, 31 July, the Egypt Committee met three times and Eden demonstrated a consummate control of detail.[13] He appears in a new light, as a war leader casting himself in the mould of Churchill. On 1 August, the Chiefs of Staff presented an alarming paper geared to a D-Day six weeks away. 'Nuclear weapons', they said, 'will not be used, but no other restrictions will be placed on the attack of military targets.'[14] In four days the country had moved to the brink

---

9   TNA: CAB 134/4107, C. M. (56) 54th Conclusions.
10 Eden, *Full Circle*, p. 557. In this category he included not only Rab but also Macmillan, who later opposed his handling of the crisis.
11 Thomas, *The Suez Affair* (London: Weidenfeld & Nicolson, 1966), p. 63.
12 TNA: CAB 134/4107, E. C. (56) 3rd meeting, 30 July 1956.
13 Particularly at the first meeting – TNA: CAB 134/.4107, E. C. (56) 5th meeting.
14 TNA: CAB 134/4107, E. C. (56) 5., 1 August 1956.

of a war in which only the use of nuclear weapons was not envisaged. To Rab's amazement, the other members of the Egypt Committee accepted this assessment and discussed emergency powers that the government would assume.[15]

The reaction of press and public – in addition to Eden's own outrage – demanded that 'something be done' quickly. It was soon pointed out that 1956 marked the twentieth anniversary of Hitler's reoccupation of the Rhineland. Almost immediately, Eden moved from a posture of planning simply to reclaim the canal to an overt determination to oust Nasser, whom he now described in the same terms as the pre-war dictators. Macmillan described Nasser as 'an Asiatic Mussolini';[16] the *Daily Herald* declared 'No More Hitlers'; Hugh Gaitskell in the House of Commons drew the same parallel: 'It's all very familiar. It is exactly the same that we encountered from Mussolini and Hitler in those years before the war.'[17]

In this frame of mind, Eden cabled President Eisenhower on 27 July, urging a firm stand. Otherwise, he argued, 'our influence and yours throughout the Middle East will, we are convinced, be irretriev-ably undermined'. As a first step, Eden urged that Britain, France and the United States confer on 'how we can best bring the maximum pressure to bear on the Egyptian government'.[18] The President im-mediately[19] called a meeting at the White House at which it was de-cided that Deputy Under-Secretary of State Robert Murphy should be dispatched to London to 'see what it's all about and hold the fort'.[20] At the end of the meeting, Eisenhower dictated a response to Eden, urging that 'the maximum number of maritime nations affected by the Nasser action should be consulted quickly' and suggesting that 'there are one or two additional steps that you and we might profitably consider'.[21]

---

15 TNA: CAB 134/4107, E. C. (56) 8th meeting, 1 August 1956.
16 Bodleian: MMS Macmillan, dep d27. Diary entry for 27 July 1956.
17 Hansard, 4 August 1956, vol. 557, col. 1613.
18 *Foreign Relations of the United States (FRUS)*, 1955–1957, vol. XVI, doc. 5. Eden to Eisenhower, 27 July 1956.
19 At 1700h (Washington time), 2200h in London.
20 Murphy, *Diplomat Among Warriors* (Garden City, New York: Doubleday & Co, 1964), p. 379.
21 State Department Central Files, 974.7301/7-2756, cited at *FRUS* p. 12.

Eden had appointed Selwyn Lloyd Foreign Secretary to succeed Macmillan. Lloyd had little experience of foreign affairs. Appointed Minister of State at the Foreign Office by Churchill in 1951, he had protested, 'I do not speak any foreign language. Except in war, I have never visited any foreign country. I do not like foreigners.'[22] Eden, with far greater experience in diplomacy, thus maintained his hold on the handling of the crisis. His approach from the start was that the use of force would be inevitable, indeed, that force was the only thing that Arabs understood. Nasser, he thundered, 'must not be permitted to have his hand on our windpipe'.[23] In this posture he had no stronger supporter than Macmillan.

On 27 July, the day after he received the news, Eden made a cautious statement in the Commons, keeping all options open. The Cabinet would meet immediately after the House rose, he added, and he would keep the House informed at every stage.[24] Hugh Gaitskell and Clement Davies confirmed the support of the Labour and Liberal parties, condemning 'this deplorable action'.[25]

When Murphy arrived in London on 29 July he quickly assessed the fire-breathing mood of the Egypt Committee. He 'was left in no doubt that the British government believed that Suez was a test which could only be met by the use of force'.[26] Eden, he felt, 'had not adjusted his thoughts to the altered status of Great Britain, and he never did'. Macmillan, by contrast, with whom Murphy had worked closely in Algiers during the war, was more attuned to Britain's post-war role.[27]

Macmillan was not slow to capitalise on his relations with Murphy – and, through Murphy, with Eisenhower, the wartime Commander-in-Chief in Algiers. To recreate the atmosphere of their former collaboration, Macmillan hosted a small dinner party on 29 July at 11 Downing Street. Present were Murphy, Macmillan and Earl Alexander of Tunis, the former commander of land forces under Eisenhower

---

22 Lloyd, *Suez 1956: A Personal Account* (London: Jonathan Cape, 1978), p. 4.
23 Clark, *From Three Worlds*, p. 166.
24 Hansard, 27 July 1956, vol. 557, cols 777–9.
25 Ibid., loc. cit. cols 778–9.
26 Murphy, *Diplomat Among Warriors*, p. 379.
27 Ibid., p. 381.

in the North Africa theatre. To Murphy the two Englishmen seemed calm and resolved in their determination to take military action to reclaim the canal.

Macmillan confided to his diary that his and Alexander's goal had been to 'frighten Murphy out of his life'.[28] They certainly succeeded in making apparent to him, and through him to Eisenhower, the fundamental difference between the British and American positions. At a hastily convened tripartite conference between British, French and American delegations, Murphy made the American position clear. Whatever position the three countries took 'should have the broadest possible base and carry the benefit of an affirmative world opinion'.[29]

On 31 July, Murphy cabled Washington on the progress of the tripartite talks. Both Eden and Macmillan, he reported, had told him that 'the British government has decided to drive Nasser out of Egypt ... and that Parliament and the British people are with them'.[30] In the first days of the crisis, Macmillan had referred to his wartime association with Eisenhower and 'both Macmillan and Field Marshal Alexander ... urged repeatedly that [the] President as their former Commander-in-Chief fully appreciate the finality of British decision. Macmillan several times expressed the wish that he could explain all this orally to [the] President.'[31]

Murphy's cable alarmed Eisenhower. Eden's position, the President felt, was 'very unwise'. He decided that Dulles should depart for London immediately. Dulles gave his opinion that the British, who had gone to war in 1914 and 1939 before having American military support but confident that this would follow, were planning to do the same over Suez.[32] Eisenhower cabled Eden, urging restraint and adding that 'public opinion here and, I am convinced, in the rest of the world would be outraged' if no conference were held to resolve the dispute.[33]

Dulles arrived in London on 1 August and was immediately

---

28 Bodleian: MSS Macmillan, d27.13. Diary entry for 30 July 1956.
29 *FRUS*, 1955–57, vol. XVI, doc. 21. Murphy to Dulles, 29 July 1956.
30 *FRUS*, 1955–57, vol. XVI, doc. 33. Murphy to Dulles, 31 July 1956.
31 Ibid., loc. cit.
32 *FRUS*, 1955–57, vol. XVI, doc. 34. Memorandum of Conference, 31 July 1956.
33 Ibid., doc. 35. Eisenhower to Eden, 31 July 1956.

subjected to pressure from Eden and Macmillan. The Prime Minister explained that Britain wanted American military support and was certainly counting on moral support. Urged by Dulles to find a diplomatic solution, he agreed to 'give a conference a try' if it could take place quickly.[34]

Macmillan played an altogether longer hand, hosting a meeting at 11 Downing Street, attended by Dulles, Murphy and Winthrop Aldrich, the American Ambassador. Ostensibly, he wanted to discuss the economic implications of the crisis, but he ranged much more broadly, urging that 'If the final result was to be the destruction of Great Britain as a first-class power and its reduction to a status similar to that of Holland, the danger should be met now.'[35] In a conversation with three senior American diplomats, in an atmosphere that was 'most informal, intimate and cordial', Macmillan spoke as Chancellor, former Foreign Secretary and, in wide-ranging geopolitical discussion, in the manner of a future Prime Minister. According to Aldrich, this was a vital meeting in the attempt to harmonise British and American policy. Macmillan, encouraged by the talk, recorded his feeling that 'Dulles & co are moving towards our point of view.'[36]

The British press saw Dulles's mission as an American attempt to harness Britain. Predictably, there was an eruption of jingoistic anti-American feeling. Leaders in *The Times* rebuked Washington for seeking conciliation and castigated Eisenhower for 'quibbling over whether or not [Nasser] was legally entitled to make the grab' as this would 'delight the finicky and comfort the faint-hearted'.[37]

By the time that Rab returned to action, the differences between the bellicose French and British positions, on the one hand, and the more cautious American stance were being trumpeted in the press; Eden, supported to the hilt by Macmillan, was resolved to drive Nasser from power; and the differing attitudes of the protagonists were assuming fixed positions. Rab, despite his view that Dulles's views were

---

34 Ibid., doc. 42. Memorandum of Conversation Eden–Dulles, 1 August 1956.
35 Ibid., doc. 46. Memorandum of Conversation Macmillan–Dulles et al., 1 August 1946.
36 Diary entry for 1 August 1956.
37 *The Times*, 31 July and 1 August 1956.

'expressed, though not consistently held',[38] inclined to agree with him and saw the restraint of the Prime Minister as his principal task. He was not helped by Dulles's occasional apparent support of British military intervention. The outspoken and frequently undiplomatic American Secretary of State, Churchill once observed, 'was the only case he knew of a bull carrying his china shop around with him'.[39]

Initially, Eden's bellicosity was echoed in Cabinet and the Commons. Gradually, however, Gaitskell and the Labour Party adopted the position that force must be a last resort and that Britain must not act in violation of the United Nations charter or in such a manner that would cause her to be branded an aggressor. None of this cut any ice with Eden, who was determined, in the words of Foster Dulles, 'to make Nasser disgorge what he was attempting to swallow'.[40] Amazingly, the Prime Minister remained convinced that, in spite of the clarity of Eisenhower's warning letter of 31 July, 'the President did not rule out the use of force'.[41] When Rab attended the Cabinet of 2 August, where it was decided to use force 'if negotiations failed within a measurable time',[42] he saw the divergence of Anglo-American interests, leaning personally to the American position. Having never quite shed the label of 'appeaser' after his support for Chamberlain in 1938–40, however, he knew that he must tread carefully to avoid renewed abuse from the right of the party.

Accordingly, he adopted a posture of partial accord with Eden, agreeing that there should be international supervision of the canal but opposing the use of force. His position was in almost every respect that of Eisenhower and Dulles, but he never put his views across forcefully. Seeing his role as one of restraining Eden, he used the same tactics as Dulles, placing obstacles in the way of military action, or in his own words attempting to put Eden in 'a political straitjacket'. The upshot,

---

38 Butler, *The Art of the Possible*, p. 187.
39 The unpredictability of Dulles's comments and his swings towards bellicosity are analysed in Graebner, *The New Isolationism: A Study in Politics and Foreign Policy Since 1950* (New York: Ronald Press, 1956). A persuasive explanation is that he was determined to show that he was a more effective Secretary of State than his predecessor Dean Acheson.
40 Butler, *The Art of the Possible*, pp. 188–9.
41 Eden, *Full Circle*, p. 436.
42 Thomas, *The Suez Affair*, p. 55.

of course, was that he was blamed for his posture at every point as the crisis unrolled.

While Rab remained equivocal, torn between loyalty to the Prime Minister and abhorrence of Eden's appetite for military action, Macmillan was increasingly active: questioning the plan proposed by the Chiefs of Staff;[43] chairing a meeting at 11 Downing Street to consider organisational arrangements for control of the canal;[44] circulating a cogent and comprehensive paper on the use of Egyptian sterling balances.[45]

This paper had been prepared by Sir Leslie Rowan, a senior Treasury official, and now Rab must clearly have appreciated the disadvantage he suffered by not heading a department. Although senior to Macmillan, he lacked the resources to challenge the Chancellor's new-found, wide-ranging authority. Eden, Lloyd and Macmillan provided impetus in Cabinet and Committee meetings while Rab, as Lord Privy Seal, was periodically charged with ascertaining the attitudes of Conservatives in the Commons and similar staff tasks.[46] His role was more akin to that of the Chief Whip than that of Deputy Prime Minister.

On 8 August, Eden broadcast to the country, drawing a parallel between Nasser's behaviour and that of Mussolini and Hitler. 'We all know this is how fascist governments behave,' he said, 'and we all remember, only too well, what the cost can be in giving in to fascism.' Rab was appalled by the demonisation of Nasser and the suggestion that the Egyptian regime bore any resemblance to Hitler's Germany. There was a clear difference, he believed, between securing international control for the canal and the overthrow of Nasser. One might imply the other, but there was no necessary linkage.[47] Nor did Eden's broadcast represent sensible diplomacy. It succeeded in ensuring that Nasser refused to attend the 22-nation Suez conference in London, called by Britain, France and the United States. In a press conference

---

43 TNA: CAB 134/4107, E. C. (56) 8, 7 August 1956.
44 TNA: CAB 134/4107, E. C. (56) 9, 7 August 1956. Salisbury was present at this meeting but, although he was senior to Macmillan in the Tory hierarchy, Macmillan took the chair.
45 TNA: CAB 134/4107, E. C. (56) 11, 7 August 1956.
46 TNA: CAB 134/4108, C. M. (56) 67th Conclusions, 26 September 1956; C. M. (56) 77th Conclusions, 2 November 1956.
47 Butler, The Art of the Possible, pp. 188–9.

on 12 August, he charged that 'The proposed conference has no right whatsoever to discuss any matter falling within the jurisdiction of Egypt' – a rational statement that was hard to refute. Indeed, in a statement released on 13 August, the Labour shadow Cabinet accepted that the nationalisation of the canal was not wrong *per se*. It was its arbitrary manner that caused anxiety. From that premise they condemned any military action that was not conducted under the auspices of the United Nations.

Eisenhower and Dulles saw the 22-nation conference as a delaying tactic and on 16 August the latter was able to report to the President that a calmer atmosphere prevailed. Both Britain and France, he believed, now recognised 'the inadequacies of their military establishments to take on a real fighting job of this size'.[48] The conclusions of the conference were predictable: participants agreed on an association of Egypt and certain foreign powers in the administration of the canal. As Egypt had refused to participate in the conference, the conclusion was somewhat academic.

Detailed military plans were presented and discussed while, ostensibly, efforts were made to resolve the crisis. The assumption that those efforts would fail underlay Committee meetings in the first half of August.[49] Cabinet Secretary Sir Norman Brook submitted a timetable for likely events after the London conference. The fundamental premise was that the decisions of the conference would be rejected by Nasser and that an assault force could then sail from the United Kingdom on 7 September.[50] 'If we were to take military action', Brook declared, 'it would be to do so only in circumstances which enabled us to secure the maximum concurrence of other nations.'

On 23 August, at the end of the conference, Sir Robert Menzies, the Australian Prime Minister, offered to travel to Cairo to report the conclusions of the conference to Nasser. While he was in Cairo his position was fatally weakened by Eisenhower, who, asked at a press conference whether the United States would support Britain and

---

48 *FRUS*, 1955–1957, vol. XVI, doc. 86. Dulles to Eisenhower, 16 August 1956.
49 For example, TNA: CAB 134/4107, E. C. (56) 13th Meeting, Minute 3, 9 August 1956.
50 TNA: CAB 134/4107, E. C. (56), 19, 14 August 1956.

France if they insisted on the decisions of the 22-nation conference, replied: 'Well, I'm not going to comment on the contents of that proposal while it's being discussed in Cairo. I will repeat what I've said, I think, each week before this body: the United States is committed to a peaceful solution to this problem.'[51]

Eisenhower thus cut the ground from under Eden's and Menzies's feet by signalling to Nasser that he no longer needed to fear invasion by an American-led coalition...

Throughout that month, Eden made warlike noises and was restrained – or at least delayed – by Dulles and Eisenhower while Rab performed a similar role in London. According to William Clark, Eden's Press Secretary, Rab was 'discouraged by the whole outlook' and 'a very damping influence'. In particular, he was repelled by the plans to bomb Cairo which, he felt, 'may really revolt the conscience of the nation'.[52] Clark described in March 1956 Eden's posture as 'the classical position of having two rival claims to the succession who could be relied on to keep the other down'. As a result, 'All these three, Eden, Macmillan and Butler, watched each other like hostile lynxes.'[53]

The rivalry between Rab and Macmillan may have been apparent to the initiated, but it was not yet blazoned about the press. Macmillan made an early public promenade on 22 August, walking from 11 Downing Street to the Foreign Office and back to No. 10, acknowledging the cheers of the crowd. 'He is clearly cutting himself a big swathe at the moment', Clark wrote in his diary, 'in the expectation that he might – just might – succeed Eden.'[54]

While Macmillan presented a warlike face to bellicose voters, Rab had the less glamorous role of restraining Eden, presenting reasons why the use of force was both immoral and illegal – an accusation that Eden was at pains to rebut.[55] Slavishly supported by Lloyd, the Prime Minister took the moral high ground, claiming that Britain's

---

51 *Public Papers of the Presidents*, Dwight D. Eisenhower 1956, p. 737; *FRUS*, doc. 171. 5 September 1956.
52 Clark, *From Three Worlds*, p. 178.
53 Ibid., p. 164.
54 Ibid., pp. 177–8; Diary entry for 22 August 1956,
55 TNA: CAB 134/4107, E. C. (56) 26, 18 August 1956.

sole aim was to uphold the principles of the 1888 Convention. 'Our incidental object of overthrowing Nasser', wrote Lloyd in a memorandum, 'almost certainly can be achieved by inflicting a complete defeat on the Egyptian armed forces.'[56] Rab's inconvenient insistence that Britain not act unilaterally but refer the matter to the United Nations was legally correct, but fine legalistic distinctions ran quite counter to the first wave of jingoistic indignation at Nasser's action. As the month progressed, moreover, Gaitskell and the Labour Party distanced themselves from Eden, withdrawing their original support for an immediate military response and insisting that the matter be referred to the United Nations.

This development, while welcome to Rab and others who strove to stay Eden's hand, raised separate concerns. Dulles reported to Eisenhower that the withdrawal of Labour Party support might encourage Nasser to stand firm in the hope that the Conservative government would fall.[57] Rab was well aware that, if the government did fall, he would be branded as the culpable 'appeaser' who had brought it about. In Washington, too, the prospect was viewed with alarm as the Republican administration feared the return of the Labour Party.[58] Dulles stressed to Gaitskell the importance of national unity.[59]

As Ian Gilmour said of Rab, he would have done his country a great service if he could have kept Eden in a political straitjacket, 'but by October Butler had run out of straitjackets'.[60] Moreover, Rab himself felt constrained. As the affair dragged on with no resolution in sight, and with Washington making it increasingly clear that Eden's rhetoric was arrant hyperbole,[61] Rab repeated the same measured advice to the Prime Minister. It was not what Eden wanted to hear. In normal

---

56 TNA: CAB 134/4107, E. C. (56) 28, 20 August 1956.

57 *FRUS*, doc. 97. Dulles to Eisenhower, 19 August 1956.

58 At a National Security Council (NSC) meeting, chaired by Vice-President Nixon on 30 November, Nixon admitted to being 'scared to death at the prospect of Bevan in a position of power in a future British Government.' (*FRUS*, doc. 626). See Chapter 15.

59 *FRUS*, doc, 129. Memorandum of Conversation Eden–Dulles, 24 August 1956.

60 *Oxford Dictionary of National Biography*, Suez section, para 2.

61 Eisenhower wrote to Eden, commenting that the Prime Minister's talk of Suez as 'an ignoble end to our long history' reminded him of Churchill in the Second World War. 'This is where I came in,' he commented to Dulles. *FRUS*, doc. 192.

circumstances such a clash results in the resignation of a dissenting minister, yet Rab not only did not resign but failed to speak out openly against the course that Eden and his supporters, of whom Macmillan was the most vociferous, had adopted. On 2 September, Eisenhower wrote to Eden stressing the need for 'assurance of permanent and efficient operation of the canal with justice to all concerned'. He differentiated between this noble goal and treating Nasser as 'a menace to the peace and the vital interests of the West'.[62] This was in essence what Rab had consistently advised Eden.

Towards the end of August, Macmillan subtly modified his position. Without diluting his support of Eden, he circulated a twelve-page memorandum addressing the economic consequences of the crisis. He emphasised the need to persuade the United States to 'take still stronger action' to support sterling – a realistic but not necessarily pessimistic assessment that prepared the ground for Macmillan to withdraw support later.[63] In Cabinet on the following day, there were the first signs of doubt of the wisdom of Eden's bellicosity when Monckton, the only Cabinet minister later to resign over Suez, questioned the resolution to use force. Salisbury countered this with the familiar parallel of the 1930s. 'If the encroachments of a dictator were not checked at the outset,' he warned Monckton and other potential doubters, 'when comparatively little strength was needed to check them, the ultimate reckoning involved a far greater convulsion and a much greater sacrifice.'[64] There it was again: the flat assertion that Nasser was an Egyptian Hitler, an assertion that Rab, suspected appeaser, was powerless to rebut.

Instead, Rab, acknowledging that the national interest was paramount, stressed the need for 'the greatest measure of support they could command in Parliament and in the country'. The parliamentary situation, he warned, was certain to be difficult as there were elements that would oppose the use of force. Eden brushed Rab's caution aside, summing up baldly that 'it was evident that the Cabinet were united

---

62 *FRUS*, doc. 181. Eden to Eisenhower, 6 September 1956.
63 TNA: CAB 134/4107, E. C. (56) 35, 27 August 1956.
64 TNA: CAB 134/4107, C. M. (56) 62nd Conclusions, 28 August 1956.

in the view that the frustration of Colonel Nasser's policy was a vital British interest which must be secured, in the last resort, by the use of force'.[65] Small wonder that Rab cast around to find another straitjacket.

In early September, the United States attempted to impose restraint, as Lloyd reported to the Cabinet that Eisenhower was strongly opposed to military action and was now uncertain of the value of referring the matter to the United Nations.[66] Dulles, he added, had devised another scheme to avoid or postpone invasion. This was the Suez Canal Users' Association (SCUA),[67] which brought delegates from eighteen nations to London for a second conference. Nasser denounced SCUA as 'a device to lead the members down the path to war, for which the British and the French are preparing'.[68] In due course the plan achieved little and Britain now resolved to refer the matter to the Security Council before the Soviet Union did so.[69]

In the last week of September, Macmillan flew to the USA for talks with the International Monetary Fund and, visiting Eisenhower in the White House, impressed the President, who felt that 'he talked very much more moderately [about Suez] than he had anticipated'. The two agreed that 'probably the British didn't know exactly how they were proceeding themselves'.[70] Thus Macmillan stealthily began to move away from vocal support of Eden's stance. Chancellor and President had great mutual respect and the perceived opinion of the latter would be important if Eden should be forced to step down. Macmillan will have been fully conscious of this; maintaining Eisenhower's support could be a trump card that Rab did not possess.

The impression that Macmillan skilfully created during this period, as he prepared to distance himself from Eden, was that of himself as statesman, a man who saw the wider picture. This was how he had portrayed himself in the early-August meeting with Dulles, Aldrich

---

65 TNA: CAB 134/4107, C. M. (56) 62nd Conclusions, 28 August 1956.
66 TNA: CAB 134/4108, C. M. (56) 64th Conclusions, 11 September 1956.
67 In Britain the association was referred to as 'CASU'.
68 *FRUS*, doc. 232. Dulles to Eisenhower, 19 September 1956.
69 *FRUS*, doc. 254. Memorandum of Conversation Coulson–State Department, 22 September 1956.
70 *FRUS*, doc. 264. (Eisenhower Library, Whitman File, Eisenhower Diaries).

and Murphy. In Washington, he radiated the same executive confidence; he and Eisenhower would discuss strategy while Eden and Selwyn Lloyd busied themselves with detail. That quality, whether real or perceived, was to become a trademark of Macmillan in the five years ahead.

We can only speculate at what point Macmillan recognised the possibility of his succeeding Eden. His tenure of the Ministry of Housing had been a spectacular success, incidentally causing Rab embarrassment as the Treasury struggled to meet the cost of that success. When Churchill stepped down in 1955, there was no doubt that Eden would take over – despite Churchill's belated concern that his chosen successor was perhaps unsuited to the job. Three years older than Eden and almost nine years older than Rab, Macmillan could not afford to wait long for Eden to retire.

Eden's persistent ill health encouraged him that his chance might come earlier than expected. By the end of 1955, when Eden meekly accepted his terms for going to the Treasury[71] and Rab committed 'political suicide' by accepting the post of Lord Privy Seal, Macmillan must have scented power, accurately judging that he could position himself as a legitimate contender.

During 1956, Eden became 'consistently incensed by Macmillan's exceeding of his ministerial role'.[72] So much so that Macmillan was not invited to the first emergency meeting on 26 July. As Macmillan lay in bed at 11 Downing Street, reading *Northanger Abbey*, Eden worked in the engine room next door. The crisis was an unexpected boon for Macmillan.

So violent was the reaction of public and press to Nasser's action that it would have been folly to seem an appeaser. Macmillan was quite the reverse, more hawkish even than the Prime Minister. To have vacillated, to have quibbled over legalities, as Rab did, would have been abhorrent to diehard Tories. Yet, even as he supported Eden, Macmillan threw out his own diplomatic lines – with Dulles, with Murphy

---

71 TNA: PREM 5/228, Macmillan to Eden, 24 October 1955.
72 Pearson, *Sir Anthony Eden and the Suez Crisis: Reluctant Gamble* (London: Macmillan, 2003), p. 33.

and Aldrich. When he flew to the United States on 20 September, he began the process of disengagement from Eden, not yet in Britain but in the larger forum of American perception.

His visit was a spectacular success. Flying to Indianapolis, he visited the small town of Spencer, where his mother had grown up, and gave a bellicose speech to assembled Indiana dignitaries, all of whom will have been conscious that Eisenhower too grew up in the Midwest.[73] From Indiana, Macmillan returned to Washington, where he conferred with the President and Sir Roger Makins, the British Ambassador, the next day.

To Makins, Mac seemed over-confident of American support,[74] on his return unrealistically predicting to Eden that Ike was 'really determined to bring Nasser down'.[75] The more he assured Eden of Eisenhower's support, the more the Prime Minister would be wrong-footed if things went wrong. It was a gamble, but given Eden's precarious health and his own ability to reverse his position later for economic reasons, it was a gamble worth taking.

How clearly did Rab see these ominous signs? Enough to cause him to take two steps which are otherwise inexplicable. At the party conference in Llandudno in October, Rab aligned himself solidly with Eden, declaring that he had 'served under five Prime Ministers ... and [had] never known the qualities of courage, integrity and flair more clearly represented than in our present Prime Minister'.[76] A few days later, on 18 October, Rab returned to London and, in a meeting at 10 Downing Street, acquiesced to Eden's increasingly lurid plans to retake the canal. It was an irrevocable and, as it turned out, disastrous miscalculation.

According to Rab's own account of the meeting, Lloyd gripped his arm and described how he had been 'wafted to Paris in the wake of the Prime Minister to attend a conference with Mollet and Pineau', the French Foreign Minister.

They had discussed the ever closer line-up between Jordan, Egypt and

---

73 The Eisenhower family home, where Ike grew up and is buried, is in Abilene, Kansas.
74 Thorpe, *Supermac*, p. 346. Interview with the author.
75 TNA: PREM 11/1102, Macmillan to Eden, 26 September 1956.
76 Bodleian: 1956 Conservative Party Conference Report, p. 124.

Syria and the consequences of a pre-emptive strike by Israel, and it had been suggested that if war broke out in the Middle East between Israel and Egypt, Britain and France would jointly intervene in the canal area to stop hostilities … I was impressed by the audacity of thinking behind this plan but concerned about the public reaction … and in all the circumstances I said I would stand by him [Eden].[77]

Lloyd confirms Rab's account, adding the damning sentence that indicated the collusive and dishonest nature of the pact. 'The feeling was', he recalled, 'that although we should continue to seek a negotiated settlement, it was possible, or indeed probable, that the issue would be brought to a head as a result of a military action by Israel against Egypt.'[78]

Lloyd was clearly aware that such military action was neither possible nor probable; it was certain. On 1 September, General Moshe Dayan, the Israeli Chief of Staff, had been approached by Admiral Barjot of the French General Staff concerning 'co-ordinated action' against Egypt.[79] At subsequent talks in Paris, Dayan learned that France and Britain had collectively planned Operation MUSKETEER, but that American pressure on Britain had caused the British to pull out. The British Foreign Office, Dayan commented, was 'passively waiting for some miracle' to solve the crisis.[80]

On 18 October, when Lloyd was 'wafted' to Paris, Mollet and Pineau had won British support for a collusive plan that could legitimately place an Anglo-French force in Egypt. The next step was to ensure that Israel would co-operate. Mollet contacted Israel's Prime Minister David Ben-Gurion and invited an Israeli delegation to Paris. Ben-Gurion, Dayan, Shimon Peres and Mordechai Bar-On arrived in Paris on 22 October for meetings with French ministers. At 7.00 p.m., Selwyn Lloyd joined them to outline the British plan. Consistent perhaps with his statement that he did not like foreigners, Lloyd failed to impress the Israelis, as General Dayan recalled: 'His manner could not have

77 Butler, *The Art of the Possible*, p. 192.
78 Selwyn Lloyd, *Suez 1956*, p. 176.
79 Dayan, *Story of My Life* (New York: William Morrow, 1976), p. 185.
80 Ibid., p. 194.

been more antagonistic. His whole demeanour expressed distaste – for the place, the company and the topic ... His opening remarks suggested the tactics of a customer bargaining with extortionate merchants.'[81]

Rab was present at the Cabinet the following day when Eden announced that 'grave decisions would have to be taken by the Cabinet in the course of the next few days'. Discussion, he said obliquely, could not be carried further until he had consulted with the French government that evening.[82]

On 24 October, a deal was hammered out in a private villa at Sèvres, whereby the Israeli army would invade the Sinai peninsula at 0500h on 29 October; the British and French would issue a twelve-hour ultimatum, appealing to both Egypt and Israel to cease fire and to withdraw to a distance of ten miles from the canal. Egypt would be requested to accept temporary occupation of key points by an Anglo-French force. In the event of Egypt's expected rejection of the ultimatum, the British and French would start bombing Egyptian airfields at dawn on 31 October.

The arrangement had a number of unpleasant characteristics. It was collusive and dishonest; it also displayed a remarkable arrogance on the part of France and Britain. Ben-Gurion was offended by Britain's refusal to treat Israel as an equal partner in the enterprise. He stated that he was unwilling to be part of a plan in which Israel could be branded the aggressor, in which 'Israel volunteered to mount the rostrum of shame so that Britain and France could lave their hands in the waters of purity'.[83] Dayan was shocked at British unconcern towards possible destruction of Israeli cities if Egypt retaliated in force. His description of Lloyd's attitude to the Israeli delegation suggests that the British saw the Israelis as walk-on players in their production. If we want further evidence of such imperial arrogance, we can find it in Rab's description of Nasser, whom he refers to as 'a carpet trader' between East and West.[84]

William Clark, Eden's press adviser, had begun work at Downing

---

81 Ibid., p. 218.

82 TNA: CAB 134/4108, C. M. (56) 72nd Conclusions, 23 October 1956.

83 Dayan, *Story of My Life*, pp. 212, 219.

84 The expression '*un grand marchand de tapis*' was originally used by Pineau, but Rab had no difficulty in adopting it with all its clear implications of a racial slur. *The Art of the Possible*, p. 185.

Street the previous year and formed an unflattering view of the government's foreign policy. The country was 'still caught up in an imperial dream', he wrote. 'Eden's Cabinet all, not excluding Butler, with his family background of India, possessed an exaggerated view of what Britain in the mid-1950s could do on its own.'[85] The outdated Victorian attitudes of both Lloyd and Butler, contemptuous of Israelis and Arabs alike, lend force to Clark's judgement.

Lloyd was fully aware of the nature of the accord between Mollet and Eden. The picture of him gripping Rab's arm almost in panic is that of a man out of his depth in conspiracy. It is less certain how clearly Rab at first understood the conditions of the Faustian pact sealed at Sèvres. There can be no doubt, however, that after two months of attempting to restrain Eden, he decisively changed his tactics and supported military action. The most likely explanation is that he observed the growth of Macmillan's public stature, based upon a hawkish stance, and that he used this moment to change tack in order to be on the 'right' side of the fence. What he did not predict – and possibly could not have predicted – is that Macmillan would deftly vault back over that fence, leaving Eden and Rab fatally exposed on the 'wrong' side.

The agreement at Sèvres has become the point of moral balance of the entire Suez affair, and the secret agreement between Britain, France and Israel to provide apparent justification for an invasion already decided upon has been the basis for heaping shame on Eden. Such is the nature of military ventures. Had Britain and France succeeded in a lightning strike to reclaim the canal, their covert collaboration would probably have been applauded as an act of diplomatic and strategic genius. In the event, the failure of the exercise required the allocation of blame, and the charge of 'collusion' neatly fitted the bill.

Eden recognised that balance and, on 25 October, laid out the Anglo-French plan in Cabinet. Walter Monckton had resigned as Minister of Defence a week before, and others in Cabinet now expressed concern that Anglo-American relations would be permanently damaged by an

---

85 Clark, *From Three Worlds*, p. 146.

invasion. Even Eden recognised that Britain 'must face the risk that we should be accused of collusion with Israel'.[86] Yet there is no evidence that Rab spoke out or attempted to restrain Eden. Characteristically, he remained publicly loyal to the Prime Minister; ironically, that loyalty was to be his undoing.

By late October, then, the government was wedded to invasion. Efforts to resolve matters through the United Nations had stalled. Newspapers were reporting an increasing divergence between London and Washington; France and Britain were committed to a secret ruse to obtain their ends. Rab was now firmly in Eden's camp, thus distancing himself from Eisenhower; after Macmillan's emollient visit to the White House in September, this was unwise. Eisenhower was facing an election on 6 November that, inexplicably, he felt would be close. He was running on a peace ticket; he was a man of the strongest moral courage who promised a government 'as clean as a hound's tooth'.[87] The shabby pact that Britain entered into at Sèvres was quite incompatible with that image.

On 29 October, Israel invaded the Egyptian Sinai and, in accordance with the Sèvres agreement, Britain and France called on Egypt and Israel to cease fire before loosing an attack on Cairo. Eisenhower's displeasure and rising suspicion that Mollet and Eden had lied to him dominated the days before the election.

In a conference at the White House on 29 October, Eisenhower voiced his suspicion that France 'may be playing us false' over the supply of extra Mystère jets to Israel.[88] Placed in an intolerable position, as the US had pledged itself to support victims of aggression, the President declared that he would do what was right, whatever its effects on the election. On the following day, he cabled Eden that 'certain phases of this whole affair are disturbing me very much'. When Pierson Dixon, the British Ambassador to the UN, refused to consider any action against Israel and referred to the tripartite statement of May 1955 as 'ancient history', Eisenhower was convinced of the duplicity of British

86 TNA: CAB 134/4108, C. M. (56) 74th Conclusions, 25 October 1956.
87 A campaign promise when Eisenhower first ran for President in 1952.
88 *FRUS*, doc. 411. Memorandum of White House Conference, 29 October 1956.

platitudes. He made his position clear: if the United Nations branded Israel an aggressor, then the US would be obligated to help. Or, he added, if Egypt requested help from the Soviet Union, 'then the Mid-East fat would really be in the fire'.[89] In the event, the Soviet challenge came not in the Middle East but in Hungary, where Soviet forces intervened to crush the revolution on 4 November. Eisenhower, furious at being placed in a position where America could not intervene in Hungary, blamed Eden for tying his hands.

Eden replied the same day in a cable replete with falsehoods. The United Kingdom had heard of Israeli mobilisation, he claimed, and had urged restraint.[90] Eisenhower was unpersuaded and in a response dripping with irony commented that 'since we have never publicly announced any modification of the Declaration or any limits upon its interpretation, we find it difficult at this time to see how we can violate our pledged word'.[91]

That afternoon, Eden made a statement to the Commons, referring to the 'very dangerous situation' created by the 'establishment of a Joint Military Command between Egypt, Jordan and Syria, the renewed raids by guerillas, culminating in the incursion of Egyptian commandos on Sunday night'. The government learned that 'the Israel government were taking certain measures of mobilisation [and] at once instructed Her Majesty's Ambassador at Tel Aviv to make inquiries of the Israel Minister for Foreign Affairs and to urge restraint'. The previous night the government learned that Israeli forces had invaded Egypt and were in the vicinity of the canal.

The greatest danger, Eden continued, was that 'free passage through the canal will be jeopardised'. For that reason, not from any consideration of national prestige, 'the United Kingdom and French governments ... have called upon both sides to stop all warlike action by land, sea and air forthwith and to withdraw their military forces to a distance of 10 miles from the canal'.

This was followed by the greatest dissimulation of the Prime

---

89 Ibid., doc. 418. Eisenhower to Eden, 30 October 1956.
90 Ibid., doc. 421. Eden to Eisenhower, 30 October 1956.
91 Ibid., doc. 424. Eisenhower to Eden, 30 October 1956.

Minister's statement, the final dishonest twist of the Sèvres accord. Maintaining the illusion that Britain and France were merely concerned observers, striving to keep the canal open in the interests of all its users, Eden reported that an ultimatum had been issued jointly to Israel and Egypt:

> The governments of Egypt and Israel have been asked to answer this communication within twelve hours. It has been made clear to them that, if at the expiration of that time one or both have not undertaken to comply with these requirements, British and French forces will intervene in whatever strength may be necessary to secure compliance.[92]

On the following day, Rab substituted for the Prime Minister at a luncheon with the British Newspaper Editors Society. In a remarkable moment of indiscretion, conceivably tailoring his speech to what he thought editors wanted to hear, he savagely attacked the American administration for real and imagined sins. Not only were they guilty of failure to co-operate over Suez, he charged, they had also been opposed to Britain's long-term economic plans since 1951. Quite apart from Rab's persistent ingenuousness on issues of international relations, this was a most injudicious time to level criticism at Washington. As he and Clark rode back to Downing Street, Rab, according to Clark, 're-verted to his old theme that the PM was mistaken to ignore the UN'. Clark retorted that 'it was rather dangerous to be so anti-American'.[93]

During the first week of November, Rab's professed loyalty to Eden was further tested. In an Egypt Committee meeting in the afternoon of 4 November, when it appeared that Egypt and Israel had both accepted a ceasefire, members accepted that Parliament and public would not accept landings in Egypt if the fighting had already ended. In masterly understatement, the minutes record that 'it would be difficult to counter the allegation that our real objective all along had been to attack Egypt'.[94] At a Cabinet meeting that evening, when it

---

92 Hansard, 30 October 1956, vol. 558, cols 1274–5.
93 Clark, Diary entry for 31 October 1956, *From Three Worlds*, p. 202.
94 TNA: CAB 134/4108, E. C. (56) 40th Meeting, 4 November 1956.

was announced that the Israelis had attained their objectives and were on the point of ceasing fire, Rab seized on the news triumphantly and argued that there was now no point in the invasion. Eden, Rab recalled, 'said he must go upstairs and consider his position'.[95] The Cabinet was divided on the question: twelve were for continuing; Rab, Kilmuir and Heathcoat-Amory favoured postponement, while Salisbury, Buchan-Hepburn and Monckton urged an immediate halt.[96] Rab and the majority of his colleagues indicated, however, that they would accept a different course favoured by the majority of the Cabinet; only Monckton stated that he would 'reserve his position' if military action were not suspended. At the end of the discussion, information came that Israel was not prepared to accept a ceasefire on the conditions laid down in the UN resolution. No ceasefire was therefore in force and the Anglo-French operation could proceed as planned.[97]

Eden, concerned at the Cabinet split, told Rab, Salisbury and Macmillan that, if he did not have Cabinet support, 'the situation might arise that someone would have to take over from him'.[98] Rab replied that there was no one to take his place, a statement that the other two ministers endorsed.[99] Eden was shocked by the growing opposition to the use of force. Macmillan and Salisbury he regarded as 'weak sisters' who had switched sides. Of the succession he is reported to have said to Hugh Massingham of *The Observer*, 'I do not care who it is going to be, but I shall make absolutely certain it isn't Rab.'[100]

On 5 November, one day before the American election, the invasion of Port Said was launched. Maintaining his position of a reluctant belligerent, Eden wrote to Eisenhower regretting 'that the events of the last few days have placed such a strain on the relations between our two countries'.[101] Eisenhower replied, saying that he was equally

---

95 Butler, *The Art of the Possible*, p. 193. Rab was, apparently, proud of having made a telling point, despite his professed admiration for Eden's audacity. Howard (*RAB*, p. 237n) notes that Rab's account of this Cabinet is challenged by Rhodes James, *Anthony Eden*, p. 567.
96 Rhodes James, *Anthony Eden*, pp. 566–7.
97 TNA: CAB 134/4108, C. M. (56) 79th Conclusions, 4 November 1956.
98 Butler, *The Art of the Possible*, p. 194.
99 Clarissa Eden, Diary entry; Rhodes James, p. 567; Pearson, *Reluctant Gamble*, p. 159.
100 Pearson, *Reluctant Gamble*, p. 164.
101 *FRUS*, doc. 499. Eden to Eisenhower, 5 November 1956.

saddened, but loosing a clear shot across Eden's bows. 'As you say,' he wrote, 'Harold's financial problem is going to be a serious one, and this itself I think would dictate a policy of the least possible provocation.'[102]

This was more than a gentle warning. By heavy selling of sterling Washington forced London's hand. Macmillan, as Chancellor of the Exchequer, faced rapidly plummeting reserves and a fast-falling pound. He promptly contacted the IMF in New York and was stonewalled. The reply came not from New York but from Washington, bluntly informing him that the United States would not agree to buttress sterling until Britain agreed to a ceasefire.[103] Rab disingenuously referred to this elementary pressure as 'blackmail'.[104] Macmillan 'switched almost overnight from being the foremost protagonist of intervention to being the leading influence for disengagement'.[105]

Soon after the 4 November Cabinet, at which Rab had openly but ineffectually challenged Eden, came another characteristic indiscretion. More damagingly – because he spoke outside Cabinet – at a dinner with twenty influential Conservative members of the Progress Trust, Rab was forthright and openly critical of Eden's actions, 'speaking privately of some of the realities of the situation, particularly in relation to sterling, which no one had hitherto done ... Whenever I moved in the weeks that followed, I felt the party knives sticking into my innocent back.'[106]

Initially innocent of Eden's deception Rab might have been, but he was undoubtedly foolish and less than staunch in his support of the Prime Minister. Having spent two months attempting to restrain him, he chose at a critical point to support the invasion. Then, at the final Cabinet before it was launched, he challenged Eden's position openly, following it with an indiscretion guaranteed to be joyously repeated among the diehards. As William Clark scornfully noted in his diary, 'God how power corrupts. The way Rab has turned and trimmed!'[107]

---

102 Ibid., doc. 502. Draft Message, Eisenhower to Eden, 5 November 1956.
103 Macmillan, *Riding the Storm*, pp. 163–4.
104 Butler, *The Art of the Possible*, p. 195.
105 Ibid., p. 194.
106 Ibid., p. 194.
107 Clark, Diary entry for 4 November 1956, *From Three Worlds*, p. 209.

Rab at this point had the wisdom to recognise that the goodwill of Washington was a vital ingredient for any aspirant to succeed the ailing Eden and that, in this area, he was being outmanoeuvred by Macmillan. In a telephone conversation with Eisenhower on 7 November, Eden had tried to turn a deaf ear to the President's urgings to cease fire by commenting that the connection was poor. Eisenhower brushed that protest aside, asking Eden to keep in touch by phone as 'the ... connection seemed very satisfactory'.[108] Eden duly called back the next day, suggesting that he and Mollet fly to Washington for talks. At first Eisenhower welcomed the suggestion but he was soon persuaded by Dulles and Herbert Hoover Jr[109] of the State Department that such a visit would be unwelcome for the moment as it was certain to alarm America's Arab friends in the region. Eisenhower called Eden back and withdrew the invitation.[110]

On 8 November, after the UN Resolution that Britain withdraw her troops, the Cabinet met for an unvarnished and sobering statement from Lloyd. Britain 'now faced a situation in which the Suez Canal was blocked';

> ...oil supplies from the Middle East were at risk; alternative supplies from the Western Hemisphere could not be counted upon, especially in the absence of financial aid from the United States; and so long as Egypt was free to reconstitute her forces while [Britain was] bound by the ceasefire, our troops at Port Said and in Cyprus were exposed...

Additionally, the government was vulnerable in the Commons, and it was increasingly urgent that fences be mended in Washington. The British Commander-in-Chief, moreover, reported that troop morale was low as a result of confinement and of press questioning of the value of their operations.[111]

Now that the possibility that Eden would not survive the crisis

---

108 *FRUS*, doc. 527. Eisenhower to Eden, 6 November 1956.

109 Son of Herbert Hoover, President of the United States from 1929 to 1933.

110 *FRUS*, docs 539 and 540. Memorandum for the Record and telephone transcript, 7 November 1956.

111 TNA: CAB 134/4108, C. M. (56), 83nd Conclusions, 8 November 1956.

was clear, both Rab and Macmillan strove to establish themselves in American eyes as the rightful heir. During a reception at Buckingham Palace on 12 November, Rab approached Aldrich and, somewhat unctuously,

> said with great earnestness how deeply he deplored the existence of what he termed mutual misunderstandings of policy which had arisen between US and UK governments. He quite evidently was greatly disturbed by the course followed by majority of Cabinet although he did not specifically so state. He said to me, 'I have been meaning to come to see you for a long time to tell you that in my opinion you are the only man who is in a position to explain to your government in detail the various attitudes of the members of our government. Never has an Ambassador occupied a more important position than you do at the present moment.'[112]

He went on to urge Aldrich to speak to Macmillan at the earliest opportunity. On the following day, Aldrich saw Macmillan, who was keen to pay a visit to Washington to see Treasury Secretary Humphrey and other Treasury officials. Aldrich advised him to wait until Eden went to Washington and to accompany him. Macmillan registered his regret that he had had to give up the Foreign Office and that Selwyn Lloyd, 'too young and inexperienced', had taken the position. This could not, he seemed to imply, have happened on his watch.

Macmillan was now openly acting as Eden's loyal but ambivalent deputy. A week later, he and Aldrich met for an hour and a half. Aldrich concluded that he and Salisbury were motivated by

> realisation of the desperate financial position in which they will find themselves at the end of the year unless by that time they are working in the closest possible co-operation with the US in both the economic and political fields ... Perhaps the above is only another way of saying

---

112 *FRUS*, doc. 571. Aldrich to State Department, 12 November 1956.

that the British Cabinet is beginning to realise what a terrible mistake
has been made.

Throughout their conversation, Macmillan referred to himself as
'Eden's deputy' who would assume responsibility for the government
if Eden became too ill. Aldrich gathered that 'some sort of movement
[was] on foot in the Cabinet to replace Eden'.[113]

On the following day, Aldrich and Macmillan met again. Aldrich
had learned that Eden needed a break and that he would almost certainly retire in the very near future. His understanding at that point was
that Rab would become Prime Minister, Macmillan Foreign Secretary,
and Lloyd Chancellor. On the other hand, he added, Macmillan might
take over as Prime Minister. Concerning the withdrawal of British
troops, on which Eisenhower insisted before Washington made any
move to help Britain, Macmillan suggested:

> If you can give us a fig leaf to cover our nakedness I believe we can get
> a majority of the Cabinet to vote for such withdrawal without requiring
> conditions in connection with location of United Nations Forces and
> methods of re-opening and operating canal, although younger members
> of the Cabinet will be strongly opposed.[114]

Aldrich added that Macmillan was 'desperately anxious' to see the
President, a development that was discussed in the White House
on the following day at a meeting between Eisenhower, Humphrey,
Under-Secretary of State Hoover and Colonel Andrew Goodpaster,
Defense Liaison Officer to the President. Humphrey commented that,
in his opinion, Rab would be the stronger Prime Minister.[115] As Secretary of the Treasury he had much contact with Rab and, naturally,
inclined to him. Philosophically the two were close, particularly in
attitudes to government spending. The President countered that he

---

113 *FRUS*, doc. 588. Aldrich to State Department, 19 November 1956.
114 Ibid., doc. 593. Aldrich to State Department, 19 November 1956.
115 Rab in his memoir refers to his 'long-standing friendship with Humphrey' (*The Art of the
Possible*, p. 195.) That may have existed, but Macmillan, as Rab's successor at the Treasury, also
had good relations with Humphrey. His friendships with Dulles and, vitally, with Ike easily
outgunned Rab's connections.

had 'always thought most highly of Macmillan, who is a straight, fine man, and ... the outstanding one of the British he served with during the war'. Hoover, he felt, should advise Rab or Macmillan to speak to Humphrey or Hoover the following day to learn the extent of aid that could be supplied. On the question of whom Hoover should address, given 'the unknown relationship between Butler and Macmillan', it was decided that discussions would be held with both until the situation became clearer.[116] Macmillan thus achieved ostensible parity with Rab and held up his sleeve the wild card of his wartime friendship with the President.

From this point on, American initiatives were proposed to both Cabinet members. Rab was Acting Prime Minister and, given Foreign Office protocol, it is significant that Macmillan was treated as his equal. Eisenhower was not alone in favouring Macmillan; clearly Aldrich, the man on the spot in London, felt that he, rather than Rab, might succeed. This was reflected in a telegram sent to the State Department on the following day, in which Aldrich wrote, 'It was quite apparent that both Butler and Macmillan are still very anxious that Macmillan and possibly Butler also should see the President as soon as the situation has reached a point where this would be in accord with President's policy.'[117]

Hoover responded on the following day, cabling Aldrich that no meeting with Macmillan or Rab could be held before the first week in December. Moreover, the withdrawal of troops took priority before anything could be arranged.[118] Aldrich passed this on to Macmillan, who expressed his concern that 'the position of Cabinet remains precarious'.[119] The Chancellor of the Exchequer, self-appointed Deputy Prime Minister, neatly handed the blame for the division to Eden and Rab while maintaining his own objectivity. It was a *virtuoso* exercise of alarmist tactics. It was also effective, for Eisenhower promptly expressed his preference for meeting Macmillan without Rab – a meeting

---

116 *FRUS*, doc. 596. Memorandum of White House Conference, 20 November 1956.
117 Ibid., doc. 598. Aldrich to State Department, 21 November 1956.
118 Ibid., doc. 600. Hoover to Aldrich, 21 November 1956.
119 Ibid., doc. 602. Aldrich to State Department, 22 November 1956.

always conditional on the withdrawal of forces from Egypt.[120] By then it was becoming clear that Eden would probably not survive; Harry Crookshank wrote to Mac from New Zealand that he should be 'up and doing'. 'Be a good Boy Scout,' he wrote. 'Be prepared.'[121]

The issue of withdrawal became the field on which Eden, and later Rab, fought the final, dispiriting, rearguard action of the Suez affair. Whilst the end result was inevitable, the Cabinet made faltering attempts to rescue some vestige of British prestige, proposing that only token withdrawals be made until they were reassured concerning the future administration of the canal.[122] This position, however, had to be balanced with the need not to give the impression that Britain and France were delaying the clearance of the canal. When General Raymond Wheeler, a hard-line West Point graduate who had served as Deputy Supreme Commander of the China–Burma–India theatre under Mountbatten in 1944–45 with no great love for the British, took charge of the canal clearance, Britain's humiliation was complete.

In this atmosphere of uncertainty, the Prime Minister, exhausted and bitterly disappointed at the outcome, his Cabinet and party viscerally divided, the leadership of the Tories apparently uncertain, left England on 22 November to recuperate at Goldeneye, the Jamaica home of novelist Ian Fleming.

Few insiders expected him to return as Prime Minister. His successor, it was clear, would be either Macmillan, the man who saved the pound sterling, or Butler, the wavering accomplice of the man who nearly destroyed it.

---

120 Ibid., doc. 604. Memorandum of White House Conference, 23 November 1956.
121 Bodleian: MSS Macmillan, dep c.309.2. Crookshank to Macmillan, 21 November 1956.
122 TNA: CAB 134/4108, C. M. (56) 84th Conclusions, 16 November 1956; CAB 134/4108, E. C. (56) 45th meeting, 19 November 1956.

CHAPTER 15

THE LEADERSHIP, ROUND 2 –
ALLEGRO VIVACE, 1956–57

The week before Eden's departure for Jamaica brought into focus the aftermath of the adventure, the complex arrangements for withdrawal of troops and the clearing of the blocked canal. In both operations the Cabinet strove to maintain British prestige, proclaiming to the world that Britain's objectives had been achieved and that the business of restoring order to a chastened Egypt could begin. It fell to Rab to attempt the delicate political *legerdemain* of presenting a humiliating reversal as a victory. The triumvirate of Rab, Macmillan and Heath, the Chief Whip, strove to hold the party together, 'commanding admiration for its dexterity, if not necessarily for its political honesty'.[1]

The Egypt Committee recognised that 'no effective support from the United States could be expected until at least a start had been made on the withdrawal of Anglo-French forces'.[2] Equally, Eisenhower was adamant that the forces should be withdrawn before clearance work began. Once General Wheeler, General Lucius Clay and John J. McCloy, a former president of the World Bank, were appointed to oversee the United Nations clearance team, the linkage between withdrawal, canal clearance and economic assistance was underscored.

Nonetheless, the Cabinet continued to recommend that only token withdrawals should be made until they were reassured concerning the

---

1 *The Economist*, 1 December 1956.
2 TNA: CAB 134/4108, E. C. (56) 44th meeting, 15 November 1956.

future administration of the canal. Macmillan pointed out that the American intention to furnish supplementary supplies of oil to Europe was by no means certain.[3] Macmillan was the realist, fully aware that Eisenhower, more a general than a politician, would be inflexible on this issue. Rab, a practitioner of 'the art of the possible', wrongly believed that there was room for negotiation.

Meanwhile, the British press was openly speculating about foreknowledge of the Israeli intention to attack Egypt, and ministers were cautioned to avoid statements in the House of Commons before the composition and functions of the UN force were known.[4] Rab, who chaired the Cabinet in Eden's absence, found the government beleaguered. Not only had it lost American goodwill and come under attack from Commonwealth countries for lack of consultation; it was also an aggressor in the eyes of the United Nations. No course of action open to Rab would satisfy more than a third of his critics.

After Eden left for Jamaica, in the words of one historian, 'Butler, Leader of the House of Commons, took charge of the Cabinet, and Macmillan took control of the government.'[5] Whilst this may appear too neat an aphorism, it perfectly describes the roles of the two protagonists. Put differently, Rab did the work of a managing director while Macmillan took the role of chief executive. It was Rab who had the responsibility for disengagement, 'the odious duty of withdrawing the troops, re-establishing the pound, salvaging our relations with the US and the UN, and bearing the brunt of the criticism from private members, constituency worthies and the general public for organising withdrawal, which was a collective responsibility'.[6] He referred to this mending of fences as 'the most difficult of [his] career'.

Recalling that period later, Rab elaborated:

There was in the party a great deal of doubt about our stopping hostilities … Of course I was left with the very difficult job, first of all, of helping

---

3   TNA: CAB 134/4108, C. M. (56) 84th Conclusions, 16 November 1956.
4   TNA: CAB 134/4108, C. M. (56) 85th Conclusions, 20 November 1956.
5   Freiberger, *Dawn Over Suez* (Chicago: Ivan Dee, 1992), p. 201.
6   Butler, *The Art of the Possible*, p. 194.

stop the run on the pound which became very severe at that time. That I did with the aid of long-distance calls to Mr Humphrey, my friend and the Secretary of the American Treasury … What really excited the hostility of the Conservative Party was the withdrawal. Many of them were quite ready to see the United Nations force come into Suez … The difficulty was that the force wasn't strong and it wasn't ready … and therefore I got, during the period I was acting Head of Government, a lot of resentment from the Conservative back-benchers.[7]

It is no wonder that Rab specifically remembered the attitude of the backbenchers; the date of 22 November must have been permanently graven on his memory as the day on which Eden's difficulties became his own. First he chaired a Cabinet and reported that there was a strong body of opinion among supporters of the government in the Commons that Britain should not withdraw without a firm assurance that her objectives had been achieved. He therefore proposed repeating the offer to withdraw one battalion, a suggestion that the Cabinet approved, inviting him to make such a statement in the House of Commons.[8]

When Rab did so that afternoon, he came under attack both from Tory backbenchers and from the opposition concerning withdrawal from Egypt and the arrival of the United Nations peace-keeping force at Port Said. 'Her Majesty's Government,' he said, 'as an earnest of their intention to withdraw from Egypt as soon as the conditions they have specified are completed, have welcomed the arrival of United Nations troops in Port Said and have stated that they are prepared to withdraw a British battalion.'[9]

However clothed, this was clearly an effort 'to cut our losses', as Nigel Birch wrote to him.[10] For the retreat Rab incurred the wrath of the right-wing Tories; for not making the retreat unconditional he was castigated by the opposition. 'We are obliged to the Lord Privy

---

7   Interview with Thames Television, reproduced in *The Day Before Yesterday*, p. 143.
8   TNA: CAB 134/4108, C. M. (56) 87th Conclusions, 22 November 1956.
9   Hansard, 22 November, vol. 560, cols 1941–4.
10 Letter, Nigel Birch to Rab, 22 November 1956. Trinity College: Butler Papers, RAB, G30.

Seal', Gaitskell observed with irony, 'for at last giving us some further information about Her Majesty's Government's attitude in this vital matter.' He asked in the same incisive vein, given that the United Nations had called on Britain to withdraw, 'whether, in all these circumstances, and in view of the very dangerous economic prospect that lies ahead, he will swallow his pride and withdraw the British troops?'[11]

Maintaining his position that Britain had acted throughout with the highest principles – a position that was becoming increasingly difficult to hold – Rab spoke of 'an exceptional step ... animated, I believe, by great courage and with the right motives'. With such language he tied himself irrevocably to Eden and to future indictments of the Prime Minister's duplicitous policy and actions.

On the same evening, Rab and Macmillan attended a meeting of the 1922 Committee to address members on the subject of the Middle East. Philip Goodhart, in his history of the 1922, describes the meeting as 'one of the classic confrontations in the history of the 1922 Committee'.[12] It was by now common knowledge that a change of leadership was imminent and that the meeting would be a 'beauty contest' for the two contenders to succeed Eden. Ian Orr-Ewing[13] recalled the occasion vividly:

> The room was absolutely crowded, every single backbench Conservative MP was there. We'd been told that we were going to be addressed for ten minutes, first by Rab Butler who would then answer one or two questions, and secondly by Mr Harold Macmillan who would also answer one or two questions. Both had taken a good deal of trouble with their speech. Harold Macmillan was the master of a short speech, both in timing and in every way, and in ten minutes he produced a very good atmosphere and a very confident result. I think a great number, I should think 90 per cent of the people as they went out of that room, would have supported Harold Macmillan.[14]

11   Hansard, 22 November 1956, vol. 560, cols 1943–4.
12   Goodhart, *The 1922* (London: Macmillan, 1973), pp. 174–6.
13   MP for Hendon North. Later Lord Orr-Ewing.
14   Interview with Thames Television, reproduced in *The Day Before Yesterday*, p. 161.

Enoch Powell, who was also attending the meeting, recalled the evening as 'one of those ghastly memories that I've got from twenty years in politics'. In typically dispassionate manner, he saw the occasion as a chess game in which Rab was simply outmanoeuvred:

> In the absence of the Prime Minister, ill, perhaps fatally ill, two potential successors looking for the position that would enable them each to down the other, and doing it with a complete show of *bonhomie*, unity and goodwill … One saw the difference in style, in character, of the two men, the different pose, if you like, of the two poseurs. But Rab lost the chess game, in that by the end of the year the people in the party on the whole believed that it was he and not Harold Macmillan who had counselled withdrawal … This wasn't so and was, to the best of my knowledge, rather the reverse; but Rab ended up on just the wrong spot on the chess board.[15]

Rab maintained later that he had 'made very few arrangements or dispositions',[16] yet the clear memory of Lord Orr-Ewing was that both he and Macmillan had taken trouble with their speech. For Powell, both he and Macmillan were 'poseurs'. Observers cite many moments when Rab 'lost the battle' and this was demonstrably one such. In practice, the choice of Eden's successor was handled by the Cabinet and not by the backbenchers. But the confrontation passed into 1922 folklore and was definitive of the attitudes that backbenchers had towards Macmillan and Rab thereafter.

Rab struck the backbenchers as feeble, unconvincing, a 'weak sister'; Macmillan was virile, at ease with the new world structure and the American President, eager to define Britain's role in that world – using once more his familiar theme that Britain's statesmen could play the role of Greeks to the Romans of Washington. As Heath's biographer neatly described Tory attitudes, the party was determined not to be

---

15   Interview with Thames Television, reproduced in *The Day Before Yesterday*, p. 161. Heffer, *Like The Roman: The Life of Enoch Powell* (London: Phoenix, 1999), records that Powell described the occasion as 'one of the most horrible things that I remember in politics' (p. 210).

16   Ibid., p. 160.

ashamed of Suez. Macmillan would brazen it out better and restore
relations with Washington.[17] A particularly satisfying thrust for Mac
must have been when he referred to 'the long adventure of politics, full
of hard knocks but still a game more worth playing than any other'.
The long adventure had lasted since Rab's letter to *The Times*;[18] the
hard knocks were Macmillan's years without preferment; the game was
one that Rab, no sportsman, did not play with the same adroitness as
Macmillan. As Mac delivered that tug on Rab's gallows, he hoisted his
opponent on his own petard.

Two days later, the General Assembly of the United Nations
overwhelmingly voted in condemnation of the actions of Britain
and France;[19] pressure was increased on the government to withdraw
from Port Said. Macmillan recognised that only this would persuade
Washington to step in to halt the slide of sterling. Aldrich reported
to the State Department that anti-American feeling was widespread
in Britain to the point that 'we are thought of by the British public as
enemies of Britain working against them with the Russians and the
Arabs instead of as allies'.[20] This attitude did Rab further damage in all
quarters as he was now blamed both for his association with the invasion and for 'caving in' to unpopular American demands. Macmillan
managed to avoid the calumny heaped on Rab by virtue of his having
predicted exactly this outcome and having, even belatedly, opposed
the invasion.

Another question that concerned observers – politicians, press and
public alike – was troubling Churchill. Asked by his doctor Lord
Moran why Eden had left the country, he admitted to being shocked,
adding 'And I'm an Anthony man.' Rab, in the position of deputising for a Prime Minister who had bolted, could be nothing but 'an
Anthony man', damaging his credibility in Britain and in Washington,
whose views, ironically, he had at first echoed. Churchill appeared to
make the same connection. He was 'very doubtful' that Eden would be

---

17 Campbell, *Edward Heath*, p. 97.
18 *The Times*, 27 May 1930. See Chapter 4.
19 By sixty-three votes to five.
20 *FRUS*, doc. 614. Aldrich to State Department, 26 November 1956.

able to carry on when he returned. 'I'd like to see Harold Macmillan Prime Minister,' he mused.

Macmillan had been wooing Churchill assiduously, visiting him at Chartwell, letting it be known that he would never serve under Rab. 'Macmillan is telling journalists that he intends to retire from politics and go to the morgue,'[21] wrote Brendan Bracken to Beaverbrook on 7 December. Further distancing himself from Eden and Rab, and letting it be known in the time-honoured manner of a candidate that he was not a candidate, Macmillan established himself, in the view of insiders, as the Prime Minister in waiting. He had the support that mattered in Washington; Rab might be on excellent terms with his former opposite number, George Humphrey, but Macmillan had the support of bigger guns in the White House and at the State Department. He also had the support of Churchill. The impression was that Rab's job, simply, was to clear up the mess that he and his boss had created in order for Eden to retire and Macmillan to take over.

The last week of November heightened that impression as events crowded on the unfortunate Rab's head. The Cabinet met daily and it seemed that each day brought another crisis. If Rab had been able to step in and provide solutions, he might have emerged with his reputation unscathed. As it was, the interrelated nature of the problems entailed that either the government would maintain its support in the Commons by delaying withdrawal   at the cost of alienating Washington and world opinion – or it would withdraw immediately, very possibly causing the government to fall. As the man in charge during Eden's absence, it was Rab who would be blamed for either unacceptable outcome.

On 26 November, the Cabinet considered a cable from Lloyd that, after discussions with the UN Secretary-General, there was no advantage to be gained from deferring withdrawal.[22] On the following day, Monckton reported on his visit to Port Said; while reports had indicated that 100–200 Egyptians had been killed, it now seemed that

---

21 'The morgue' is the House of Lords. Bracken to Beaverbrook, House of Lords Record Office, BK C/17. Cited by Thorpe, *Supermac*, p. 353.

22 TNA: CAB 134/4108, C. M. (56) 88th Conclusions, 26 November 1956.

this estimate was inaccurate and several hundred had died. Egyptian stories of British atrocities, moreover, were gaining currency.[23] On 28 November, as the Cabinet strove to save face by delaying or phasing withdrawal, Macmillan pointed out the unwelcome truth that only immediate withdrawal would placate Washington. During November, gold and dollar reserves had fallen to an extent 'that would be a considerable shock both to public opinion in this country and to international confidence in sterling'. He urged a prompt announcement of Britain's intention to withdraw. Rab accepted the inevitability of withdrawal and summed up the Cabinet view that, in the light of Macmillan's economic statement, Britain 'should announce, in the next few days, that we were now prepared to withdraw the Anglo-French force from Port Said as rapidly as possible, in the faith that the United Nations had now accepted responsibility for securing the [original British] objectives'.[24] The problem, of course, was that such faith entailed a grossly optimistic assessment of the truth. In modern political parlance, it was heavy 'spin'. When the Cabinet returned to the question in the first of two meetings on the following day, Lloyd addressed the issue while Macmillan remained silent.[25] He knew that the need to placate the White House would determine the course of action that the Cabinet adopted; the 'spinning' of it was Rab's problem and not his.

In the second Cabinet that day, Rab suggested that Britain press the UN Secretary-General for 'more positive assurances on the points about which public opinion in this country was exercised, particularly the clearance of the Suez Canal'. In assuming responsibility for public relations, Rab assumed responsibility for the 'spin', seeking some face-saving formula but returning to the reality that no further pressure could be put on the UN or on Washington.[26] It was now not only Eden who would shoulder the blame; Rab had undertaken an impossible task while Macmillan had spoken a self-evident truth in urging immediate withdrawal.

---

23 TNA: CAB 134/4108, C. M. (56) 89th Conclusions, 27 November 1956.
24 TNA: CAB 134/4108, C. M. (56) 90th Conclusions, 28 November 1956.
25 TNA: CAB 134/4108, C. M. (56) 91st Conclusions, 29 November 1956.
26 TNA: CAB 134/4108, C. M. (56) 92nd Conclusions, 29 November 1956.

In Washington, Rab's efforts to maintain order while he extricated Britain from Egypt were being viewed pessimistically. At a meeting of the National Security Council on 30 November, Hoover had given his opinion that if Rab could reverse policy without a change of government it would be 'a masterful stroke'. Humphrey agreed, adding that 'the possibilities, for good and for evil, that could come out of the present situation were such that they could scarcely be exaggerated'. It was 'touch and go whether the Victorians or Moderns would end up in control of the Tory Party'. This prompted Vice-President Nixon, chairing the meeting, to ask if Washington could do anything to help the Tories. 'He expressed himself as scared to death at the prospect of Nye Bevan in a position of power in a future British government.'[27] At that meeting, the decision was taken that the United States should assure Britain of financial support. At the same time, however, the US government should not overdo that assurance of support, as this would 'make it harder for Butler to line up the Conservative Party behind the … statement of British withdrawal'.

Eisenhower was almost certainly angling to move Eden out and Macmillan in. Macmillan was equally certainly aware of this but, counter to allegations of Byzantine plots, he did not force the pace by urging military action solely to embarrass Eden. He simply allowed events to take their course, giving Eden the latitude to destroy himself. Eisenhower had the greatest respect for Churchill, the war leader. When he took office in 1953, Churchill, albeit in decline, had returned as Prime Minister and for two years the wartime colleagues were in power. Eden took over in 1955, high in Ike's estimation as Churchill's able and loyal lieutenant. On 17 November, however, speaking to Dulles, Eisenhower confessed that he had started 'with an exceedingly high opinion of [Eden] … and then [had] continually to downgrade this estimate'.[28] What could be more natural than that the torch should pass, admittedly with interruptions, from FDR to Ike, from Churchill

---

27 *FRUS*, doc. 626. Minutes of NSC Meeting, 30 November 1956.
28 Memorandum of a Conversation with the President. 17 November 1956. Eisenhower Library, John F. Dulles Papers, White Memorandum Series, Box #4. Cited by Freiberger, *Dawn Over Suez*, p. 199.

to Macmillan, and the Anglo-American special relationship flourish as before? Later in November, Ike wrote to Churchill, hoping that

> *this one may be washed off the slate as soon as possible and that we can to-gether adopt other means of achieving our legitimate aims in the Middle East. Nothing saddens me more than the thought that I and my old friends of years have met a problem concerning which we do not see eye to eye. I shall never be happy until our old time closeness has been restored.*[29]

On 1 December, the issue of Egyptian casualties surfaced once more in Cabinet. It was now confirmed that 300 Egyptians had been killed in the Port Said area; moreover, 'neutral opinion in the world was tend-ing to give credence to the far higher figures quoted by the Egyptian government'. An unwelcome request to maintain a strategic reserve in Cyprus had been received from Paris, a request certain to infuriate the Conservative right. Rab woefully confessed that 'it was not easy to find reasons for rejecting the proposal'. There were also differences between London and Paris on how to word the announcement of withdrawal. Rab took on the responsibility of agreeing the content of the announcement with the French Foreign Minister.[30]

At a second Cabinet on the same day, discussion resumed over how Rab should present the situation to the Commons on 3 December. It was a delicate balancing act: how to portray the outcome as a victory for Britain, who could now withdraw, having achieved her objectives; how to square that 'victory' with the issue of British subjects expelled from Egypt; how to avoid the problem of British dependence on oil from the Middle East; and how to 'recognise with appreciation' the American statement that they would support the UN in resisting any attempt to introduce 'external forces' or to impede the UN force.[31] To weave these incompatible position statements into a credible speech was a challenging puzzle. However he approached the task, Rab was certain to be accused of deceit. His decision publicly to support Eden

---

29 Eisenhower, *Waging Peace* (Garden City, NY: Doubleday, 1965), pp. 680–81.
30 TNA: CAB 134/4108, C. M. (56) 94th Conclusions, 1 December 1956.
31 TNA: CAB 134/4108, C. M. (56) 95th Conclusions, 1 December 1956.

in an enterprise of which he fundamentally disapproved was about to cost him dear. One may speculate as to how clearly Macmillan foresaw this outcome, but it is certain that he was well pleased with the difficulties that faced Rab.

By the end of November, the Cabinet had agreed to withdraw all troops and Rab told Aldrich that, subject to agreement by the French, he would so inform the Commons on 3 December. His announcement followed a statement by Selwyn Lloyd which sparked off a series of violent exchanges.[32] Rab was assiduously factual, confirming the decision of the British and French governments to withdraw from the Port Said area without delay. The context in which it was delivered, however – when it was accepted that Britain had suffered a defeat, and when Lloyd had been verbally savaged in his statement – was, to say the least, unpropitious. It redounded even further to Rab's disadvantage, as the question inevitably was asked – why had Rab, as head of the government *pro tempore*, not made Lloyd's statement himself?

On 4 December, Macmillan spoke in the Commons, describing the run on sterling and the diminishing reserves. In contrast to the previous day's statement by Lloyd, it was a strong speech, in Macmillan's words, 'an immediate explanation from me both of the significance of these figures and of government policy'. He administered the bad news, offset by the encouraging statement that the problem was not caused by any weakness in Britain's trading position. 'But', he added, 'the closure of the Suez Canal and of the Iraq Petroleum Company pipelines must adversely affect our balance of payments, especially if these interruptions are prolonged.' The message was clear: the Suez affair was directly responsible for the economic problems; with no underlying balance of trade problems, however, and a moratorium on payment of interest on American and Canadian loans, he would have the room to solve those temporary problems without an additional Budget. Macmillan spoke confidently, handling questions from Gaitskell, Wilson and Healey with assurance. The contrast between

---

32 Hansard, 3 December 1956, vol. 561, cols 877–95.

the Chancellor of the Exchequer on the one hand and Rab and Lloyd on the other was marked.[33]

Reginald Bevins, Parliamentary Secretary to the Ministry of Works, summed up that contrast when he spoke of Rab's apparent indecision during Suez:

> In the case of Suez, Rab had appeared to be devious, even in the House of Commons itself. Macmillan had tried and failed, but Butler hadn't even tried. Secondly, those who knew Butler well knew that it was almost impossible to get a decision out of Rab on anything, however important. It was like getting blood out of a stone and there is one quality a Prime Minister mustn't have and that is the inability to make quick decisions.[34]

Bevins's view of Rab as indecisive was a recurring criticism. On the occasion when firm decisiveness was most needed, either to support or oppose Eden's policy, Rab was found wanting. After Général Challe put to Eden the French plan of 14 October, to invite Israel to attack across the Sinai, Rab was chronically indecisive. According to Sir Richard Powell, Permanent Secretary at the Ministry of Defence: 'Butler behaved in typical Butlerian manner of agonising over anything, wondering if it was right or it wasn't. He certainly went through all that and expressed himself dubious about the thing from time to time. But that was just the makeup of the man.'[35]

Once Eden left the country and Rab's task was clearly defined, he did, in fact, handle the withdrawal and recovery efficiently, but his performances in the Commons were lacklustre. In a Vote of Confidence debate on 5 and 6 December, Bevan, congratulating Lloyd on 'having survived so far', accused Rab of 'Freudian lapses' when he addressed the Commons.[36] The government, Bevan charged, had consistently given different reasons for the invasion. In a devastating speech he

---

33 Hansard, 4 December 1956, vol. 561, cols 1050–66.
34 Interview with Thames Television, reproduced in *The Day Before Yesterday*, p. 160.
35 Suez Oral History Project: Interview with Sir Richard Powell. Pearson, *Reluctant Gamble*, p. 142.
36 Hansard, 5 December 1956, vol. 561, col. 1268.

took the government to task for a series of untruths told and justifica-
tions manufactured, for appealing to 'the unthinking and unreflective
who still react to traditional values, who still think that we can solve all
these problems in the old ways'. The government, he conceded, would
survive the vote of confidence, but

> It will take us very many years to live down what we have done. It will
> take us many years to pay the price. I know that tomorrow evening hon.
> and right hon. Members will probably, as they have done before, give
> the Government a vote of confidence, but they know in their heart of
> hearts that it is a vote which the government do[es] not deserve.[37]

Bevan was right. After a two-day debate the government survived
with a majority of 327 to 260.

The last days before Eden's return brought further difficulties, frustration and humiliation for Rab, who had operated on the assumption
that, once Britain acceded to American demands, all would be well
and the Special Relationship would resume. On 12 December, in a
Cabinet at which Macmillan was not present, he reported that Lloyd
was unhappy with progress of clearing the canal. General Wheeler
had followed Eisenhower's instruction that clearance would not
begin until the Anglo-French force was withdrawn, which, in British eyes, meant that the USA and Egypt were collaborating to heap
further opprobrium on Britain. At the same meeting, Rab announced
that the French had refused to accept a withdrawal date earlier than
22 December, which 'exposes us to criticism from the United States
that we had not honoured the understanding on this subject'. Since it
was on this understanding that Washington had guaranteed support
from the IMF, Rab was once again placed in the position of having to
offend either his government's supporters or Washington; nor was his
position improved when it became clear that Wheeler had no intention of using British salvage ships in the clearance operation.[38]

---

37 Ibid., cols 1282–3.
38 TNA: CAB 134/4108, C. M. (56) 99th Conclusions, 12 December 1956.

As a final blow to British prestige, the Cabinet learned that Britain would have no legal justification for retaining Egyptian prisoners of war once the fighting ceased. It had been the government's intention to hold prisoners until such time as Egypt released the canal contractors' employees seized by Egypt. Legally, Britain would be obliged to return the prisoners while Egypt retained the civilian contractors' staff as a bargaining counter. That was certain to be ill-received by the British press and public and, once more, it was Rab who would be blamed for the loss of face. At a Cabinet on the following day, Rab, doubtless with some relief, proposed that the handling of this issue be discussed after Eden's return.[39]

Eden returned after three weeks in Jamaica on 14 December to be greeted by the newspaper headline 'Prime Minister Visits Britain'[40] and frank suggestions from *The Times*, *Manchester Guardian* and *The Economist* that he resign. When he appeared in the Commons on 17 December, only one Member rose to applaud him. Rab nonetheless later maintained that:

> When Eden came back from Jamaica it wasn't clear that he wasn't going to continue as Prime Minister at all. I thought he was going on and, to be frank, in the particular competition for being Prime Minister, I had made very few arrangements or dispositions, as they say in the military way, and I was totally surprised after Christmas when Eden informed me he was going to Sandringham to tender his resignation.[41]

Between Eden's return and his informing Rab of his decision to resign, the Prime Minister maintained his position that there had been no collusion and, even more remarkably, that Britain had not suffered a tactical defeat. The government was trapped in further dishonesty when a report from Sir Edwin Herbert revealed that 650 Egyptians had been killed in Port Said, 800 seriously injured and 1,000 slightly injured. The Cabinet Minutes state coyly that the government would need

39 TNA: CAB 134/4108, C. M. (56) 100th Conclusions, 13 December 1956.
40 *Forward*, a weekly publication with a left-wing bias, 14 December 1956.
41 Interview with Thames Television, reproduced in *The Day Before Yesterday*, p. 160.

'to decide what publicity they should give to the revised estimates'.[42] Some progress was made on the exchange of prisoners for contractors' staffs, but there continued to be bad blood between London and Washington over canal clearance.[43] Above all, there was no change in the British attitude that Nasser and his government deserved less consideration than Britain – an attitude tragically shared by Eden and Rab.

On 20 December, the day before the House adjourned for the Christmas recess, the Prime Minister was questioned closely by Gaitskell as to the exact date that France and Britain had resolved to intervene. Eden's responses were evasive and misleading; he only managed to avoid further embarrassment when the Speaker closed down the Question hour in accordance with the House Standing Orders. As Harold Wilson pointed out, the House had been denied the presence of the Prime Minister for three and a half weeks and was now about to adjourn for several more weeks. In vain did Desmond Donnelly[44] protest that 'the integrity of the House of Commons and of the country' was involved. Question Time came to an end and Eden was saved by the bell.[45]

Under these circumstances, it beggars belief that Rab remained unaware of Eden's imminent departure. Rab was not naturally devious, nor was he as perspicacious as Macmillan, but after twenty-seven years in Parliament he was scarcely ingenuous in politics. He had witnessed the fall of Chamberlain, observed the intrigues in the Labour Party to dethrone Clement Attlee. He must have had an awareness of his own proximity to the throne when Churchill stepped down, yet he solemnly stated on television that he was 'totally surprised' by Eden's decision.

In his memoirs, the period between Eden's return and Macmillan's accession – almost a month and a period of immense importance to Rab's future – is covered in one paragraph. Was he unable to come to terms with his failure to succeed Eden? Was he reluctant to admit that

---

42 TNA: CAB 134/4108, C. M. (56) 102nd Conclusions, 17 December 1956.
43 TNA: CAB 134/4108, C. M. (56) 103rd Conclusions, 19 December 1956; C. M. (57) 1st Conclusions, 3 January 1957.
44 Desmond Donnelly (1920–74), Labour Member for Pembroke.
45 Hansard, 20 December 1956, vol. 562, cols 1456–63.

he had played his cards poorly? That he had dithered and appeared spineless? He has no difficulty admitting that 'there were many on the back benches who would oppose my succession; there was no similar anti-Macmillan faction'.[46] Or had he already concluded that the game was lost, that Macmillan had swept the board at the 1922 Committee meeting on 22 November? If that were so, then better that he should be seen to be outmanoeuvred by a devious manipulator while he, Rab, went about doing the Prime Minister's bidding. That he should appear surprised by Eden's decision, affect to be unprepared, yield to the 'better prepared' opponent without having engaged himself in the contest. That method of concession would best preserve his self-respect.

Ultimately, Rab was undone by two hard facts. The first was wholly concerning his character and his standing with Tory diehards. To them, Eden had acted patriotically and to criticise Suez was an unpatriotic act. This was the tenor of the Tory defence of Eden in the Commons on 20 December.[47] Rab, despite his ultimate support of Eden's 'audacity', was known to be opposed to the enterprise and was less than discreet about it. Nigel Nicolson saw this as the main cause of his undoing.

> Butler threw away his chance, I think, of becoming Prime Minister by his extraordinary ambivalent attitude to the Suez Crisis. One didn't know from day to day whether he was in favour or not. In all his public speeches he supported the Prime Minister up to the hilt. But one heard that behind the scenes he was taking his own different attitude; that he hadn't known until too late what was going to happen, and that he thought the whole thing had been grossly mismanaged. This point of view percolated down to the backbench members and he gave the impression that he was presented with a poisoned chalice ... But everybody thought, and some perhaps even knew, that his whole instinct was to oppose Sir Anthony Eden on this.[48]

---

46 Butler, *The Art of the Possible*, p. 195.
47 Sir Henry Studholme and Dame Florence Horsbrugh notably accused the opposition of trying to bring discredit on Britain by attacking Eden. Hansard, 20 December 1956, vol. 562, col. 1459.
48 Interview with Thames Television, reproduced in *The Day Before Yesterday*, p. 160.

The second consideration was the presence of Macmillan, who had grown in stature enormously in five years and who, as Chancellor of the Exchequer, had a very real responsibility to act in the country's economic interests, even if those were counter to Britain's strategic plans. Nicolson's comments are once more perceptive:

> Of course, it was a strange thing that Macmillan was the first to say – let's go in; and the first to say – let's get out. So you can say that Macmillan was the arch-criminal in the whole Suez operation. And yet, somehow or other, he managed to give the impression that he was the only man in Eden's absence, in Eden's illness, who could handle this ghastly situation. And so he became Prime Minister, and I thought quite rightly.[49]

After Parliament retired for the Christmas recess, events moved rapidly to their *dénouement*. At Chequers on 27 December, Eden consulted Lord Kilmuir, the Lord Chancellor, about what course he should take. Kilmuir urged him to stay, but believed that Eden would disregard his advice.[50] Significantly, that advice was sought privately from Kilmuir rather than from Rab, after a luncheon at which Rab had been present. When Eden's doctors advised him that to continue in office might finally be too much for his health, he asked Salisbury to speak to the doctors and give him totally objective counsel. Salisbury did so and reported to Eden that he must step down. It was ironic that the two friends had resigned together from Chamberlain's government in 1938 and that it was Salisbury who now told Eden that his position was untenable – whether on strictly medical rather than political grounds is unknown.

On 7 January, Eden chaired his last Cabinet and on the following day travelled with his wife to Sandringham, where he informed the Queen of his intention to resign. On the following day, the Queen went to London, ostensibly to see her dressmaker, in order to receive

---

49 Ibid., loc. cit.
50 Thorpe, *Supermac*, p. 358; Kilmuir, *Political Adventure*, p. 283.

the Prime Minister's resignation at the Palace and to invite her choice as successor to form a government.

According to Eden's record of events, he recommended a successor to the Queen, a confidence that, quite properly, he never disclosed. He noted that 'the Queen made no formal request for my advice but enabled me to signify that my own debt to Mr Butler while I have been Prime Minister was very real'.[51] Writing to the Queen's Private Secretary, Sir Michael Adeane, in 1970, he dismissed accounts that he had not advised Her Majesty. However, because conversations between Monarch and Prime Minister should be confidential, he continued, 'I do not propose to state here what that advice was, except to say that the course subsequently followed was consistent with that advice.'[52]

It is difficult to suggest any motive that Eden, by then Lord Avon,[53] might have had for obfuscating the question. Although he stops short of stating that he recommended Macmillan, the two statements, taken together, clearly imply that he acknowledged his debt to Rab but was unable to recommend him as his successor. Whether he went so far as to recommend Macmillan is less clear, but, for the second statement to be true, he cannot have endorsed Rab.

On his return from Sandringham on 9 January, Eden officially informed the Cabinet that he would offer his resignation to the Queen that day and all Cabinet members except Rab and Macmillan were asked their preference. There were just two contenders; Salisbury, who suffered from rhotacism, asked ministers simply whether they preferred 'Wab' or 'Hawold'.

Salisbury had never championed Rab. Their differences dated back to 1938 when Salisbury, then Viscount Cranborne, had resigned, while Rab supported the policy of appeasement. Julian Amery remembered that ministers were individually summoned to the Cabinet room by

51 Avon Papers, Note on Resignation Audience, AP20/33/12A. Cited by Thorpe, *Supermac*, p. 359.
52 Avon Papers, The Earl of Avon to Sir Michael Adeane, 27 November 1970, AP23/2/20A. Cited by Thorpe, *Supermac*, p. 359.
53 In July 1961, more than four years after his resignation. It was customary for retiring prime ministers to be offered an earldom, generally upon resignation. Clement Attlee, for example, accepted the title 'Earl Attlee' three weeks after he handed over the leadership of the Labour Party in November 1955.

Salisbury, starting with known Macmillan supporters. Preferences were noted in two columns on a sheet of paper visible to ministers as they were questioned. Thus the 'Macmillan' column had an early boost and the choice appeared to be unanimous.[54] In the event, the outcome was not unanimous but overwhelming.[55] All but two preferred Macmillan.[56]

This preference was not restricted to the Cabinet. Backbenchers, particularly since the evening of 22 November, were firmly aligned behind Macmillan. Ted Heath, the Chief Whip, told Salisbury that the Suez Group was implacably opposed to Rab. As Rab himself observed, there was a strong anti-Rab faction, while Macmillan had no group solidly opposed to him.[57]

The Queen received advice on the morning of 10 January – from Salisbury, who reported the Cabinet's and party's preferences, and from Churchill, who later told Rab that he had chosen 'the older man'. If there is a message to be extracted from those three words, it is probable that Churchill saw Macmillan as steadier under pressure, a quality that Rab had recently demonstrated that he lacked.

Achieving success with apparently effortless ease is traditionally a cardinal British virtue – certainly among Old Etonians who served in the Grenadier Guards. Macmillan may have been conspiring endlessly from the moment he recognised that Eden would have to go

---

54 Letter from Lord Amery to D. R. Thorpe, 6 February 1975, cited in *Supermac*, p. 746, note 118.

55 Lord Salisbury's account of the transition is recorded in a memorandum '1957', preserved among his papers. Hatfield House: Salisbury Papers, File B: 1956–60. Cited by Thorpe, *Supermac*, p. 745, note 104.

56 At the time, unlike the Labour Party, the Tories held no formal elections to choose a leader. Instead a series of 'soundings' took place, a mystical process intended to divine the consensus of the party. Candidates were not supposed to promote themselves (Hailsham's major crime at Blackpool in 1963) but to 'emerge' in a subdued manner to become the clear choice of the majority of the party.

In 1957 the process was manipulated by Salisbury in favour of Macmillan. Nonetheless, it was generally accepted that Macmillan was the first choice of the Cabinet and that there was a violent anti-Rab faction. Despite mutterings about apparent discrepancies, once Salisbury and Churchill advised the Queen to send for Macmillan, the 'soundings' were generally accepted as representative.

It was not only an unscientific process but, conducted in an atmosphere of oppressive secrecy, was susceptible to every kind of manipulation by what Macleod called 'the Magic Circle'. In 1963, two facts most clearly 'emerged': that there was widespread opposition to Rab and that Home was 'acceptable' to the majority of the party. After 1963 and what was widely regarded as an outrageously rigged process, the Conservatives adopted a more conventional system.

57 Butler, *The Art of the Possible*, p. 195.

– according to one historian, as early as 16 November[58] – but he was outwardly unflappable, not overtly too ambitious. At least, that is the impression that his public relations machine generated. Richard Crossman described his manner perfectly: 'The studied Edwardian elegance of his despatch-box manner, the mannered witticisms and the whole style of party polemics which he has so consciously adopted – everything about him disconcerted me.'[59]

Yet that quality of calm and superior confidence, almost of languor, was to make a substantial contribution to his remaining in office rather longer than the six weeks that he forecast to the Queen.

Beneath that urbane and detached exterior, Macmillan was the more calculating of the two contenders, vastly better equipped for the cut and thrust of a leadership contest. Powell rightly saw the confrontation as a game of chess in which Rab was simply outplayed. To extend that analogy, Rab was playing the game without a queen. The vital piece that Macmillan possessed was his position as Chancellor of the Exchequer; he was to employ that to maximum effect when he urged a change of strategy for purely economic reasons; he had, to use his own words, 'a figleaf to cover his nakedness'. Rab had indeed committed 'political suicide' when he allowed himself to become a Minister Without Portfolio. To use a different metaphor, he became a loyal staff officer while Macmillan commanded an army.

Clarissa Eden wrote to Rab on the morning that Macmillan went to the Palace: 'Just a line to say what a beastly profession I think politics are – and how greatly I admire your dignity and good humour. Yours ever, Clarissa.'[60]

Rab treasured this 'balm' and dutifully gave his loyalty to the new Prime Minister. He suffered another disappointment immediately when Macmillan decided to keep Lloyd at the Foreign Office, as he 'felt that one head on a charger should be enough'.[61] When Churchill came to power in May 1940, he had temporarily retained many

58 Thorpe, *Supermac*, p. 365.
59 Article in the *Sunday Telegraph*, 9 February 1964.
60 Butler, *The Art of the Possible*, p. 196.
61 Ibid., p. 196.

of Chamberlain's men, including Rab, in their positions. Now Rab, hoping to be Foreign Secretary, suffered from a similar decision. In his memoirs, he acidly comments that Macmillan's 'memory played him false' when he suggested that Rab chose the post of Home Secretary.[62] That thrust was yet another Rabism.

Ultimately, such Rabisms contributed to his undoing. His acquiescence to the statement that Eden was 'the best Prime Minister we've got', his indiscretion to the assembled members of the Progress Trust, his alienation of Macmillan in 1930 – three items in a long list of unfortunate comments – undid him in 1956–57. His enemies had long memories, reaching back to the pre-war days when he was seen as 'flabby and morally too'.[63] Despite his obvious ability and untiring efforts to overcome the government's difficulties during Eden's absence, there was no 'Butler Group', no solid cadre of supporters on whom he could rely.

Macmillan, by contrast, enjoyed not only wide support among Tory MPs; he also had the solid support of Eisenhower, a vital ingredient for Eden's successor. It is impossible to imagine Rab sitting in the White House, strategising and enjoying a glass of Bourbon with the President. Macmillan had an easy friendship with Ike, forged in the war, a field on which Rab never played. Rab's milieu was among liberal intellectuals, not a group that appealed to right-wing knights of the shires. Every sketch that one reads of Rab's character portrays his idiosyncratic mannerisms, his shyness, his greater comfort with papers than with people. Eccentricity can be a winning trait, but, combined with intellectual arrogance, it hampered him in comparison with the more 'clubbable' Macmillan. No one doubted Rab's ability; few Cabinet colleagues – one, to be exact – preferred him as Eden's successor.[64]

Rab's own comments in retrospect highlight the distance between

---

62 See Macmillan, *Riding the Storm*, p. 186. Macmillan in a diary entry for 3 February 1957 wrote that the office of Foreign Secretary was a burden 'from which I think he really shrank in today's circumstances'. Bodleian: MSS Macmillan, d28*.

63 Colville, *The Fringes of Power: 10 Downing Street Diaries, 1939–1956*, p. 124.

64 The lone vote for Rab came from Patrick Buchan-Hepburn. Selwyn Lloyd expressed no preference, as he told Rab over dinner on 7 September 1960. (Trinity: Butler Papers, RAB, G36.31.) Buchan-Hepburn paid for his support of Rab, as he was dropped from the Cabinet by Macmillan. Thorpe, *Supermac*, p. 361 and note.

him and the mainstream of the party – a distance that he himself created. In an interview with Thames Television he spoke objectively about 'the party' as if it were a separate organism, something of which he was not a part. 'What really excited the hostility of the Conservative Party', he accurately stated, 'was the withdrawal.'[65] This remoteness from the *camaraderie* of the party, from the atmosphere of the smoking room, incurred, he admitted, 'a lot of resentment from the Conservative back-benchers at that time'.

By 12 December, when Dulles and Humphrey came to London, Macmillan was firmly in control of saving the pound. Rab was not present at meetings between them, and Macmillan reported to Rab – by letter – on the talks. Unlike Rab, who had seen American pressure as blackmail, Macmillan took the sanguine, realistic view that this was akin to a commercial deal. The aspect of the salvage operation of which Rab was most proud, was, in the event, handled by Macmillan.

Amid Rab's unfortunate comments, his tactical blunders and his indiscretions, what were Macmillan's thoughts? At what point did he see with clarity that he could seize the crown? His biographer believes that the thought had not occurred to him before the Suez Crisis.[66] Certainly he viewed with detachment the succession of 1953, observing that Monckton would not serve under Rab, whom he considered 'a slab of cold fish' and that Rab was 'able and sincere but almost pathologically ambitious'.[67] Clearly – and quite reasonably – Macmillan had no thoughts of succeeding Churchill, although he marked Rab down as a certain contender in a later contest.

To his biographer Mac admitted that 'My belief is, when you get a chance, take it. It was always my philosophy. Chance played such a role in my life – Winston, the war, Algiers, housing … which made me Prime Minister.'[68] To the same biographer Rab admitted that Macmillan had seen that chance before he did and was quicker than he to notice the state of Eden's failing health.[69] Even if he had noticed

---

65 Reproduced in *The Day Before Yesterday*, p. 143.
66 Horne, *Harold Macmillan, vol. 1* (London: Macmillan, 1988), p. 454.
67 Bodleian: MSS Macmillan d14. Diary entries for 3 and 6 July 1953.
68 Conversation between Macmillan and Alistair Horne, *Harold Macmillan, vol. 1*, p. 454.
69 Ibid. Interview of Lord Butler by Alastair Horne.

and 'made his dispositions', it is extremely doubtful that he could have supplanted Macmillan, whose deft manoeuvres were difficult to imitate. One after another, Rab's colleagues comment on his ambivalence. And, interestingly, one after another, despite Macmillan's description of him as 'almost pathologically ambitious', they cast doubt on his resolve to reach for the top.[70]

Fundamentally, as Harold Nicolson recorded, it was Munich that reappeared to derail Rab's ambition. 'If Rab had not been so weak about Munich', he wrote, 'and Harold Macmillan had not been so strong, Winston would have given different advice to the Queen.'[71] In the context of Suez, that weakness was fatal, final evidence to support Maudling's comments.[72]

As much as Gaitskell said of Nasser, 'It is all very familiar', so Tory diehards had the same feelings about Rab – and they never saw fit to change their opinions. This was 'the Magic Circle' that Iain Macleod railed against;[73] this was the group that Maudling dubbed 'Blue Blood and Thunder'.[74] They had picked their man on 22 November. On 10 January he was to be found reading Jane Austen ('very soothing')[75] until the time came to don his morning coat for a 2 p.m. appointment at the Palace. Rab, having heard results of the soundings from Ted Heath, was spied by a press cameraman walking alone on the Embankment.

'The best thing to do in the circumstances,' he explained.[76]

---

70 Anthony Head, John Boyd-Carpenter, Nicholas Henderson and Macmillan himself questioned Rab's lust for the top job. From the other side of the Commons, George Brown, himself a frustrated aspirant to 10 Downing Street, was convinced that Rab simply didn't want it enough.
71 Harold Nicolson, *Diaries and Letters*, vol. 3, p. 328.
72 See opening sentence of Chapter 14.
73 In an article in *The Spectator*, 17 January 1964.
74 Maudling, *Memoirs*, p. 64.
75 Macmillan, *Riding the Storm*, p. 184.
76 *Daily Sketch*, 11 January 1957.

CHAPTER 16

HOME SECRETARY, 1957–62

The five years following Macmillan's accession saw Rab's fortunes steadily decline. The chart of his standing showed periodic surges but, viewed from the armchair of history, the trend was inexorably downward.

After Macmillan became Prime Minister, Rab was flooded with letters expressing the view that he was, as one wrote, 'the only man who was a fit follower for Sir Anthony'.[1] The prevailing, possibly sincere, sentiment was that 'you have plenty of time yet'. The tributes are revealing, reflecting the view that Rab, above all others responsible for the rebuilding of the Conservative Party in the post war years, had been betrayed by his colleagues. Expressions like 'too upright and kindly for politics', 'good Christian gentleman', 'stoic and noble', 'such a good loser', '*reculer pour mieux sauter*' permeate the correspondence. To Rab, the team player, one tribute must have seemed particularly apposite, regretting 'the raw deal you have had from so-called friends and colleagues, most of whom would have been out on their ears long ago if it had not been for the way you have so unselfishly served the interests of the Tory Party since the war. I am disgusted.'

Such letters must have given Rab consolation that his work for the party had not gone unnoticed. The fact remained, however, that his parliamentary colleagues had chosen another leader. He may

---

1 Trinity: Butler Papers, RAB, G31. – all the letters quoted are from that file.

have suspected that his opportunity had eluded him, that it had been unfairly denied him, but Macmillan's age gave him hope that he had one more chance to reach Downing Street. To achieve this would require clear seniority and visibility. The Foreign Office was the stage on which he could best perform, but this Macmillan was determined to deny him.

Offered the Home Office, he chose to soldier on, not quite abandoning hope. Later, when Macmillan asked him if he had considered taking a peerage, he treated the question with contempt. But he never quite answered it. As early as 1957 he considered retirement and a Cambridge Mastership. The temptation recurred in 1959 when Dr R. M. Jackson wrote to Rab, suggesting that he offer himself for the Mastership of St John's. Rab declined, claiming reluctance to sever connections with Saffron Walden and the government. Whilst Butlers had long-standing connections with Cambridge, and St John's had a fine tradition, he was not ready to be put out to pasture.[2] In October 1958, Rab did accept the post of High Steward of Cambridge University, an entirely ceremonial office used principally by the university to honour a distinguished alumnus.[3]

His own reflections for public consumption were quoted by *The Sun*: 'It was very close – closer than most imagined. But let us say that the best man won … Those who miss the bus must resign themselves to walking. But, looking on the bright side, those forced to walk are often in better health.'[4]

Rab's private analysis was that three issues had determined the outcome: 'The reaction of Conservative MPs after visiting their constituencies at Christmastime; the attitude of the younger members of the Cabinet; and the *ambience* and connections of the present incumbent of No. 10.'[5] Rab was neither an Etonian nor a blue-blooded landowner, and he had seemed *vieux jeu* to younger colleagues. That last fact must

---

2   Trinity: Butler Papers, RAB, A186, Rab to R. M. Jackson, 22 April 1959.
3   Trinity: Butler Papers, RAB, G33.110.
4   Trinity: Butler Papers, RAB, G31.43; *The Sun*, 14 January 1957.
5   Trinity: Butler Papers, RAB, G31.70.

have made him doubt that he would have another chance, but he resolved to stay the course and project a more 'modern' image, even if the Home Office was not the stage he would have chosen to do so. Between the premierships of Churchill (1910–11) and James Callaghan (1967–70) no Home Secretary became Prime Minister. The average age of incoming Home Secretaries was fifty-seven. Rab, at fifty-four, was younger than average, but premature retirement from the mainstream was probably Macmillan's plan for him.

The new Prime Minister selected his Cabinet with care. Having persuaded the right wing of his party and the country at large that retreat from Suez had been a victory, he saw his role as threefold: to improve the position of Britain in the modern world, projecting her as an honest broker between the USA and the USSR; to achieve tangible results of that role by arranging a summit conference; and to improve the domestic economy as never before. None of these objectives involved the Home Secretary.

Knowing that he needed to include Rab in his Cabinet, yet determined to keep him down, Macmillan assumed from the outset of his administration the air of an international statesman, fortunately able to depend on support from more earth bound colleagues such as Rab. International travel was an important part of the projection of this *persona*, as was the emerging phenomenon of television. Rab, by now no longer the slim young man of the 1930s, still unprepossessing in his dress,[6] appeared pedestrian beside the elegant Edwardian figure of the Prime Minister. Cartoonists had fun playing on the word 'butler' to describe the relationship between the two: Macmillan, the dashing aristocrat, and Rab as his faithful butler-retainer. While Mac circled the globe on assignments of weighty importance, Rab stayed home 'holding the baby'.[7]

---

6   Chips Channon, a sharp *arbiter elegantiae*, described Rab's clothes as 'really tragic'. *Chips*, p. 164. Diary entry for 9 September 1938. Rab objected to little in Chips's diaries, but took exception to this criticism. Butler, *The Art of Memory*, p. 53.

7   The phrase, used in an unfortunate off-the-cuff remark by Rab, was reported in the *Daily Telegraph* of 7 January 1958.

"HELLO SIR! EVERYTHING'S ALL RIGHT. THE BABIES ARE DOING FINE, LORD SALISBURY WISHES TO BE REMEMBERED, DR. A. SENDS HIS LOVE AND I HOPE YOU TOO ARE HAVING FUN — WITH SIR ROY..."

Cartoon by Victor Weisz ('Vicky') which appeared in the Evening Standard *on 19 June 1960. Reproduced by kind permission of Solo Syndication.*

The first such occasion arrived in January 1958 when Peter Thorney-croft, the Chancellor of the Exchequer, determined on a full-scale confrontation with the Prime Minister over a £50 million increase in government spending estimates, announced his resignation. This was immediately followed by the resignations of two Treasury Ministers, Enoch Powell and Nigel Birch. Macmillan, about to set off on a six-week tour of the Commonwealth, refused to be perturbed by the resignations of the entire Treasury team. He announced Thorneycroft's replacement and the two junior ministerial appointments before setting off, as scheduled, on the first leg of his tour, commenting that he needed to settle 'little local difficulties' before he left. It was left to Rab to settle lesser appointments.

This attitude of condescension, a mannerism that came easily to Macmillan, was characteristic of relations between the two men throughout Rab's time at the Home Office. In June 1958, Rab urged a rebuilding of prisons, writing Macmillan a firm, forthright letter:

> *The longer I remain here, the more it is borne in on me that the main part of my duty consists in taking what steps I can to carry out long overdue reforms in our penal system. I would go further and say that I shall be unable to fulfil my mission here unless I find it possible to press forward a comprehensive plan of penal reform.*[8]

Macmillan replied with an insouciance as casual as Rab's convictions were heartfelt. 'I am all for it,' he wrote. 'No doubt it will cost money, but I do not suppose the money will be spent very quickly. I take it, it will be mostly be [*sic*] building new prisons, but they will take some time, especially if the Ministry of Works has anything to do with the plans.'[9] The message was obvious: 'We statesmen occupied with world affairs have more important things to worry about than new prisons. Have your prisons by all means, but I doubt that this will happen very soon.'

Macmillan consistently adopted an attitude of casual tolerance towards Rab's initiatives at the Home Office. At one Cabinet meeting, during a prolonged discussion of prostitution and homosexuality, Macmillan

> allowed it to take its course without any attempt to intervene. In the end Butler reproved me for my lack of interest in the long debate … However, I denied the charge of inattention. 'No, no,' I replied. 'I quite

---

8   Trinity: Butler Papers, RAB, G 32. Butler to PM, 27 June 1958.
9   Ibid., Macmillan to Butler, 28 June 1958.

understand what it is you want to do. You want to popularise abortion, legalise homosexuality and start a betting shop in every street. All I can say is if you can't win the Liberal nonconformist vote on these cries you never will.'[10]

Rab himself commented on this posture of Macmillan, describing the Prime Minister's attitude to his reformism as 'a similar spirit of indulgent scepticism as Churchill had shown fifteen years earlier towards my work for education'.[11] This was perceptible again in the summer of 1959, when a group of senior ministers gathered to discuss an early draft of the election manifesto. As Rab recalled:

> We had reached the passage which stated, in unexciting but I thought unexceptionable language, certain of my legislative aims for the next Parliament. 'We shall revise some of our social laws, for example those relating to betting and gaming and to clubs and licensing, which are at present full of anomalies and lead to abuse and even corruption.' The Prime Minister picked up the document, held it out two feet from his face, hooded his eyes and said very slowly, 'I don't know about that. We already have the Toby Belch vote. We must not antagonise the Malvolio vote.'[12]

This comment, apparently designed to belittle the importance of Rab's proposals, came close to being a public insult. The witticism was greeted with sycophantic chuckles and, when Edward Heath, the Chief Whip, brought the assembled ministers back to business, Macmillan once again treated Rab as a tiresome junior. 'Well, this is your province, Rab,' he said languidly. 'I suppose you think it's all right.' There was no further discussion.

Rab, eschewing the cardinal sin of splitting the party, hid his emotions. In the immediate aftermath of his disappointment in January he had allowed his bitterness to show in an interview with Derek Marks

---

10 Macmillan, *Tides of Fortune*, p. 732.
11 Butler, *The Art of the Possible*, p. 197.
12 Ibid., pp. 197–8.

of the *Daily Express*. Shocked by Rab's 'anguished candour', Marks tore up his notes and abandoned the story.[13] To his own papers Rab confided his feeling that he had been 'unfairly treated by the party hierarchy',[14] while in public he stated categorically that he 'would certainly not desert the ship at a time like this'.[15] Underscoring that loyalty, he seconded Salisbury's proposal of Macmillan as party leader at a meeting on 22 January, referring to the 'many years in opposition and in office Harold Macmillan and I have worked in close partnership'. They had been 'shoulder to shoulder throughout the time the last Prime Minister was away'. Indeed, Macmillan, 'with his great historical sense and imagination ... referred to [Rab and himself] as the two Consuls'.[16]

Rab stresses in his memoirs that he was not 'Home Secretary *tout court*', and this is assuredly true, as Macmillan heaped other roles on Rab in those years. At different times Rab was Deputy Prime Minister, First Secretary of State, Leader of the House and Chairman of the Party. Towards the end of the Macmillan era, moreover, he succeeded in settling the tangled affairs of the Central African Federation. Yet, despite these responsibilities conferred – and systematically withdrawn – Macmillan neither increased Rab's power base in the party nor gave any commitment or indication that Rab might succeed him. Indeed, on the one occasion that the subject was discussed, Macmillan suggested that, 'At your age, you had better be king-maker rather than king.'[17] As Rab commented, that was a strange remark from a man nearly nine years his senior.

Perhaps the most wounding rebuff came in November 1957, when Macmillan created and chaired a Steering Committee with Rab as deputy chairman. Perceiving this as a move to strip him of his role as party policymaker, Rab protested, writing, 'As you know, I have had certain responsibility for this area since 1945 under your two

---

13 Hill, *Both Sides of the Hill* (London: Heinemann, 1964), pp. 208–9.
14 Trinity: Butler Papers, RAB, G 31. Note of 18 April 1957.
15 *Daily Express*, 11 January 1957.
16 *The Times*, 23 January 1957.
17 Butler, *The Art of the Possible*, pp. 196–7.

predecessors and was responsible for the policy statements, which were not unattended by a meed of success.'[18]

The sarcastic tone of the memorandum probably elicited no more than a curled lip from Macmillan. As to the content, Rab spoke no less than the truth. But eight years had passed since Rab's formulation of policy had built the foundations of the 1951 victory, and the balance of power in the party had shifted. Since the end of austerity, the Prime Minister was no longer concerned with Rab's reformist constructs of the post-war era. Two of Rab's pre-1951 acolytes – Maudling and Macleod – were members of the committee, but both were now Members of Parliament in their own right, with their own ambitions.[19] Rab's influence in determining policy was decidedly truncated.

The irony is that Rab was an extremely effective and conscientious Home Secretary. From the first he treated the post differently from his immediate predecessors, urging research into the causes of crime rather than argument over forms of punishment. On a range of issues – capital and corporal punishment, prison reform, treatment of young offenders, prostitution, homosexuality, betting and gaming – Rab made it clear that he planned reform.

Soon after the Christmas recess he addressed the House on the Homicide Bill, already in committee stage when he took over at the Home Office. This curious and controversial Bill specified types of murder in retribution for which the death penalty would be applied. The governing criterion was not to be the heinousness of the crime but a definition of the types of homicide that would be deterred by the existence of the death penalty. Debate soon turned to types of murder and the issue of murder by poison surfaced as a special case. Rab argued cogently that it was wise 'to remember that the Bill was not drafted necessarily to take into its scope the types of murder which strike people as being particularly heinous. That is because we do not believe that a line can be drawn, by Statute, between the more heinous and the less heinous.'[20]

18 Trinity: Butler Papers, RAB, G32. Rab to PM, 11 November 1957.
19 See Macmillan, *Pointing the Way*, p. 5.
20 Hansard, 23 January 1957, vol. 563, col. 267.

This line of reasoning, argued Samuel Silverman, was 'the *reductio ad absurdum* of the retentionist case'. If the government prevailed, the number of murderers executed would fall from twelve a year to two and a half. The argument that the death penalty protected Britain from unlimited murders was ludicrous, he argued. 'Let us make an end of it … let the new brooms sweep clean, and let the first thing they sweep away be this intolerable, mischievous, unrealistic and fundamentally dishonest Bill.'[21]

In spite of arguments for abolition, the Bill passed into law and Rab initially accepted the retention of the death penalty for the killing of policemen or prison officers. By nature, however, a reformist, intellectually bedevilled by the ever-present question of proof of guilt and the possibility of judicial error, he revised his views during his time at the Home Office.[22] In truth, he was in a difficult triangulated position, poised between a Prime Minister who betrayed little interest in home affairs, a Tory Party with a substantial contingent of 'hangers and floggers', and his more liberal parliamentary supporters, led by Iain Macleod. Privately, he hoped and believed that the Bill was a temporary backlash and that public sentiment would ultimately turn against hanging in all cases.[23]

From the very outset he admitted to the House that the Home Office was spending a pitifully small amount of money on research leading to prison reform. Useful work had been done on Borstal training, approved school training and probation, but more work was needed on imprisonment itself. Rab therefore proposed to give first priority to expanding the research programme. In a dig at the right wing, he indicated that to rely on experience alone was not enough. Statistics and sociology – not words calculated to appeal to the knights of the shires – were essential to a proper study of prison administration,

---

21 Ibid., cols 277–8.
22 Butler, *The Art of the Possible*, p. 202. He states that he 'began to see that the system could not go on.'
23 As Anthony Howard points out, however, before Rab left the Home Office, having 'seen that the system could not go on', he had sent more condemned murderers to the gallows than any other post-war Home Secretary. The statistic was first quoted by Auberon Waugh, writing in the *Sunday Telegraph*, 12 April 1981. Howard, *RAB*, p. 253.

particularly long-ignored and urgent issues such as overcrowding and understaffing.

Any Member listening to that speech will have had no doubt that Rab was planning fundamental reform not only of the prison system but of the sentencing policy of courts and the very basis of collaboration between the judiciary and the executive. Remand centres would be introduced, which would serve to keep young people out of prison and be 'real centres of research into the broader question of juvenile delinquency'. As Rab proceeded through his speech, it was clear that the first root-and-branch reform of the justice system for thirty years was imminent. Rab's concluding remarks described his vision, incorporated two years later in the White Paper, *Penal Reform in a Changing Society*:[24]

> Here, I begin to look some way into the future, perhaps … to dream a little. At any rate, I am coming to an end. I believe that we might one day come to think of our prisons not as places of punishment, though that they must be since deprivation of liberty must always be a punishment; not only as places where offenders are trained to be better men and better citizens, which is what they seek, however imperfectly, to be now; but also as places where an offender could work out his own or her own personal redemption by paying his or her debt not only to the society whose order he has disturbed, but to the fellow members of that society whom he has wronged.[25]

This ringing idealism was greeted by a certain scepticism among insiders. Since 1948, the Permanent Under-Secretary at the Home Office, Sir Frank Newsam, elliptically described by Rab as 'an original', had dominated successive Home Secretaries. The notion of reform, unless such reform was instigated by Newsam, was fanciful. His record was impressive; his exercise of power awe-inspiring.

When severe storms caused flooding on the east coast in 1953, damaging 24,000 houses, Newsam took control of the emergency

---

24 White Paper Cmd 645, published on 2 February 1959.
25 Hansard, 13 March 1957, vol. 566, cols 1140–55.

operation, directing both civilian rescue services and troops. Rab wrote that 'Newsam had almost literally taken charge of the country ... and secured achievements that would have surprised Canute.'[26] In the following year, when Antoni Klimowicz, a 24-year-old Pole who had stowed away aboard a Polish ship, attempted to disembark and seek political asylum, he was held on board the ship by the crew. Newsam arranged for a writ of habeas corpus to be issued and sent a posse of police officers to board the ship and free Klimowicz. A diplomatic incident threatened to explode, but Newsam stuck to his guns and Klimowicz was allowed to stay in Britain.

By 1957, Newsam, born in 1893, was beyond retirement age and Rab, keen to run his own department, recognised that appointing a new Permanent Under-Secretary was an essential first step. Newsam, however, had served in the Home Office since 1920 and Rab hesitated to make such a significant change. In June, however, his hand was forced.

Gwilym Lloyd George, Rab's predecessor, had taken Newsam's advice and authorised the tapping of the telephone of Billy Hill, a well-known London gangster. Routine intercepts had revealed conversations between Hill and his barrister, Patrick Marrinan. These had been disclosed to the Bar Council by Lloyd George, an action that provoked cries of outrage at state intervention from opposition benches. Rab, placed in the position of defending – or at least defusing – the actions of Lloyd George and an authoritarian civil servant, made a statement in the Commons, defining the powers of the state. Telephone tapping, recognised by Parliament as necessary, could be authorised only by the Secretary of State in matters of national security or to prevent serious crime. Rab assured the Commons that this instance would not be treated as a precedent and that 'this necessary but distasteful power' would not be abused.[27]

Gaitskell, sensing an issue that could be used to advantage against a Tory government, distinguished between state security, in which the Labour Party recognised the need for telephone tapping, and crime

---

26 Butler, *The Art of the Possible*, p. 199.
27 Hansard, 7 June 1957, vol. 571, cols 1565–6.

detection, which exposed the thin end of the wedge. Supported by Jo Grimond, the Liberal leader, he pressed for a full-scale inquiry. Under pressure, Macmillan and Rab appointed a committee of three Privy Councillors chaired by Lord Birkett[28] to consider and report upon the use of telephone tapping and to recommend when and how information so obtained should be used.[29]

For Rab, the affair was an unwelcome scandal, not of his making but nonetheless moving the Home Office to centre stage. Two decisions flowed from the incident: first that Newsam should be persuaded to retire, which Rab achieved by arranging for him to become a Knight Grand Cross of the Bath in the Queen's Birthday Honours and to retire on 30 September. Second, Rab recognised that he be aware of what he called 'rats' – 'incipient causes of trouble that might blow up on the floor of the House at a few hours' notice and, if badly handled, could affect the standing and reputation of the whole government'.[30] By spending more time in the smoking room of the Commons, he maintained closer touch with the mood of the party.

One such potential cause of trouble was the imbroglio over the allegation by Harold Wilson that the decision to raise the bank rate had been prematurely leaked. A tribunal was established in November and duly reported on 21 January 1958. In Macmillan's absence, Rab moved that the House accept the report's conclusions that there was 'not a shred of evidence' to implicate any of those whom Wilson had alleged to be involved. Everyone who had prior information about the raise, the tribunal concluded, had held the information confidential. Rab's motion to the House was presented in magisterial fashion, a reproof to Wilson and the opposition for misuse of parliamentary privilege. Rab succeeded not only in presenting the tribunal's findings with almost Churchillian oratory, but also, in a manner uncharacteristic of his normal debating style, in pouring righteous scorn on the smear tactics of the opposition.[31]

---

28 Norman Birkett QC, the eminent barrister who had recently retired as a Lord Justice of Appeal.
29 Statement released from 10 Downing Street, 28 June 1957. *The Times*, 29 June 1957.
30 Butler, *The Art of the Possible*, p. 199.
31 Hansard, 3 February 1958, vol. 581, cols 815–30.

During the Prime Minister's Commonwealth tour in early 1958, Rab's star waxed. He was suddenly seen in weighty meetings, conclaves, luncheons and dinners around the country: chairing a long Cabinet to discuss Civil Estimates on 14 January; lunching with Selwyn Lloyd and Dag Hammarskjöld, Secretary-General of the United Nations, on 16 January; announcing the appointment of new ministers on 17 January; stating that the government would 'stick out and do [their] job' in an interview with Robin Day in a new ITN series, *Tell the People*, on 19 January; lunching with Prince Souvanna Phouma, Prime Minister of Laos, on 20 January; granting asylum to three Hungarian families who had stowed away on *The Highland Monarch* from Brazil in late January; receiving a deputation of forty women from the Association for Moral and Social Hygiene to discuss the Wolfenden Report's recommendations on prostitution on 29 January; speaking on relations with the Communist *bloc* to the Oxford University Conservative Association on 31 January; debriefing Selwyn Lloyd on his return from Ankara on 2 February; speaking in the Commons on conditions under which nuclear bombs be carried over England by the RAF or USAF on 4 February; finally receiving Macmillan on his return and staying overnight with him at Chequers on 14 February. The Prime Minister's absence had provided a thrilling stage for his right-hand man.

A week after Macmillan's return, however, came Nemesis. During a twice-delayed ceremony to install Rab as Rector of Glasgow University on 21 February, the Home Secretary was pelted with eggs, tomatoes, soot, fire extinguisher foam and lavatory paper, and was hit full in the face with a bag of flour. As *The Times* delicately expressed it, 'The students speedily made it plain they had no taste for listening to Mr Butler's theme of continuing British greatness in a changing and competitive world.'[32]

Rab's sensible reaction was to play down the incident; his error came, however, when he commented, 'I understand youth. I have children of my own and like to feel that I haven't lost touch.'[33] To the diehards,

---

32 *The Times*, 22 February 1958, p. 6. For an eyewitness account, *Evening Standard*, 21 February 1958.
33 *Daily Mirror*, 22 February 1958.

the response was quite inadequate; this was a time for birching rather than understanding. To more progressive Tories, the comment was simply the feeble reaction of a middle-aged duffer. To the entire party, the humiliating spectacle of a 55-year-old man in full academic regalia being barracked and pelted with vegetables divested Rab of the *gravitas* he had acquired during the previous month. It 'immortalised the right's impression of him as a well-meaning but ineffective reformer being satisfactorily brought up short against the social effects of his own policies'.[34]

In March, Rab appeared on television in a BBC *Panorama* broadcast together with Canon Collins and Michael Foot, prominent anti-nuclear campaigners, who aggressively attacked him. Viewers wrote to Rab complimenting him on his 'kindly manner, patience and steadfastness, his underlying strength of conviction', his 'sense of confidence, patient statesmanship, dignity and aplomb'. Desmond Donnelly, himself prominent in the Campaign for Nuclear Disarmament, wrote that Rab was thrown to the lions, but the lions came off worse. 'In no other country', he wrote, 'would the Deputy Prime Minister have submitted himself to public questioning from such a group.'[35]

There is a certain irony in the comment as it was precisely that submission – as at the University of Glasgow – that damaged Rab's image. It is difficult to imagine the wily Macmillan taking such risks. Supporters of Rab might admire his 'calm serenity, dignity and argument', but he was caught in a squabble over a highly emotive subject – the hydrogen bomb – and no one in his position could gain from that in the public eye.

Throughout 1957 and 1958, the principal problem faced by the government was the alienation of the middle class, 'the backbone of the party'. Tories saw the concerns of the electorate as, first, that the cost of living was too high, second that the burden of taxation was too great, and third, that the new Rents Act would result in more notices to quit and rent increases.[36] Rab argued that the Tories had already brought

---

34 Howard, *RAB*, p. 262.
35 Trinity: Butler Papers, RAB, E9.56.
36 Trinity: Butler Papers, RAB, E6.2.3.

Income Tax down from 31 per cent under Labour to 25 per cent and that it was still falling. As to the Rents Act, it was necessary and would take time to have any effect. There was, he argued, no cause for alarm.[37]

If there was kudos to be gained from an improving economy, Macmillan made sure to garner it for himself and took pains to prevent Rab from projecting himself as his deputy.[38] In August 1958, about to leave for visits to Greece and Turkey, he wrote to Rab urging him not to change his plans to spend a week in Scotland. Selwyn Lloyd, he assured him, would be in London from the 9th to 11 August and the Lord Chancellor would also be available. Rab, therefore, need not miss the beginning of the grouse-shooting season. Rab replied to Macmillan on the same day, accepting the suggestion, a tactical error that allowed Macmillan to manipulate him.[39]

In October, the Conservative conference in Blackpool provided the stage for the clash between the Home Secretary and Tory 'hangers and floggers'. In a calmly reasoned speech Rab held the right wing at bay, systematically working through a checklist of issues, any of which could have blown up in his face. He did not support flogging or birching young offenders. Instead, he proposed new detention centres to 'de-Teddify the Teddy Boys'. Young criminals would have to prove their worth to gain their liberty. An overhaul of the prison system was needed, principally to eliminate overcrowding.

Addressing the perennially emotive issue of capital punishment, he doubted that a new Homicide Bill could be introduced during the current session. On the question of flogging he said simply, 'The Government are not prepared to reimpose flogging for crime that has decreased since flogging was abolished.' He did not intend to put the

---

37 Trinity: Butler Papers, RAB, E6.2.5.

38 In his memoirs Macmillan more than once refers to Rab as 'Rab Butler, who presided over the Cabinet and acted as my deputy during my absence.' He is careful not to refer to Rab as his permanent deputy. With the gratuitous comment that 'the domestic front … was one of constant anxiety', he proceeds to record his obligation to 'the second member of the government, Rab Butler', who was 'universally accepted as my deputy'. Again, he avoids describing Rab as 'my deputy'. He links Rab with Heath, saying, 'Together with the Chief Whip, Edward Heath, Butler managed the House of Commons in my many absences.' (*Riding the Storm*, pp. 702–3.)

39 Trinity: Butler Papers, RAB, G33.2.

clock back 100 years. Regarding prostitution, penalties were 'ridiculously small', and he would welcome an early debate on the Wolfenden Report. Overall, he would continue his own review of crime, rather than escape his responsibilities by appointing a commission. Penal reform would not be purely idealistic but would 'create in criminals a wholesome dread of punishment and give them a reasonable hope of redemption'. As *The Times* reported, 'with his usual artistry in tactical command, he had merely retreated on to prepared positions and then not budged a yard'.[40]

In September 1957, the Wolfenden Committee on homosexual offences and prostitution recommended that 'homosexual behaviour between consenting adults in private should no longer be a criminal offence'. Its publication set in motion a drive by the police to remove prostitutes from Britain's streets. Fourteen months after the publication of the report, Rab spoke in the House, intimating that the government would, in general, follow its recommendations, although more time was needed to look into the causes of homosexuality and to frame legislation that would neither expose an innocent woman who behaved indiscreetly to arrest, nor impose on the police an impossible burden of proof.[41] *The Times*, reporting on the debate, commented that 'Mr Butler himself was at his best and that is very good indeed.'[42]

The Street Offences Act, introduced the following August, was a disappointment to the Association for Moral and Social Hygiene. This organisation had been formed by Rab's great-aunt Josephine Butler, who fought long and hard for the principle that prostitutes were entitled to the protection of the law as much as any other citizen. At a time when genteel ladies never spoke of 'the social evil', this took enormous courage.[43] Rab was vice-president of the Association but, after his active promotion of the Act, he was asked by the Association to step down.

In July 1957, Macmillan made a rousing speech, attacking the 'doctrinaire nightmare' of Socialism and boasting, 'Let us be frank about

40 *The Times*, 10 October 1958.
41 Hansard, 26 November 1958, vol. 596, cols 365–82.
42 *The Times*, 27 November 1958.
43 At the time the Bill became law, the *Yorkshire Post* published an excellent profile of Rab's great-aunt on 18 August 1959.

it – most of our people have never had it so good.'[44] This was the theme of the election campaign that led to the Conservative majority of 100 in the election of 8 October 1959. The economic boom that had begun in that year continued and carried the Tories to victory in the election on 8 October, a remarkable comeback from the post-Suez doldrums. Almost immediately, Macmillan began his reorganisation of the government. On the following day he offered Rab the chairmanship of the party, a thankless position which Rab rashly accepted. His biographer attributes Rab's acceptance of the post to his preoccupation with personal affairs.[45]

Since Sydney Butler's death in 1954, Rab had become close to her cousin by marriage, Mollie, the wife of explorer August Courtauld. Indeed, Sydney had predicted that, after her death, Rab and Mollie would marry. When August, crippled by multiple sclerosis, died in March 1959, Rab and Mollie decided to marry. The *Daily Express* carried the teasingly ironic headline 'Rab plans quiet wedding to mother of six'.[46] The pair were married in Hertfordshire on 21 October, and, after a brief honeymoon in Rome, Rab was back in the Commons for the first day of the new Parliament, on which the Queen's Speech announced the Betting and Gaming Bill that he was promoting.

The Bill had aroused widespread controversy but, as the *Daily Sketch* pointed out, the existing laws were absurd and the Bill would pass after much opposition:

> Police spend precious hours and days swooping on private card parties and ganging around to catch bookies. The betting laws are so stiff with humbug and puritanism so you might expect Butler's Bill to get an easy passage.
>
> Nothing of the kind.
>
> Massed against it will be powerful sections of the church and moral welfare societies as well as the usual diehards who believe that people can't be trusted.

---

44 In a speech at a Tory rally in Bedford to mark twenty-five years' service by Mr Lennox-Boyd, the Colonial Secretary, as MP for Mid-Bedfordshire, 20 July 12957.

45 Howard, *RAB*, p. 269.

46 *Daily Express*, 15 October 1959.

The Bill would pass, however, the *Sketch* argued, as the clinching argument would be the waste of police time under the existing system.[47]

One almost immediate result of Rab's second marriage was the decision to purchase a holiday home in the Hebrides. During 1960, he and Mollie explored possibilities and in January 1961 they found Frachadil, the rambling farmhouse that was to be their refuge for twenty years. For Rab, the remoteness of the Isle of Mull, its informality, its quality of being 'a separate kingdom' that induced 'a slowing down of life, of time itself' in carefree holidays, was an undiscovered joy.[48] He was able to relax to the point that he was able to listen to music with pleasure, a pastime that he had previously scorned.[49]

The period immediately following the 1959 election is crucially important to understanding Macmillan's and Rab's relations and to the ever-present question of succession. Rab was an extremely able Home Secretary and, although Macmillan overloaded him with responsibility, he continued to do all that was demanded of him, almost as if it were a personal challenge. He was fully aware that the chairmanship of the party was an invitation to the lions' den, as he pointed out to Macmillan, saying that the question of flogging was 'a subject of very great interest to the party. They seem to have poured all their emotions into this receptacle.'[50]

Nonetheless, he accepted the offer. Very soon there was speculation that his position in the party was slipping, an erosion attributed to his continued refusal to bring back the birch. There had been a number of issues that provoked controversy: phone tappings; the threat of sanctions unless IRA outrages ceased; criticism from Lord Winterton that Rab was too soft with criminals. Yet, according to the *Daily Sketch*, Rab

47 *Daily Sketch*, 26 October 1959.
48 Mollie Butler, *August and Rab*, pp. 50–59.
49 Rab detested theatre, cinema and concert hall alike, preferring the circus for entertainment. On one occasion he and Mollie were invited by the French Ambassador to a performance of Anouilh's *L'Invitation au Château* in which one actor plays the parts of two very different twins. At the final curtain call, when the actor was greeted by wild applause, Rab enquired, 'Where's the other one?' The Queen, a fellow guest, turned to Mollie and remarked, 'I thought that Mr Butler understood French.' When Mollie said that he did, Her Majesty commented, 'Well he didn't seem to understand what was going on tonight.' Mollie Butler, *August and Rab*, pp. 72–3.
50 Trinity: Butler Papers, RAB, G35.8, Rab to PM, 5 January 1960.

was still positioned to follow Macmillan into No. 10.[51] *The Guardian* also saw the appointment as significant for Rab's future prospects.[52] The temptation is, however, to believe that Macmillan wished the opposite effect, that the exposure of Rab to the constituencies would bring the differences over corporal punishment to the fore and undermine Rab's position as Home Secretary. Walter Terry of the *Daily Mail* asked, 'Will Rab surrender to the floggers?'[53] A Gallup poll in March claimed that 78 per cent of people supported flogging for crimes of violence and 74 per cent wanted judges to be given more power to hang.

On 9 March 1960, Rab recorded his feelings about holding down the three jobs.[54] It is illuminating, both as a personal memoir and for the light it casts on his feelings about Macmillan and his ambitions. The first point he makes is that the offices of Home Secretary and Leader of the House are easily combined, as 'so many of the presences coincide'. 'The only weakness of the Home Office angle', he wrote, 'derives from the many extraordinary incidents which occur overnight and which lead to intense political interest.' In other words, Macmillan had handed him a hot potato – of which Rab was acutely aware. Colleagues commented, however, that Rab, rejuvenated by his second marriage, seemed to have regained his energy.

The chairmanship of the party, he wrote, 'was only undertaken because there was a gap owing to Hailsham's illness and because the Prime Minister wished me to do it'. His life, Rab conceded, was made more difficult 'by the very strong feelings of a huge section of the party in favour of birching or flogging. I find this especially among the women members of our committees wherever I go.' This always surprised Rab as it seemed to be quite alien to the real business of politics. He concluded that 'The unforeseen exposures of the three jobs … are the most difficult to reconcile with equanimity.'

During this period he was 'called into perpetual consultation on major issues by the PM'. These consultations largely concerned the

51 *Daily Sketch*, 18 December 1959.
52 *The Guardian*, 14 January 1960; Trinity: Butler Papers, RAB, G35.11.
53 *Daily Mail*, 3 February 1960.
54 Trinity: Butler Papers, RAB, G35.100.

Budget, from which Macmillan was anxious that any bad news or talk of strict measures should be excluded. Rab commented that Derick Heathcoat-Amory, the Chancellor, 'does not wish to remain in office indefinitely since I do not think he likes the ultimate and unending responsibility'. He was right; Heathcoat-Amory was replaced two months later by Selwyn Lloyd.

The parallel between Heathcoat-Amory's position in 1960 and Rab's experience in 1955 is notable. The former was being pressured to maintain a positive spin on the Macmillan boom, much as Rab had been pressured by Eden to remain upbeat in the economic measures and the first Budget before the 1955 election. Clearly Macmillan saw it as vital that the notion of 'Never-Had-It-So-Good' should be maintained at all costs.

With a certain concealed *Schadenfreude*, Rab described the other problems facing Macmillan: the difficulties with the railway unions; American policy of arming Germany and other European countries with 'these hideous nuclear bombs'; anxiety about Chancellor Adenauer's *Ostpolitik*; finally, the publication of the Eden memoirs were embarrassing Macmillan as 'bits of what happened are revealed and other bits are not'. Rab's apparent objectivity as he surveyed his position and Macmillan's anxieties masks a satisfaction that it was he whom Macmillan consulted to banish the lonely isolation of office. Then, more than ever, holding down three disparate and important functions within the party, he must have seen himself as Macmillan's natural successor. Within the House of Commons there was no one with the same stature or experience. Surely, he must have said to himself, it is now just a matter of time.

Changes, he knew, were imminent, as Derick Heathcoat-Amory had decided to leave politics altogether. Rab turned to two long-standing friends, Michael Fraser and James Ramsden, for tactical advice. Fraser, Rab's deputy at the CRD, sent Rab a crisp, incisive memorandum in which he identified three possible courses of action: to become Foreign Secretary, to return to the Treasury or to stay at the Home Office. Each of the first two options had advantages and disadvantages and Fraser reluctantly concluded that Rab was better off staying where he was.[55]

---

55 Trinity: Butler Papers, RAB, G36.27, Fraser to Rab, 21 April 1960.

Ramsden took the view that Rab's appointment of Home to the Foreign Office would be masterly 'not only because it gives the PM the kind of person it would suit him to have there, but because it wouldn't do to have anyone there but you, unless it were a peer'.[56] In a second letter, he urged Rab not to canvass Macmillan for the position of Foreign Secretary, nor to do 'anything off your own bat to alter the present set-up, which reflects so much credit on you and gives the world the least possible excuse to snarl at you, in the role of loyal and devoted colleague'.[57]

Rab followed Ramsden's advice, writing to Macmillan on 31 May, offering to return to the Treasury, if Macmillan wanted that, but felt that to be most helpful he should take on less rather than more. The Commonwealth Relations Office, which Macmillan had suggested, was tempting, but, in the balance, he should prefer no move at all.[58] When he learned of Macmillan's decision to replace Lloyd with Home, he repeated his preference to carry through the programmes he had initiated. He would, of course, do anything that the Prime Minister requested.[59]

Wildly different interpretations of the succession now appeared in the press. The *Daily Mail* ran a headline 'Now Watch Butler Soar',[60] while the *Yorkshire Post* stated authoritatively and inaccurately that he had turned down the job of Foreign Secretary because he wanted to retain the position of Party Chairman.[61] Interestingly, the *Evening News* assured readers that whoever became Foreign Secretary would challenge Rab's position.[62] Whatever the newspapers might say, Rab sensed that Macmillan was planning to oust him – or, at least, to reduce his status in the party. With the public, however, Rab's popularity was such that his persuasive television broadcast just before the Ludlow by-election in November was watched in 7,123,000 dual-channel homes.[63]

56 Trinity: Butler Papers, RAB, G36.10.
57 Trinity: Butler Papers, RAB, G36.11, Ramsden to Rab, 24 April 1960.
58 Trinity: Butler Papers, RAB, G36.26, Rab to PM, 31 May 1960.
59 Trinity: Butler Papers, RAB, G36.15, Rab to PM, 2 July 1960.
60 *Daily Mail*, 14 July 1960.
61 *Yorkshire Post*, 8 July 1960.
62 *Evening News*, 12 July 1960.
63 Trinity: Butler Papers, RAB, G36.50 and G36.55.

The issue of flogging returned to the news during April and May 1961. For a month the issue was reinflated by a meeting of 3,000 Tory women in Central Hall, Westminster, where the assembled worthy ladies demanded the return of corporal punishment. They scolded Rab for his distaste for birching, urging him to 'Come down out of the clouds and be a man.'[64] Over the following days, a revolt appeared to be brewing in the House of Lords as Lord Parker, the Lord Chief Justice, demanded that courts should have the power to order the birch or cane[65] and Earl Winterton questioned Rab's ability to discharge his duties as Home Secretary. The burden of three offices (Home Secretary, Leader of the House and Tory Party Chairman) was too great, he argued. Rab should surrender the Home Office to a younger man.[66] On 16 May, the Lords finally settled the matter and on the following day *The Guardian* hailed 'Mr Butler's victory'.[67] The overt revolt in the Lords had been quelled, but Rab was far from confident that the matter had been finally laid to rest.

It had not. Moreover, the summer of 1961 was a period of acute discomfort for Rab, stimulated by the leak of an off-the-cuff remark made at a private dinner in Madrid, where he and Mollie were guests of the Spanish Foreign Secretary. Rab politely but incautiously expressed a hope that closer relations could be established between Franco's Spain and Western Europe. British newspapers reacted in differing but universally critical fashion. Was Rab attempting to endear himself to the right, a first move in a leadership bid?[68]

The most incisive questions were asked by Deryck Winterton of the *Daily Herald*, who examined Rab's words as symptomatic of a far broader question. His column opened with the challenging concatenation of three propositions: 'Exactly what makes Mr Richard Austen Butler tick has always been something of a mystery. And that is probably why he is not Prime Minister. Tory MPs like to have their leaders more cut and dried.'

---

64 *Daily Express*, 20 April 1961.
65 *Daily Herald*, 2 May 1961.
66 *Yorkshire Post*, 3 May 1961.
67 *The Guardian*, 17 May 1961.
68 *East Anglia Times*, 1 June 1961; Trinity: Butler Papers, RAB, L70.

Why, Winterton wondered, had Rab 'dropped his latest brick in Spain'? Two intriguing possibilities, far from cut and dried, offered themselves: 'Was he loyally trying to prepare the way for Lord Home? Was he disloyally trying to queer Lord Home's pitch?' (Home was due to pay an official visit to Spain soon afterwards.) It is a mark of Rab's quality of opaqueness that both of these possibilities seem plausible. Behind each of them lurks what Winterton called 'the deeper question … his fulsome praise of the mean and beastly rule of Franco recalls that before the war Butler was an appeaser, a man of Munich.'

There it was, once again, twenty-three years after Munich, the label that Rab never shed. However much Rab achieved for his party or his country, the loyal but misguided support for Chamberlain's policy could be brought out and polished to be used against him. Unsurprisingly, this was the thrust of the attack in the Commons, conducted by Healey, Gaitskell and Konni Zilliacus.[69]

The goad of pre-war appeasement was enduringly effective and the Madrid episode also fuelled the public perception of him as indecisive. Because he reflected long and hard over the morality of such questions as corporal punishment, hanging, life imprisonment, he was portrayed as a Home Secretary who could not come to grips with battling crime. This growing mood was sensed by the press and expressed bluntly by the *Sunday Times*. After a parliamentary year of unremitting work, Rab's popularity had ebbed, an article alleged, because of 'that most dangerous of political vices, indecision'.[70]

Meanwhile, youth crime was increasing and Rab wanted both to curb the rise and to be certain that young people were being treated fairly. He deplored the knee-jerk reaction of the right that young people alone were responsible, blaming 'good-time parents' rather than 'latch-key children' for the trend.[71] His solution, the introduction of remand centres, was disparagingly referred to as 'The Youth Jail that is not a

---

69 Hansard, 30 May 1961, vol. 641, col. 33.
70 *Sunday Times*, 11 June 1961.
71 *Sunday Pictorial*, 9 July 1961.

Jail: A New Move in Our Penal System'.[72] In this, as in other issues, he sought the cause of crime more than other Home Secretaries.[73]

As the conference approached, the press licked its lips in anticipation of a head-to-head confrontation between Rab and the 'hangers and floggers'. Speculation flourished: Rab might go to the House of Lords; he might leave the Home Office; Macmillan was grooming Lloyd to replace him; he would definitely lay down one of his responsibilities. 'Laying down one of his responsibilities' was effectively a euphemism for leaving the Home Office, and, when the *Daily Mail* pronounced that Rab could not hold on to all his jobs, the implication was clear.[74]

At the Brighton conference, Rab faced fifty-eight resolutions critical of his policy on crime and punishment and sixty-five resolutions demanding stiffer penalties. Dramatic headlines heralded the confrontation, 'Tories face split over birch'.[75] The widespread concern over the crime wave and the potential split over corporal and capital punishment were presented as a trial of Rab himself; the outcome would decide his future.[76] Amid the speculation a strategically managed leak prompted a headline in *The Times*, 'Mr. Butler may leave Party HQ: Possible post for Mr. Macleod'.[77] If, as the detail and accuracy of the article were impressive, the source of the information was the Prime Minister's office, the purpose was a neatly executed knifing of Rab.

When, later that day, the reshuffle took place, the predictions of *The Times* proved accurate. Macmillan offered Macleod the Duchy of Lancaster and the Leadership of the House; Macleod also asked for the chairmanship of the party as a condition of his moving.[78] There followed 'Macleod Up, Butler Down' comments in the press. As *The Guardian* expressed it, Rab was simultaneously promoted and

---

72 *Evening Standard*, 11 July 1961.
73 *The Guardian*, 18 July 1961. He had emphasised this in the Eleanor Rathbone Memorial Lecture that Rab delivered at Reading University on 12 February 1960. He urged 'research on a scale never before attempted in this country. Alas, it lacks the romantic appeal of journeys to the bed of the ocean or to the moon. But the difficulties are surely as great.' (Trinity: Butler Papers, RAB, G35.)
74 *Daily Mail*, 14 September 1961.
75 *Daily Mirror*, 27 September 1961.
76 *Sheffield Telegraph*, 27 September 1961.
77 *The Times*, 9 October 1961.
78 Fisher, *Iain Macleod* (London: Andre Deutsch, 1973), p. 199.

demoted, assuming responsibility for overseeing the European Economic Community (EEC) negotiations while being stripped of two offices. The difficulty with that bland evaluation was that there was effectively nothing for him to handle in relation to the EEC as Heath was responsible for the demanding negotiations. Rab, simply, was sacrificed on the altar of solidarity in Macmillan's Cabinet. In the search for an explanation or a *quid pro quo* for Rab's sacrifice, it was suggested that Rab had shed the two offices in exchange for an undertaking from Macmillan that he would support him for the leadership.[79] Unfortunately, the very reverse was the case. Rab had been ousted from the two responsibilities that kept him close to the centre of power. In time, but not yet, Macmillan would remove him from his remaining office too.

The issue of the leadership overshadowed Rab's triumph at the conference, where he spoke persuasively against flogging in what Macleod described as the best speech he had ever heard from Rab.[80] Only fifty hands were raised to support corporal punishment, whereupon his stock began to rise again. 'Butler is still the favourite,' declared *The Observer*, but this opinion was based on wishful thinking.[81] Rab's naturally bitter disappointment was inflamed by the perception that Macleod was now heir-apparent. 'The favourite to succeed Macmillan', trumpeted the *Daily Mirror*, 'the potential new heir' and 'the Tories' man of the future' came from the *Daily Express* and the *Daily Mail*.[82] A reference in *The Economist* to Macleod as 'the best next Prime Minister we've got' produced a predictably resentful reaction from Rab. When Parliament reassembled on 17 October, Macleod expected to move into the room traditionally occupied by the Leader of the House. Rab, however, refused to give it up and, after a stand-off that lasted for several days, Macleod was moved into another room and Rab remained in occupation.[83]

The most divisive legislation to be introduced during this period

---

79 *Daily Mail*, 12 October 1961. There was no such arrangement. Macmillan disingenuously commented to Rab that he needed a younger man, 'if he could find the right one.' (Bodleian: MSS Macmillan d45.69–70. Diary entry for 16 September 1961.)
80 Mollie Butler, *August and Rab*, p. 70.
81 *The Observer*, 15 October 1961.
82 All articles appeared on 10 October 1961.
83 Fisher, *Iain Macleod*, p. 203.

was the Commonwealth Immigrants Act. Immigration from the West
Indies had been dramatically increased after the United States passed
legislation in the 1950s to limit immigration from the Caribbean. By
1961, resistance to unrestricted entry by Commonwealth citizens had
grown in Britain and a Gallup poll found that 67 per cent of those
polled favoured imposing a limit. As Rab pointed out, the motives of
many respondents were doubtless 'not honourable', but it was clear
that only by imposing quotas could there be successful integration of
immigrants into the community. When the Bill received its second
reading in November, Gaitskell launched a savage assault on the Bill
and the government, specifically on Rab and Macleod. That they had
allowed the Bill to be drafted, that they had not made any threat of
resignation, had allowed the first Fascist victory in Britain.[84] Gaitskell's
speech was brilliantly caustic. Rab's performance was wooden, but the
government achieved the necessary votes and breathed more easily.

In March 1962, Macmillan effectively truncated Rab's term at the
Home Office when he created a new Central African Office and
offered it to him. From March until July, despite retaining the title
of Home Secretary, Rab was principally occupied with the Central
African Federation. March also brought a crushing defeat for the government in the Orpington by-election, which Liberal Eric Lubbock
won with a 22 per cent swing away from the Tories. At the root of the
government's unpopularity was disillusion with the erosion of living
standards after the optimism of 1959.

Selwyn Lloyd's deflationary measures of the previous year, including
a 'pay pause', had alarmed professional families and his proposals for
the 1962 Budget in April were overruled in Cabinet. After a continuing
slide in the government's popularity that spring, a dispiriting third
place in the Derby by-election and a 'spectacular'[85] swing away from
the Tories in local elections, Macmillan worked throughout June to
develop an incomes policy.[86]

---

84 Hansard, 16 November 1961, vol. 649, cols 792–803.
85 Macmillan's own description, *At the End of the Day*, p. 65.
86 Remarkably, he excluded Selwyn Lloyd from the formulation of *Incomes Policy: A New Approach*,
    working closely with Hailsham and Roy Harrod. Diary entries for 11 and 12 June 1962.

In early July, Rab and Macleod urged Macmillan to take steps to reflate the economy and to replace Lloyd, whose advocacy of government policy on television was unconvincing. Macmillan reacted with uncharacteristic zeal, with no talk on this occasion of 'a little local difficulty'.[87] In what became known as 'The Night of the Long Knives' he replaced seven Cabinet ministers. Maudling was the big gainer, replacing Lloyd at the Treasury, while Rab acquired the largely symbolic title of 'First Secretary of State', but lost the Home Office. The last of his three previous responsibilities was taken away, but his role as Macmillan's deputy seemed secure. Macmillan's position, by contrast, was perilous; the purge of the Cabinet was seen as desperate flailing.

When, in January, Rab and Macmillan lunched at Buck's, the Prime Minister had prophesied, 'Either I shall decide [to retire] before the election, in which case it all falls on you or else it will be a year or two after the election, in which case it will not be so certain.'[88] Orpington seemed to bring that election closer and, despite Macmillan's 1959 triumph, a decision to retire might be taken for him. Rab at last had the scope to achieve a success in foreign affairs and Macmillan's words of January must have rung in his ears as he prepared to fly to Southern Rhodesia.

---

87 The speed with which Macmillan acted may have been caused by a leak on 12 July. Rab had lunched with Lord Rothermere on the previous day and a substantially accurate prediction of the reshuffle appeared in the *Daily Mail* on the following day, 12 July 1962.

88 Trinity: Butler Papers, RAB, G38.16, note of 24 January 1962.

CHAPTER 17

THE POISONED CHALICE, 1962–63

The first British colony to acquire independence after the Republic of Ireland in 1922 was the Gold Coast, becoming Ghana in 1957. Over the next six years, Nigeria and Sierra Leone followed. To European settlers, however, events in those three countries appeared unconnected with independence movements elsewhere on the continent.

The jewel in Britain's African crown was Kenya, where about 30,000 white settlers, subsidised successively by Labour and Conservative governments, were confident that their way of life would continue indefinitely. Wholesale imprisonment had contained the Mau-Mau rebellion of 1952 and, in spite of systematic atrocities, white owners of Kenya's fertile soil saw events in West Africa as remote from their country. Plans were drawn up in 1959 for Kenya, Tanganyika and Uganda to acquire independence in the 1970s,[1] but white rule seemed assured for at least a decade.[2]

Further south lay the protectorates of Northern Rhodesia and Nyasaland and the self-governing colony of Southern Rhodesia. During 1952, meetings were held in London to establish a federation of the three countries. African representatives from Northern Rhodesia and Nyasaland boycotted the meetings, convinced that Southern Rhodesia's racial policies would be extended to the northern protectorates. Their concerns were substantiated by Sir Godfrey Huggins, Prime Minister of Southern Rhodesia, who declared at a press conference in

---

1   Fisher, *Iain Macleod*, p. 142.
2   In the event, Tanganyika became independent (as Tanzania) in 1961; Uganda and Kenya followed suit over the next two years, Uganda in 1962 and Kenya in 1963.

January 1953 that there would be no Africans in the future Federation's administration, as 'they are quite incapable of playing a full part. If you had studied them you would realise how hopeless they are.'[3]

The Central African Federation was formed in 1953, against the wishes of the vast majority of Africans, but hailed by Europeans as the only practicable means by which the three Central African Territories could achieve security for the future and ensure the well-being of all their peoples. Northern Rhodesia and Nyasaland were overseen by the Colonial Office, while Southern Rhodesian affairs were handled by the Commonwealth Relations Office. Southern Rhodesia also differed from her northern neighbours in that the ratio of white settlers to Africans was greatly higher.[4] The Federation was governed by a Governor-General and a Prime Minister, Sir Raphael (Roy) Welensky.

Welensky, the thirteenth child of a Jewish father from Vilna and an Afrikaner mother, is often likened to Ernest Bevin. He left school at fourteen, worked for Rhodesia Railways, was professional heavyweight boxing champion of Rhodesia at the age of nineteen, and came into politics through the trades unions. A protégé of Huggins, he succeeded his mentor as the Federation's Prime Minister in 1956.

In March 1958, the Northern Rhodesia government issued a White Paper containing proposals for the constitution. Welensky objected to the document as 'it offered no advance whatever towards self-government' and in its proposals for the franchise was 'a flagrant violation of democratic principles'.[5] Adding to his concerns, Dr Hastings Banda returned from London to Nyasaland in July as leader of the Nyasaland African Congress Party. From the outset, Banda was committed to the secession of Nyasaland from the Federation, responding to a reporter who asked if he intended to use violence that he did not mean 'with violence but one can't exclude that if we are not allowed to get out of it'.[6]

---

3   Mason, *Year of Decision: Rhodesia and Nyasaland in 1960* (London: Institute of Race Relations, Oxford University Press, 1960), p. 48.

4   In 1960 Southern Rhodesia had a white population of 223,000 (7.3 per cent); in Northern Rhodesia (76,000) and Nyasaland (9,300) the ratio was much lower and there was a more realistic acceptance of the ultimate inevitability of majority rule.

5   Welensky, *Welensky's 4000 Days* (London: Collins, 1964), p. 89.

6   Ibid., p. 100.

Despite Welensky's objections, as his first election as Prime Minister was imminent, the British government insisted on issuing its own White Paper. This was released on 17 September and Welensky told a press conference that the White Paper's proposals were 'fundamentally unacceptable' as they represented no advance towards responsible government. By coincidence, Rab was staying with Courtauld relatives in the Eastern Highlands of Southern Rhodesia[7] and he visited Welensky in Salisbury to discuss the issue unofficially. He offered, without commitment, to put Welensky's view on the Federation to Lord Home, the Commonwealth Secretary, and Macmillan.

Welensky was impressed by Rab's unexpected offer of help and over the following months the two exchanged frank letters.[8] Rab remained in touch with Welensky, warning him in March 1959 in a cable of the mood in Westminster:

> *I have seldom seen Members of all parties so genuinely worried as they are now. It isn't that some Africans have been killed after violence and riots – we have had plenty of experience of that – but a deep uneasiness that events in Nyasaland may destroy all the hopes we have built on a federation demonstrating to the world a working partnership between European and African. This has been very dear to us in the Conservative Party because we believe it is the greatest venture in our imperial history.*[9]

On 3 February 1960, Macmillan made his celebrated speech to the South African parliament in Cape Town. 'The wind of change', he said, 'is blowing through this continent. Whether we like it or not, this growth of national consciousness is a political fact.' The speech was greeted by silence in Cape Town and outrage by the right wing of the Tory Party in Westminster. To Rab, as well as to Macleod, Hailsham and progressive Tories, the speech merely expressed an obvious truth. Macleod, the new Colonial Secretary, saw it as a green light for reform.

Macleod decided early on to focus on Nyasaland, where the

---

7   Trinity: Butler Papers, RAB, G33.46; Rab to PM, 11 September 1958.
8   Trinity: Butler Papers, RAB, G33.47.
9   Trinity: Butler Papers, RAB, F86.11.

European population was tiny and where, in March 1959, a state of emergency had been declared. Dr Banda, the presumptive leader of an independent Nyasaland, had been imprisoned; Macleod, believing him to be the only capable African leader who, if he remained in jail, would be seen as a martyr by his supporters, pressed for his release. Opposed by the Governor, by Welensky, and by several members of his own Cabinet, Macleod threatened to resign. When Banda was finally released on 1 April 1960, Macleod immediately met him and urged him to maintain order among his supporters, offering the carrot of a constitutional conference that would consider Nyasaland's secession from the Federation.[10]

In the Central African Federation's constitution it was specified that within not less than seven and not more than nine years a Review Commission would be appointed to study the Federation's working. On 21 July 1959, Macmillan had announced that an Advisory Commission was to be appointed under the chairmanship of Lord Monckton to prepare 'for the 1960 review, on the constitutional programme and framework best suited to the achievement of the objects contained in the Constitution of 1953'.[11]

The Monckton Commission soon concluded that 'hatred of the Federation in the Northern Territories was almost pathological and that it was widespread, sincere and of long standing'.[12] Once the Committee accepted that nothing in constitutional theory made the right of secession incompatible with the federal concept, quoting Professor Wheare that 'There are cases where to grant the right to secede is to ensure that states will never exercise it,'[13] Home abandoned all hope for the Federation and considered it doomed.[14] Macmillan saw the problem as intractable: if the government leant too much to the European side, African confidence in the government would be undermined;

---

10 Fisher, *Iain Macleod*, p. 159.
11 Hansard, 21 July 1959, vol. 609, col. 1072.
12 Birkenhead, *Walter Monckton* (London: Weidenfeld & Nicolson, 1969), p. 347.
13 Wheare, *Federal Government*, pp. 90–92. Cited by Birkenhead, op. cit., p. 354.
14 Rab disputes this view, claiming that Home expressed 'hope that there was still at least a chance of saving something from the Federation'. (*The Art of the Possible*, p. 210.) Home, however, wrote to Lord Birkenhead that, after the report of the Monckton Commission, he had no hope that the Federation could be preserved. Birkenhead, *Walter Monckton*, p. 359.

Macleod would resign; the party and government would be split in two. If it leaned to the African side, Europeans would have no faith in the government; Home and others would resign; the party and the government would be split in two.[15]

In July 1960, Duncan Sandys took over from Home as Secretary of State for Commonwealth Relations. Predictably, Macleod and he came into conflict. Macleod's intransigence over issues affecting the Federation, moreover, led to a cooling of relations with the Prime Minister, and in the reshuffle of October 1961, Macmillan replaced him with Maudling. Despite initial optimism that Maudling, relaxed and as informal in manner as Macleod was correct, would ease the problems between the Colonial and Commonwealth Offices, within three months Macmillan, commenting that Maudling was *plus noir que les nègres*,[16] was looking for another solution. Cabinet Secretary Norman Brook suggested that he appoint one minister to handle the combined responsibilities of the Offices for the Central African Federation and its individual territories.

Macmillan's diaries in late 1961 reflect concern for Rab's well-being. By January, however, he recorded, after the Christmas recess, 'Dined with Butler, who has been away in Scotland for a holiday. He seemed much better in health and spirits.'[17] 'On reflection', Macmillan wrote later, 'it became clear to me that I must try to persuade Butler to accept this onerous and distasteful task.'[18] After initial resistance, Rab yielded to Macmillan's and Home's persuasion and, confident that he could re-establish mutual trust with Welensky, agreed to take a two-week fact-finding trip to Central Africa in May. Macmillan wrote to thank Rab for taking on a 'thankless but challenging job'.[19]

On the following day, Rab wrote a record of his conversation with Macmillan. The Prime Minister played him beautifully, first hinting that the succession was still there for Rab. Home, he said, did not want it; Selwyn Lloyd had held two of the Great Offices

---

15 Bodleian: MSS Macmillan, dep d41*.64–5. Diary entry for 4 February 1961.
16 Bodleian: MSS Macmillan, dep d44*.106–7. Diary entry for 10 January 1962.
17 Bodleian: MSS Macmillan, dep d44*.113–14. Diary entry for 15 January 1962.
18 Macmillan, *At the End of the Day*, p. 321.
19 Trinity: Butler Papers, RAB, G38.1.

as Foreign Secretary and Chancellor, but, said Macmillan, 'When
he comes onto a platform nobody felt that here comes the leader
of England.' Rather quaintly, Macmillan compared Rab's mission in
Central Africa with his own experience in North Africa during the
war and, in a Mac-like twist, he added, 'If you take this on you will
be like Bonar doing all the work for Lloyd George.' The proposition that Rab might succeed Macmillan as Bonar Law had taken
over from Lloyd George in 1922 was doubtful – a fact which cannot
have escaped Rab.[20] Nonetheless, he accepted the post. Macmillan
was delighted, recording in his diary, doubtless for posterity, the self-
justifying comment that Rab was 'obviously much better in health
and spirit since he gave up the Chairmanship of the Party and Leadership of the House of Commons'.[21]

Rab was not without his own apprehensions about the task. He had
concluded from the Monckton Report that the Central African problem was 'much more complicated than India' but he believed that his
own experience of India's problems equipped him for the task, recording:

> I approach this situation with appropriate modesty. I am not doing it simply
> as escapism from a long period of home social issues at the Home Office. Nor
> because of frustration after nine years of acting head of the Government ... I
> am doing it ... because I feel here is the open window for which I have been
> waiting and one for which my early Indian experience, my curious knowl-
> edge of the personalities and the sense of destiny propel me.[22]

Macmillan accordingly announced in the Commons that he had
'invited my right hon. Friend the Home Secretary to undertake this
responsibility' and that 'from 19 March, all the existing responsibilities
of the Commonwealth Secretary for the Federation and for Southern
Rhodesia, and those of the Colonial Secretary for Northern Rhodesia
and Nyasaland, will be exercised by the Home Secretary'.[23]

---

20 Trinity: Butler Papers, RAB, G38.2, 10 March 1962.
21 Bodleian: MSS Macmillan, dep d45*.57–8. Diary entry for 9 March 1962.
22 Trinity: Butler Papers, RAB, G38.6, 11 March 1962.
23 Hansard, 15 March 1962, vol. 655, cols 1545–6.

The announcement was greeted by shocked surprise. Gaitskell asked if 'the Prime Minister [was] aware that this is one of the most extraordinary statements that has ever been made in my recollection by any government'. Was the Prime Minister convinced that Mr Butler, 'the best Home Secretary we have',[24] was also 'the best Colonial Secretary and the best Commonwealth Relations Secretary, as well as being the best minister in charge of the Common Market?' This 'fiddling around with ministerial responsibilities', Gaitskell suggested, illustrated the government's inability to make up its mind about the Federation. Macmillan retained his habitual calm while implied criticism came at him from all sides of the House.

The appointment was better received in Africa, where 'Welensky, Whitehead, Banda, and even Kaunda seem[ed] pleased.'[25] Welensky believed that Macmillan had given the job to Rab in the hope that he would fail to preserve the Federation and that this would tarnish Rab's public image.[26]

A public opinion poll taken the previous October at the time of the reshuffle had indicated that 36 per cent of the electorate favoured Rab as the next Prime Minister, despite Macleod's popularity and his dramatic promotion in the Cabinet reorganisation. His closest contenders – with 19 per cent and 18 per cent – were Selwyn Lloyd and Peter Thorneycroft.[27] If Macmillan wanted Rab not to succeed him, then a well-publicised failure in Central Africa would be helpful. Indeed, it was difficult to see how Rab could best navigate between Scylla and Charybdis. If he succeeded in dismantling the Federation he would again run foul of the right wing of his own party. If Welensky remained in control of the Federation he would be tarred with the brush of racialism. A Salisbury newspaper, designed mainly for an African readership, ran a headline 'Federation Must Go'. Rab, it said, was 'taking on a dying

---

24 The repeated dig at Rab for his deliberately ambiguous response when he was asked if Eden was 'the best Prime Minister we have' recurred frequently in the press, to Rab's discomfiture.
25 Bodleian: MSS Macmillan, dep d45*.67. Diary entry for 14 March 1962.
26 Welensky, *Welensky's 4000 Days*, pp. 361–2.
27 As an aside, in that poll Edward Heath, the only one of six possibilities mentioned to the public who actually became Prime Minister, was tipped by just 1 per cent of those polled.

baby and need only address himself to one question: why federation has failed to work after a trial of eight and a half years'.[28]

Federation, the article argued, had failed to work for three reasons: 'The continuing suspicion and fear of the Africans that they will be dominated by a white minority; failure to achieve an agreed federal solution involving the majority of the people; and the fact that federation was based on imposition' and 'No amount of persuasion by the British Government or of force by the Federal Government can now make it acceptable to Africans.' Rab's best course, it continued, would be to 'formulate a positive plan which has all the overwhelming economic advantages of association between the three territories and none of the political disadvantages'. A first step would be to return education, health and agriculture to the territorial governments. As things stood, the paper charged, the move was part of a plan orchestrated by Welensky.[29]

Rab's acceptance of the burden suggests that, to some extent at least, he saw the appointment in positive terms. It would have been totally justifiable for him to have refused the appointment; there could have been no recriminations if he had pointed to his responsibilities as Home Secretary and the minister with oversight for Britain's negotiations to join the EEC, a matter central to Macmillan's policy for the future. Instead, he scarcely hesitated. He recorded that in April he was approached by Sir Archibald James, his former PPS, who pointed out to him that he had been given 'a wonderful opportunity of cashing in with those Conservatives who might well be instrumental in forwarding my own personal interests'. If he succeeded in dismembering Northern Rhodesia in such a way that the whites retained control of the valuable copper mines, he would incur everlasting gratitude from the right.[30] Rab failed to rise to this insidious suggestion. His explanation of his decision, that it 'involved the livelihood and liberty, the expectations and emotions of 9 million people',[31] is probably the truest explanation for his accepting the challenge.

---

28 *African Daily News*, 16 March 1962.
29 Reported in *The Times*, 17 March 1962.
30 Trinity: Butler Papers, RAB, G38. Notes of conversation with Sir Archie James and others, 4 April 1962.
31 Butler, *The Art of the Possible*, p. 208.

Immediately he was appointed, Rab asked Sir Albert Robinson, the Federation's High Commissioner in London, to come to see him. The meeting went well and Robinson reported to Welensky that he was sure that there would be 'a more relaxed atmosphere' and that Rab's 'sympathetic attitude [would be] a great help'.[32] Most importantly, Rab was acutely aware that speed was of the essence, but he resolved not to be pressured into hasty solutions, as he felt Macleod had been. Welensky was glad to receive Robinson's positive reaction. He had a high opinion of Rab at their first meeting, but understood political realities. He feared that Rab was coming to Africa as 'a liquidator not a negotiator'.[33]

Rab was cautiously optimistic. The situation in Nyasaland complicated matters, but, despite the Monckton Commission's conclusions, he held out hope that the two Rhodesias might be persuaded into some form of true – not merely economic – union, and that, once the problems posed by Nyasaland had been resolved, this might form the basis of future discussions. Nonetheless, he was determined that any such resolution would be reached by collective bargaining and he was incensed that Sandys, during a February visit to all three countries of the Federation, had travelled to Zomba to meet with Banda. He had seen a record of this meeting, which indicated that Sandys had told Banda that the secession of Nyasaland would be accepted by Britain. Rab made it clear to Robinson that 'whatever may have been said in Nyasaland, [he intended] to tell Banda that he won't get unilateral secession, and that whatever we do will have to be part of a general settlement. And I assure you that we shall do nothing without the most exhaustive enquiry.'[34]

Welensky was impressed by Rab's approach. 'He has a very incisive intelligence,' he wrote.

He seems almost glacial in his manner, but he is a man of deep feeling and almost impenetrable reserve. He is orderly, precise and quick-thinking.

---

32 Welensky, *Welensky's 4000 Days*, pp. 330–31.
33 Ibid., p. 337.
34 Ibid., pp. 332–3.

He is very flexible in negotiation, but when he has reached a decision he does not change it … I think that Rab Butler was the best British minister I dealt with in the years from 1957 onwards, and he had the roughest, most unpleasant job.[35]

When Rab visited Salisbury in May, he told Welensky of the Sandys/ Banda meeting in February, and that no record of the discussion of secession existed in either the Colonial Office or the Commonwealth Relations Office. At first, Welensky was reluctant to believe that as early as February 1962 the British government was negotiating with Banda behind his back. Later that month, when Sandys visited Salisbury, he lunched with Welensky and, without mentioning his meeting in Zomba, said simply that 'Britain had lost the will to govern.'[36] A decisive man of clear-cut likes and dislikes, Welensky continued to trust Rab despite his conviction that the majority of Macmillan's Cabinet wished to see the Federation dismantled.

Rab too, perhaps, was reaching that conclusion. Not only had Sandys given Banda the impression that unilateral secession was an option for Nyasaland; Rab was further angered by the United Nations' decision to send a team of investigators to London to discuss Southern Rhodesia with the British government – an action agreed to by the Foreign Office without reference to him. Home may have suggested to Rab that the Federation might be saved, yet his true opinion, expressed to others, was that it was doomed. Home and Macmillan were very close and, while Home was a thoroughly honourable man, Rab thought he might be acting as Macmillan's catspaw. As Rab surveyed the difficulties of the job he had taken on he must have wondered if he was about to slip on an enormous banana skin.

Gaitskell had not tempered his initial reaction to the announcement of Rab's appointment. Intensely suspicious that the government would cobble together a deal that allowed Nyasaland to secede and then sell out Northern Rhodesia and the country's mineral assets to

---

35 Ibid., p. 331.
36 Ibid., pp. 318–9; Sampson, *Macmillan: A Study in Ambiguity*, p. 181.

a government of white settlers in Salisbury, he pressed for an early debate on Central Africa. Rab, anxious to be seen to be treating the matter urgently, proposed to make an announcement during the debate after the Easter recess. Inactivity would be 'highly dangerous', he said. He proposed that a 'full and exhaustive' enquiry be conducted. This would have the double advantage of defusing any criticism from the opposition that the government was papering over cracks, and of postponing any action until after the 'full and exhaustive' study had been conducted.

Even that seemed precipitate to Welensky. Would it not be better, he pleaded with Rab, for him to come to Africa for his initial inspection visit in early May before making any statement at all? As Lord Alport described the position, the entire problem was 'bedevilled by Nyasaland's relationship with the Federation'. Once that was resolved, things would be easier and it would be possible to strengthen the economic and political association between the territories. A position, in other words, exactly congruent with Gaitskell's suspicions.

At a meeting on 25 April, Alport gave Welensky a draft of Rab's proposed announcement. It was an anodyne statement that nonetheless opened the door for Nyasaland's withdrawal. Welensky felt betrayed once more and implored Alport to stay Rab's hand; he believed that Rab's announcement accepted the break-up of the Federation and gave the initiative to its opponents.[37]

Rab and Mollie arrived in Salisbury on 11 May. 'He was at all times friendly and frank,' Welensky recalled,

and displayed none of the built-in prejudices to which we had become accustomed. He listened courteously; he made no easy, flattering or headline-catching promises; and he gave the same serious consideration to the opinions and feelings of the European minority as to those of the African majority. He did not give the impression that the solution to our problems was a simple affair of head-counting.[38]

37 Welensky, *Welensky's 4000 Days*, pp. 336–7.
38 Ibid., p. 338.

Rab visited Banda and Kenneth Kaunda, leader of the United National Independence Party in Northern Rhodesia, and returned to Salisbury for three days. When he left, Welensky and his ministers 'felt genuinely encouraged to believe that Britain still had some desire to maintain close bonds between the Territories of the Federation'. 'We are prepared to negotiate', he said, 'but there can be no question of letting Nyasaland out unless and until we have reached agreement with the British government about the future of the Rhodesias.'[39]

When Banda visited London in early July, Rab realised – late in the day – the extent of his hatred for the Federation and that secession must ultimately be granted. Kaunda applied increasing pressure on Northern Rhodesia, threatening widespread civil disturbance unless his demands were met. Later that month, when Macmillan made his sweeping Cabinet changes in 'The Night of the Long Knives', the Prime Minister proposed that Rab give up the Home Office. *Prima facie*, this made eminent sense, if Rab were to concentrate his energy on Africa, but Rab was appalled by the suggestion, comparing its implications with the treatment that he had received from Eden in 1955. 'I have been on a limb before with a minute staff', he wrote, 'and found it difficult to keep things going … I should lose a lot in precedence and efficiency if I were simply associated with Africa, and a small piece of it at that.'[40]

Macmillan's comment of January regarding Bonar Law and Lloyd George was now revealed as disingenuous. Rab saw clearly that he was about to be sidelined and handed a poisoned chalice.[41] He was to have Central Africa and nothing else; the succession was not going to 'fall on Rab' as Macmillan had intimated. It was already up for grabs, whenever the election was to be held. By August 1962, no longer holding any illusions about Macmillan's motives and determined to settle the future of the Federation in an equitable manner, Rab was embroiled in the detail of Nyasaland's relation to the Federation. In a top secret document, 'Preliminary Outline of Advisers' Proposals', he addressed pressure applied by Nyasaland on the Federation. Simply,

---

39 Ibid., p. 340.
40 Trinity: Butler Papers, RAB, G38.13, Rab to PM, 11 July 1962.
41 See Chapter 16: Trinity: Butler Papers, RAB, G38.16, 24 January 1962.

the Malawi Party ministers refused to discuss any co-operation with the two Rhodesias until Nyasaland was granted the right to secede.[42]

This remained the dominant issue through the Commonwealth Prime Ministers' Conference in London in September and the Nyasaland constitutional conference in late November. On 2 December, Banda returned to Nyasaland and announced that full internal self-government was to be granted. In Northern Rhodesia, the Governor called upon the African Nationalists to form a government. Kenneth Kaunda of the National Independence Party and Harry Nkumbula, leader of the African National Congress, formed a coalition. On the following day, Winston Field's Dominion Party was returned in the Southern Rhodesian general election. Although the party aimed to preserve some form of economic link with Northern Rhodesia, it too wanted to end the Federation. On 19 December, Rab announced the acceptance in principle of the secession of Nyasaland. Welensky reacted with a threat to do all in his power to resist the break-up of the Federation. 'The British Government have ratted on us,' he charged. 'They have gone back on the most solemn undertakings and intentions … They have been guilty of an act of treachery.'[43]

In truth, the government was unable to perform as planned. The Federal Government never made any real effort to fulfil their side of the contract, involving partnership with Africans. If the British government had supported the Federation, it would have resulted in a bloody revolution of millions of Africans. The Federation would have emerged with a perhaps decimated and hostile population – and its economy destroyed.[44]

Welensky protested that Rab had not consulted him, as agreed, before announcing Nyasaland's right of secession.[45] Rab had been assiduous in ensuring lengthy consultation; he had, moreover, delayed the announcement to avoid embarrassing Welensky at the time of the Southern Rhodesia elections. Nonetheless, Welensky declared that it

---

42 Trinity: Butler Papers, RAB, F86.43.
43 Franklin, *Unholy Wedlock: The Failure of the Central African Federation* (London: George Allen & Unwin, 1963), pp. 225–6.
44 Ibid., p. 226.
45 Franklin adds the comment that, to Welensky, 'consultation' meant 'getting my own way'.

was his intention 'to fight it out'. He denied any intention of action against Britain. If, however, Britain attempted to force its will on the Federation, that would be a different matter. At all events, it was an unrealistic scenario – but one couched in enough ill-will to guarantee the end of the Federation.[46]

Still Rab wrestled with Nyasaland's right to secede and, as part of his visit to Central Africa, he spent two days in Zomba and Blantyre in late January 1963. At the end of the trip he devoted an hour and a half to meeting Banda before returning to Salisbury.[47] After the visit, he was gratified to be told that African leaders considered him to be trustworthy and also to be a wise administrator. He was solemnly informed that Africans referred to him as 'Njobvu Yeikuro' – literally meaning 'large elephant' with an implied meaning of 'sagacious beast'.[48]

By early March, when Welensky received an invitation to London for talks to begin on 26 March, the demise of the Federation was widely predicted. At the first meeting, Rab said unhappily, 'If we were free to decide, we would like to see the closest links between the Rhodesias.' It was clear, however, that, to Rab's discomfiture, Kaunda was calling the tune in Northern Rhodesia. When they met again on 29 March, Rab, looking 'wan and grey and ill', informed Welensky of his intention to make an announcement that 'No Territory can be kept in the Federation against its will, and it follows from this that any Territory must be allowed to secede if it so wishes.' In other words, as Welensky and the Southern Rhodesians feared, Northern Rhodesia was to be allowed to secede from the Federation.[49] Welensky and his party had been invited to lunch with Macmillan, but after this statement Welensky asked Rab to have an official notify the PM that 'neither I nor any member of my delegation will be able to go to this luncheon today. I don't want to be discourteous, but I cannot accept the hospitality of a man who has betrayed me and my country.'[50]

---

46 Franklin, *Unholy Wedlock*, pp. 227–9.
47 Trinity: Butler Papers, RAB, G40.1.
48 Butler, *The Art of the Possible*, p. 214.
49 The Southern Rhodesian government's certainty that Britain would 'betray' them is described by Ian Smith in *The Great Betrayal* (London: Blake, 1997), pp. 49–54.
50 Welensky, *Welensky's 4000 Days*, pp. 356–9.

All that remained was for Rab to perform the obsequies and dissolve the Federation, to which end a conference was arranged at Victoria Falls in late June. Headlines such as 'Orderly Dissolution Is Mr Butler's Aim'[51] and 'Central Africa: The Last Act'[52] sent Rab on his way. He arrived at Victoria Falls on 28 June and immediately buckled down to business. Meeting all leaders individually before the opening of the conference,[53] he stressed that discussion should be restricted to the affairs of the Central African Federation and not intended to cover the internal affairs of any single country.

Welensky, preparing to leave Salisbury, said that his delegation was approaching the talks in a spirit of co-operation, aimed at 'devising the most effective machinery to work out solutions of the problems associated with the dissolution of the Federation and the reversion of responsibilities to the territorial governments ... consistent with an orderly and equitable disposal of the Federal Government's responsibilities.'[54]

Despite his assertion of co-operation, however, Welensky had remained determined to accept no British hospitality since he cancelled his luncheon appointment with Macmillan in March. He declined an invitation to lunch with Rab on 27 June and on the following day refused to attend a reception for delegates and the press.[55]

There was speculation that he was hatching a plot to replace Field and unilaterally declare Southern Rhodesia independent.[56] While Welensky was publicly aloof although remaining friendly with Rab in private,[57] Rab succeeded in placating Northern Rhodesian leaders Kaunda and Nkumbula, who had demanded the return of almost all Ministries affecting Northern Rhodesia. The conference agreed to establish working parties to settle the return of federal functions to

---

51 *The Guardian*, 27 June 1963.
52 *Daily Telegraph*, 28 June 1963.
53 Rab was all business from the moment he arrived. Meeting Winston Field in the courtyard of his hotel, he suggested a meeting that evening. 'Will 6.30 suit you?' he asked. 'I think we had better meet in my room.'
54 *The Times*, 27 June 1963.
55 This was inevitably greeted by headlines in the *Daily Telegraph*, 'Welensky Snubs Rab'.
56 *The Guardian*, 1 July 1963; Trinity: Butler Papers RAB,L90.
57 Mollie Butler, *August and Rab*, p. 64.

territorial responsibility, a breakthrough regarded as a minor diplo-matic triumph.[58]

Rab insisted that Southern Rhodesia could achieve independence only if fully representative government were provided for in a new constitution agreed between the country's two communities. His persistence paid off but underscored the failure of the experiment in multiracial living, bringing the struggle between white power and African nationalism into clearer focus. Responsibility for that, however, could hardly be laid at Rab's door.

Field felt that Southern Rhodesia's best route to independence was to bury the Federation rather than to keep it alive until Britain yielded to his demands.[59] Recognising that the need to give African Southern Rhodesians a bigger voice at the polls was a *sine qua non* of a British grant of independence, he forced Rab's hand, ensuring that Britain would gain little approbation from the African world.

The outcome was, all observers agreed, a triumph of practical common sense, but scarcely a cause for liberal rejoicing. A great deal of potential wrangling lay ahead but the decision to wind up the Federation by 31 December 1963 was a necessary first step. By astute and resolute statesmanship, Rab achieved the apparently impossible task of, as *The Economist* described it, 'taking Central Africa to pieces without its blowing up in his face'.[60] Even Welensky found himself able to put a positive spin on the outcome. As he left the conference room, looking solemn, he commented, 'Well, we had to have a funeral, so the arrangements were admirable.' In a television interview, however, when asked for the root cause of the break-up of the federation, he was blunt. 'I unhesitatingly give the palm to Harold Macmillan,' he said. 'His wind of change has betrayed the white man up and down this continent … The present leaders have been in office too long, that is all that is wrong.'

Welensky felt no animus towards Rab, believing that 'If he had been given a reasonable chance, the story might have been a different

---

58 *The Times*, 29 June 1963.
59 *The Times*, 4 July 1963.
60 *The Economist*, 5 July 1963.

one.' He believed that Rab acted decently and had no idea of Sandys's undertakings to Banda. Macmillan, on the other hand, he considered devious in the extreme with the 'most complicated mind' he had encountered. Did Macmillan, he wondered, hope that by giving Rab the responsibility for the Federation he would break Rab's reputation? 'It was a stinking kettle of fish that was handed to him, and he has my sympathy, not my resentment.'[61] 'The Federation was destroyed,' said Sir Roy, 'not by our avowed enemies but by those who called themselves our friends and said that they believed in what we had built. They killed it slowly, in the dark and by stealth; and they wept hypocritical tears as they finished the deed.'[62]

It was with a justifiable sense of pride that the First Secretary of State returned in early July to England, where he received a letter from Arthur Lytton Sells, a language scholar who had been a Cambridge don at the time of Rab's Fellowship at Corpus. Lytton Sells told Rab that he was 'delighted to hear of your success in Rhodesia – a success that would have been unbelievable if anyone but you had achieved it.' 'It would be a good thing for the country', he added, 'if you became PM before the next Party conference.'[63] With Macmillan's government mired in scandal from the Profumo affair,[64] that outcome seemed eminently possible.

---

61 Welensky, *Welensky's 4000 Days*, pp. 361–2.
62 Ibid., p. 45.
63 Trinity: Butler Papers, RAB, E19.9.10.
64 John Profumo, War Minister, had been involved in 1961 in an affair with Christine Keeler, an aspiring model – an affair that he denied in the House of Commons in March 1963. Keeler may have been conducting a simultaneous affair with a Soviet naval attaché and the scandal, with society, security and sexual angles, became a *cause célèbre* that came close to bringing down the government and probably contributed to the election result in 1964.

CHAPTER 18

WILL THERE BE BLOOD? THE LEADERSHIP, ROUND 3, 1963

When Macmillan assumed the premiership, he said to the Queen, half in jest, that his administration might last for no more than six weeks. Six years later, he considered the question of who might succeed him. Despite the economic boom that Britain had enjoyed, recent scandals made it likely that Macmillan would bequeath to his successor as unattractive a climate as he had inherited from Eden. As he weighed the government's options in the summer of 1963, the primary question facing him was whether he should lead the party at the next election – which needed to be called before 9 October 1964. Potential successors were circling and that led Macmillan to the subsidiary question: if he were to step down, who should succeed him?

In early 1963, Rab, as Deputy Leader, was heir apparent, but Macmillan doubted that his accession would be automatic, as Randolph Churchill loyally recorded. 'It can be argued', he maintained, 'that Macmillan did all he could during his seven years as Prime Minister to advance the fortunes of Butler. Of course he did not take the decisive step, which would have ensured the success of Butler, of resigning.' Macmillan's growing concern was that Rab 'would not be acceptable to large and influential sections of the party ... in the House of Commons and the country'. He also doubted, according to Churchill, that Rab could lead the party to win a general election.[1]

Churchill's judgement is undoubtedly the official Macmillan

---

1   Randolph Churchill, *The Fight for the Tory Leadership* (London: Heinemann, 1964), p. 94.

version, which can be roughly paraphrased as: 'Did all I could to help him. Gave him every chance. But at the end of the day he didn't have what it takes and the fellows knew it – in the House and other chaps in the country. Shame, but there it is.'

Macmillan had, it is true, ostensibly eased Rab up the ladder toward the premiership. Randolph Churchill, faithfully describing Macmillan's official posture, believed that. So did Lord Swinton. Iain Macleod fundamentally disagreed; that shrewd observer argued that 'From the first day of his premiership until the last, Macmillan was determined that Butler, though incomparably the best qualified of the contenders, should not succeed him.'[2] Edward Heath also contradicts Churchill's assertion:

> My first thought upon hearing Alec Home deliver (Macmillan's) resignation statement to the conference on 10 October was that Rab Butler would, once again, fail to make it to No. 10. I had already sensed that Macmillan wanted to keep Rab out, although he never said as much. He had come to regard Rab as an indecisive personality yet, however much the Prime Minister might have tried to orchestrate the outcome from his sickbed, it was ultimately the party's decision, and when Redmayne consulted the parliamentary party, both peers and MPs, they simply wouldn't have Butler. Too many on the right despised him for moving the party to the left. Others, like Macmillan, simply saw him as indecisive.[3]

Randolph Churchill, working from the premise that Macmillan fully supported Rab, needed to propose another reason why he ultimately found Rab unsuitable. Rab, he explains, now almost sixty-one, was too old. The Profumo affair stimulated a demand for greater vigour at the top, for less complacency and drift. Rab endorsed this and subtly criticised Macmillan, saying on television on 8 July, 'I think I am pretty well aware that people want us to give a fresh impression of vigour and

2   *The Spectator*, 17 January 1964.
3   Heath, *The Course of My Life*, p. 253.

decision before the next election.' Maudling, the most likely candidate of the younger generation, not unnaturally criticised the government because they had 'not been successful in obtaining the allegiance of the younger generation of voters, because we have not yet found a way of talking to them in language they understand or in terms of the ideals they cherish'.[4]

That may have been so, and early in 1963 there broke out what Rab later described as 'the absolute rage of fire which worked through the Conservative Party in favour of a younger man'.[5] And if a younger man was called for, which of the promising new men best fitted the bill? Maudling, Macleod, Heath? Maudling, whom Macmillan tended to favour, was, arguably, too young at forty-six.

It was perfectly logical, therefore, that Hailsham should appear to Macmillan as the most suitable candidate at the age of fifty-six. A fine orator, a first-class brain, 'a man who knows how to think and act'. If Hailsham were to run, he would be required to relinquish his peerage, an option open to him after the passage of the Peerage Act at the end of July. The Prime Minister's choice of Hailsham to travel to Moscow to sign the Nuclear Test-Ban Treaty, given his inexperience in that area, was a clear signal of his good standing in Macmillan's eyes. By September, Macmillan was happy with him as his successor and on 30 September, as the Conservative conference drew near, he so informed Hailsham.[6]

The Conservative Party appeared beleaguered in the late summer of 1963. Since the Orpington by-election had been lost to the Liberals by almost 8,000 votes,[7] few things had gone right for Macmillan's government. In January 1963, President de Gaulle had contemptuously dismissed Britain's sixteen-month-long negotiations to join

---

4 Sampson, *Macmillan: A Study in Ambiguity*, pp. 227–8.
5 Interview with Kenneth Harris, published in *The Listener* on 28 July 1966. Given that this was said almost three years later, it is quite possible that this was the rationalisation for his rejection that Rab had chosen to adopt.
6 Randolph Churchill, *The Fight for the Tory Leadership*, pp. 94–5.
7 The by-election on 14 March 1962 had seen a swing of 21.9 per cent against the Conservatives. Eric Lubbock, the Liberal candidate, won 22,846 votes against Conservative candidate Peter Goldman's 14,991. Although the result was initially hailed as the beginning of a Liberal revival, the vote was more an anti-Tory than pro-Liberal statement.

the EEC;[8] the Vassal and Profumo affairs had badly damaged the government; and, by the time that Lord Denning's report was published in September,[9] the Tories trailed Labour in opinion polls by nineteen points.[10]

Macmillan was conscious of the need not to cling to power for too long. 'The untidiness of Churchill's departure was constantly in his mind.'[11] On 25 July, he addressed the 1922 Committee and raised the issue of the succession. There were two interrelated matters: his successor and the timing of his own stepping down. The imminent election linked the two: would he lead the Tories into the next election? To win that election, the Conservative Party needed to appear strong and united; 'Policies needed to be forward-looking, highly political in content and, if possible, strongly contrasted to those of the Socialists.'[12]

Macmillan then let the genie out of the bottle with the spectre of rivalry. In his notes for the address he wrote,

> The transition from one leader to another man has got to be smooth and the party must know its mind. I tell you, frankly, that I should be most reluctant to lay down my responsibilities until I was sure that the party, under its new leader, was going to be more certain, more strong, more united than it was before the change.[13]

The Prime Minister was urging the 1922 Committee to take nothing for granted; the obvious successor was by no means the right one. He

---

8   De Gaulle told Macmillan personally of his intention to veto Britain's entry at a meeting in Rambouillet in December 1962. On 14 January, he held a press conference, at which he spoke of the problems that Britain's membership would cause the community and effectively dashed British hopes of membership.

9   The Denning Report, a 70,000-word report on the Christine Keeler and John Profumo affair, was presented to Parliament in September 1963. By then the affair had been so closely followed and pruriently reported that the Report was an immediate bestseller, and crowds flocked to buy copies on the day of its publication.

10 D. R. Thorpe, 'The October 1963 Conservative Party Conference', *Conservative History Journal*, vol. II, 2, Autumn 2013.

11 Horne, *Harold Macmillan, 1957–1986*, p. 531.

12 From Macmillan's notes for the address; quoted by Goodhart, *The 1922*, p. 188.

13 Ibid., p. 189.

was effectively knifing Rab in front of an audience not disposed to promote him. His notes continue:

> I appreciate that where there is not an heir apparent, I must be sure that in due course one is forthcoming, and I give you my word that I shall not give up until I know that, by the various proper methods of communications which are open to us, the party will accept a man who may be called as my successor, and accept him with goodwill and with the certain knowledge that their views have been fully assessed and taken into account.

In the 1957 succession, the backbenchers had not been canvassed. In 1963, Macmillan assured them that they would be consulted – in the full knowledge that Rab was not their leader of choice. With this simple paragraph Mac made it clear that he shared that view and that another candidate needed to be found. Once the backbenchers joined the circle of electors, Rab's electability ebbed fast.

John Morrison, long-standing chairman of the 1922, was conducting his own research. At the end of June, just before Rab left for the Victoria Falls conference, Morrison had called on him with the depressing news that 'the chaps won't have you'. When he returned, Rab spoke to friends on the Executive who confirmed what Morrison had said. This was supported by another *Daily Telegraph* poll that showed Maudling with a commanding lead: of 100 Members polled, seventy-one supported Maudling, nine Rab and five Hailsham.[14] Rab, persuaded that the party would elect a younger man, indicated to Maudling that he would be glad to serve under him.

Macmillan's awareness of the need for decision was sharpened by a memorandum that greeted him when he returned to London from shooting grouse in late August. Lord Poole, Joint Party Chairman, wrote to warn him that the Parliamentary Party wanted a change in leadership before the next election. He doubted if a decision could be delayed until after the Christmas recess 'without doing irreparable

---

14 Ibid., p. 191.

harm to the party'.[15] Again the Prime Minister pondered the succession; again he failed to find a clear solution. In his diary he recorded that 'perhaps another leader could do what I did after Eden left. But it cannot be done by a pedestrian politician.'[16]

The two candidates that Macmillan considered were Hailsham and Maudling. Presumably considering Rab 'a pedestrian politician', he omitted him from the field. Hailsham, he felt, had 'vision and moral strength' and would be able to restore party fortunes better than Maudling, 'admirable' though Maudling was. As for the party, 'The "backbenchers" (poor fools) do not seem to have any idea, except "a young man".' When he called Rab in to talk with him on 10 September, he concealed his intentions, 'for [Rab] is not discreet'. He inferred from Rab's comments that he would 'accept the premiership if there was a general consensus of opinion for him. But he doesn't want another unsuccessful bid.' Macmillan, convinced that Rab was better cast as king-maker than king, concluded that 'He would prefer to be Warwick[17] (which he could be) and not try to be King (which he can't)' and that, on the whole, he would support Hailsham.[18] When Macmillan spoke to Home the following week, Home too supported Hailsham but feared that it would split the party.[19]

'Supermac' might have been moribund, but he was still in Downing Street, with no need to call an election until the following year. The more he considered his options and his legacy, the more he became convinced that he should lead the Tories into that election before stepping down. He discussed resignation with Dorothy and, on Sunday 6 October, with his son Maurice and Julian Amery, both of whom argued that Macmillan would be rendering a splendid last service by

---

15 Memo, 28 August 1963, Macmillan Archive. Cited by Horne, *Harold Macmillan, 1957–1986*, p. 531.

16 Bodleian: MSS Macmillan, dep d50*. 63–4. Diary entry for 10 September 1963.

17 The reference is to Richard Neville, Earl of Warwick during the Wars of the Roses. He earned the title 'The King-maker' by obtaining the crown first for Edward IV of York and later restoring the Lancastrian King Henry VI to the throne. See Chapter 16 above; Butler, *The Art of the Possible*, pp. 196–7.

18 Bodleian: MSS Macmillan, dep d50*.74. Rab also recalls Macmillan making that observation at Chequers in about 1960.

19 Bodleian: MSS Macmillan, dep d50*.84. Diary entry for 18 September 1963.

staying on and taking the responsibility rather than saddling his successor with it by handing over power before the election.[20] This view was shared by Swinton, who was in favour of Mac's stepping down in January – but only if Hailsham would succeed him. He warned Mac that Rab 'would ... lose the election disastrously' and that 'Maudling would be worse electorally'. Rab, Swinton believed, would support Hailsham but Macmillan concluded that 'If it cannot be got by agreement, [he] ought to stay on at whatever inconvenience to [himself].'[21] The longer he stayed, of course, the worse Rab's chances of succeeding him would become.

Persuaded by the argument that he would serve the party best by remaining at the helm, Macmillan temporised, telling Hailsham that he had not yet decided whether to remain in office until an election but that Hailsham should be ready to succeed him. To Martin Redmayne, the Chief Whip, he indicated that he was inclining to the view that he would fight an election and would announce his decision on the last day of the Conservative conference in Blackpool.[22] On the evening of 6 October, Macmillan dined alone with Home and told him of his plan to carry on. If he announced on 12 October his decision to retire in early January, a leadership contest would begin immediately. This would be dangerously divisive when Wilson was emerging as an impressive and youthful Leader of the Opposition. On the following day, when Macmillan and Rab talked about the leadership, the Prime Minister sensed that Rab clearly wanted him to carry on 'for – in his heart – he does not expect the succession and fears it'.[23]

This astute comment was reinforced by a letter that Macmillan received from his brother-in-law James Stuart. Stuart had been on what he called 'a pub crawl', sounding out MPs informally about the Prime Minister's options. 'Rab', he wrote, 'may be relying on loyalty and fatalism to result in [the leadership] falling into his lap.'[24] With his view

20 Randolph Churchill, *The Fight for the Tory Leadership*, p. 95.
21 Bodleian: MSS Macmillan, dep d50*.112–3. Diary entry for 30 September 1963.
22 Randolph Churchill, *The Fight for the Tory Leadership*, p. 96.
23 Bodleian: MSS Macmillan dep d51*. Diary entry for 7 October 1963.
24 Stuart to Macmillan, 5 October 1963, Macmillan Archive. Cited by Horne, *Harold Macmillan 1957–1986*, pp. 537–8.

of Rab reinforced by Stuart, with his son and son-in-law urging him to stay at the helm, and with a reaction to Lord Denning's report less adverse than he had expected, Macmillan seized the nettle and decided to remain in place. He resolved to announce his decision in Blackpool on the following Saturday.

During the night of 7 October, Macmillan suffered excruciating pain from an enlarged prostate gland and on the following day, fearing that his condition was debilitating, if not terminal, reached the decision that he must resign, a decision heartily endorsed by his doctors. In the morning he presided over a Cabinet meeting but made no reference to his condition or his decision. Later, however, he informed Rab and Home privately that he would be out of action for some months and might not lead the party into the next election.[25] The BBC that evening announced simply that the Prime Minister had been admitted to hospital and that Rab would take charge in his absence, with no comment or speculation on his long-term plans. Without warning, the battle for the succession began.

It was an unusual battle, both in that it was not easy to recognise the opposing forces and in that the battlefield was unconventional. Since the passage of the Peerage Act in July, moreover, the number of potential contenders had been increased by the possible appearance of Hailsham and Home as electable commoners. The Conservative conference, irreverently referred to by Rab as 'the annual seaside outing of the hangers and floggers',[26] was not typically the stage on which aspirant leaders paraded. The prospect of turning the conference into an American-style convention appalled the party faithful. Contenders chose their tactics carefully.

Rab, deputising for Macmillan at the conference, took a statesman-like approach. On 9 October, he arrived in Blackpool and moved into the suite reserved for the Prime Minister. From there he telephoned Macmillan to stress that the conference was a rally and absolutely

---

25 Rab apparently gained the impression that he was again to hold the fort, possibly for two or three months but that Macmillan had not taken the decision to retire. Howard, *RAB*, p. 310.

26 Ian Gilmour, 'Butler, Richard Austen', *Oxford Dictionary of National Biography*, para 28.

not a stage for a leadership election. This was a canny move. If Mac's resignation were announced during the conference it would favour Hailsham and Home, both of whom had standing outside the Parliamentary Party. If it were delayed until Parliament reassembled, Butler and Maudling, the two leading candidates in the Commons, would enjoy the advantage. Rab recognised this and was anxious to avoid a crude show of convention-style lobbying.

Hailsham had no such inhibitions. At the outset he publicised his candidacy – by announcing his intention to disclaim his peerage; by feeding his infant daughter in the foyer of the Imperial Hotel, populism that more discreet colleagues saw as vulgar; by allowing Randolph Churchill to distribute buttons emblazoned with a large 'Q'. Churchill worked the conference halls, enthusiastically pressing buttons into delegates' hands, not omitting to press one into Rab's. Rab calmly disposed of it in a litter bin.[27] By such shamelessly hucksterish electioneering Hailsham swiftly eliminated himself. From his hospital bed Mac shook his head in wonder and sorrow: 'Hogg had it in his hand but his undignified behaviour in Blackpool and the parading of baby and baby food finished him. Nor should he have talked of giving up his peerage and going into the House of Commons.'[28]

In June, Maudling had been the frontrunner. The *Daily Telegraph* carried a report of a poll of fifty MPs and calculated that, extended across the party, it would have resulted in Maudling's receiving 147 votes, against fifty-six for Hailsham, forty-two for Heath, twenty-eight for Rab, twenty-one for Powell and seven each for Home and Macleod.[29] Maudling was certainly the backbenchers' choice, the *Telegraph* maintained. 'In the inner circle of the 1922 Committee,' the article continued, 'it is reliably estimated that between 60 and 70 per cent of Conservative MPs are ready to support Mr Maudling.'[30] Maudling now kept a lower profile – so low that his speech to the conference was uninspiring enough to put him out of the running.

---

27 Fisher, *Harold Macmillan*, p. 235. Cited by Horne, *Harold Macmillan, 1957–1986*, p. 547.
28 Bodleian: MSS Macmillan, dep d51*.13–14. Diary entry for 14 October 1963.
29 *Daily Telegraph*, 20 June 1963.
30 This sentence is dutifully reported and not challenged by Philip Goodhart in his history of the 1922 Committee. *The 1922*, p. 187.

The recollection of Nigel Birch, MP for West Flintshire,[31] is that by the time of the conference Maudling was no longer a serious contender but was a candidate that many hoped would provide a satisfactory compromise solution between the opposing factions of Hailsham and Rab. 'Blackpool was unprecedented in the sense that a Prime Minister resigned in the middle of it,' he recalled:

> And unprecedented also in the sense that there was no certain front runner, which is rather unusual in our party. Now the frontrunners were Lord Hailsham and Rab Butler. But the trouble about them was that those who liked Rab didn't like Hailsham, and those who liked Hailsham didn't like Rab. So I thought when the conference opened that perhaps the best would be Maudling. Reggie Maudling had a very important speech, and he made rather a flop of it. His weakness is that he cannot lift a big audience and he couldn't lift them then.[32]

Rab's tactic of remaining above the fray, playing his 'mandarin, fastidious role',[33] was ineffective, for he suffered from one overwhelming defect: he lacked charisma, ever the competent, even brilliant administrator; never the inspiring leader. Harold Wilson wickedly described him as 'the churchwarden turned caretaker', adding with savage condescension, 'Poor Rab! He's got the worst liability you can have in politics, the look of a born loser.'[34] Rab had no image, no endearing sartorial eccentricity, no Churchillian cigar, no Gannex mackintosh. Physically, he had allowed himself to expand in recent years; he lacked the lean and hungry look of an ambitious conspirator. As a realistic alternative to the opposing figures of Maudling and Hailsham, he failed to inspire. In King Edward's Hospital for Officers, Macmillan heard the news from Blackpool and summoned Lord Home to his bedside.

There was no obvious candidate to succeed him, Macmillan told Home. Since no one was emerging, he was beginning to think that it might be

---

31 Later Lord Rhyl.
32 Thompson, *The Day Before Yesterday*, p. 218.
33 Horne, *Harold Macmillan 1957–1986*, p. 549.
34 Hansard, 20 December 1956, vol. 562, col. 1461.

necessary for Home to disclaim his peerage, to enter the Commons via a by-election at Kinross and West Perthshire and take over. He then drafted a message to the conference, indicating that he would not be able to attend nor would he lead the party at the next election. On the following morning, Home flew to Manchester and was driven to Blackpool, where he read the Prime Minister's message to the conference. On the same evening, Maudling and Home were interviewed by Robin Day. Home played his cards close to his chest, revealing nothing. As Home walked away, Maudling smiled and said to Day, 'Well, Alec is obviously going to run.'[35]

Over the following twenty-four hours, Home gained considerable ground without appearing to take the offensive or even to appear as a combatant. Taking a walk to escape the conference, Martin Redmayne and Selwyn Lloyd, who was strenuously promoting Home, encountered a gnarled pensioner, a committed Labour voter who told them that Home was the right man to lead Britain. This almost Shakespearean augury was followed by the appearance of Nigel Birch, who flew to Blackpool and put the word out that Home was willing to be drafted. With canny coyness, Home opened his speech in a Foreign Affairs debate, 'offering a prize to any newspaperman this morning who can find a clue in my speech that this is Lord Home's bid to take over the leadership of the Conservative Party'. That evening, Ian Trethowan of the BBC shrewdly observed that Home had 'now emerged as the man who may be drafted into the premiership between Mr Butler and Lord Hailsham'. The political correspondent of the *New York Times*, observing Home's demeanour and his sudden emergence as a candidate, chuckled and told Dennis Walters, a Hailsham lieutenant, that Home behaved throughout like an American compromise candidate at an American political convention.[36]

John Boyd-Carpenter, a strong Rab supporter who believed that 'Rab's hour had come at last',[37] dined on 9 October with 'Juby' Lancaster, the local MP, very much a member of the 'Inner Circle'. When the suc-

---

35 Thorpe, 'The October 1963 Conservative Party Conference', *Conservative History Journal*, vol. II, 2, Autumn 2013.
36 Ibid.
37 Boyd-Carpenter, *Way of Life*, p. 173.

cession was discussed, Lancaster was genuinely astonished to learn that Boyd-Carpenter and his wife were unaware that the matter had been settled in favour of Home. 'It's all arranged,' said Lancaster simply.[38]

The week began with the assumption that there were three serious candidates, a lineup neatly described by Sir Gerald Nabarro. 'Effectually,' he said, 'there are three probable contestants in the succession. Butler, donnish, dignified and dull; Maudling, matey, manly and moneywise; and Hailsham, ebullient, erudite and erratic. The mantle of the premiership should fall on Hailsham.'[39] That view was shared by Macmillan in the weeks before the conference, but by Saturday, the last day of the conference, there were two views: the view of the press, that Hailsham was gaining on Rab and that Home was a possible compromise candidate; and the view of Tory insiders that the succession was already stitched up in favour of Home. Those who adhered to the latter view saw no necessity to disabuse reporters of their now outdated opinions. Silence aids stealth and Macmillan had once more deployed stealth to maximum effect.

Central to Macmillan's stealth was the lead that he had given to the 1922 Committee. On 31 July, the day that the Peerage Act became law, Morrison approached Home and suggested that party unity might require him to stand. After initially rejecting the idea, Home accepted that it might be the case and responded that, in that case, he would make an appointment with his doctor for a check-up.[40]

Before Saturday's mass rally at the conference, the 1922 Executive Committee met at the Bona Vista Hotel to discuss the question which was by then dominating the conference. At the outset, two members still supported Maudling, despite his lacklustre speech of the previous day, and two supported Hailsham. The general tenor, according to the Committee's historian, was almost unanimous. 'The rest leaned heavily towards Lord Home … as the one candidate likely to promote party unity at a time when party unity was essential.' To consolidate Home's position, 'The Executive agreed on a form of consultation within the

38 Ibid., p. 174.
39 Randolph Churchill, *The Fight for the Tory Leadership*, pp. 102–3.
40 Goodhart, *The 1922*, p. 191.

party that would be phrased in a way most likely to accentuate Lord Home's strengths.' Members were asked for their first and second preferences, and whether they felt 'particularly opposed' to any of the four candidates. Home, it was assumed, would do particularly well on the second preference.[41]

The existence of several candidates made the succession vastly more complicated than in 1957 when it was a simple choice, in Salisbury's words, between 'Wab' and 'Hawold'. It had created 'a partial political vacuum'. Under Morrison's leadership, the 1922 Executive Committee had the confidence to step forward and fill it.[42] Within the 1922, however, there were dissenters. Macleod and Powell were lobbying for Rab, whose lukewarm response baffled his supporters. They were unaware of Morrison's informing him that 'the chaps won't have you'. Even as he went through the motions of acting as Macmillan's *locum*, of behaving like a future Prime Minister, Rab suspected that his chances of succeeding were doomed.

On Saturday 12 October, Rab lowered his standard and effectively left the battlefield. He and Mollie lunched with the Homes and during the meal Home remarked casually that he would be visiting his doctor during the following week as he had been approached 'about the possibility of … becoming Leader of the Conservative Party'. Despite the considerable speculation that had been taking place about Home's possible candidacy, the news came as a surprise to Rab. The morning newspapers had for the first time treated Home as a possible solution to a deadlock, but both newspapers and bookmakers had been erratic and wide of the mark. Now, for the first time, Rab confronted the reality of solid, embodied opposition to his succession. Unsurprisingly, his address to the general assembly of the conference was uninspiring, not at all the call to action expected from a leader.

'Butler fails to rouse Tories' was the theme common to many Sunday papers the following morning. Most now recognised that Home was 'emerging'. *The Observer* spoke of Home as 'the most likely successor to

---

41 Ibid., p. 195.
42 Ibid.

Mr Macmillan'. The *Sunday Telegraph* concluded that the race 'seemed to be narrowing to two men: the Earl of Home, the compromise and universally acceptable but reluctant candidate; or Viscount Hailsham, backed by powerful groups in the party hierarchy, but with some bitter opponents among some backbench MPs and ministers'. Whilst the *Sunday Express* still favoured Rab, it added that 'Lord Home is being widely tipped here tonight'. Most outspoken was the *News of the World*, which predicted that 'The Earl of Home can become Prime Minister if he wants to. Some Cabinet ministers, bitterly opposed to Lord Hailsham, are ready to back Lord Home as a "stop Quentin" move.' Rab had demonstrably slipped back in the race. Maudling had been eliminated. The amiable Home was a novelty that journalists were delighted to seize on. Rab was old news that they were happy to discard.[43]

The new week opened with the *Express* group remaining loyal to Rab. 'Butler's the Man', trumpeted Monday's headline. The *Daily Telegraph* and *The Guardian* also appeared to be returning to the conventional view of Rab as Macmillan's successor; each carried a picture of Rab, the country squire. Betting shops still treated him as the favourite, offering odds of 4–5 on him; Home remained an outsider at 100–8. Away from the frenzied plotting of Blackpool, more conventional opinions held sway.

The Prime Minister, however, wanted no conventional solution, no process by which Rab would automatically succeed him. On 14 October, he dictated a memorandum to Rab, recommending that the Cabinet, the other Conservative MPs, the Conservative peers and the constituency parties be sounded as to their choice for the leadership. By widening the field for the soundings he ensured that Rab's critics on the backbenches would have a say in the choice of leader. To have entrusted the matter solely to the Cabinet would probably have been to Rab's benefit. The Cabinet unanimously approved Macmillan's memorandum. Odds now lengthened to 5–4 against Rab and shortened to 6–1 against Home.

---

43 The Sunday papers on 13 October 1963 were full of speculation, often contradictory ideas within the same newspaper. In the light of how much momentum the pro-Home movement had gathered in forty-eight hours, it is remarkable that fewer journalists saw the writing on the wall.

Unsurprisingly, Rab was critical of Macmillan's suggested procedure for taking soundings. In a typical Rabism he described Lord Dilhorne's soundings as 'a large clumber spaniel sniffing the bottoms of the hedgerows'.[44] Yet, he still did not promote himself, prevented, possibly, by the public-school tradition of self-abnegation. Rab was popular with the general public, but fully aware of the opposition to his succession. It was simplest to behave as Macmillan's natural heir.

On Tuesday and Wednesday a steady stream of senior MPs visited Macmillan in hospital. Reporters strove to extract inside information, but little solid fact emerged from the party. Undaunted by rumour, the *Daily Express*, alone among the dailies, continued to maintain that Butler was the clear choice of the party. Rab, the paper claimed, had the support of 38 per cent; Hailsham had 27 per cent, and Home 10 per cent. The *Daily Telegraph* never quite abandoned Rab and now saw the contest as a face-off between him and Maudling.

On Thursday 17 October, the soundings were completed. The constituencies believed that animosity between pro-Butler and pro-Hailsham supporters was so great that only a compromise candidate such as Home could unite the party. The Cabinet was reported by Dilhorne as being preponderantly for Home;[45] backbenchers narrowly favoured him; in the Lords, pro-Home feeling was overwhelming.

At midnight, a group, including Maudling and Macleod, gathered at Enoch Powell's house. Determined to stop Home, they approached Macmillan to seek a two- or three-day delay in announcement of a successor. It was already too late. Hailsham also mounted a 'Stop Home' effort, meeting with Rab and Maudling at Rab's Treasury office on Friday. He urged Maudling to join him in saying that he would serve under Rab and proposed a meeting at 6.00 that evening with Home. Macmillan correctly assessed the Maudling and Macleod threat as a feint. 'Perhaps Butler realised that he was merely being used as a "stooge"', he reflected, 'and that the young men would desert him as soon as they had broken Lord Home.' Home must appeal to Rab's ambition, Macmillan believed. 'Pin

44 Sampson, *Macmillan: A Study in Ambiguity*, p. 233.
45 Macmillan recorded, 'In Cabinet ten for Home; three for Butler; four for Maudling; two for Hailsham.' Diary entry for 17 October 1963.

down Butler and Maudling,' he urged Home. If Rab took the Foreign Office and Maudling the Treasury, 'the game would be in his hands'.[46]

Macmillan, the succession now assured to his satisfaction, sent his resignation to the Queen, who visited him in hospital that morning. Begging leave not to give Her Majesty a direct recommendation for a successor, Mac read his memorandum written the previous evening, explaining the procedure followed for taking soundings, analysing the four leading candidates and detailing the findings of the four enquiries. 'The whole contest', Macmillan wrote,

> has been publicised as one between Mr Butler and Lord Hailsham … Nevertheless, it soon emerged that there were very strong opponents of each. There were those for instance who thought that Mr Butler with all his qualities was a dreary figure who would lead the party to inevitable defeat or to a worse defeat than was necessary … On the other side there were those who thought that Lord Hailsham, in spite of his great qualities, was somewhat unpredictable. This included the more old-fashioned people who are shocked at the gimmicks and inescapable advertising which play an important role in political life.[47]

After disposing of the other candidates, Macmillan's memorandum turned to Lord Home:

> When we come to the position of Lord Home it is noticeable that apart from being the first choice of very large groups … he seems to be the second choice of everybody. Nobody is against him … If your Majesty would make this choice you would incur no blame and would be held to have chosen a man generally supported by all the various sections to whom a minister must look for the support of his administration.

At 12.56 the Palace announced that the Queen had received the Earl of Home in audience and invited him to form an administration. When

---

46 Bodleian: MSS Macmillan, dep d51*. Diary entry for 18 October 1963.
47 Macmillan's 'Thursday Memorandum' to the Queen is reproduced in full in Thorpe, *Supermac*, pp. 621–6.

the 6.00 meeting with Hailsham, Butler and Maudling took place, Rab did not press himself forward as Hailsham had wished; Maudling did not rally to Rab. The meeting fell apart.

By the morning of Friday 18 October, the press finally recognised the drift of opinion. At opposite ends of the political spectrum, the *Daily Herald* and *The Times* continued to believe that Rab would ultimately finish on top – although the *Daily Herald* also ran an article titled 'Home May Ditch Rab'. The *Daily Telegraph*, *The Guardian* and the *Daily Mail* saw Home's election as a *fait accompli* and dutifully applauded it. It was left to *Private Eye* ten days later to announce:

> The death occurred on October 18th, 1963 of the Conservative Party. The Conservative Party had been suffering from severe Macmillan for the last seven years and although this had finally cleared up, its condition was so debilitated as a result that a sudden attack of Lord Home caused its immediate demise.

Private Eye expressed with characteristic disdain the shock caused by the 'emergence' of Home. The *Daily Telegraph* had published a Gallup poll the previous week that showed the public's belief that Rab would win by a small margin over Hailsham and Maudling. Most ominously, however, it also indicated that 50 per cent of the public had no preference. Political journalists tried to inject some ideology into the contest, portraying it as a choice between the 'old' Tory Party represented by Butler and the 'new' party characterised by Maudling. In truth, however, they were flogging a dead horse; the public cared little for the contest. Only when the outsider romped home did the issue become the subject of widespread debate. Macmillan had achieved his ends, orchestrating a surprising result – precisely the one he wanted – and, if *Private Eye* is to be believed, could relax 'happy in the knowledge of a lifetime's work well done, a country served and an old colleague stabbed ruthlessly in the back'.[48]

Enoch Powell later recalled Rab's inertia when, Powell believed, the leadership was within his grasp. In an interview for Thames Television

---

48 *Private Eye*, No. 49, 1 November 1963.

he referred to 'a well-known tag of Tacitus about a rather undistin-
guished Roman Emperor, that he'd have made a splendid Emperor
if he'd never been one'.[49] The opposite, he argued, applied to Rab,
who 'would have made a splendid Prime Minister if he'd ever been
one'. Then, in his typically academic, somewhat Jesuitical style, Powell
distinguished between 'the qualities of being a Prime Minister and
becoming a Prime Minister'. In order to become Prime Minister, he
continued,

> a man must be ready to shoot it out. He must be ready to see his rivals
> off, no matter how. He mustn't mind blood on the carpet. You see, Rab
> Butler had it in his hands. He could have had it for one shot and we
> … gave him the weapon. We said, 'You see, Rab, look at this, this is a
> revolver; we've loaded it for you, you don't have to worry about loading
> it.' … Rab said … 'Will he bleed?' We said, 'Well yes, I'm afraid when
> you shoot a man he does tend to bleed.' 'Oh,' said Rab, 'I don't know
> whether I like that, but tell me something else, will it go off with a
> bang?' We said, 'Well, Rab, I'm afraid we must admit you know, a gun
> does make rather a bang when it goes off.' Then he said, 'Well, thank you
> very much, I don't think I will. Do you mind?'[50]

Powell's analysis is ruthlessly accurate. How he moved from that picture of indecision to see Rab as a potentially excellent chief executive is, however, puzzling. The outburst of splenetic indignation when
Home 'emerged' was not so much that Rab had not become leader as
that Home had. Rab became as much a symbol of what might have
been as Home was a symbol of Old Etonian conspiracy. Powell was
too shrewd a politician to admit to simple indignation that Home had
become Prime Minister; that would not have been constructive. So
the negative 'Stop Home' movement, which failed, was reclothed as
outrage that Rab had been passed over and conspired against. Yet in

---

49 Powell's reference is to Tacitus, writing about the Emperor Galba, '*Omnium consensu capax
    imperii nisi imperasset.*' *Histories*, I, 49.
50 Interview with Enoch Powell, *The Day Before Yesterday*, p. 219.

his own words, criticising Rab's faint-heartedness, Powell raised the very question that Rab's father had raised four decades before.

That question is one that Rab, unsurprisingly, chose not to address when he recalled the events of October 1963. In an interview with Thames Television, he identified the Profumo affair as the event that caused a sea change within the Tory Party. 'It really was quite extraordinary', he recalled, 'how a gust of wind swept the Commons and the Conservative Party in favour of a younger leader.' John Morrison, the chairman of the 1922 Committee, indicated that a younger man was needed and that Maudling, a married man, would be preferable to Heath, a bachelor. 'I was told at the time', he continued, 'that my claims were obviously in the ring, but that I was too close to Macmillan, and too much regarded as being with the old regime, and they would really prefer it to go to a younger leader. It did lead eventually to the succession of Mr Heath, after a short period with Alec Douglas-Home. It might have been better, really, if they'd decided to go for the younger leader from the start.'[51]

Rab refers to this supposed desire for a younger leader several times but it is inconceivable that this was something new, brought on by the Profumo incident. If there was such feeling, was Rab not aware of it? Did he not understand the need to rejuvenate the party – something he himself had understood at the time of the Long Knives? Or is this rationalisation, effectively blaming his failure to succeed Macmillan on Macmillan's handling of the Profumo affair, which suggested complacency and stimulated a wish for a young leader? There were other stimuli, of course – a younger Leader of the Opposition in Harold Wilson; the excitement that surrounded John Kennedy, the youthful President of the United States. The invocation of the Profumo affair and Macmillan's handling of it is a useful barb to use against Macmillan, effectively suggesting that it was Rab's proximity to Macmillan that ruled him out of contention.

Rab correctly believed that Macmillan wanted to carry on.[52] It was only when his doctors told him that he would need an operation and

---

51 Thompson, *The Day Before Yesterday*, p. 217.
52 Ibid., p. 218.

that he could not continue that he reluctantly stepped down. Rab seems to have assumed that, if he simply carried on as normal, Mac's mantle would fall on him. Accordingly, he installed himself in the suite in Blackpool originally reserved for Macmillan and acted as *locum* Prime Minister. He assumed that he would enter the race by virtue of his position and that he needed to do little, if anything, to promote himself. Once Hailsham made his rash bid for prominence and the party, including Macmillan, turned against him, Rab surely felt that he was the frontrunner and that it was merely a question of beating Maudling, something that his experience would probably assure. The emergence of Home, what Lord Rhyl refers to as Macmillan's 'swapping peers in mid-stream', was unexpected; indeed, according to Rab, he learned about it from Home at lunchtime on Saturday, shortly before he was to make his speech. Quite correctly, he saw this as a serious threat and failed to impress his audience.

It has become accepted wisdom that, if Rab had refused to serve under Home, Home would not have been able to form a credible government. But that is far from certain. If Rab had led an insurgency against Home, he might have succeeded in bringing him down – and destroying the Tory Party at the same time. That was not Rab's *modus operandi*, as Powell observed. Home might well have been able to form a government without Rab, but not in the teeth of Rab's determined opposition. And if the party were radically split, with three or four key ministers refusing to serve, there loomed the very real possibility that the Queen would send for Wilson.[53] As it was, Home offered Rab the plum of the Foreign Office, the one post that, as Macmillan knew, would attract Rab; this overcame any resistance that Rab might have had. To fight to become PM in the teeth of obviously relentless opposition to him was not only out of character; it was certain to split the party; the leadership moreover was probably something that, at the age of almost sixty-one, despite his former ambition, he no longer wanted as passionately as before.

---

53 Wilson rejected that idea as the Tories had a large majority. Wilson, *The Governance of Britain* (London: Weidenfeld & Nicolson, 1976), p. 26.

Macmillan had recognised the importance of Home's offer. Whilst he did not want to see Rab at the Foreign Office – the post that he had denied him in 1957 – he realistically believed that it would be the price of Rab's support. 'It will be terrible for Rab,' he admitted. Lord Poole, the Party Chairman, brushed aside Macmillan's profession of regret with the astute comment that Rab already knew that he had no chance.[54]

Both were correct. It was 'terrible' for Rab and, as Poole dismissively judged, he never had a chance. There was no solid, substantial group of Rabbites, no rousing principle behind which supporters could rally. By not exerting himself he gained no support but he was able to make things less 'terrible' by leaving the question open. If the mantle fell on his shoulders, he would accept it willingly. If it did not, he had the fig-leaf of having preserved party unity to protect his self-esteem. Because he had not played and lost, he was always able to speculate what might have been, had he played. This may have been the kindest outcome.

For two days in Blackpool things seemed to be moving steadily in Rab's direction: Hailsham eliminated himself by vulgar exuberance; Maudling disappointed his audience with a too-technical speech. Then, unexpectedly, Macmillan, seeing the course that events were taking, promoted Home, adding a question to the survey of Members' preferences. Once Home had the gloss of the official compromise candidate, Rab's chances steadily, irretrievably evaporated.

Macmillan was determined to stop Rab from becoming Prime Minister.[55] Harold Wilson wrote bluntly that Macmillan 'seemed markedly allergic to the idea of being succeeded by Mr Butler and took some part in ensuring that he was not'.[56] But it involves a long logical leap to argue that Macmillan acted out of pure malice, that he 'ruthlessly stabbed Rab in the back'. Mollie was quite prepared to make that leap; she 'vowed privately never to speak to Harold Macmillan again'.[57]

---

54 Thorpe, *Supermac*, p. 577.
55 From Macmillan's determination that Rab should not succeed him has arisen the allegation that he 'fixed' the process of consultation. This is not the case; the soundings taken were thorough and correct. It was the anti-Rab feeling, contrasted with the almost universal acceptance of Home, that determined the outcome.
56 Wilson, *The Governance of Britain*, p. 41.
57 Mollie Butler, *August and Rab*, pp. 82–3.

Macmillan consistently asserts that Rab simply didn't want the top job enough – indeed, that he feared it. George Brown, another frustrated aspirant for Downing Street, agreed with Macmillan's analysis.[58] Rab's own actions can only be fully explained in that light. A loyal deputy is not always the right choice as successor.

Years later, over a glass of whisky at Trinity College, Cambridge, Rab asked John Boyd-Carpenter, 'Do you think that if I had stood firm in 1963 I would have been Prime Minister?' When Boyd-Carpenter replied in the affirmative, Rab said with a sigh, 'I think so too.'[59]

---

58 George Brown, *In My Way* (London: Victor Gollancz, 1971), p. 60.
59 Boyd-Carpenter, *Way of Life*, pp. 178–9.

CHAPTER 19

FOREIGN SECRETARY, 1963–64

Rab's question to Boyd-Carpenter amounted to wondering whether, if he had refused to serve, he would have succeeded in blocking Home's accession. Many Tories feared that he would do just that, and divide the party by 'standing firm'. Predictably, Rab did nothing of the kind, for which he received praise from his old colleague Harold Balfour, who wrote, 'I think your bearing and decision in the circumstances are those of a great, unselfish and generous man.'[1] From Sir Sydney Roberts, former Master of Pembroke, Cambridge, came a touching reminiscence:

> I wonder whether you remember an evening in the Old Library about 40 years ago when, as Secretary of the French Society, you cajoled me into proposing a motion which ran something like, '*Que la politique est néfaste*'.[2] I have been acutely reminded of it in the last few days and deplore the way in which you have been treated. Of course I know that your magnanimity will triumph over any disappointment.[3]

As in 1957, tributes and compliments flowed. Throughout all the letters there is a recurrence of expressions like 'no justice in what has happened', 'great dignity', 'cruelly used by fortune', and demonstrably, as one letter among many expressed it, 'you have a tremendous following

---

1   Trinity: Butler Papers, RAB, B32.3.18. Balfour and Rab were two of the signatories to the letter to *The Times* of 28 May 1930, but they had drifted apart since 1945.
2   'How politics is evil!'
3   Trinity: Butler Papers, RAB, B32.3.20.

of ordinary, decent people'. 'No one without your high sense of duty',
wrote one constituent, 'could have faced with such outward equanimity the final result.' Paul Channon, son of Rab's friend Chips, took a
pragmatic view. Assuming that Rab's ambitions for Downing Street
were finally thwarted, he suggested that Rab accept a peerage and
become Foreign Secretary in the House of Lords. That he accepted
the Foreign Office and remained in the Commons suggests that even
then he had hopes that Home might be forced out and that he still had
the slimmest chance of replacing him.[4]

Between Rab and Douglas-Home there was studied politeness.
Rab wrote him a letter that was never sent, pledging his full support.[5]
Douglas-Home, ever the gentleman, wrote Rab a note on 22 October, regretting that events had caused him 'to hurt even in the tiniest
degree any one of my friends'. He expressed deep gratitude for Rab's
loyalty and 'inestimable admiration for his courage'.[6] After days of
frantic manoeuvre the *Sunday Times* delivered its post-mortem judgement on the week's events. One comment in particular seemed to sum
up backbenchers' feelings. 'Nigel Birch's dislike of the PM', the article
stated, 'was equalled only by his distrust of Butler.'[7]

In 1957, after his initial disappointment at Macmillan's preferment,
the office he most coveted had been the Foreign Office. Nearly seven
years later, his appointment to that post was ambiguous. It was the
job he had desperately wanted Macmillan to offer him; on the other
hand, by 1963–64 it was cold comfort, a consolation award rather than
a glittering prize seized on the way to the top.

Not unnaturally, this failed to excite him as he entered what he
suspected would be his last year in government. He foresaw that the
Tories led by Douglas-Home would lose the next election, due to be
held in 1964. Gaitskell died in January 1963 and was replaced by Harold
Wilson. There would, Rab was certain, be renewed calls for a younger

---

4   Trinity: Butler Papers, RAB, G40.106.
5   Trinity: Butler Papers, RAB, G40.124.
6   Trinity: Butler Papers, RAB, G40.127.
7   *Sunday Times*, 20 October 1963.

Tory Leader – Maudling, Heath or Macleod[8] – to counteract Wilson's image of youthful dynamism. Rab was decidedly not of the future but looked to the past, endlessly rehashing the 1963 leadership contest, seeking reassurance that he had been right not to split the party.[9]

That commitment to party unity did not, however, prevent him from uttering a typical Rabism when he seconded Douglas-Home as party leader in November. 'Sir Alec has the great advantage of looking and being ageless', he said, 'and I am quite certain that he will make a direct appeal to the young, and that we shall in fact be a government young in heart under his leadership.'[10] Considering that, a mere ten days before, *Private Eye* had published its obituary of the Tory Party, featuring a caricature of Douglas-Home as a death head,[11] the suggestion that he appealed to the young was either absurd or teasingly wicked.

In contrast to 1951, when, as the incoming Chancellor of the Exchequer, he had eschewed his official residence at 11 Downing Street in favour of his and Sydney's house in Smith Square, he moved into the Foreign Secretary's official home as soon as possible. Rab was too devoted a public servant to abuse the privileges of office but there are recurring hints during the year that he served Douglas-Home that one attraction of the Foreign Office was that its benefits appealed greatly to Mollie. Overseas travel, the pomp of a grand residence, and, above all, the challenge of redecorating and furnishing it to her taste – these were massively attractive to her, as her own memoir makes clear.[12]

Rab was punctilious, dedicated to his 'boxes', a model of efficiency. But by the time he acquired the post that he had coveted for almost a decade, his enthusiasm for the job was spent. Nicholas Henderson, his Private Secretary at the Foreign Office, describes Rab as an 'addict' to his boxes, yet abidingly indecisive. That apparent indecision, however,

---

8   In 1963, Macleod was still a contender. When Randolph Churchill published *The Fight for the Tory Leadership* and Macleod responded with his account of the 1963 struggle in *The Spectator* (on 17 January 1964) he alienated himself permanently from the 'Magic Circle' whom he derided.

9   Howard, *RAB*, p. 324. The source was an interview between Anthony Howard and Lord Carrington, Minister without Portfolio at the Foreign Office, on 1 June 1981.

10   *The Times*, 12 November 1963.

11   In its issue of 1 November 1963.

12   Mollie Butler, *August and Rab*, pp. 86–92.

Henderson describes as the result of a positive process of deciding. Rab, sensing that an issue might be explosive, would avoid taking a definitive position. He compared himself to Pierre Bezukhof in *War and Peace*; his critics described his methods as '*reculer pour mieux reculer*'.[13]

On minor issues he wavered endlessly. Henderson describes him asking several times if he needed to go to a National Day cocktail party at the Moroccan Embassy. Henderson reassured him that he need not attend. Rab asked again as he left the Foreign Office, even telephoned Henderson from home to be certain. The following morning, when Henderson suggested that he write to the Moroccan Ambassador to apologise for his unavoidable absence, Rab said simply, 'Oh, I went.'[14]

Rab had acquired a reputation for indecisiveness early in his spell at the Treasury. Yet he had ultimately made weighty choices to implement policy. As First Secretary of State he had handled the dismemberment of the Central African Federation, a task whose completion demonstrated his diplomatic ability. Yet, in the last year of his lifetime in government, holding the office most congruent with his talents, he had less taste for executive action. Henderson draws a picture of Rab at his most elliptical, enjoying the bafflement of officials and reporters when he let slip a deliberate indiscretion or *non sequitur*.

Towards the Prime Minister he was never disloyal, but was frequently condescending, commenting that 'Alec [was] not bad' at chairing a meeting.[15] It is as if at the end of his political career he decided to become a caricature of himself, as if he chose insouciance and impenetrability as his shield against showing his feelings or his disappointment. It was an unfortunate posture for, as Rab retreated behind the protection of his *bons mots*, he increasingly alienated himself from colleagues. His posture of being 'a good loser' was, observers suspected, a convenient mask that could be disposed of at any time. Rab had not done anything that might have divided the party in 1963, yet his commitment to the new Cabinet seemed lukewarm. He thought

---

13 Henderson, *Inside the Private Office* (Chicago: Academy Chicago, 1987), pp. 72–4. The expression *reculer pour mieux sauter* (to withdraw, the better to advance) was adapted for Rab to mean 'to withdraw, the better to withdraw'.

14 Ibid., p. 73.

15 Ibid., p. 80.

Douglas-Home unqualified intellectually to be Prime Minister; while he never stated that publicly, it was as though that assumption were a known fact, shared with his audience. Rab's besetting sin of intellectual arrogance marred his record of loyalty in the year he served Home.

When President John Kennedy was assassinated in Dallas on 22 November, Rab said at the next Cabinet meeting that 'Our forward plans must inevitably be based on the assumption that United States leadership would be less positive than hitherto.'[16] Rab never quite accepted that Lyndon Johnson belonged in the White House. When he and Mollie travelled to Washington with the Douglas-Homes in February 1964, Mollie, seated next to LBJ at a White House dinner, 'was inundated with signatures from the President on every scrap of paper that he could lay his hands on, place cards, menus etc.'.[17] It is easy to imagine how Rab's lip curled at Johnson's behaviour and how much pleasure it later gave him to recall the incident. Johnson seemed to Rab the prime example of the vulgar Texas politician, an image enhanced by an incident when Rab returned to Washington in April.

Johnson was infuriated by Britain's decision to sell Leyland buses to Cuba. Rab maintained somewhat disingenuously that buses were not strategic weapons and the sale should not be of concern to the United States. The President maintained his position that Britain should boycott Cuba and cancel the order. Reaching in his pocket, he brandished a large wad of dollars. If Britain was so hard up that she needed to trade with Cuba, then Rab should cancel the order and send the bill to LBJ at his ranch in Texas. He would pay for the cancelled order himself.[18] Once again, it is easy to imagine how Rab retold this anecdote and equally easy to guess how Johnson felt toward the British Foreign Secretary.

On 17 January 1964, *The Spectator* published an article by Iain Macleod on the leadership crisis. Randolph Churchill had stated in his book *The Fight for the Tory Leadership*, a work cravenly sympathetic to

16 TNA: PREM 11/4408, PM to Ormsby-Gore, 2 December 1963.
17 Mollie Butler, *August and Rab*, p. 88. Mollie calmly put them all in her handbag as if it were the most natural thing in the world to be showered with signed mementos.
18 TNA: PREM 11/4789, Rab to PM, 29 April 1964.

Macmillan, that 'Macmillan did all that he could during his seven years as Prime Minister to advance the fortunes of Butler.' Macleod flatly contradicted this statement, maintaining that the very opposite was Macmillan's purpose. This, Macleod argues, explained Macmillan's actions – why he put the three young likelies – Maudling, Heath and Macleod (whom in Vatican parlance he termed *papabile*)[19] – into very responsible positions to see what emerged; why, rather than turn to Butler, he began to promote Hailsham.

Macleod recalled how, after the Blackpool conference, he returned to London and how he and Maudling both assumed that the mantle would fall on Rab. When Macleod joined Reggie and Beryl Maudling for lunch, Rab was mentioned often, Hailsham little, Home not at all. 'It is some measure of the tightness of the Magic Circle', Macleod wrote acidly, 'that neither the Chancellor of the Exchequer nor the Leader of the House of Commons had any inkling of what was happening.' In Macleod's view, the decisive roles were played by Macmillan and Redmayne. 'I am certain', he conceded, 'that they acted at each stage in the interests as they saw it of the sort of Tory Party in which they believe. So did I.'[20]

In an analysis of Macleod's article, *The Guardian* commented that 'There was real support for Sir Alec Douglas Home throughout the Tory Party but for the first time since Bonar Law the party is being led from the right.' To have ignored Rab as a potential Prime Minister demonstrated that the Tories could not find a leader in the House of Commons and, as a consequence, 'gravely weakened the House of Lords'.[21] Many Tories, according to Macleod, shared Macmillan's view 'that Butler had not in him the steel that makes a Prime Minister nor the inspiration that a leader needs to pull his party through a fierce general election'. Macleod disagreed with that analysis but, on his own admission, had accepted the possibility of Hailsham succeeding

---

19 The word 'papabile' is used by Vatican watchers to describe cardinals who, in their opinion, might become the unanimous choice for the Papacy.
20 *The Spectator*, 17 January 1964; Trinity: Butler Papers, RAB, G43.2.
21 Trinity: Butler Papers, RAB, L93.

Macmillan. Once again, we can see not so much a pro-Butler faction as a determination to stop Home.

Macleod's article reopened the controversy over the leadership that had temporarily been closed – by Rab who wearily confessed to reporters, 'Well, it is something to have been almost Prime Minister.' The renewed discussion of the events of Blackpool further harmed Rab, as they enhanced the image of a losing candidate, a man twice passed over. Rab, already prone to rehash the events of 1963 and wonder aloud whether he had done the sensible thing, was encouraged to keep the issue alive. This finally consigned him to the ranks of the superannuated, as Alec Douglas-Home, condemned as being of the old guard, a postscript to the Edwardian era, was, in fact, seven months younger than Rab.

It gave him a certain satisfaction to speak French to the French Minister of Foreign Affairs, Couve de Murville, at their meeting in The Hague – an initiative that surprised Couve[22] and delighted the *Daily Mirror*, which ran a headline 'Friends Again – Thanks to Rab'.[23] He was gratified to learn from Dean Rusk that, in spite of Johnson's dismissive attitude towards Britain, the special relationship was still valued at the State Department. He describes as his 'most ambitious objective' the attempt to 'explore world issues with the Soviet Union'.[24]

Despite his stated opinion that British Prime Ministers, especially Churchill and Macmillan, had been too concerned with achieving dramatic results in negotiations with the Kremlin, Rab too saw his visit to Moscow as an opportunity to put his own stamp on his time in office – a tenure which, as he feared and predicted, was to last a brief year. Since 1945, and more urgently since Suez, definition of Britain's global role was at the centre of foreign policy. Redefining the wartime alliance of Britain, the USA and the USSR was an elusive fantasy that Churchill, Macmillan and Eden failed to realise. Despite his veneer of realism, Rab suffered from similar 'objectives ... still dancing as

---

22 Butler, *The Art of the Possible*, pp. 252–3.
23 *Daily Mirror*, 25 October 1963.
24 Butler, *The Art of the Possible*, pp. 257–60.

images on the horizon'.[25] In terms of practical politics, however, he was fully aware that the Soviet leaders regarded Home's ministers as a 'lame-duck' government and were already preparing themselves for doing business with Wilson and his team. That recognition increased his sense of detachment.

From 26 April to 7 May, Rab, accompanied by Mollie, took the only long trip undertaken during the year. After the stay in Washington – and the confrontation with the President over selling buses to Cuba – the party continued to Hawaii, Tokyo and, after much vacillation and discussion, to Manila. It was a remarkable trip, principally because its purpose was far from clear. Again, there is the temptation to wonder if Mollie's love of foreign travel played a part in the justification for the excursion.

There was an absurd sequel. In Tokyo, Rab bought a camera and, on a routine visit to the Foreign Office, a Customs official established that duty was owed and submitted to Rab a demand for £7 4s 6d (£7.22 ½p). This enraged Rab who proposed to take the matter up with the Chancellor. His staff implored him simply to pay the demand and let the matter die; fortunately wisdom prevailed and Rab sent off a cheque in payment.[26]

Whilst relations between Douglas-Home and Rab remained perfectly cordial and professionally correct, there was no personal affection between the two. It is inconceivable that the Prime Minister was unaware of Rab's casual indiscretions, his condescending manner of loyalty. In October 1963, Rab was a valuable, even perhaps necessary, ally. That shelf-life was short, however, and by early in 1964 Douglas-Home had consolidated his position and made dispositions for a younger front bench, whether or not the Tories won the 1964 election. Rab, while not sulking in his tent like Achilles, was doing little to endear himself to his Cabinet colleagues. When he returned from the Washington–Tokyo–Manila trip, Paul Channon warned him of plots to erode his sphere of influence. By August, *Newsweek* predicted that

25 Rab's expression for the frustration of his foreign policy goals – *The Art of the Possible*, p. 260.
26 Trinity: Butler Papers, RAB, E.20.1.

Rab would have no place in a future Conservative Cabinet[27] and that he would take an academic post – an accurate prediction as, according to Anthony Howard, Douglas-Home had already promised Christopher Soames the Foreign Office if the Tories won the election.[28] Rab promptly denied any intention to leave politics, saying that there was 'absolutely no truth' in the *Newsweek* story.[29]

Yet Rab, the senior party strategist, ceased to exist when Home awarded to Heath the chair of the Advisory Committee on Policy, a post that Rab had held since 1945. Together with his removal from the Conservative Research Department, this was symptomatic of Rab's eclipse. As his power and influence contracted, so did his interest in and, consequently, his value to the Tory Party. Not only did he allow the waters to close over him after October 1963; he seemed almost to encourage it. He would do what could reasonably be expected of him – and he would take pleasure in the reduction of those expectations. He took little part in day-to-day issues and no part at all in the debate over Retail Price Maintenance (RPM) that dominated the summer.

As Nicholas Henderson recalled, his last weeks at the Foreign Office were sad.[30] He urged that the 1964 election be delayed as long as possible but otherwise was scarcely involved in strategy. There is, however, a certain 'chicken and egg' quality to the relationship of lack of interest and lack of employment by the party. This was accentuated when Rab, in his one appearance at a Tory press conference, spoke of 'a strong undercurrent of Labour',[31] for which he was accused of defeatism.[32] The manifesto and the thrust of the campaign owed little to him – and he appears not to have been unhappy with that distance. He was quoted in news bulletins only seven times, as against Home (66), Maudling (38), Hogg (25) and Wilson (125).[33]

Late in the day, however, Rab again succeeded in infuriating

---

27 *Newsweek*, 24 August 1964.
28 Howard, *RAB*, p. 333. The source is a conversation between Soames and Howard on 19 June 1985.
29 *The Times*, 19 August 1964.
30 Henderson, *Inside the Private Office*, p. 84.
31 *The Times*, 5 October 1964.
32 Butler and King, *The British General Election of 1964* (New York: Macmillan, 1965), p. 118.
33 Ibid., p. 170.

colleagues by a classic piece of indiscretion – described by Randolph Churchill as 'his own death-wish and death warrant'.[34] To suggest, a week before polling day, that support for the Tories was ebbing – a trend that would cost them the election – was the ultimate sin in the eyes of Central Office.

Travelling to Darlington, where he was to make two speeches, Rab was interviewed by George Gale of the *Daily Express*. According to the article published the following day,[35] he favoured Gale with several Rabisms, few of which had any lasting impact. Less dismissable, however, was the comment that 'We're running neck and neck. I'll be very surprised if there's much in it – say twenty seats either way. But things might start slipping in the last few days.' As always, there was an effort to find some wisdom, the deeper understanding that Rab possessed, that caused him to anticipate by twenty-four hours what the newspapers were going to say. Ever subtle Rab, his supporters argued, had blunted the impact of an adverse story.[36]

Home and his colleagues were less inclined to credit Rab with subtlety and regarded it as, at best, foolishness; at worst, disloyalty. David Ormsby-Gore wrote to Douglas-Home after the Tories suffered a narrow defeat:[37] 'How tantalising a result. So near and yet so far. Almost anything could have tipped the balance, Khrushchev's removal twelve hours earlier, China's nuclear explosion thirty-six hours earlier or just Rab keeping his mouth shut for once.'[38]

Characteristically, Douglas-Home telephoned Rab a few days after the story appeared, telling him 'not to bother about that stupid *Express* story. It couldn't have mattered less.'[39] That Rab had also told Gale that

---

34 *Evening Standard*, 10 October 1964.

35 *Daily Express*, 9 October 1964.

36 Rab did say some remarkably inexplicable things at this stage in his career. During a visit to Moscow he asked the rector of Moscow University if the university received financial assistance from the state. In the Soviet system, the rector replied, the state met all expenses. Rab's supporters in the press praised him for his subtlety, implying that the rector had walked into a trap cunningly set by Rab. The equally improbable notion that he predicted a close race with support for the Tories slipping is in the same manner of apologia.

37 The Labour Party was elected with an overall majority of four seats.

38 Hirsel Archive, Ormsby-Gore to PM, 16 October 1964. Cited by Thorpe, *Alec Douglas-Home* (London: Sinclair-Stevenson, 1996), p. 369.

39 Henderson, *Inside the Private Office*, p. 84.

Douglas-Home found Heath 'a bore' was, perhaps, more damaging. Heath, future Tory leader and Prime Minister, was not a man to forget insults. His biographer noted with understatement, 'He afterwards explained that he had only meant that Home was fed up with RPM; but the unflattering implication lingered.'[40]

Rab shared with Douglas-Home a love of shooting; both were keen sportsmen and good shots; their wives were good friends. Yet there was always a distance between the two men, a distance that Douglas-Home made no moves to close once he became Prime Minister. Rab's influence may have been on the wane, but Douglas-Home kept him at a respectful distance. Rab might, just might, be a rallying point for anti-Home forces; Macleod's article had demonstrated the depth of resistance to 'old' Tory values.

Like Macmillan before him, therefore, Douglas-Home tempted Rab to move to the upper house, holding out an earldom as incentive. This was a remarkable offer for a man who had not been Prime Minister; Rab was more than a twice-defeated candidate for party leader; he was the architect of the thirteen years of Tory rule that had just ended. Douglas-Home, his close colleague since the 1930s, recognised this and understood Rab's frustrated chafing at his position in 1964. Yet Rab refused the offer. Thanking Douglas-Home, he wrote a letter of simple yet puzzling logic:

> I feel … that this is not the time to leave the Commons. If it was an expanding moment of my career, I might take a different line, but there are so many difficulties ahead that I think they ought to be faced and that I should not, so to speak, retire. I am very attracted by the idea of helping you over the foreign scene, and this will be a great personal pleasure to me.[41]

The refusal embarrassed Home who, confident that his offer would be accepted, had planned the future of the Tories without significant

---

40 Campbell, *Edward Heath*, p. 164.
41 Trinity: Butler Papers, RAB, G42.

participation from Rab. The party was in disarray, perhaps more serious than in 1945, but Rab was 'too old to pull any clever ideas out of
his hat to rescue them'.[42] This was an open secret with the press, a
fact made clear when *The Times* carried a story headlined 'Sir Michael
Fraser to be Deputy Chairman of the Tory Party' with the sub-head,
'Speculation over Mr Butler's Future Role'.[43]

Within the party there was no speculation. The message was clear:
younger men would make the running; Rab's position as Deputy
Leader no longer existed. In December, in a speech that turned out
to be his final significant address in the Commons, he had a distinctly
outdated look, opening with a reminiscence of Ernest Bevin's *tours
d'horizon* in the 1945–51 Labour government. It was ill judged to challenge Wilson over his recent visit to Washington, asserting, 'I will …
be opening the foreign affairs debate as I used to in the old days.'[44]

One week later, the Commons adjourned for the Christmas recess,
regathering on 19 January 1965. Apart from a question on 21 December
concerning British subjects in Congo,[45] his nostalgic speech of five
days before marked his swansong. Despite his professed determination
to carry on, he finally bowed to the obvious and the inevitable.

By January, his situation had changed. Douglas-Home had not succeeded in his attempt to move Rab gracefully from the Commons and
it was left to his successor to lure Rab definitively from the front line
of politics.

---

42 Proudfoot, *British Politics and Government 1951–1970* (London: Faber & Faber, 1974), p. 173.
43 *The Times*, 23 October 1964.
44 Hansard, 16 December 1964, vol. 704, col. 401.
45 Hansard, 21 December 1964, vol. 704, col, 860.

CHAPTER 20

CAMBRIDGE AND AFTER, 1965–82

Harold Wilson famously claimed after Labour's narrow victory in 1964 that, if the Tories had been led by Rab, they might well have won. With Douglas-Home's accession, Rab's influence and interest may have declined, but the new Prime Minister was well aware of his popularity with the electorate. Wilson did not see Rab as an active threat; merely his presence in the Commons was a potential irritant that he would be better off without. The new Prime Minister, moreover, felt that Rab had been treated disgracefully by the Tories. 'Looking for a scapegoat,' he later wrote, 'they settled on him, using a report of an apparently injudicious conversation between him and a *Daily Express* journalist.'[1]

On 23 December, when Rab, Mollie and the family were about to head up to Mull for Christmas and the New Year, Mollie fielded a phone call from 10 Downing Street; the Prime Minister was trying to reach Mr Butler. Since Rab was at a shoot in Essex and would not be meeting Mollie until later that evening at King's Cross, Mollie arranged for a car to meet Rab from his train at Liverpool Street and take him to Downing Street. Naturally, she was agog to know what the Prime Minister wanted that occasioned urgent phone calls.

Her curiosity was satisfied when Rab appeared at Smith Square, 'filling the front door in his brown travelling overcoat and leading

---

1 Wilson, *The Labour Government 1964–1971: A Personal Record* (Boston, MA: Little, Brown, 1971), pp. 75–6.

Bella, our much loved Dandie Dinmont'.[2] Rab, brow furrowed, baffled and conflicted *à la* Rab, told her that Wilson proposed to recommend to the Queen that he become Master of Trinity College, Cambridge. That the post was a Crown Appointment meant that the Queen herself would be a co-agent in the departure of Rab from the House of Commons – for Wilson offered a life barony to accompany the appointment.

If Lord Home had touched a nerve in Rab's body with his offer of the Foreign Office in 1963, how much greater a stirring of the emotions must have occurred a year later when the finest, grandest, richest, most prestigious and most visible of all Oxford and Cambridge colleges should have fallen, ripe and luscious, into his lap? The propitious retirement of Lord Adrian, the current Master, the opportunity to abandon the shadowing of foreign policy, the facile congruence of all Rab's non-political ambition into a simple offer – what could possibly impede his acceptance?

Rab asked the advice of many colleagues, torn between the plum of academic appointments and the irreversible reality that to accept would be to end his political career. He would never again have red boxes to peruse, top secret memoranda that came to him by right. From consummate insider he would overnight become an observer from a distant viewpoint. After nearly forty years in the Commons, it was a complex decision.

Lord Dilhorne suggested to Rab that he should accept Wilson's offer of a peerage as 'it may be years before you get another opportunity of doing so'. Dilhorne commented that 'Wilson is far cleverer and more able than Attlee'. In other words, there might be a long period of the Socialists in power and Rab should grab the peerage while he could.[3] The common tenor of advice from friends was that Trinity would bring 'peace of mind after all your travails'. Archbishop Fisher wrote that it would be a welcome 'port after stormy seas'.[4]

Yet it was not until mid-January that Rab told Wilson of his

---

2   Mollie Butler, *August and Rab*, p. 93.
3   Trinity: Butler Papers, RAB, B35.1.
4   Trinity: Butler Papers, RAB, B35.2.22.

willingness to accept the offer, if it were made. On 25 January, the Prime Minister wrote:

> After very careful thought I have come to the conclusion that if you should be willing for me to do so, I should submit your name to the Queen for this appointment ... It would give me much pleasure also if you will allow me to submit your name to Her Majesty for a Life Peerage.

On the same day, Rab replied to Wilson, accepting both offers.[5] The Queen signified her approval and Rab was appointed to succeed Lord Adrian when he retired on 30 June.[6] The academic post was caviare to a descendant of Montagu Butler. The title also had a topical significance. Home had offered him an earldom, whose acceptance would have been a reward for his services to the Tories in government. The *Yorkshire Post* suggested that he might have been awarded a viscountcy but for the new Labour government's opposition to any more hereditary honours.[7] The life barony, lower down the scale of precedence, was acceptable to Rab as it was offered by a Labour Prime Minister for a task he was about to undertake. The title was not a political payoff nor a golden handshake to ensure his departure; it reflected the importance of his new appointment.

On 6 February 1965, *The Economist* commented astutely, if somewhat obliquely:

> Mr Butler thus returns to Trinity as perhaps the only man in history who is generally blamed for not quite becoming Britain's Prime Minister. Some contemporaries will say that is the final condemnation of the present-day Tory Party, that they could not quite accept this man as their leader. But historians will pronounce that without him, during these last extraordinary two decades, it would not have been natural for so large a

5   Trinity: Butler Papers, RAB, C34.7.
6   Trinity: Butler Papers, RAB, C34.9.
7   *Yorkshire Post*, 1 February 1965. Trinity: Butler Papers, RAB, C35.2.1.

part of the decisive middle section of intelligent opinion to associate the concept of progress with a party which calls itself Conservative.[8]

In the same week, the *Glasgow Herald* summed up Rab's departure, commenting equally astutely that 'It is not the true consummation of his long and brilliant career in politics and his unequalled work for the Conservative Party ... The fairest judgement may be that he contributed to his own bad luck.' And on the same day, on 1 February 1965, the *Daily Express* ran an article, coining for the first time the tag that would thereafter attach to Rab – 'The Best Prime Minister We Never Had'.[9] This was a view that *The Guardian* did not share. Peering into what might have been, their correspondent aired the more realistic but no less sympathetic assessment that Rab could have declined to serve under Home and that might have brought Home down, but 'such a ruthless Butler would not have been the true Butler. And the true Butler, with his reputation for gently barbed ambiguity, may well be better suited to academic retirement than to Downing Street.'[10]

An unusual ally in this view was the *Daily Mirror*, which spoke no less than the truth: 'His academic ancestry ... and his own sparkling performance at Cambridge did him no good in the Tory Party – which is always suspicious of brains and especially of chaps who are "too clever by half".'[11]

Rab, the article concluded, had the wisdom of a serpent but no fire in his belly. He was 'happy to be out'; Mollie was 'delighted at his decision to quit politics'.[12] In an ending to a political career, Rab went from Whitehall to the Fens with greatly less blood spilt than is normal in such exits from centre stage. Yet, if Rab felt he was leaving an arena of savage ambition for the calm of academe, he reckoned without the politics of the Senior Common Room.

Sometime undergraduate at Pembroke and, forty years before, a Fellow of Corpus Christi, Rab had presumed to allow his name to be

---

8 Trinity: Butler Papers, RAB, C35.3.
9 Trinity: Butler Papers, RAB, C35.4.
10 *The Guardian*, 1 May 1965; Trinity: Butler Papers, RAB, C35.6.1.
11 *Daily Mirror*, 1 February 1965; Trinity: Butler Papers, RAB, C35.8.
12 *Daily Sketch* and *Evening Standard*, 2 February 1965; Trinity: Butler Papers, RAB, C35.14.

presented to the Queen as a prospective appointee to the Mastership of a college to which he did not belong. Why, certain Trinity Fellows asked, should the Mastership of their college be offered as token amends for a displaced Foreign Secretary?[13] 'We're not here to cushion the fall of failing politicians,' commented one Fellow. 'That's not what the Mastership is for.'[14] Was it really the case that Her Majesty would offer the Mastership to a man from a lesser college? Lord Adrian was a distinguished physiologist; Lady Adrian was a widely respected philanthropist. Rab and Mollie had, it might generously be conceded, acquired some capital, but it was in an entirely different currency, a coinage that had no market at Trinity.

In 1951, C. P. Snow published *The Masters*, a novel whose subject is the election of the Master in a Cambridge college. In 1963, a stage version of the story began an eight-month run at the Savoy Theatre. The process and the political issues in a Master's appointment were, therefore, no longer arcane but were the stuff of popular discussion. Rab's appointment was highly topical. Rarely can such an appointment have been the subject of so much public opinion and general approval. Like it or not, the Fellows of Trinity had a much loved celebrity on his way to the Master's Lodge.

According to Patrick Duff, the Vice-Master, interviewed by Anthony Howard, Downing Street had been less than tactful in its handling of the appointment. There had been no more than cursory sounding of Trinity dons and inadequate dialogue leading up to the appointment. The Vice-Master only heard the identity of the new Master from the Prime Minister's office after reading the news in that morning's newspapers.[15] Soon enough, however, the general mood in Trinity became one of acceptance; the feeling that 'we are lucky to have you here' prevailed[16] as Fellows shed their parochial objections in the face of unparalleled public approval of Rab's return to Cambridge. He received over a thousand letters of congratulation from all walks of British life. All approved of his taking the Mastership and saw the Life Peerage as

13   *The Guardian*, Trinity: Butler Papers, RAB, G35.6.4.
14   The remark from Peter Laslett, a left-wing don, was quoted by *The Observer* on 7 February 1965. Cited by Howard, *RAB*, p. 343.
15   Interview, Professor Patrick Duff and Anthony Howard, 19 February 1986; *RAB*, p. 343.
16   Trinity: Butler Papers, RAB, B35.2.9 and B35.2.11.

no less than his due. He was widely welcomed by Cambridge dons and by fellow peers in the House of Lords. Lord Adrian himself wrote to register his pleasure at Rab's appointment. He had heard immediately after Home became Prime Minister in October 1963 that Rab might come to Trinity, but had been concerned, he wrote, as he had heard a rumour that Rab had turned the offer down.[17]

Rab had experience of academic administration, having been Chancellor of the universities of Sheffield and Essex. Moreover, Mollie and Rab between them had strong connections with Trinity. Mollie's first husband August had been an undergraduate in the college; their son Christopher was one of the College Chaplains; and their son William was still a Trinity undergraduate. Rab's great-uncle Montagu had been Master, while Sir James ('Jim') Butler, the historian after whom Rab had spoken at his first Union debate forty years before, was still a Fellow of the college. Mollie herself recalled that in her youth she had 'attended six successive May Weeks and six Trinity May Balls'. 'But, of course,' she added, 'to be the Master's wife was something else.'[18]

That was self-evident – and perhaps the most impressive aspect of Rab and Mollie's tenure of the Master's Lodgings at Trinity was the manner in which, after initial resistance, Lord and Lady Butler were accepted as an important working team by Fellows, undergraduates and college staff alike. Mollie assumed a maternal, pastoral role and she is the one more vividly remembered by Trinity's junior members. Rab was ever present, a somewhat magisterial figure playing a ceremonial *persona* in College. It was Mollie, with her extraordinary memory for people, their names, and their likes and dislikes, who welcomed undergraduates to the Lodge and put them at their ease. Every Sunday a large group of undergraduates and their guests went for drinks at the Lodge, which very quickly became an expression of her elegant but unpretentious taste. If Sydney had been the iconic politician's wife, Mollie was pitch-perfect in the role of Master's Lady.[19]

---

17 Trinity: Butler Papers, RAB, B35.2.9 and B35.2.142.
18 Mollie Butler, *August and Rab*, p. 97.
19 These impressions of Mollie as Master's Lady are gained from interviews with Trinity graduates who were up at Cambridge in the late 1960s and early 1970s.

In a very short time she redecorated the Lodge, whose condition and appearance had deteriorated under the Adrians, creating an elegant backcloth for Rab's pictures and treasured mementos of his career. In the drawing room hung a Monet, a Manet, a Renoir and a Cézanne. On corridor walls she placed the originals of cartoons by Giles, Vicky, Illingworth, Cummings and Low, succeeding in creating a home in which Rab regularly entertained College Fellows to drinks after Sunday dinner at High Table.[20] By building the physical environment that showcased the new Master, she enabled Rab to feel totally at home and to distance himself from the hostile jungle of Westminster. By July 1965, he was sufficiently removed emotionally to coin a cynical Rabism, referring to Heath's election to the Tory leadership as 'a tribal levée'.[21]

In November 1966, Rab received an intriguing letter, offering him a challenging project:

Next summer Charles is due to take his General Certificate of Education examination at Advanced Level in two subjects – History and English Literature.

For some time his future education has been under discussion and after hearing his preferences I invited the Archbishop of Canterbury, the Prime Minister, Lord Mountbatten, the Chairman of the Vice Chancellor's Committee and the Dean of Windsor to give me their advice. They all agreed that if he was reasonably qualified he should attend a university, which is what he wants to do.

We have naturally thought a good deal about the choice of University and College and, after taking many considerations into account, we have decided to ask you if Trinity College, Cambridge, of which you are Master, would accept him in the autumn of 1967.

Yours sincerely,

Elizabeth R[22]

---

20 There is a delightful, short account of dining at Trinity by Kenneth Rose, 'An Evening at Trinity' in Mollie Butler, *A Rabanthology* (York: Wilson 65, 1995), pp. 81–3.

21 Trinity: Butler Papers, RAB, G.45.

22 HM The Queen to Lord Butler, Master of Trinity College, Cambridge, 16 November 1966.

Rab was flattered and delighted but not unaware of the potential political problems. If he were to make a commitment on behalf of Trinity and
the prince failed his A-level papers, would Trinity be obliged to take
him? Would there be an outcry that the eldest son of the Queen was
taking a place that could be occupied by a better, more academically
minded undergraduate? Things had changed since his great-uncle, the
Prince of Wales (later Edward VIII and Duke of Windsor) had been
an undergraduate at Magdalen, Oxford. Rab wrote an undated memo,
making it clear that Trinity would take responsibility and that in no circumstances would his admission deny entry to another undergraduate.[23]

Rab was unaware at the time that the decision to send the Prince
of Wales to Trinity was the result of almost a year of discussion and
soundings, conducted largely by Dr Robin Woods, the Dean of Windsor. After a dinner party at Buckingham Palace on 22 December 1965,
at which the Prime Minister, the Archbishop of Canterbury, Earl
Mountbatten, Sir Charles Wilson, Dr Woods and Sir Michael Adeane
had discussed the prince's future education, Woods had been asked
by the Queen to recommend a college. Cambridge was preferred to
Oxford, largely because of its proximity to Sandringham, where the
prince had his own cottage on the estate, and Woods presented Her
Majesty with a shortlist of five colleges. Both George VI and his
brother, Prince Henry, the Duke of Gloucester, were Trinity men and
the final choice of Trinity was welcomed by the Queen.

The prince invited Rab to tea at Buckingham Palace in December
and the two discussed what course of study would be most suitable.
The conventional view was that he should study British constitutional
history but Rab felt strongly that he should follow his own wishes;
there would be plenty of time to deal with the constitution later; this
was a short period never to be repeated in the prince's life. He should,
as far as possible, live the life of a normal undergraduate, attending
lectures, living in college and – a proposal that shocked the Palace –
take final examinations.[24]

---

23 Trinity: Butler Papers, RAB, G46.3.
24 Holden, *Charles, Prince of Wales* (London: Weidenfeld & Nicholson, 1979), pp. 136–7.

Whether he knew it or not, Rab was offering Prince Charles the same advice as his cousin J. R. M. Butler had given to Lord Stamfordham, Private Secretary to King George V, concerning the Duke of York and the Duke of Gloucester in 1919. Jim Butler had been concerned that the princes would not gain enough of the 'slower maturing advantages that university life has to offer' if they only stayed up for one year. Moreover, if they lived out of college they would miss the opportunity of mixing with 'other minds of similar interests'.[25]

Jim Butler's advice had been disregarded but, nearly fifty years later at a time when the monarchy was less remote, more visible than it had been before the war, Rab's advice prevailed with Prince Charles and his parents. The prince settled on a degree course in Archaeology and Anthropology, and was thus destined to become the first Heir Apparent to hold a university degree.

Left-wing dons at Trinity, while they might deplore the existence of a monarchy, accepted that, if a monarchy existed, the best place to send a prince was Trinity. Thus a curious pride surrounded Prince Charles's choice of their college, and it was generally accepted that Rab's standing at the Palace had brought it about. A minor protest erupted when, by allowing the prince to have a small kitchen area in his rooms, Rab further delayed the building of a long-scheduled bathroom on the same staircase. This was largely a *pro forma* grumble.

Rab took seriously the responsibility of being *in loco parentis* to the Heir Apparent. He must have reflected on what had made his own undergraduate career both a success and a challenge, its pleasures and disappointments, and formulated an idea of what it could be for Prince Charles. He also needed to represent authority, but not to enforce rules dogmatically. Thus he looked the other way when the prince violated the rule forbidding undergraduates to keep a car in Cambridge during their first year. Charles, driving his MGB and accompanied by his detective – known to Trinity undergraduates as 'Oddjob' – became a familiar sight.

---

25 Butler to Stamfordham, 16 November 1919; Royal Archives: George V. o. 1595/1. Cited by Frankland, *Prince Henry, Duke of Gloucester* (London: Weidenfeld & Nicolson), p. 50.

On the role of the monarchy, the importance of its remaining above politics, however, Rab was adamant. When the prince, impressed by a persuasive Socialist with rooms on his staircase, asked Rab if he might join the University Labour Club, Rab responded violently. 'Hell no,' he blurted, and then explained the necessity of the prince's remaining above the clash of political parties.[26]

Recognising that the prince would be alone in a unique fashion, unable to talk to his peers with any degree of frankness, Rab set aside for him forty-five minutes before dinner on days that he was in Cambridge. He would be available to discuss or advise on any issue that might be raised and, to emphasise that availability, he gave Charles a key to a side entrance to the Lodge, enabling him to use the 'secret staircase' leading to Rab's study.[27]

Rab felt strongly that the *mores* of Cambridge rather than Palace protocol should be the compass for Charles's undergraduate years. This was, of course, an impossible goal, but Rab was implacable in his insistence that 'balcony jobs', public relations exercises that were part of the rebranding of the monarchy in the 1960s, should disrupt the prince's university career as little as possible. When it was decided that Charles should spend a term at Aberystwyth University before his investiture as Prince of Wales, Rab protested at the time being taken from his work towards his final examinations. In his view, Charles had been pressured into switching from Archaeology and Anthropology to History – an academic error – and now his performance in the Tripos was to be undermined by public relations exercises. Charles was making an important statement as the first Heir to the Throne to sit a public university examination; the Throne itself, he felt, was undermining the prince's statement with gestures that could have waited until his Cambridge career was completed.

In the circumstances, Rab probably influenced the prince as much as any outsider could have done. He persuaded him of the difference between an interest in Socialism and membership of a political party;

26 Holden, *Charles, Prince of Wales*, p. 139.
27 Ibid., p. 138.

he registered his disappointment that Charles made his friends among the polo-playing aristocracy rather than among the wider social mix of Trinity. He saw the prince's Cambridge years as, perhaps, the only period in which a 'normal' life would be possible, and he encouraged that 'normality' wherever possible.

In one area of the prince's life there was a continuing prurience: constant speculation followed his relations with young women until he married Lady Diana Spencer. It was at Cambridge that he learned to relax with women and it was through Rab that he took his first tentative steps. Rab was writing his memoirs and had engaged Lucia Santa Cruz, daughter of the Chilean Ambassador, as his research assistant. Anthony Holden describes the friendship that developed between her and the prince as 'the kind of puppy-love most men experience in their teens', adding that 'until he met Lucia, his circumstances had prevented the adolescent adventures all too familiar to lesser mortals'.[28] Even the slightest attention paid to a female provoked gossip in the press and hints of a deep attraction. Rab, observing the prince's interest in Lucia Santa Cruz, was able to ease the mechanics of their meeting by giving Lucia a key to the Lodge and the use of a room away from prying eyes — both of the press and of Charles's contemporaries who might be tempted to offer a scoop to a newspaper.

Anthony Holden, in his first biography of Prince Charles, quotes Rab as saying, 'The prince asked if she might stay in our Lodge for privacy, which request we were very glad to accede to.' This suggestive but relatively innocuous remark was expanded by other writers to suggest that Rab somehow 'pimped' for Charles, and one account quotes Rab as saying that 'Charles and Lucia spent many nights in the bedroom of the Master's Lodge that was given over to them for privacy.'[29]

In speaking of the romance at all Rab had violated the code of secrecy that surrounded the Prince of Wales; in his later book, *King Charles III*, Holden wrote that Rab

---

28 Ibid., p. 199.
29 Spoto, *The Decline and Fall of the House of Windsor* (New York: Simon & Schuster, 1995), p. 369.

was quite as much a personal 'guru' to the young Charles as was Dickie Mountbatten or ... Laurens van der Post. But it is disappointingly characteristic of the older Charles to have disavowed Butler's influence when it was detailed in the author's earlier volume, *Charles, Prince of Wales*. This may be partly because of the excitement caused by Butler's revelation that he had encouraged a liaison between the virgin Prince and ... Lucia Santa Cruz ... who has subsequently gone down in history as the Prince of Wales's first 'real' girlfriend. But it also shows an ungrateful streak in Charles, a man quite as prepared to disown specific influences as to cultivate them.[30]

This alleged ingratitude was to come later; throughout Charles's time at Trinity his relations with the Master were cordial and mutually respectful. When the Prince of Wales was away from Cambridge in Aberystwyth he wrote to Rab, expressing how much he was missing the stimulus – and the elegance – of Trinity.[31] A year later, Rab wrote him a note before the Tripos, wishing him well in the examinations and offering him the use of the Master's garden for a post-Tripos party on 14 June. Charles responded with thanks for the note of encouragement and for the offer of the garden. When it was all over and Charles was awarded an adequate degree in the second division of Class II, he wrote to Rab with gratitude:

> *I can now put KG and BA after my name. I would like to thank you for all the personal trouble you took over my welfare – academic and otherwise. You were most kind and your hospitality will always remain a happy and long-lasting memory for me.*
>
> *My greatest relief is that you are spared incarceration in the Tower and can continue your endless good work at Trinity. Many thanks again.*
>
> *Yours very sincerely, Charles*[32]

The reference to a 'KG' is to the award of the Knighthood of the Garter, an honour bestowed on Charles in 1958. When Rab too was admitted

---

30 Holden, *King Charles III* (New York: Grove Press, 1988), p. 109.
31 Trinity: Butler Papers, RAB, G46.3; 8 May 1969.
32 Trinity: Butler Papers, RAB, G46.

to the Order of the Garter on 23 April 1971, this was seen as an act of gratitude for his attention during the prince's university years.[33]

The work of Lucia Santa Cruz as Rab's research assistant bore fruit in 1971 with the publication of his autobiography, *The Art of the Possible*. The book is a perfect example of Rab's style – laconic, elliptic and literary, making few concessions to the ill-read reader. The structure of the work owes much to Peter Goldman, Rab's long-time colleague in the Conservative Research Department. In the short preface Rab shows his hand on two occasions: first, with a reference to Duff Cooper's autobiography, a concise work, published in 1955, comprising twenty-three short chapters and widely praised as a model of clarity. The second reference is a deft Rabism, as he wrote, 'I have eschewed the current autobiographical fondness for multi volume histories, and have preferred a single book which is not too heavy for anyone to hold up and doze over in bed.'[34]

Since February 1966, volumes of Macmillan's autobiography had appeared in print and, by the time that Rab's memoir was published, the fourth volume, *Riding the Storm*, had just appeared. By then, Macmillan had covered the years up to 1959 and two more volumes were ultimately published to complete the opus. Rab's patronising comment on 'the current autobiographical fondness for multi-volume histories' was a satisfying dig at the former Prime Minister. Indeed, the economic style of Rab's memoir was the feature most admired by Enoch Powell.[35]

Rab had pondered long and hard on the style he might adopt for his memoirs. In November 1967, he delivered the Romanes lecture in Oxford's Sheldonian Theatre, taking as his subject 'The Difficult Art of Autobiography'. It was, in typical Rab fashion, an elusive lecture, demonstrating his wide literacy, moving with ease from Leonard Woolf to Saint Augustine to Marcus Aurelius. From the latter's third book of *Meditations*, he quoted what, perhaps, was close to his own philosophy of life:

---

33 *Cambridge Evening News*, 23 April 1971.
34 Butler, *The Art of the Possible*, p. xi.
35 In a review in the *Daily Telegraph*, 12 July 1971. See also Mollie Butler, *A Rabanthology*, pp. 75–80.

If you do the work on hand following the rule of right with enthusi-asm, manfully and with kind-heartedness, and allow no side issues to interrupt, but preserve the divinity within you pure and upright, as if you might even now have to return it to its giver – if you make this firm, expecting nothing and avoiding nothing, but are content with your present activity in accordance with nature and with old-fashioned truthfulness in what you say and speak – you will live a happy life, and there is no one who can prevent this.[36]

In accepting the Mastership of Trinity, Rab had accepted that he was leaving the spotlight, that he would be at the centre of a very different court, a *milieu* suited to his donnishness, his mannerisms and intellec-tual flourishes. Once he left the political stage he definitively set aside the habits of thirty-six years of party politics. Politicians still crossed the stage, but it was his stage and they came at his invitation. The court he established at Trinity was his own creation, no papal palace at Avignon, but Rab's domain. He did, however, remain something of a maverick. At a private dinner party in Cambridge in 1969 he made 'an extremely witty and rather donnish speech of introduction which stopped barely short of being openly insulting, not only to the leader of the party [Edward Heath] but to many of those still prominent in its affairs who had been not mere colleagues but friends, includ-ing Macleod, Powell and Maudling'.[37] It was incidents like this that prompted Macleod's painfully accurate comment that 'Rab loves being a politician among academics and an academic among politicians; that is why neither breed of man likes him all that much.'[38]

Once Prince Charles had gone down and Rab faded once more from public gaze, he became, if not obscure, then certainly less prominent, less symbolic. He enjoyed the role of a widely admired and respected Master of the most admired and respected Cambridge college. Trinity

36 'The Difficult Art of Biography', *The Romanes Lecture* (Oxford: Clarendon Press, 1968), deliv-ered in the Sheldonian Theatre, 22 November 1967, p. 25.
37 Cosgrave, *R. A. Butler: An English Life*, p. 6.
38 Ibid., p. 21.

undergraduates of the early 1970s, too young to remember Rab's years in the spotlight, recall him as benevolent but remote.[39]

That remoteness was partially caused by Rab's habitual shyness and, as he aged, by a vagueness that Charles Moore, a Trinity undergraduate in the late 1970s, characterised as 'Rab's anecdotage'.[40] Moore remembers Rab as perfectly friendly but frequently rather bemused in the presence of undergraduates, whose names he never remembered as Mollie did. 'He might not have known my name,' Moore recalls, 'but I was a familiar face, and he would take me aside at parties in the Lodge and recount anecdotes.' On one occasion, Rab left a party in the Lodge to go to bed, and a few minutes later guests were treated to the sight of a naked Master wandering towards his bedroom at the end of the corridor.

This was not the only sign of Rab's apparent loss of grip. A greatly more dangerous symptom of his not getting any younger occurred in December 1973. Presenting the Booker Prize at a dinner at the Café Royal, he made two off-the-cuff jokes about 'Jew-boys', 'causing Lord Weidenfeld, the winning publisher, to glower and the literary editor of *The Observer* to storm out'.[41] Rab thereafter tended to avoid London and the limelight.

Cambridge, perhaps his most natural habitat, finally became his real home. He played host to visiting dignitaries, frequently politicians of all parties, coming at his invitation. The Master's Lodge at Trinity became a centre for political recollection rather than a hothouse of political action. Rab's life became simpler, more Cambridge-centered. When he and Mollie acquired Frachadil, they sold their house in Smith Square and took a flat in Whitehall Court as their London home. Rab's seventieth birthday came, and he decided that he wanted to spend a further five years at Trinity.

This was far from automatic, as the Fellows of the college had the power to renew or deny the Master's appointment. Trinity tradition was that an academic should hold the post and there was an attempt to persuade Rab not to offer himself for re-election in 1972. Once word of this

---

39 Private interviews with Trinity graduates.
40 Interview with Charles Moore, 19 June 2015.
41 *Evening Standard*, 29 November 1973. Rab's apology for his remarks was referred to in the *Jewish Chronicle*, 7 December 1973. The account quoted here is from the obituary of Martyn Goff, *Daily Telegraph*, 26 March 2015.

reached Rab's ears, however, he deftly outflanked the delegation of senior Fellows who had come to propose his retirement and, in the subsequent election, was unanimously accepted as Master for a further five years.[42]

Yet he knew that that December 1977, his seventy-fifth birthday, would mark the end of his Cambridge tenure, and the prospect saddened him more than he would have imagined possible in 1965. He began to prepare for a sedate and definitive retirement from the 'perfect and unalloyed happiness' of Trinity.[43] For Trinity Fellows and undergraduates Rab's presence in the Lodge 'had been a little special'.[44] He brought distinction and celebrity to the appointment; Mollie provided a welcoming elegance. It was a successful joint enterprise.

In 1947, Rab had inherited Gatcombe Park from his father-in-law, Sam Courtauld. This elegant eighteenth-century manor house, set in 730 acres, was used less and less by Rab and Mollie, who greatly preferred to spend their time on Mull. In the summer of 1976, Rab sold Gatcombe to the Queen, who wanted to give it to Princess Anne and her husband Mark Phillips. The story broke on 24 June with intense and inaccurate speculation as to the price that Her Majesty paid. Estimates ranged from £300,000 to £750,000, generally reflecting the political bias of the newspaper concerned. The more left-wing a paper's posture, the higher the price quoted. As *The Times* commented,

> Some Labour MPs reacted angrily at the purchase of the house (the Press Association reports). Mr Ronald Thomas (Bristol North West) said: 'In the economic crisis, when working people are having to take considerable cuts in their standard of living, I find this example of the flaunting of wealth appalling and, indeed, almost obscene.' Several Labour MPs later tabled a Commons motion saying the provision of 50 houses for families in need would have been a much more worthy investment.[45]

---

42 This story is undocumented but was widely believed and is congruent with Trinity tradition. When the Fellows voted over three-quarters of the Senior Common Room cast a vote and all of them elected to retain Rab for a further five years.

43 Butler, *The Art of the Possible*, p. 1.

44 Interview with Charles Moore, 19 June 2015.

45 *The Times*, 24 June 1976.

Rab, naturally, did not disclose the price but commented simply, 'I'm glad it's going to a nice family.' Later, however, he did comment that Her Majesty drove a very hard bargain.[46]

The sale of Gatcombe neatly financed the purchase from Mollie's son Julien of Spencers, the house at Great Yeldham where Mollie had lived with August until her first husband's death in 1959. Appropriately, in retirement Rab would move back to the constituency that he had represented from 1929 to 1965. Leaving Trinity would be a wrench, but the Master entered into a ceremonial round of farewells in good cheer.[47]

His activities outside Cambridge had gradually contracted as he settled into a cultured and comfortable life in Great Court beside the River Cam. A butler and private chef in the Lodge made for a certain elegance. As one colleague commented, 'We had a slippered duke in the Lodge for thirteen years, and it was lovely.'[48] With Mollie playing the role of duchess, Rab's last job may have been the one to which he was most suited.

Sadly, it had to come to an end and in December 1977 Rab wrote to Jim Callaghan:

> *Dear Prime Minister,*
>
> *Since I have reached my seventy fifth birthday, I offer to the Crown my resignation of the Mastership of Trinity. The Statutes lay down that the Master should retire at seventy but you may remember that I was extended by ninety-one Fellows to seventy-five.*
>
> *I am deeply indebted for the privilege of having been appointed and shall be finishing off the academic year as is customary.*
>
> *I am glad to say that the College is in good shape and has had excellent results in all spheres.*
>
> *Both my wife and I have enjoyed our contact with the young men and not least with the Prince of Wales during his time here.*
>
> *Yours sincerely,*
>
> *Butler*[49]

---

46 Howard, *RAB*, p. 356. Comments made by Rab to Howard during interviews.
47 Howard, *RAB*, pp. 356–7.
48 J. A. Weir, 'Lord Butler', *Cambridge Review*, 7 May 1982. Cited by Howard, *RAB*, p. 349.
49 Trinity: Butler Papers, RAB, P5.

The letter was not strictly necessary, but Rab was Rab. He could not have left Trinity without dotting the 'i's and crossing the 't's in acknowledging his gratitude to the office that had appointed him, even if the occupant had changed.

With this modest letter Rab brought his association with Trinity to an end. Ever the educator, it was to the young men of the college that he doffed his cap. Fourteen years after the crushing events surrounding the Blackpool conference, he could look back on a long and successful tenure. He had converted those Fellows who doubted the purpose of his appointment, who had seen their college being used as the donor of a consolation prize to a thwarted politician. Lord Butler of Saffron Walden had found, after a career of huge promise and equally searing disappointment, a role that was his least controversial and, ultimately, his most natural.

So natural had it been that Rab had deviated from his original plan to be a frequent speaker in the House of Lords. In the event, he revisited Parliament rarely and, each time, to plead a specific cause close to his heart. As an agent for the interests of Trinity and as defender of the principles of the 1944 Education Act, he chose the issues to address and spoke his mind plainly.

As agent for Trinity, Rab spoke for fourteen minutes in June 1976, presenting Trinity's case against the nationalisation of Felixstowe Docks, a development in which Trinity had a substantial interest. The college had spent over £1 million in providing roads, underpasses, lighting and services on the 300 acres it owned and took pride in the development. This was not an instance of playing politics or angling for personal or private gain, he maintained. The revenue from the docks – one-sixth of the total endowment of the college – was being used to further education. Trinity itself had twenty Nobel Prize winners in the scientific field (compared with twenty-one won by the whole of France) and was supporting a scheme to share its wealth with less well-endowed colleges. The best prospects for Felixstowe Docks were under the ownership of European Ferries and not as a nationalised entity controlled by the British Transport Docks Board.[50]

---

50 Hansard, House of Lords, 22 June 1976, vol. 372, cols 193–8.

He returned to this subject in the Lords in October, restating objections to the Bill, arguing that private management by European Ferries would be more likely to maintain the position of Felixstowe as a world leader among container ports than the Dock Board.[51] On the second occasion he was supported by Lord Cross of Chelsea, an honorary Fellow of Trinity, and the Bill was denied a third reading by 147 votes to seventy-one.

By the time that Rab spoke out to defend the principle of free school buses, which had been central to his Education Act, the political landscape had totally changed. Edward Heath had fallen from the Tory leadership and had been replaced by Margaret Thatcher. Four years later, Callaghan's government fell and the Tories were back in power. When the Thatcher government proposed an Education Bill containing a clause enabling local authorities to impose charges for the use of school buses, Rab opposed the inclusion of that clause vigorously. First, however, in Rabish style, he faintly praised the Prime Minister:

> Only recently the leader of the party to which I have belonged for about sixty years had a great success in France. The French have discovered for the first time since Joan of Arc that it was possible to be a woman and a statesman. I notice that none of the French press – not even *Le Canard Enchaîné*, to which I am a subscriber – made this allusion, so I hope that they will take this copy from me in the House of Lords. The right honourable lady also made a very good speech in England. She has had a very difficult time.[52]

In what was to be Rab's last speech of any substance in the Lords, he was more discursive than he had been in his prime. His age and detachment from politics were beginning to show in his manner of delivery. Yet he finished his speech with moving oratory, a paean to the rural areas of Britain, from which the school bus service might be withdrawn. The Conservative Party, he said, had always been strongest when it supported

---

51 Hansard, House of Lords, 22 October 1976, vol. 375, cols 1708–13.
52 Hansard, House of Lords, 13 March 1980, vol. 406, col. 1218.

the rural areas. The rural tradition perpetuated by Disraeli, Salisbury and Baldwin 'was true Conservative rural policy and philosophy'. As to the clause of the Bill that would cancel rural school bus services, he said simply, 'I feel, I am sorry to say, like Martin Luther: "Ich kann nicht anders." I can do no other. I ask noble Lords to do no other.'[53]

Rab was manifestly slowing down. In his last years at Trinity observers had found him increasingly distant, even suffering incipient senility. In truth, his health had slipped away rapidly and concerns about his heart, about diabetes and polyps in his intestine effectively grounded him after 1979.[54] His final public appearance, at which he was frail but in good cheer, was at the unveiling of his portrait in the National Portrait Gallery on 13 January 1982.

At about this time, Mollie was told by Rab's doctors that, contrary to their first opinion, the polyps were malignant, and she and they kept this from Rab. His condition worsened rapidly in January and February and he died on 8 March, with his family around him.

His funeral service was held in the parish church of Saint Mary the Virgin, Saffron Walden on 13 March 1982. Mollie describes Rab's religious faith as 'certain and simple'. He had been brought up to believe in the teachings of the church and had never deviated from them. The service was appropriately simple, beautifully congruent. Opening with Psalm 121, 'I will lift up mine eyes unto the hills, from whence cometh my help', it included two apposite readings.

The first lesson, from the Book of Wisdom, included four verses that made up a polysyllogism, a logical form common in Stoic philosophy:

> The beginning of wisdom is the most sincere desire for instruction,
> and concern for instruction is love of her,
> and love of her is the keeping of her laws,
> and giving heed to her laws is assurance of immortality,
> and immortality brings one near to God;
> so the desire for wisdom leads to a kingdom.

---

53 Hansard, House of Lords, 13 March 1980, vol. 406, col. 1224.
54 The crescendo of health problems that began in September 1980 is described by Mollie in *August and Rab*, pp. 140–49.

The second lesson was no less well chosen. From Saint Paul's Epistle to the Romans four verses were read, which equally forcefully urge faith in the face of adversity:

> No, in all these things we are more than conquerors through him who loved us. For I am convinced that neither death, nor life, nor angels, nor rulers, nor things present, nor things to come, nor powers, nor height, nor depth, nor anything else in all creation, will be able to separate us from the love of God in Christ Jesus our Lord.

The service came to an end with William Cowper's well-known and simple hymn, 'God Moves in a Mysterious Way'. Even at his last, Rab Butler was able to bestow a Rabism on the congregation. In the third stanza are the four lines that he had mischievously invoked in the House of Commons as the Archbishop of Westminster anxiously followed the Second Reading of the 1944 Education Act in the Distinguished Strangers' Gallery:

> Ye fearful saints, fresh courage take;
> The clouds ye so much dread
> Are big with mercy and shall break
> In blessings on your head.

His Service of Thanksgiving, conducted by the Dean of Westminster in Westminster Abbey on 5 April, was something of a *reprise* of Rab's favourite scriptures and hymns. The reading from Romans was once more the first lesson, following 'God Moves in a Mysterious Way'.

Psalm 91 followed, a statement of absolute personal faith in God:

> He that dwelleth in the secret place of the most High shall abide under the shadow of the Almighty ... Thou shalt not be afraid for the terror by night; nor for the arrow that flieth by day ... A thousand shall fall at thy side, and then a thousand at thy right hand; but it shall not come nigh thee ... Only with thine eyes shalt thou behold and see the reward of the wicked. Because thou hast made the Lord, which is my refuge, even the most High, thy habitation.

The second lesson, from Philippians IV, might have been Rab's simple benediction to those he loved:

> Finally, beloved, whatever is true, whatever is honourable, whatever is just, whatever is pure, whatever is pleasing, whatever is commendable, if there is any excellence and if there is anything worthy of praise, think about these things. Keep on doing the things that you have learned and received and heard and seen in me, and the God of peace will be with you.

The address by the Reverend Harry Williams, Dean of Trinity in the late 1960s,[55] spoke of Rab's conviction that 'a house divided against itself cannot stand'. That principle, above all others, above his own ambition, had guided his entire life. 'It was always for unity and harmony that Rab ceaselessly worked.' Referring to his humility, his modesty, his wicked humour, often mistaken for malice by the uninitiated, the address moved to the final quarter of Rab's life and his marriage to Mollie: 'They complemented each other in a way and to a degree that I have never seen in any other married couple. Indeed, it is almost impossible to think of Rab without Mollie or Mollie without Rab.'

With the seventeenth-century German hymn 'Nun Danket Alle Gott', Rab's love of Austria and Germany was remembered. In a short and intensely personal service, invested with the Gothic grandeur of the royal abbey, Rab's remarkable life and his enduring dedication to principle were celebrated.

Later in the year, Trinity held an unusual and personal memorial in the chapel on 21 November. This took the form of a poetry reading, punctuated by psalms, an anthem and a lesson. The selection of readings mirrored Rab's broad, eclectic tastes, including works by Christina Rosetti, Shakespeare, Keats, Matthew Arnold, Thomas Hardy, Euripides, Plato, Kipling and John Betjeman. The last two stanzas of 'Expectans Expectavi', a poem by Rab's cousin Charles Sorley, had been

---

55 There is a tender and moving description of Harry Williams in Mollie Butler's *August and Rab* at p. 102 and a note of his leaving Trinity at p. 111.

set to music by Charles Wood in 1919 and this was sung as the anthem at the centre of the reading. After the *Apology* of Socrates, the strains of Handel's 'The Arrival of the Queen of Sheba' filled the crowded chapel to bring the reading to a majestic close.

CHAPTER 21

OMNIUM CONSENSU CAPAX IMPERII NISI IMPERASSET[1]

With those words ('Everyone agreed that he'd have made a good Emperor if he'd never been one') Tacitus described the Emperor Galba, a judgement recalled by Enoch Powell, who believed that its converse applied – that the vast majority of the electorate rightly thought that Rab, had he been given the chance, would have been an exceptional Prime Minister. The thrust of argument in this book is that, had that come to pass, then the same would have been said of Rab as of Galba.

One parliamentary pundit observed that 'He always looks as if he will be the next Prime Minister until it seems that the throne may actually be vacant.'[2] Other paradoxes abound. 'Anyone who understands Rab Butler', a Cabinet colleague remarked, 'must be gravely misinformed.' Butler, another article commented, is the enigma of British politics.[3] More obliquely, a new lobby correspondent was given the advice: 'There are two rules to remember: never believe anything Rab Butler tells you, and never ignore anything he tells you either.'[4] Brendan Bracken described him to Beaverbrook colourfully as 'a curious mixture of Gandhi and Boss Tweed'.[5]

---

1   Tacitus, *Histories*, 1. 49. See Chapter 18.
2   *Time*, 18 October 1963.
3   'Butler Profile', an article by Arthur L. Gavshon of Associated Press; Trinity: Butler Papers, RAB, G43.16.
4   Mollie Butler, *A Rabanthology*, facing p. 20.
5   Cosgrave, *R. A. Butler: An English Life*, p. 14. William 'Boss' Tweed (1823–78) was Congressman for New York's fifth district and boss of the Tammany Hall machine.

It has become an established truth that this impressively competent and erudite politician, thrice thwarted in his ambition to enter
10 Downing Street, was unfairly cheated by a combination of anti-
intellectual bias and the envy of his colleagues. Rab has become 'The
Best Prime Minister That Britain Never Had'. It is a handle applied
as automatically to his name as 'the Conqueror' to that of William I.

So secure has the image become that its logical implications – that
Rab was brought down by conspiracy, that he was 'too clever by half'
for the knights of the shires, that his opponents were antediluvian vil-
lains, that a cabal of Old Etonians knifed Rab to ease the way for Alec
Douglas-Home – have all in some measure been accepted as contribu-
tory truths. Criticisms of Rab, such as that of Lord Kilmuir, that in
1957 'Rab had no one to blame but himself' are treated as prejudice
rather than balanced opinion. 'Many at that time', Kilmuir continues,
'considered that his habit of publicly hedging his political bets was too
great a weakness and this had accordingly damaged his position in the
Conservative hierarchy and in the parliamentary party.'[6]

Despite his respect for and friendship with Rab, Kilmuir was adamant that the right man was chosen to succeed and that, had Rab
succeeded Eden, a serious schism would have rent the party. If this
was true in 1957, it was the more true six years later when there were
calls for a younger leader and when two new candidates entered the
contest from the House of Lords. Ted Heath had no doubt that Rab
would fail once more in 1963, both because Macmillan was determined
to keep him out and because 'too many on the right despised him for
moving the party to the left. Others like Macmillan simply saw him
as indecisive.'[7]

The charge of indecision may at first seem a curious criticism of the
man who single-mindedly drove the 1944 Education Act, who rede-
fined the Tory Party between 1945 and 1951, and who won retrospective
praise as Chancellor of the Exchequer when *The Economist* referred to
him as 'the last real policy-making Chancellor'.[8] He was universally

---

6 Earl of Kilmuir, *Political Adventure*, p. 286.
7 Heath, *The Course of My Life*, p. 253.
8 *The Economist*, 27 June 1970; Trinity: Butler Papers, RAB, G46.5.

regarded as serious (although the *Daily Herald* admitted that 'he has his lighter moments'[9]) and 'the hardest worker in British politics'.[10] It was Rab who, in an interview with the *Yorkshire Post*, displayed an intellectual grasp of Conservative policy that depended not upon rigid doctrine but which was able to adapt to changing circumstances, always to reflect the traditional attitudes of a substantial part of the electorate.

In that wide-ranging interview, Rab was at his best. Many of the party's objectives would take more than the span of one government to achieve. Doubling the standard of living for all sections of society, for example; bringing the standard of living in the Commonwealth up to the standard in Britain; achieving *détente* with the Soviet Union. These were projects for the long term, underpinned by the strengthening of national character, upholding of moral standards, wider opportunities in education and youth services.

Only a dynamic society, he argued, could survive in the modern world. Tories saw such dynamism emerging from a society that had freedom to develop individual talents and ideas. With a well-educated populace, traditional class structure would be overtaken and a more equitable society would emerge. Prosperity politics was not enough. Instead, full employment, generous social services and modern comforts should be, to use Churchill's expression, a springboard and not a sofa.[11] Central to the society that Rab outlined was a strong moral code, particularly the influence of family life. He returned to this theme more than once, emphasising the centrality of the Church of England to the Conservative Party. To a great extent, this highlighted the differences between Conservative and Labour, but his answers also expressed the sincerity of his own religious beliefs and ideals.[12]

At face value, Rab's expressed definition of principle reflected the very nature of leadership: a certainty of purpose, combined with a shrewd grasp of realities. Three years after that interview, Rab displayed

---

9   *Daily Herald*, 22 July 1941.
10 *Sheffield Telegraph*, 19 July 1961.
11 Churchill had used the phrase to lament the slowing down of the Allied invasion of North Africa in 1942–43. 'I had intended North Africa to be a springboard and not a sofa.'
12 *Yorkshire Post*, 9 May 1960; Trinity: Butler Papers, RAB, G35.138.

remarkable determination and statesmanship in resolving the problem of the Central African Federation. Yet within a few months the Tories rejected him for the last time and precipitated his departure from politics.

In the face of this persistent and resolute opposition, it is difficult to argue that Rab was the natural choice whose ascent was checked by malign conspiracy. His enemies were not alone in preferring Macmillan; many of his friends also doubted his suitability for the top job. The principal reasons adduced are his indecision, a duplicitous ambition and his lack of 'steel'. Any one of these, it can be argued, was enough to disqualify him from the highest office.

The third criticism, that he lacked 'steel', the expressed reason for Macmillan's determination to block him, is, *prima facie*, the most powerful. Whilst Rab at one level understood the realities of politics, his views regarding the right of succession betray a naïve set of assumptions. There are no friends at the top; how could he have been unaware of that?

Rab's comment to the Canadian press regarding the Tory leadership in March 1953 reveals an attitude to promotion – the principle of 'Buggins' turn' – that is more typical of civil servants than politicians. The Civil Service – in common with any structured organisation – distinguishes between managerial and executive roles. Rab was a phenomenally good manager, one of the most competent chairmen imaginable. The Education Act of 1944, the winding-up of the Central African Federation in 1963 – those and a score of other applications of 'the art of the possible' demonstrate that ability. But skilful management is not always accompanied by the decisive qualities required of a chief executive. Rab loved nothing better than the craft of piloting a Bill through the House of Commons, for which he had the necessary attention to detail, pertinacity and drive. But that is a task that the competent chief executive officer delegates – as Macmillan did.

Ted Heath commented on Rab's intellectual ability and its practical limitations:

He was, indeed, a complex personality. Of his intellectual ability there was no doubt whatever … Yet on numerous occasions I detected a certain insecurity when he would ask me to resolve a question about procedure or policy ... I found that he was, above all else, an organiser of ideas rather than a judge of how far it was politically expedient to implement them.[13]

Heath's distinction between 'an organiser of ideas' and a judge of political expediency illustrates in simple, stark contrast the difference between Macmillan and Rab, the difference between fashioning policy and implementing decisions handed down by the Cabinet. In the early 1950s, a similar power struggle was being acted out in the Labour Party. Clement Attlee delayed his retirement, largely to ensure that he was not succeeded by Herbert Morrison. Attlee was determined to block Morrison, a charismatic and competent manager, principally because he thought him an excellent Number Two who would be a catastrophe as party leader. Five years later, Macmillan wrestled with the problem of retaining Rab's loyalty as Number Two, while blocking his advance. Macmillan never believed that Rab had the ability to devise and implement difficult policy decisions.

Officials at the Treasury found him indecisive and liable to question a decision they thought had already been reached. For a leader, the ability to reach a decision and stick with it is a vital asset. Macmillan had it; Rab, despite his 'rare treasure house of a mind',[14] did not. His namesake, Lord Butler of Brockwell, a future Cabinet Secretary, recalls Rab's telephoning a young resident clerk at the Foreign Office during the Profumo crisis, asking for his advice – an action that betrayed extraordinary indiscretion along with indecision.[15]

That quality of indecision was apparent to Enoch Powell after the 1963 leadership crisis, and there is ample evidence of crippling hesitation over both major and minor matters. At one end of the scale is vacillation over Suez; vastly less important but equally illustrative was his indecisiveness over a minor decision during the Commonwealth Conference in May 1960. Rab was to host a luncheon, and the

13 Heath, *The Course of My Life*, p. 254.
14 Cosgrave, *R. A. Butler: An English Life*, p. 10.
15 Interview with Lord Butler of Brockwell, 5 January 2015.

caterers Searcy Tansley sent a number of sample menus. Rab perused each menu and wrote 'perhaps' on most of the items, writing 'yes' only against scampi and crème brûlée. For a competent and decisive Cabinet minister, these should not have been challenging questions.[16]

Such indecision is frequently a symptom of insecurity. A second common symptom is the tendency to make contemptuous judgements of colleagues – in short, Rabisms. Time and again we find examples of Rab's disdain for members of his party – not merely the 'hangers and floggers', but successively for party leaders – for Churchill, whom he characterised as capable of being 'extraordinarily stupid';[17] of Eden, 'the best Prime Minister we have'; of Macmillan, whom he mocked for his tendency to pose as both the descendant of Scottish crofters and the brother-in-law of the Duke of Devonshire. It beggars belief that Rab was unaware of his ability to give offence to influential colleagues.

As to duplicitous ambition, Rab's besetting sin was that he defied the etiquette of candidacy by being a permanent candidate. Ambition is an accepted quality in politics; showing that ambition is less easily forgiven. Deryck Winterton of the *Daily Herald* expressed colleagues' attitudes succinctly, writing: 'It is also true that he can never look at any Great Office of State without being sure that he could do better than the present occupant. He could be right. Butler's mistake is that he does not keep the conviction to himself.'[18]

That astute comment points to one reason why so many Tories rejoiced when Rab stumbled. For the rank and file of the party, less cerebrally endowed backbenchers, Rab was simply 'too clever by half'. As Baldwin had warned Rab the undergraduate, intellectualism was a sin, a sin that Rab was never at pains to conceal.

No one who saw Rab at work doubted his ability, his determination or his focus. Even at the time of his departure from the Exchequer he saw the introduction of the October Budget as a matter of honour. He was capable of loyalty both to the Ministry he served and to individual colleagues. Not a natural leader himself, he could be a naturally loyal

16 Trinity: Butler Papers, RAB, G35, 107–9.
17 Archie Brown, *The Myth of the Strong Leader*, p. 90. Interview with Rab on 23 September 1966.
18 *Daily Herald*, 30 May 1961.

follower. As Clark observed to Eden, 'What Butler needed was love and a feeling of being wanted.'[19] In return, Rab gave loyalty; sadly, that loyalty was not always well placed, not always reciprocated.

To Churchill he demonstrated remarkable loyalty when he agreed to hold the fort after the Prime Minister's stroke in 1953; a more determined politician would have insisted on a permanent change at the top. To Eden he was consistently and fundamentally loyal, despite his doubts over Suez. In 1955, he sacrificed his own integrity in the interests of an election Budget. In the following year, he destroyed his standing in the Tory Party first by opposing the invasion, later by his too-close association with Eden, whose catastrophic policy Rab was left to dismantle. Macmillan, who played Rab brilliantly, bestowing and removing appointments with baffling frequency, treated his First Secretary of State with humiliating condescension, yet knew he could rely on him.[20]

It was an earlier loyalty, however, that most contributed to Rab's undoing; after 1938 he was from then on tarred with the brush of appeasement. In his memoirs he maintains that he was 'not ... a prime mover in the complex and dramatic events' of 1938–39. He was, he appears to suggest, an errand boy for the policymakers, 'a sceptical spectator'.[21] He justifies Chamberlain's policy on the parallel arguments that Britain was too weak to fight and that, in any event, the country would not have gone to war to uphold the integrity of Czechoslovakia, adding for good measure that Britain, unlike France, was not bound to the Czechs by any treaty. He accepts Wheeler-Bennett's convenient conclusion that the Munich settlement, the sacrifice of 'a smaller power to slavery', was shameful but inevitable. From the outset, he maintains, Chamberlain foresaw the subsequent invasion of Prague, and this far-sightedness, apparently appeasement, was a gambit that gave Britain time to rearm.

In maintaining that he had accepted Chamberlain's policy merely to gain time for rearmament he distorted the facts, grossly misrepresenting his responsibility and attitudes in 1938. As Patrick Cosgrave points

---

19 Clark, *From Three Worlds*, p. 152.
20 See for example Bodleian: MSS Macmillan, d33*, 105; d34.79; d30.111.
21 Butler, *The Art of the Possible*, p. 66.

out, 'Butler did not merely go along with appeasement; he worked hard, long and enthusiastically for it, and there is very little evidence in public records for the time that he took the slightest contemporary interest in the rearmament programme to which he devotes such emphasis in his memoirs.'[22] Rab's commitment to appeasement was well known, not only among the German diplomatic community but also to British Intelligence. Rear Admiral John Godfrey, Director of Naval Intelligence, organised a meeting in 1939 with Count von Schwerin, head of the English Department of the *Abwehr*. The meeting's purpose was to send a clear message to Hitler that Britain would honour her commitments if Germany attacked Poland; Godfrey invited Rab to attend as his presence would lend force to the message.[23]

Appeasement was not the sole cause of Rab's undoing.[24] There were more direct causes for his rejection in both 1957 and 1963. It was, however, always there, the blemish that he could never quite reason away. To Macmillan, for whom absence of military service was a grievous fault, the label of appeaser may well have been enough to block his ascent. The combination of his wavering support of Eden during Suez and his support of Chamberlain in 1938–39 amounted to overwhelming evidence of faulty judgement. Appeasement was a rod that his enemies could always use to chastise him.

As a young man, Rab never doubted that he would succeed. Things came easily to him; he knew that intellectually he outshone his peers. Languages – particularly German – were puzzles that he quickly solved. He grew up in a family whose tradition of success was constantly before him. Monty represented Empire, a whole lineage of public servants, many of whom had been knighted for public service. India was the arena in which his father, his uncle Harcourt and his maternal uncle Dunlop had flourished. Rab, it was assumed, would do the same.

The first check to his ascent came at Cambridge, where his third year, during which he turned twenty-one, was unfortunate. Over-work,

---

22   Cosgrave, *R. A. Butler: An English Life*, p. 43.
23   TNA: ADM 223/466.
24   This argument is developed by Paul Stafford (1985), 'Political Autobiography and the Art of the Plausible', *The Historical Journal*, 28, pp. 901–22.

over-commitment to Union Society business, relentless ambition – all combined to bring on a nervous collapse and the decision to postpone Part II of the Tripos until 1925. His third year would be, if not a sabbatical, greatly less demanding. How much that setback affected him is hard to gauge. It was quickly compensated for by a resounding first in Part II and the offer of a Fellowship at Corpus. After a potentially serious setback he was back on track.

There are similarities between the collapse at Cambridge and the chastening experience of the failure of appeasement. Rab knew that his career hung by a thread and it was only Churchill's cautious treatment of the Chamberlainites that saved it. Rab was also aware that he had considerable work to do after 1941 to re-establish himself and, as in his fourth year at Cambridge, he drove himself and excelled. He desperately needed to be admired for his achievements – a need that an uncharitable observer might attribute to narcissism.

Rab's apparent intellectual arrogance may have been due to a shyness, even a lack of confidence stemming from the Cambridge collapse.[25] In an article for *Everybody's Magazine*, Laurence Thompson described Rab as 'a man of extreme complexity'. 'Unwrapping Butler,' he wrote, 'one finds a series of watertight compartments.' Rab's apparent self-confidence, he speculated, was perhaps assumed 'because it is politically useful to give an appearance of knowing what you are doing' or, equally possible, it might be 'a mask for shyness, even for a certain self-distrust'.[26]

That article was written in 1957, two and a half years after Sydney's death – a blow from which Rab never totally recovered. By the time that he married again, in 1959, his best chance to lead the Tory Party had come and gone. In 1956 and 1957, when he most needed Sydney's resolve by his side, he was alone. It was during that period that he appeared at his most cynical, most prone to utter self-destructive Rabisms.

---

25 Howard at *RAB*, p. 370 suggests an insecurity. Rab also tended to see both sides in any argument and this contributed to his self-doubt and frequent indecisiveness.

26 Laurence Thompson in an article for *Everybody's Magazine*, May 1957. Rab read and approved the article with minor alterations of emphasis. Trinity: Butler Papers, RAB, E6.2.35.1–9.

Kenneth Galbraith, President Kennedy's close adviser and Ambassador to India, shared with Rab a joyful irreverence for pomposity and, perhaps, a tendency to mock others a little too readily. When he wrote the introduction to the American edition of Rab's memoirs, he attributed the eclipse of Rab's ambitions to his habit of looking 'on his own role and that of others with ill-concealed amusement'. Rab, he observed, 'could never view himself with the terrible solemnity of the truly determined politician'. Sadly, however, 'it is the solemn men who make it'.[27] Rab would probably have been more comfortable in the company of JFK, his brother, Mac Bundy, Dick Goodwin and Kenneth Galbraith than in the Conservative Party of the 1950s and 1960s.

From the start of his political career, Rab's apparent intellectual arrogance spawned Rabisms; observers attributed complexity rather than malice to his many quotable comments, for Rab, paradoxically, was the least malicious of men. As achievement followed achievement, it seemed inevitable to observers like Chips Channon that Rab would succeed in reaching the very top. Yet, almost as soon as he held office, the doubts began to circulate.

His spell at the Board of Education reinforced confidence in his ability but failed to dispel the doubts. From 1945 to 1951, he reshaped Tory policy, but the very notion of policy further alienated the right wing. When his upward ascent was checked in 1955, and Suez caught him wrong-footed in 1956, his enemies were jubilant.

Rab's behaviour during Suez was not, in fact, as vacillating as it seems. Fundamentally opposed to the use of force and less determined than Eden that Nasser must be destroyed, he came around to supporting Eden as the right thing to do. The timing and the manner of his reaching the decision to support the Prime Minister, however, were clumsy and could be interpreted – indeed, were interpreted – as rank opportunism. Macmillan, by contrast, seemed decisive and logical; certainly the members of the 1922 found him the more plausible.

Thus Rab, reviled by the left over Munich, was now reviled by the

---

27 Introduction by Professor J. K. Galbraith to *The Art of the Possible* (Boston, MA: Gambit, 1972), p. x.

right over Suez. That analysis, somewhat glib, does not incorporate the greatest single factor – that Rab had no solid following in the Parliamentary Party. There was no loyal group that he could depend on to support him in a contest with Macmillan. Although he received many letters of sympathy when he was passed over, in the higher reaches of the party – where it ultimately mattered most – only Patrick Buchan-Hepburn gave Rab his vote.

Rab lost the contest and went not to the Foreign Office but to the Home Office, from which, as he gloomily recorded, only Churchill in the twentieth century had moved on to Downing Street. Many letters to Rab consoled him by pointing out that his time would come. Maybe that sentiment was genuine as Rab was still only fifty-four. If Macmillan were contemplating winning an election in 1960 and then stepping down before the next one, Rab would be a very credible candidate, aged sixty-one and with two of the Great Offices of State behind him.

As a potential party leader, he had broad popular appeal – and was cognisant of that. As far as the public was concerned, he had served Churchill and Eden well in 1955 without being a contender for the succession. One professional observer commented that he seemed 'severe and a little aloof', but that was nothing new. He was confident that he would command public support as leader – if only he could *become* leader.

If, on the other hand, Macmillan fought and won an election in 1964, Rab's position as heir apparent would evaporate and at least two of the young men whom Rab had brought up – Macleod and Maudling, not to mention Heath – would be plausible candidates, radiating the aura of the new, improved Tory Party. Rab might have another chance, but it would be in a very narrow window.

To Macmillan's surprise, Rab succeeded in dismantling the Central African Federation without bloodshed. With that behind him and the titles of Deputy Prime Minister and First Secretary of State, Rab must have been confident, when Macmillan went into hospital, that this time he would carry off the crown.

Tony Benn comments in his diaries that Rab did not want the Peerages Bill to pass as it might bring Hailsham and Home back to the

Commons. If that was written before October 1963, it was perspicacious. At the time, the popular Hailsham, who combined an outgoing
and positive personality with a first-class mind, would have seemed
the greater threat. He wanted to be Prime Minister and showed it,
whereas there was no indication that Home had any such ambition. If
Rab is to be believed, before he realised that Home posed a threat, the
choice had already been made.

Time and again, it seems, Rab was a frontrunner until late in the
day but, in the home stretch, his support slipped away. Despite his
ability, he lacked charisma, that essential element of leadership. Just as
his written work often seems to lack a central theme, and his spoken
words had a certain ambiguity, so, as a potential leader, he failed
to inspire.

The 'natural leader', according to one definition, is 'one with special,
even supernatural gifts whose leadership [does] not depend in any way
on institutions or on holding office'. Instead, followers make an act
of faith; they 'bestow charisma on leaders, when that person seems to
embody the qualities they are looking for'.[28]

The lack of that charismatic leadership further lessened Rab in his
colleagues' eyes. The 'turning and trimming' that William Clark so
despised; the overt ambition and adjustment of principle; the moral
indecisiveness, all combined to make colleagues reject him as a leader,
however great his intellectual ability. Had Rab succeeded Eden, it is
easy to imagine him confronted, like President Jimmy Carter, with
choices that overwhelmed him; easy to imagine his very leadership
derailed by his own understanding of the gravity of the choice.

Even when intellectual ability and charisma combined, as they did
with Hailsham, that was not necessarily enough to carry the possessor
to Downing Street. Hailsham's ambition was too shamelessly vulgar
for the Parliamentary Party; Rab's ambition involved too much devi-
ousness and moral adjustment. Neither, in the final analysis, was what
the party wanted or needed. Despite Macleod's horrified protests, it
may be that what it most needed in 1963 was Alec Douglas-Home.

---

28 Archie Brown, *The Myth of the Strong Leader*, p. 4.

Whilst Rab was immensely popular with the electorate, his colleagues instinctively recognised this ambiguity. When the time came to follow a leader over the top, they hesitated. Macmillan sensed this, and when his own resignation was accelerated too rapidly for Maudling, Macleod or Heath to succeed, he set the 'Stop Rab' movement in motion. That it worked so effectively is testimony to the gravity of doubts about Rab.

There was an inevitability about Eden's succeeding Churchill. Three and a half years later, Rab was confident that he was in the same position as Eden had been in 1953: he expected the crown to pass naturally to him. When he was passed over in favour of Macmillan, Rab railed against the party, his colleagues, even against the Queen, whom he irrationally blamed for her action in sending for Macmillan. Later, recalling that mood of having been betrayed, he uttered the words that Dennis Walters remembered and used as the title for his own memoirs:

> Whatever you do if you intend to get on in politics, never show that you have been wounded. In politics you must always keep running with the pack. The moment that you falter and they sense that you are injured, they will turn on you like wolves, biting and savaging you.[29]

Perhaps the greatest irony is that the job for which he may have been most suited eventually came to him as a consolation prize. Rab's intellect and vision might have made him as important a shaper of the world as Dean Acheson had been as Secretary of State a decade before. The similarities of intellect and of world view are obscured by the principal difference between the two. Acheson had no desire for the top job or for the business of politics. Rab did have such ambition and that ambition, manipulated cynically by a hostile Prime Minister, ultimately prevented him not only from becoming Prime Minister, but also from performing his natural role on the world stage. By the time he did become Foreign Secretary, his career was almost over – his ambition spent. It was an unimportant interlude. The contrafactual scenario of

---

29 Walters, *Not Always With the Pack* (London: Constable, 1989), p. 16.

Rab, without ambition for Downing Street, serving a Prime Minister whom he admired as Acheson admired Harry Truman is an attractive one indeed.

After a Herculean effort at the Board of Education and his sterling work at the Conservative Research Department, Rab was rewarded with the Exchequer when the Tories returned to power in 1951. The presence of Eden and his experience with foreign affairs automatically excluded any other candidate from the Foreign Office. This was unfortunate for, as William Clark pointed out, Eden 'possessed an exaggerated view of what Britain in the mid-1950s could do on its own'.[30] A government committed to establishing Britain's role in Europe, based on realistic co-operation with, rather than subservience to, the United States could have positioned Great Britain solidly at the centre of the European Community. There might have been no humiliation at the hands of de Gaulle, no equivocation about the country's role. Rab, as Foreign Secretary in the late 1950s, would have been the perfect minister to implement such policy.

The issue of Britain's joining the European Community illustrates Rab's cerebral approach to diplomacy. Initially opposed to British membership, he pondered long and hard, eventually reaching the conclusion that Britain should join. He accordingly invited Macmillan to dinner at Buck's, where he solemnly informed him of his conversion. Macmillan recalled that

> He told me that in spite of (a) the farmers, (b) the Commonwealth, (c) the probable break-up of the Conservative Party, he had decided to support our joining the Common Market. It was too late to turn back now. It was too big a chance to miss, for Britain's wealth and strength. But we must face the fact that we might share the fate of Sir Robert Peel and his supporters.[31]

---

30 Clark, *From Three Worlds*, p. 146. Whilst Clark does not exclude Rab from the group of post-war imperialists around Eden, he implies that Rab's imperialist ideas applied only to India.
31 Bodleian: MSS Macmillan, dep d46.110. Diary entry for 21 August 1962.

This is a perfect cameo of Rab: loyal lieutenant, punctilious analyst, vacillating executive.

To read the moral certainty of Rab's instincts and to contrast these with the apparent uncertainty of the man whom Clark described as needing to be wanted is to underscore the paradox. Persuaded from an early age that he could achieve whatever he set out to do, driven by Sydney who would 'make him Premier', denied the leadership in 1953, thwarted in 1957, resentful towards real and imagined enemies, Rab remained focussed on the leadership he sought and failed to grasp, rather than on how he could best have served himself and his country. Yet he himself deplored that 'Everybody writes about me as a possible successor … Nobody ever writes about what I do.'[32]

In that curious and inaccurate complaint, one can detect once again Rab's debilitating insecurity. Leading newspapers dedicated many column inches to Rab's achievements in the various Ministries he occupied. Not unnaturally – as leadership contests make for good stories – they also speculated incessantly as to his future. In so doing, they deflected attention from the most intriguing unfulfilled possibility – that Rab, at a critical time in Britain's history, was the best Foreign Secretary that Britain never had, the man best qualified to implement a far-reaching and innovative foreign policy after Eden's accession.

Curiously, Harold Macmillan may have recognised Rab's suitability. In June 1960, casting about for the best person to succeed Home at the Commonwealth Office, he recorded in his diary that Rab had refused the offer of the Foreign Office.[33] Like several of Mac's diary entries, this was assuredly written for posterity, in this case to defend himself against any charge that he had blocked Rab. It is highly improbable that Rab refused in 1960 the Ministry that he had most wanted in 1957. Indeed, Macmillan recorded that he had 'tried to steer [Rab] off the F. O. to which he had some leanings'.[34] With the explanation that 'one head on a charger was enough', Macmillan retained a weakened

---

32 Recalled by Chris Patten, 'R. A. Butler – What We Missed'. Mollie Butler, *A Rabanthology*, p. 111.
33 Bodleian: MSS Macmillan, dep d39*.78–9. Diary entry for 28 June 1960.
34 Bodleian: MSS Macmillan, dep d28*.8–9. Diary entry for 3 February 1957.

Foreign Secretary, enabling him – like Eden before him – to control foreign policy.

Whilst Rab Butler was decidedly not the best Prime Minister that Britain never had, there is persuasive evidence that he had the necessary diplomatic, political and negotiating skills to have implemented the government's foreign policy from 1955 to 1963. He amply demonstrated those skills in bringing the Central African Federation to its natural end without civil war or bloodshed. In Rab we see a remarkable combination: a voracious appetite for work, determination, loyalty to principle, an ability to interpret broad guidelines imposed from above, and considerable cerebral ability in their application. We see a Metternich of pre-1820, a diplomat of wide vision and ability. Sadly, the events of 1938 and 1939 had effectively excluded Rab from that office. Only Churchill could have reinstated him – and Churchill, with his own challenging agenda as the new Prime Minister in 1951, had no intention of letting Rab near foreign affairs. Nor, for different reasons, had Eden or Macmillan.

Rab's complaint that the press endlessly speculated on whether he might take over as Leader was heartfelt, but for that speculation, once again, he had only himself to blame. Time and again he was given the broadest of hints that 'the chaps wouldn't have him', on the last occasion just months before the tragicomic Blackpool conference of October 1963. Yet he continued to see himself and present himself as a contender for the leadership. Unable to relinquish his ambition, he drove himself relentlessly, to the point of endangering his health. Macmillan's diaries contain periodic concerns for his well-being; Welensky records him looking 'wan and grey and ill'; Ian Smith commented that before the Victoria Falls conference Rab felt too ill to fly to Salisbury for a pre-conference meeting.[35] As he had done at Cambridge forty years before, even after his second marriage in 1959, Rab allowed responsibilities to be piled on him until he came close to collapse.

Rab saw diplomacy, the entire realm of politics, as 'the art of the possible' – the title he gave to his own memoirs and which he used in

---

35 Although Smith believed that this was a 'diplomatic' illness. *The Great Betrayal*, p. 53.

a letter to Archbishop Amigo in connection with his greatest triumph, the 1944 Education Act.[36] His tragedy is that until the last he believed that his ability would be suitably rewarded – and that he showed it. As a result, he met stalwart resistance from those determined to keep him out of Downing Street. That fatal ambition, combined with misplaced loyalty, erratic judgement and, in no small measure, his own insecurity, consistently denied him the Foreign Office, the Office of State to which he was most suited.

---

36 On 16 September 1942 he concluded his letter to the Archbishop, writing, 'I have been very conscious in putting forward the proposals above, that they constitute *l'art du possible* in the world in which we live.' Clifton, *Amigo: Friend of the Poor*, p. 214.

SOURCES

Primary Sources:

The Papers of Richard Austen Butler, Trinity College, Cambridge, 210 boxes.

The Papers of Harold Macmillan, Bodleian Library, Oxford, 1314 shelfmarks.

Conservative Party Archive, Papers of R. A. Butler, Bodleian Library, Oxford, 37 shelfmarks.

James Chuter Ede, unpublished diary, 12 vols, Add MSS 59690-59701 (British Library).

CAB and PREM files, The National Archives, Kew.

Department of State, Indexed Central Files, Washington, DC. Collected in US State Department, *Foreign Relations of the United States, 1955–1957*, Vol. XVI (see below).

Secondary Sources, Select Bibliography:

Adelman, Paul, *The Decline of the Liberal Party 1910–1931*, 1982, London: Longman.

Alport, Lord, *The Sudden Assignment*, 1965, London: Hodder & Stoughton.

Aster, Sidney, *1939*, 1974, New York: Simon & Schuster.

Attlee, Earl, *As It Happened*, 1954, London: Heinemann.

Avon, Earl of, *Memoirs*, 3 vols, 1960–1965, London: Cassell & Co.

Ball, Stuart (ed.), *Parliament and Politics in the Age of Churchill and Attlee: The Headlam Diaries 1935–1951*, 1999, London: Cambridge University Press.

Beer, Samuel, *Modern British Politics: A Study of Parties and Pressure Groups*, 1965, London: Faber & Faber.

Benn, Tony, *Years of Hope: Diaries, Letters & Papers 1940–1962*, 1995, London: Arrow.

_____, *Out of the Wilderness: Diaries 1963–1967*, 1988, London: Arrow.

Bevan, Aneurin ('Celticus'), *Why Not Trust the Tories?*, 1944, London: Gollancz.

Bevins, Reginald, *The Greasy Pole*, 1965, London: Hodder & Stoughton.

Birkenhead, Earl of, *The Life of Lord Halifax*, 1966, Cambridge, MA: Houghton Mifflin.

_____, *Walter Monckton*, 1969, London: Weidenfeld & Nicolson.

Boyd, Francis, *Richard Austen Butler*, 1956, London: Rockliff.

Boyd-Carpenter, John, *Way of Life: The Memoirs of John Boyd-Carpenter*, 1980, London: Sidgwick & Jackson.

Brown, Archie, *The Myth of the Strong Leader*, 2014, London: Bodley Head.

Brown, George, *In My Way*, 1971, London: Victor Gollancz.

Bullock, Alan, *The Life and Times of Ernest Bevin*, vol. 2: *Minister of Labour 1940–1945*, 1967, London: Heinemann.

Bury, Patrick, *The College of Corpus Christi and of the Blessed Virgin Mary: A History, 1822–1952*, 1952, Cambridge: C.C.C.

Butler, D. E. and King, Anthony, *The British General Election of 1964*, 1965, New York: Macmillan.

Butler, Sir Geoffrey, *The Tory Tradition*, 1957, London: Conservative Political Centre.

Butler of Saffron Walden, Lord, *The Art of the Possible*, 1971, London: Hamish Hamilton.

_____, *The Romanes Lecture*, 1968, Oxford: Clarendon Press.

_____, *The Art of Memory: Friends in Perspective*, 1982, London: Hodder & Stoughton.

Butler, Mollie, *August and Rab: A Memoir*, 1987, London, Weidenfeld & Nicolson.

_____ (ed.), *A Rabanthology*, 1995, York: Wilton 65.

Cairncross, Alec, *Years of Recovery: Economic Policy, 1945–51*, 1985, London: Methuen.

Campbell, John, *Edward Heath: A Biography*, 1993, London: Jonathan Cape.

Cazalet-Keir, Thelma, *From the Wings*, 1967, London: The Bodley Head.

Charlton, Michael, *The Price of Victory*, 1983, London: BBC.

Charmley, John, *Duff Cooper*, 1986, London: Weidenfeld & Nicolson.

Churchill, Randolph, *The Fight for the Tory Leadership*, 1964, London: Heinemann.

_____, *The Rise and Fall of Sir Anthony Eden*, 1959, London: Mac-Gibbon & Kee.

_____ (ed.), *Europe Unite: Speeches 1947 & 1948*, 1950, London: Cassell.

Churchill, Sir Winston, *The Second World War*, vol. 2, *Their Finest Hour*, 1949, London: Cassell.

_____, *The Second World War*, vol. 3, *The Grand Alliance*, 1950, London: Cassell.

Clark, William, *From Three Worlds*, 1986, London: Sidgwick & Jackson.

Clarke, Peter, *A Question of Leadership: Gladstone to Thatcher*, 1991, London: Hamish Hamilton.

Clifton, Michael, *Amigo: Friend of the Poor*, 1987, Leominster: Fowler Wright.

Colville, John, *Footprints in Time*, 1976, London: William Collins.

_____, *The Fringes of Power*, 1985, London: Hodder & Stoughton.

_____, *The Churchillians*, 1981, London: Weidenfeld & Nicolson.

Conservative and Unionist Central Office, *Return to Greatness*, 1947–1949, London.

Cooper, Chester, *The Lion's Last Roar: Suez, 1956*, 1978, New York: Harper & Row.

Cooper, Duff, *Old Men Forget: The Autobiography of Duff Cooper, Viscount Norwich*, 1955, London: Rupert Hart-Davis.

Cosgrave, Patrick, *R. A. Butler: An English Life*, 1981, London: Quartet Books.

Cradock, Percy, *Recollections of the Cambridge Union*, 1953, Cambridge: Bowes & Bowes.

Craig, Gordon and Loewenheim, Francis, *The Diplomats 1939–1979*, 1994, Princeton, NJ: Princeton University Press.

Cudlipp, Hugh, *Walking on the Water*, 1976, London: The Bodley Head.

Dalton, Hugh, *The Fateful Years: Memoirs 1931–1945*, 1957, London: Frederick Muller.

Danchev, Alex and Todman, Daniel (eds.), *War Diaries 1939–1945: Field Marshal Lord Alanbrooke*, 2001, London: Weidenfeld & Nicolson.

Dancy, John, *The Public Schools and the Future*, 1963, London: Faber & Faber.

Dayan, Moshe, *Story of My Life*, 1976, New York: William Morrow.

Dell, Edmund, *The Chancellors: A History of the Chancellors of the Exchequer, 1945–90*, 1997, London: HarperCollins.

Denning, Lord, *Lord Denning's Report*, 1963, London: HMSO.

Dickie, John, *The Uncommon Commoner*, 1964, London: Pall Mall.

Dilks, David (ed.), *The Diaries of Sir Alexander Cadogan*, 1972, New York: Putnam's.

Dirksen, Herbert von, *Documents and Materials Relating to the Eve of the Second World War: The Papers of Herbert von Dirksen (1938–1939)*, Vo. 1, 1948, Moscow: Foreign Languages Publishing House.

Dixon, Piers, *Double Diploma: The Life of Sir Pierson Dixon*, 1968, London: Hutchinson.

Dow, J. C. R., *The Management of the British Economy 1945–1960*, 1968, Cambridge: Cambridge University Press.

Eden, Sir Anthony – See Avon, Earl of.

Eisenhower, Dwight D., *Mandate for Change: The White House Years, 1953–1956*, 1963, Garden City, NY: Doubleday.

_____, *Waging Peace: The White House Years, 1956–1961*, 1965, Garden City, NY: Doubleday.

Eubank, Keith, *Munich*, 1963, Norman, OK: University of Oklahoma Press.

Evans, Sir Harold, *Downing Street Diary: The Macmillan Years*, 1981, London: Hodder & Stoughton.

Feiling, Keith, *The Life of Neville Chamberlain*, 1947, London: Macmillan.

Fisher, Nigel, *Iain Macleod*, 1973, London: Andre Deutsch.

_____, *Harold Macmillan*, 1982, Littlehampton Book Services.

Franklin, Harry, *Unholy Wedlock: The Failure of the Central African Federation*, 1963, London: George Allen & Unwin.

Freiberger, Steven, *Dawn Over Suez*, 1992, Chicago: Ivan Dee.

Gilbert, Martin and Gott, Richard, *The Appeasers*, 1963, Boston, MA: Houghton Mifflin.

Gilmour, Ian and Garnett, M., *Whatever Happened to the Tories*, 1998, London: Fourth Estate.

Gold, Ann (ed.), *Edward Boyle: His Life by His Friends*, 1991, Basingstoke: Macmillan.

Goldman, Lawrence, *The Life of R. H. Tawney: Socialism and History*, 2013, London: Bloomsbury.

Goodhart, Philip (with Branston, Ursula), *The 1922: The Story of the Conservative Backbenchers' Parliamentary Committee*, 1973, London: Macmillan.

Graebner, Norman, *The New Isolationism: A Study in Politics and Foreign Policy Since 1950*, 1956, New York: Ronald Press.

Graves, Robert, *Goodbye to All That*, 1960, Harmondsworth: Penguin Books.

Hailsham, Lord, *The Door Wherein I Went*, 1975, London: Collins.

_____, *A Sparrow's Flight: The Memoirs of Lord Hailsham of St Marylebone*, 1991, London: Fontana.

Halifax, Earl of, *Fullness of Days*, 1957, New York: Dodd Mead.

Harris, Ralph, *Politics without Prejudice: A Political Appreciation of the Rt Hon Richard Austen Butler*, 1956, London: Staples Press.

Hart-Davis, Duff (ed.), *King's Counsellor*, 2006, London: Weidenfeld & Nicolson. (See Lascelles, Sir Alan.)

Healey, Denis, *The Time of My Life*, 1990, New York: Norton.

Heath, Edward, *The Course of My Life*, 1998, London: Hodder & Stoughton.

Heffer, Simon, *Like The Roman: The Life of Enoch Powell*, 1999, London: Phoenix.

Henderson, Nicholas, *Inside the Private Office: Memoirs of the Secretary to British Foreign Ministers*, 1987, Chicago: Academy Chicago.

Hennessy, Peter, *Whitehall*, 1989, London: Secker & Warburg.

_____, *The Prime Minister, the Office and its Holders since 1945*, 2001, London: Macmillan.

_____, *Never Again: Britain 1945–1951*, 1993, London: Jonathan Cape.

_____, *Having It So Good: Britain in the Fifties*, 2007, London: Penguin.

Hill, Lord, *Both Sides of the Hill*, 1964, London: Heinemann.

Hoffman, J. D., *The Conservative Party in Opposition 1945–51*, 1964, London: MacGibbon & Kee.

Holden, Anthony, *Charles, Prince of Wales*, 1979, London: Weidenfeld & Nicholson.

_____, *King Charles III: A Biography*, 1988, New York: Grove Press.

Home, Lord, *The Way the Wind Blows*, 1976, London: Collins.

Hoopes, Townsend, *The Devil and John Foster Dulles*, 1973, Boston, MA: Little, Brown.

Horne, Alistair, *Harold Macmillan*, 2 vols, 1988, London: Macmillan.

Howard, Anthony, *RAB: The Life of R. A. Butler*, 1987, London: Jonathan Cape.

_____ and West, Richard, *The Making of the Prime Minister*, 1965, London: Jonathan Cape.

Hughes, Emrys, *Macmillan: Portrait of a Politician*, 1962, London: George Allen & Unwin.

Iremonger, F. A., *William Temple, Archbishop of Canterbury*, 1948, London: Oxford University Press.

Ishiguro, Kazuo, *The Remains of the Day*, 1989, London: Faber & Faber.

Kilmuir, Earl of, *Political Adventure: The Memoirs of the Earl of Kilmuir*, 1964, London: Weidenfeld & Nicolson.

King, Cecil, *The Cecil King Diary, 1970–1974*, 1975, London: Jonathan Cape.

_____, *With Malice Toward None: A War Diary*, 1970, London: Sidgwick & Jackson.

Kingseed, Cole, *Eisenhower and the Suez Crisis of 1956*, 1995, Baton Rouge, Louisiana: LSU Press.

Kirkwood, Kenneth, *Britain and Africa*, 1965, London: Chatto & Windus.

Kyle, Keith, *Suez*, 1992, London: Weidenfeld & Nicolson.

Kynaston, David, *Austerity Britain, 1945–1951*, 2007, London: Bloomsbury.

_____, *Family Britain, 1951–1957*, 2010, London: Bloomsbury.

Lamb, Richard, *The Macmillan Years 1957–1963: The Emerging Truth*, 1995, London: John Murray.

_____, *The Failure of the Eden Government*, 1987, London: Sidgwick & Jackson.

_____, *The Drift to War 1922–1939*, 1991, New York: St Martin's.

Lascelles, Sir Alan, *King's Counsellor*, 2006, London: Weidenfeld & Nicolson.

Leaming, Barbara, *Churchill Defiant: Fighting On, 1945–1955*, 2010, New York: HarperPress.

Lloyd, Selwyn, *Suez 1956: A Personal Account*, 1978, London: Jonathan Cape.

Love, Kennett, *Suez: The Twice-Fought War*, 1969, New York: McGraw-Hill.

McCallum, R. B. and Readman, Alison, *The British General Election of 1945*, 1947, London: Oxford University Press.

Macleod, Iain, *Neville Chamberlain*, 1961, London: Frederick Muller.

Macmillan, Harold, *Memoirs*, 6 vols, 1966–73, London: Macmillan.

Mason, Philip, *Years of Decision: Rhodesia and Nyasaland in 1960*, 1960, London: Institute of Race Relations, Oxford University Press.

_____, *The Men Who Ruled India*, 1985, London: Jonathan Cape.

Maudling, Reginald, *Memoirs*, 1978, London: Sidgwick & Jackson.

Minney, R. J., *The Private Papers of Hore-Belisha*, 1960, London: Collins.

Montague Browne, Anthony, *Long Sunset: Memoirs of Winston Churchill's Last Private Secretary*, 1995, London: Cassell.

Moore, Charles, *Margaret Thatcher: Not for Turning*, 2013, London: Allen Lane.

Moran, Lord, *Churchill, Taken from the Diaries of Lord Moran: The Struggle for Survival, 1940–1965*, 1966, Boston, MA: Houghton Mifflin.

Morgan, Janet (ed.), *The Backbench Diaries of Richard Crossman*, 1981, London: Hamish Hamilton & Jonathan Cape.

Morgan, Kenneth, *Labour in Power 1945–1951*, 1984, London: Oxford University Press.

Morrison, Lord, *An Autobiography by Lord Morrison of Lambeth*, 1960, London: Odhams.

Mosley, Sir Oswald, *My Life*, 1968, London: Nelson.

Munch-Petersen, Thomas, '"Common Sense Not Bravado": The Butler–Prytz Interview of 17 June 1940', *Scandia*, 1986.

Murphy, Robert, *Diplomat Among Warriors*, 1964, Garden City, New York: Doubleday & Co.

Murray, Williamson, *The Change in the European Balance of Power: The Path to Ruin, 1938–1939*, 1984, Princeton: Princeton University Press.

Neff, Donald, *Warriors at Suez*, 1981, New York: Linden Press.

Nicolson, Harold, *Diaries and Letters*, 3 vols, 1966–68, London: Collins.

Norwich, John Julius, *The Duff Cooper Diaries*, 2005, London: Weidenfeld & Nicolson.

Nutting, Anthony, *I Saw for Myself: The Aftermath of Suez*, 1958, Garden City, NY: Doubleday.

_____, *No End of a Lesson*, 1967, London: Constable.

Olson, Lynne, *Troublesome Young Men: The Rebels who Brought Churchill to Power and Helped Save England*, 2007, New York: Farrar, Straus & Giroux.

Pearce, Edward, *The Lost Leaders: The Best Prime Ministers We Never Had*, 1997, London: Little, Brown.

Pearson, Jonathan, *Sir Anthony Eden and the Suez Crisis: Reluctant Gamble*, 2003, London: Macmillan.

Pimlott, Ben, *Harold Wilson*, 1992, London: HarperCollins.

_____, *Hugh Dalton: A Life*, 1985, London: Jonathan Cape.

Pineau, Christian, *1956 Suez*, 1976, Paris: Robert Laffont.

Proudfoot, Mary, *British Politics and Government, 1951–1970*, 1974, London: Faber & Faber.

Raczynski, Count Edward, *In Allied London*, 1962, London: Weidenfeld & Nicolson.

Ramsden, John, *The Making of Conservative Party Policy*, 1980, London: Longman.

Redcliffe-Maud, Lord, *Experiences of an Optimist*, 1981, London: Hamish Hamilton.

Rhodes James, Robert (ed.), *Chips: The Diaries of Henry Channon*, 1967, London: Weidenfeld & Nicolson.

_____, *Churchill, A Study in Failure*, 1970, London: Weidenfeld & Nicolson.

_____, *Anthony Eden*, 1986, London: Weidenfeld & Nicolson.

Roberts, Andrew, *Eminent Churchillians*, 1994, London: Weidenfeld & Nicolson.

_____, *The Holy Fox*, 1991, London: Weidenfeld & Nicolson.

Rowse, A. L., *Appeasement: A Study in Political Decline, 1933–1939*, 1963, New York: Norton.

Sampson, Anthony, *Anatomy of Britain Today*, 1965, London: Hodder & Stoughton.

_____, *Macmillan: A Study in Ambiguity*, 1967, London: Allen Lane.

Seldon, Anthony, *Churchill's Indian Summer: The Conservative Government, 1951–55*, 1981, London: Hodder & Stoughton.

Smith, Ian, *The Great Betrayal*, 1997, London: Blake.

Smith, W. O. L., *To Whom do Schools Belong?*, 1942, Oxford: Basil Blackwell.

Sparrow, Gerald, *R. A. B., Study of a Statesman*, 1965, London: Odhams.

Spoto, Donald, *The Decline and Fall of the House of Windsor*, 1995, New York: Simon & Schuster.

Stafford, Paul, 'Political Autobiography and the Art of the Plausible: R. A. Butler at the Foreign Office 1938–1939', *The Historical Journal*, 28 (1985), pp. 901–22.

Stewart, Graham, *Burying Caesar*, 1999, London: Weidenfeld & Nicolson.

Swinton, Earl of and Margach, James, *Sixty Years of Power: Some Memories of the Men Who Wielded It*, 1966, London: Hutchinson.

Taylor, A. J. P., *Beaverbrook*, 1972, New York: Simon & Schuster.

_____, *English History, 1914–1945*, 1965, Oxford: Clarendon Press.

Temple, William, *Christianity and Social Order*, 1942, (reprinted 1956), Harmondsworth: Penguin.

Templewood, Viscount, *Nine Troubled Years*, 1954, London: Collins.

Thomas, Hugh, *The Suez Affair*, 1966, London: Weidenfeld & Nicolson.

Thompson, Alan, *The Day Before Yesterday*, 1971, London: Sidgwick & Jackson.

Thorpe, D. R., *Alec Douglas-Home*, 1996, London: Sinclair-Stevenson.

_____, *Supermac: The Life of Harold Macmillan*, 2010, London: Chatto & Windus.

_____, *The Uncrowned Prime Ministers*, 1980, London: Darkhorse Publishing.

_____, 'The October 1963 Conservative Party Conference', *Conservative History Journal*, vol. II, 2.

Timmins, Nicholas, *The Five Giants*, 2001, London: HarperCollins.

US State Department, *FRUS, 1955–1957, Vol. 16, Suez Crisis*, 1990, Washington.

Vansittart, Lord, *The Mist Procession*, 1958, London: Hutchinson.

Walters, Dennis, *Not Always with the Pack*, 1989, London: Constable.

Waugh, Evelyn, *Put Out More Flags*, 1942, London: Chapman & Hall.

Welensky, Sir Roy, *Welensky's 4000 Days*, 1964, London: Collins.

Wheare, K. C., *Federal Government*, 1951, London: Oxford University Press.

Wheeler-Bennett, Sir John, *Munich: Prologue to Tragedy*, 1966, London: Macmillan.

_____, *John Anderson, Viscount Waverley*, 1962, London: Macmillan.

Williams, Philip (ed.), *The Diary of Hugh Gaitskell 1945–1956*, 1983, London: Jonathan Cape.

_____, *Hugh Gaitskell: A Political Biography*, 1979, London: Jonathan Cape.

Wilson, Harold, *The Governance of Britain*, 1976, London: Weidenfeld & Nicolson.

_____, *The Labour Government, 1964–1970: A Personal Record*, 1971, Boston, MA: Little, Brown.

Winterton, Earl, *Orders of the Day*, 1953, London: Cassell.

Woolton, Earl of, *Memoirs*, 1959, London: Cassell.

Woodward, Llewellyn, *British Foreign Policy in the Second World War*, 1962, London: HMSO.

_____, *Documents on British Foreign Policy 1919–1939*, 1946–57, London: HMSO.

Youngson, A. J., *The British Economy 1920–1957*, 1960, London: Allen & Unwin.

Ziegler, Philip, *Mountbatten: The Official Biography*, 1985, London: HarperCollins.

INDEX